Jazz on My Mind

Jazz on My Mind

*Liner Notes, Anecdotes
and Conversations
from the 1940s to the 2000s*

HERB WONG

with PAUL SIMEON FINGEROTE

Cherie—

Thank You For Keeping

Jazz on Your Mind.

I Dig Ya 'Gaten!

Paul

(with Herb)

McFarland & Company, Inc., Publishers

Jefferson, North Carolina

LIBRARY OF CONGRESS CATALOGUING-IN-PUBLICATION DATA

Names: Wong, Herb. | Fingerote, Paul Simeon.
Title: Jazz on my mind : liner notes, anecdotes and conversations from
the 1940s to the 2000s / Herb Wong with Paul Simeon Fingerote.
Description: Jefferson, North Carolina : McFarland & Company, 2016. |
Includes index.
Identifiers: LCCN 2016011063 | ISBN 9780786496402
(softcover : acid free paper) ∞
Subjects: LCSH: Jazz—History and criticism. | Musical criticism. |
Jazz musicians—Interviews.
Classification: LCC ML3506 .W66 2016 | DDC 781.6509—dc23
LC record available at http://lccn.loc.gov/2016011063

BRITISH LIBRARY CATALOGUING DATA ARE AVAILABLE

ISBN (print) 978-0-7864-9640-2
ISBN (ebook) 978-1-4766-2547-8

Front cover photograph of Herb Wong courtesty of Richard Hadlock;
front cover design direction by Kira Wong Roher

Printed in the United States of America

*McFarland & Company, Inc., Publishers
Box 611, Jefferson, North Carolina 28640
www.mcfarlandpub.com*

Acknowledgments

Thanks to the following for their contributions to *Jazz on My Mind*:

Thanks to my wife, Marilyn, and our daughters, Kira and Kamberly; and to my brother in life and in jazz, Dr. Woody Wong.

Thanks to my co-author, colleague and friend, Paul Simeon Fingerote.

Thanks to those whose contributions and efforts made this publication possible: Production assistants Quincy Fingerote (proofreading), Barbara Hickey (transcriptions), Remona Murray (research and scans), Marilyn Wong (proofreading); photographers Jim Edelen, Richard Hadlock, Andy Nozaka, Veryl Oakland; researchers Sara Cline, Larry Kelp, Suzanne McCulloch, Jay Nitschke, Sibila Savage; Tim Jackson, Timothy Orr, Jan Stotzer, Bill Wagner and the Monterey Jazz Festival; Stuart Brewster, Michael Griffin, Harvey Mittler and the Palo Alto Jazz Alliance; Jerry McBride and the Stanford University Archive of Sound; friends David Miller, Melissa Morgan, Steve Piazzale, Danny Scher, Deborah Winters; and Herb's Herd, my Palo Alto Adult School Jazz Class students, whom I taught for almost 30 years.

Thanks to those who assisted in obtaining permissions, including Frank Alkyer, Maureen Bacon, Nieves Bates, John Bishop, Anthony Brown, Raquel Bruno, George Buck, Fatima Budica, Thomas Burns, Melanie Clarkson, Paul de Barros, Patty Boyle, Madeline Eastman, Linda Fernandez, Kevin Gore, Donna Gourdol and the McPartland Family, Thomas Gramuglia, Ron Haas, Tom Hampson, James Harrod, Irv Kratka, Cem Kurosman, Jon Jang, Richard Jeweler and the Brubeck Family, Devra Hall Levy, Dave McIntosh, Charles McPherson, Alasdair McMullan, Lee Mergner, Dan Ouellette, Knut Pederson, Nick Phillips, Sandra Prince, Mike Rittberg, Sean Roderick, Anna Sala, Toby Silver, Rhett Smith, Gary Smulyan, Diana Spangler, Gerry Teekens, Tricia Tierno, Adam Tight, Henry Towns, Steve Turre, Terry Vosbein, Ana Way, Scott Wenzel, Jim Wills, Gil Wisdom.

Most importantly, my thanks to all of the young musicians who are learning, studying, playing and appreciating jazz. My heartfelt gratitude goes to their teachers, mentors, families, friends and supporters. Thank you for ensuring that the future of our music is so well placed in such capable hands.

Finally, thanks to all of you for allowing me to share the jazz that's been on my mind for seventy wonderful years.

Dig ya' later!

Herb Wong

Liner notes written by Herb Wong are reprinted courtesy of:

Concord Music Group, Inc. (Louie Bellson / *Dynamite!*; Art Blakey / *In This Korner*; Ray Brown / *SuperBass 2*; Richie Cole / *KUSH: The Music of Dizzy Gillespie*; Buddy DeFranco / *You Must Believe in Swing*; Shelly Manne / *Perk Up*; Tierney Sutton / *Unsung Heroes*).

Rhino Entertainment Company/A Warner Music Group Company (Carmen McRae / *Dreams of Life*; Mel Tormé / *It Happened in Monterey*).

Sony Music Entertainment (Woody Herman / *Woody's Winners*; Denny Zeitlin / *Shining Hour: Live at the Trident*)

Universal Music Enterprises, A Division of UMG Recordings, Inc. (Kenny Burrell / *75th Birthday Bash Live!*; Herbie Hancock / *The Prisoner*; Bobby Hutcherson / *Total Eclipse*; Oscar Peterson / *Eloquence*; Dianne Reeves / *The Palo Alto Sessions*; Buddy Rich / *Big Swing Face*; Bola Sete / *At the Monterey Jazz Festival*; Wayne Shorter / *Super Nova*; Cal Tjader / *The Prophet*).

Tracks

Preface

Paul Simeon Fingerote

In late December of 2013, Herb Wong's wife, Marilyn, asked me if I could help Herb with his memory. Unable to recall any prior mention by Marilyn of my mnemonic skills, I was left to my own devices until I heard from Herb, who clarified: "Not memory, Paul, *memories*," memories which were to become *Jazz on My Mind*.

These were the memories Dr. Herb Wong had made over seven decades as a reigning force in jazz: 30-year DJ on San Francisco's KJAZ radio station; author of more than 400 album liner notes during the heyday of jazz; explorer of creativity in one-on-one conversations with jazz legends and legends-to-be; founder and producer with Palo Alto Records and Black-Hawk Records; founder and producer of Palo Alto and Stanford jazz concerts and festivals; co-founder and artistic director of the Palo Alto Jazz Alliance; scientist and educator, innovator and pioneer in the field of jazz education; member of the Jazz Educators Hall of Fame; President of the International Association for Jazz Education.

Herb Wong and I had met through our mutual work with the Monterey Jazz Festival. Herb covered the event as a journalist for 56 years and, for 30 of those years, I was the festival's marketing and public relations director.

With our common connections in jazz and path-crossing careers; with our shared respect for words and joint sense of humor; with our mutual love of family—considering each other as such—Herb and I developed a personal relationship over the years, a relationship that extended over and above our professional association.

So it was only natural for Marilyn to have approached me with her request to help Herb write this book.

Complicating our mission of memorializing Herb's memories was the understanding—which we all shared at the outset—that Herb had terminal cancer with less than a year to live.

For our first meeting on the book project, I sat down with Herb and Marilyn in the living room of their longtime home, a classic Eichler located on a leafy lane in Menlo Park, California. I came to the table with an agenda in hand, mapping out the steps we needed to take in order to complete the book over the next twelve months.

On my return to my office in Monterey, I received a frantic phone call from Marilyn, letting me know that the latest prognosis had given Herb less than *four* months to live—not the year I had planned out in my agenda—and that Herb was unaware of this depressing new development.

In response, I accelerated the schedule of my meetings with Herb while maintaining the facade of our twelve-month to-do list. I had hoped that the year I had projected for the project's completion might help prolong Herb's positive outlook on life, if not Herb's life itself.

Herb's job was to select the liner notes, articles and conversations he wanted to include in our book. My job was to interview Herb and record his accounts of the artists—in addition to his insights on jazz—then weave it all together into the pages of *Jazz on My Mind*.

Instrument by instrument, artist by artist, story by story, we worked our way through Herb's selections and Herb's recollections.

I was enlightened by his encyclopedic knowledge of jazz; educated by his thesaurus-like language and way with words; fascinated by his tales from behind-the-scenes; and always aware that, at any moment, Herb might die.

The highlight of those meetings occurred for me when, during our interviews, Herb would pause, close his eyes, and then seem to disappear for a moment without saying a word—a rarity for Herb Wong. Concerned at first, I soon sensed that, at those unforget-table times, Herb was not merely recalling memories, he was reliving moments from a lifetime of jazz on his mind.

Herb and I were able to complete our conversations a week before Herb completed his life, Easter Sunday, April 20, 2014.

As Dr. Herb Wong was wont to say in closing—and as I am privileged to paraphrase here—Dig ya' later, Herb, dig ya' later!

Introduction

Herb Wong

Jazz has been on my mind for more than seventy years, from the 1940s through the early 2000s, the years that embrace the glory days of the golden age of jazz.

I started writing reviews of jazz albums when I was 14 years old, playing piano at Sunday school in exchange for use of the back page of our church's newsletter—space made available to me by our minister for the publication of my earliest efforts as a nascent jazz critic.

Both the minister and I thought we got the better of the deal.

Since then, I have written over 400 liner notes and articles based on dozens of conversations with jazz artists, ranging from the legends to the lesser-knowns. I focused on artists who—because of the attention they have consistently devoted to making their music consistently fresh—decidedly deserve more attention.

They range from Pepper Adams to Denny Zeitlin and read like a "Who's Who" of jazz history in between: Louie Bellson, Art Blakey, Dave Brubeck, Nat King Cole, Duke Ellington, Stan Getz, Dizzy Gillespie, Benny Goodman, Jim Hall, Herbie Hancock, Woody Herman, Milt Hinton, Billie Holiday, Milt Jackson, Elvin Jones, Stan Kenton, Shelly Manne, Marian McPartland, Carmen McRae, Art Pepper, Oscar Peterson, Joshua Redman, Django Reinhardt, Buddy Rich, Wayne Shorter, Cal Tjader, Mel Tormé, Phil Woods.

These are among the more familiar names you'll find in *Jazz on My Mind*, along with some less familiar favorites of mine—all of whom I have interviewed, profiled or written liner notes for during the launch, climb or peak of their careers.

My criteria in selecting artists for inclusion in *Jazz on My Mind* were twofold:

First, I wanted to re-emphasize the attributes of an artist's music that may be familiar to the casual listener, while stressing those attributes with which the casual listener may not be that well acquainted.

Second, I wanted to introduce the phalanx of artists who deserve greater attention, those artists who are not yet considered a part of the "great-greats" but, one day, may be.

Jazz on My Mind is not a history of jazz nor is it a jazz encyclopedia, although components of both are included in this record.

Jazz on My Mind is, instead, a fresh look back at the tradition of the jazz cannon, shedding light on the internal muscle of the music, illuminating the critical creative core that otherwise might have been missed.

At the same time, *Jazz on My Mind* is a fresh look forward, focusing on the innovative tradition of jazz, a tradition turned towards the future, a tradition that needs to be nurtured in order for it to continue to serve as the nerve center of jazz creation.

There is a flip side to *Jazz on My Mind*—not the "B" side, by any means—and that is the flip side of my life: As long as jazz has been on my mind, science has been in my soul.

The two share much in common.

Both jazz and science have rich histories. Both emphasize discovery. Both are involved with innovations built on interesting structure. Both offer challenges in different environments. They're melded, they're integrated, and you'll find both in fusion throughout the pages of *Jazz on My Mind*.

Throughout my long playing career in the world of jazz, I have been blessed with the opportunity to earn a living by working with the music I love. From jazz writer to jazz producer, manager, educator, DJ, innovator, industry leader.

It all culminates in *Jazz on My Mind* ... and it all started with the arrival of a mysterious box on the doorstep of our house in Stockton, California.

CHAPTER 1

Big Bands

Shortly after our family moved from Oakland, California, 75 miles south to Stockton, a package arrived on our doorstep. It was a heavy box, about 14 inches square, addressed to the previous owner of our new digs.

Being typical young boys of 9 and 11, my brother Elwood and I did what any young boys our age would do in this instance. With no return address visible on the box, I turned to Woody and I said, "Let's break open the box and see what's inside."

Woody, being my *younger* brother, readily complied. So we tore at the wrapping, cracked open the cardboard, and discovered inside … the rest of my life.

Record after record, big band after big band, jazz royalty after jazz royalty: Duke Ellington … Count Basie … The King of Swing, Benny Goodman. The list of big band 78s and jazz luminaries flowed on and on from that no longer mysterious, now musical box.

Both Woody and I had been classically trained on piano. But I knew when we opened that box that *this* was the music for me. "This is where the *real* music is," I said to my brother, "this is *my* music."

It was no mere coincidence that my first exposure to real jazz was in that big box of big bands. For, as I would later discover, it was the big band format that built the foundation upon which jazz would grow. It was the big band that grew the groundwork for all subsequent sizes of jazz combos that were to follow. It was the big band that started it all.

What gave birth to the big band?

From an historical perspective, big bands were the offspring of the orchestras of the '30s and '40s called "swing bands" and there were thousands of them across

Herb Wong (left) and Woody Wong as children (courtesy the Wong family).

the country. The big bands were a natural progression to follow the swing bands, a progression that followed Fletcher Henderson's concept of what a big band should consist of—sections.

Horn sections, reed sections, rhythm sections ... sections were the basis for what were called "jazz orchestras" in those days. But in the 1950s, when bebop was in full flower, they came to be called big bands. And the premier jazz orchestra of the day, the first famous big band, was led by composer, arranger and band leader, Edward Kennedy "Duke" Ellington.

Duke Ellington

The Duke Ellington Orchestra—which was looked on as more of a dignified jazz orchestra than a big band—emboweled and enhanced Ellington's compositional contributions. Compositions were the basis for the substance and sustenance of any successful jazz orchestra. And, when it came to compositions—to the color, to the tone, to the distinctiveness of each musician in the band—Duke Ellington and the Duke Ellington Orchestra had it all.

Or *almost* had it all.

In the late 1960s, while working on developing a curriculum for the Berkeley School District's primary classes, I happened to play an Ellington tune to a group of elementary school kids, asking them to write down and draw their thoughts as they listened to the music. When I read their reactions, my reaction was to read their writings to Duke.

The next time he called (Duke called frequently, often at 3:00 or 4:00 in the morning, while he was up all night composing) I was ready, with my students' essays by the bed. Marilyn answered the phone, which was strategically placed on her side of the bed, and Duke asked for me in his usual manner: "Hello, beauty. Is the beast there?"

Marilyn handed me the phone and I said, "Edward, I've been checking out your music and I have found a void in your repertoire. Let me read you something."

I read a couple of the letters to him: "When I hear Duke's music I have this deep down, brown feeling in my tummy," said one of the kids; "When I hear Duke's music, it's like giant valentines floating up in the sky," said another.

Duke listened for a moment and then said, "Who are these people? Who are these authors, these poets?"

"These are first graders," I said, "and this is what's missing, Edward: You have gained inspiration from all kinds of people, from all walks of life, but you have never drawn inspiration from young children."

There followed the longest pause I have ever experienced in a telephone conversation with Duke. Finally, he said, "Herb, I think you have found a hole in my thing and I would appreciate your help in filling that hole up as soon as possible."

And so I created an entire curriculum for primary school students based on "Take the 'A' Train," Ellington's classic rendition of Billy Strayhorn's legendary composition, with every grade interpreting the music within their natural learning curve:

The kids in kindergarten pretended to be trains; first graders used wooden blocks to build trains; second graders created a huge mural of the A Train; third graders researched stories of trains; fourth graders rode the train in a nearby park; fifth graders

Herb Wong leads Duke Ellington on his visit to Berkeley's Washington Elementary School in 1969 (photograph by Jim Edelen; courtesy Larry Kelp).

explored the history of local trains; and the sixth graders explored the science of trains by building their own steam engines.

The culmination of this unique curriculum was a concert I arranged and produced to benefit the district, starring the Duke Ellington Orchestra. It packed the Berkeley Community Theater to the rafters with kids, parents, teachers and administrators, all cheering their new-found hero, Edward Kennedy "Duke" Ellington.

Imagine: In a time when jazz in the schools was *unheard of*, we created an entire school curriculum based on a classic jazz tune. And, imagine: That tune was almost thrown out with the trash.

Duke Ellington and His Orchestra—*In Concert 1960*
Hindsight (HCD-268); 1960

The inspired concert performance by Duke Ellington's Orchestra on May 27th, 1960, in Santa Monica, California, is captured "live" on this recording. It was a sufficiently special one-nighter in that it recalled the verve of earlier recordings testifying the virtues of Ellington's peak in-person performances, swinging without mercy, aided by outstanding soloists with distinctive instrumental voices. This concert once again demonstrates his commitment to the adage expressed in the song title "It Don't Mean a Thing (If It Ain't Got That Swing)."

Through the decades of its amazingly long existence, the band regularly clocked in a tremendous amount of travel miles on the road playing one-nighters. Regarding his heavy touring schedule, Ellington once remarked: "What I'm involved in is a continuous autobiography, a continuous record of the people I meet, the places I see change…. By playing one-nighters, I can hear reactions from all kinds of audiences. You get a real contact when you play a phrase and somebody sighs."

Ellington's unrivaled fifty years of artistic development and achievement and his creative output of over two thousand compositions surely earn him the honor as the leading composer in the Western world. The universality of his commanding contributions in music also points to his development as probably the most striking evolution in the arts in America. He produced some of the most original music of the century and is, of course, firmly regarded as a genius—the greatest composer in the history of jazz.

Keying into the year of this concert, at the dawn of the 1960s—it was also the continuation of an Ellington pathway for a cumulative grand tour through the decade into the 1970s. During the 3rd Annual Monterey Jazz Festival, 1960 also brought forth the Ellington-Billy Strayhorn opus "Suite Thursday," a tribute to novelist John Steinbeck's *Sweet Thursday*, set in Monterey's Cannery Row. Other exhilarating works of the year followed, including engaging jazz re-workings of "The Nutcracker Suite" and "Peer Gynt Suite," plus the film soundtrack for the jazz themed, *Paris Blues*.

Momentum of strong interest had been renewed four years earlier when an emotion-packed performance refueled Ellington's rightful lofty position, reflected in the readers' popularity jazz polls. This healthy change of regard was due to a fiery late night impromptu jam session on stage at the 1956 Newport Jazz Festival during which tenor saxophonist Paul Gonsalves strung together 27 mind-blowing choruses between the two sections of "Diminuendo and Crescendo in Blue" (circa 1937). Subsequently Gonsalves' celebrated uninterrupted blues solo was named "the wailing interval" and intense interest in the re-visitation of the performance was sustained throughout the remainder of his life.

The program of tunes on this disc represents a balance of familiar and seldom heard selections from Ellingtonia. As for "re-creations" of his past body of works, they were not aimed at superseding the originals. Ellington viewed them as organic, and from a different perspective at different times; i.e., he refused to submit them to static treatment. In sum, these re-interpretations represent a dynamic on-going positive attitude to performing music. By the 1960s, his insight from deeper experience and wisdom gave his performances an of-the-moment freshness. Along with the cast of extraordinary soloists, the Ellington sound and voicings, this recording documents the undiminished spontaneity and the bright, hard swinging rhythm section mates of bassist Aaron Bell and drummer Sam Woodyard who delivered the requisite goods to the maestro. For this writer's taste, the unparalleled Ellington magic was luckily caught in action!

Turning to the music at hand … logically the authority of the Ducal piano with Bell and Woodyard on "Take the 'A' Train" traps attention with an immediate swing feel, reminding there is little to compare with a real live audience experience to enhance communications. If trumpeter Ray Nance's jaunty vocal laced with hipness echoes Betty Roché's wonderful 1956 vocal version, it is because it was indeed adapted by Nance. And it is a ball to listen to Nance! Enthusiasm and a keen sense of coloration infused his trumpet and cornet work. Writer Stanley Crouch describes it well: "…abetted by mutes, plungers and his refined control of open tone, (he) could juggle the puckish, the plaintive, the buffoonish, the high minded, and the translucently exotic." Dig Gonsalves' satisfying solo, the plump, fat sound of the horn sections, and the surging ensemble. And isn't it marvelous to hear Ellington's voice crediting the soloists or anything else at anytime!

Highlights of how "'A' Train" became Ellington's signature tune is interest-worthy to share. A detailed account is recounted by David Hajdu in his 1996 Billy Strayhorn biography, *Lush Life*: It began with a dispute between the radio broadcasting industry and ASCAP over a fee increase for rights to broadcast music written by ASCAP members. This conflict precipitated radio stations to give birth to BMI to compete with ASCAP. In turn, the stations wouldn't air any music by ASCAP beginning January 1941. As Ellington's most popular compositions were with ASCAP, and in order to get airplay, he asked his son, Mercer, and Strayhorn to promptly write a largely new repertoire, with composer credit to them (non–ASCAP writers). In the heat of writing, Mercer said to Strayhorn as he pulled a crunched piece of music out of the garbage: "What's wrong with this?" And Strayhorn responded: "That's an old thing I was trying to do something with, but it's too much like Fletcher Henderson." Mercer flattened it out and put it in the pile of new music. The upshot was that Ellington selected the swinging chart of "Take the 'A' Train" and the rest is history!

"Red Carpet" is the third of four parts of "Toot Suite" (1959) and is subdivided into its own three sections. Harry Carney's powerful baritone saxophone sound carries a lot of weight in the band's overall voice. Russell Procope's clarinet is followed by the shapely lines of the saxes, and Ellington's piano takes it to Booty Wood's smoothly ignited plunger solo on the "syringaphone" with speech like pattern; finally a segue goes into a walking riff while Nance's trumpet notions are fired up.

The last of the three segments of the "Newport Jazz Festival Suite" is the exciting "Newport Up." Appropriately titled, it is a high flying up tempo flight. It contains a loping parade of cool jazz riffs stretched out with some inventive repetitions and liberal solo space. Co-composed with Strayhorn, it was aimed at the 1956 festival in Newport, Rhode Island. The bass plays a prominent role and Bell gives Ellington the deep anchoring notes he wants; the drums do likewise as Woodyard's ability to drive is a quality Ellington expected. Ellington recaps the soloists pridefully.

It's a fresh surprise to hear valve trombonist Juan Tizol's well-known composition "Perdido" played with a Gerald Wilson arrangement … resulting in a more assertive leaning to bebop lines, earmarking its conception and rewarding the careful listener with different possibilities of the tune's contours. Also, it illustrates the flexibility and resourcefulness of the soloists as they merge swing into bebop. Listen to Jimmy Hamilton's conceptual adjustments on clarinet and the Gillespie-influenced trumpet statements. The tune's riff-derived melody combined with a slow paced chord pattern is simply a jam session natural.

On "Matumba" (more familiarly known as "Congo Square") there is evocation with minor key chords heard with a rhythmic feel supporting the imagery Ellington promotes in a tale of a pretty girl who stimulates erotic responses at the New Orleans site. Ellington's commentary is both informative and charming, offering the backdrop for the direction of the music. "Matumba" is a movement from the satirical tone parallel to the history of jazz—*A Drum Is a Woman*, a close collaboration of Ellington/Strayhorn. Bassist Bell is openly featured. In 1962 he told writer Stanley Dance about the challenge posed by "Matumba": "It's so unorthodox, and Sam's not playing any definite rhythm. There's no bass part there, and it took me a long time to figure out what to do. Actually I'm playing two against three on it … I didn't just come in and start doing it." This perspective reveals how Ellington had enormous confidence in his talented musicians to enlist their intuition, technical wherewithal and imagination to solve problems—finding solutions that fit and enrich the musical frameworks.

The aforementioned tour de force "Diminuendo and Crescendo in Blue" is a widely popular choice to close a concert and leaving the audience ecstatic and exhausted with glee. Paul Gonsalves shares the storied genius behind the success of "Diminuendo and Crescendo in Blue." In the face of speculations made among New York musicians about the ability of the Ellington band to make it in Birdland—a modern jazz venue with high expectations—Ellington called the tune(s) Gonsalves had never played (107 and 108 in the band book) previously. When the band had finished the first part, Gonsalves told Ellington he'd like to take some choruses between the two parts. After he blew an untold number of choruses, the audience was aroused and went crazy standing on chairs. "We didn't play it again until that time at Newport," said Gonsalves. "We were getting ready to go on when Duke called me in the wings." Ellington instructed him to "play it as long as you like." The screaming crowd was turned on emotionally—it was sensational and triumphant! And check Gonsalves' solo content and musical demeanor on this 1960 trip … it is filled with surprises and, of course, his Coleman Hawkins-influenced horn never stops swinging.

Unarguably, the Ellington Orchestra was really in top form that evening in Santa Monica. Gonsalves observed: "One night we may stink, but the next night we might sound wonderful when there's that fusion between guys who feel like playing, when everything's goin' down right, and we're playing his music the way it should be played … man, it's the greatest jazz band there is." This concert was one of those super special Duke Ellington nights!

— · — · — · — · — · — · — · — · — · — · — · —

Woody Herman

Woody Herman wasn't just another big band leader; Woody Herman created a big band culture. He paved the way, driving big bands to their rightful place in the historical jazz cannon.

He chose musicians who evidenced skills in composition and Woody supported them, giving them the freedom to express themselves as soloists. He always had dynamite soloists who helped deliver the flavor of the big bands—the driving attraction that appealed to other musicians and to the audience. It was a balance that Woody was able to achieve, kind of like having a small band inside of a big band.

Woody Herman also managed to turn my wedding reception into a performance showcase for his Herd.

Woody called me while I was on the air at KJAZ to check on bookings for the coming week; I was acting as his unofficial manager at the time. When we got to Saturday, I said, "I don't know what the *band's* going to be doing on Saturday, Woody, but I do know what *I'll* be doing. *I'm* getting married."

After a brief silence, Woody said, "Wow! To Marilyn, right? Well, the band will be there, so you'll have to get a place that will hold a thousand guests."

"Wait a minute," I said, pausing to go back on-air, "We don't have any plans like *that*, Woody. But it would be great to have the band as our guests and I'll get you the details after my show," I said, hurriedly hanging up to get back to my on-air show.

A couple of minutes later, Woody called again. "Herb, I know you will be calling on all the important people in the industry to be at your wedding, so we're going to come with our axes. We're not just going to be your guests; we will be *playing* your wedding."

And so our wedding reception—with all of our friends and all of the music industry heavyweights in attendance—was turned into a performance showcase by Woody Herman and his Herd.

Woody was delighted, I was delighted, Marilyn was delighted, and—since we've been married for 46 years, I guess it worked!

Woody Herman—*Woody's Winners*
Columbia (CL 2436); 1965; Reissued by Sony Music Entertainment

GREASY SACK BLUES

"The blues has always been part of our bag. It's reminiscent in some degree of the sharing of the Roseland bandstand by Basie and me. It has certainly left its mark on both of us."

—Woodrow Charles "Woody" Herman

Woody Herman himself has indeed been—and decidedly is—a winner. He has basked in the limelight of the winner's circle many times more than a quarter century.

Herb Wong on his 1963 KJAZ promotional visit with Woody Herman at Harrah's Lake Tahoe (photograph by an unknown Harrah's PR photographer; courtesy the Wong family).

He has been honored by jazz polls for the high musical quality of his own performances and for his respective "Herds." His outstanding recordings, from the old 78s to albums of the 1960s, are collectors' items. He has even toured foreign lands for the State Department. Woody Herman, in short, has earned the rare respect, adulation and lasting enthusiasm of countless people all over the world.

Woody's groups have been among the notably productive seedbeds for jazz musicians, who have been nurtured, trained and very often explosively introduced to the public. To cite specific cases would easily involve a long list of jazz musicians. Even in 1965 there were new talents in the Herman band whose brilliance, vigorous spirit and musicianship attracted and stirred crowds from San Francisco to the Jazz Festival in Juan-les-Pins, Antibes. This process, the subtle, complex evolution of the Herman bands under Woody's effectual leadership, has been occurring for a long time and cannot be explained by a single performance or relationship. The French have a word for it, I believe—*èpanouissement*. Although it has no exact or literal English translation, it does convey the idea of "becoming," and encompasses such nuances as growth, development, unraveling, flowering and fulfillment.

This album, recorded live at Basin Street West in San Francisco, is the realization of a long-held hope of mine. Having Woody play for the first time in Basin Street West (a spacious, attractive club that John Hammond has called one of the finest jazz rooms in the country) was a three-day jazz joyride. Album producer Teo Macero and other Columbia staffers were present during the engagement, and were rocked by this newest edition of Woody's wailing, free swinging, smoking band. Woody's stand-up firing squad nearly blew the glasses and everything else off the patrons' tables. No doubt about it, the band held its audiences spellbound.

The selections:

"23 RED"

Bill Chase wrote this blistering swinger several years ago. When I first heard it in December 1963, in Las Vegas, I hoped that it would be recorded some day. The seemingly mystic title is very simply explained. The numeral 23 and the color red are a "lucky" combination that composer Chase used at roulette tables in Reno, Tahoe and Las Vegas, when the band played there. Actually, "23" is the band's repertoire code name for the tune "Four Brothers" ("hot tunes" such as "Caldonia," identified as "24," and "Early Autumn," "21," are also "lucky" at the felt-lined tables.). This opening track is one of the album's many highlights. The trumpet-centered chart features Chase, Duško Goyković and Don Rader in a romping trumpet choir that opens with lightening excitement and explodes into Chase's shout to initiate a fascinating series of exchanges (one chorus each of two bars, two choruses of four bars and two choruses of twos.).

"MY FUNNY VALENTINE"

This version has been labeled by its arranger, Don Rader, as "My Funky Valentine." Dig Woody's low-register clarinet with its natural, warm, woody sound. Rader's open-horn work is followed by an Al Cohn-tinged tenor of Gary Klein. The trumpets screech as lead trumpeter Chase impressively penetrates the sound barrier. "My Wailin' Valentine" it is!

"NORTHWEST PASSAGE"

Woody's galloping warhorse gets a redressing job by arranger-pianist Nat Pierce. Originally recorded on March 1, 1945, by the "First Herd," it now joins the ranks of "Apple Honey" and "Caldonia," head arrangements rendered in later, contemporary versions. All we need now is "Your Father's Mustache" and "Wild Root," and the twenty-year cycle of up-tune overhauling will be nearly complete.

Woody, Nistico and Rader on mute kick it off and then Sal lashes into his long solo, much like a voracious Cro-Magnon devouring a long-sought meal. Chase's trumpet slices in, rapier-like, to boost the scorching excursion to its conclusion. A real pressure-cooker!

"POOR BUTTERFLY"

An oldie scored by Rader who, incidentally, contributed several nice arrangements during this latest tenure with Woody. Previous associations with the Maynard Ferguson and Basie bands helped pave the way for Don's current creative outpourings. Father Herman's richly beautiful alto and clarinet never dip into the commonplace. His lyrical statements can be serene and lovely, yet at the same time be buoyed up by intense sincerity and passion.

"Woody's Whistle"

This is an original blues by Duško Goyković, who wanted to "get the guys to relax and release tensions, to rid themselves of cobwebs and the hard-walking feeling of this number." The chart possesses highly interesting thematic phrases. Nat Pierce's groovy pianistics carry the line again while over it Woody sometimes sings the short commentary: "Your sister smokes … your sister smokes … smokes in bed." Nistico's wailing is followed by Duško's crying re-entry.

To close the tune, Woody blows his pocket whistle. It is not just a device for this tune; it has been a functional part of Woody's stage *accoutrement* for some time. Woody blows it to signal to members of the band that intermission is over and that it's time to regroup on the bandstand for the next set.

"Red Roses for a Blue Lady"

Another arrangement by the Yugoslavian trumpet star, Duško Goyković, this has a good Herman reed-section sound. Andy McGhee fashions a cruising, warmly attractive tenor solo.

"Opus de Funk" and "Theme (Blue Flame)"

I am delighted that this Horace Silver vehicle is included! Back in June 1955, Woody recorded Nat Pierce's arrangement of it, and here it is again a decade later—and what a swinging version it is! Nat's wonderful piano work (Woody makes a jocose reference to pianist Mary Lou Williams) forecasts the visceral swing of the performance. Gary Klein uncorks a Lester Young/Al Cohn-ish solo, and Chase reaches way upstairs to lift the elation even higher. Finally, Duško pours fresh, flaming fuel into this steamer, while the band grooves with propulsive riffs.

This was the final tune the band played that last night at Basin Street West. It was obviously inspired by the very hip crowd-gathered there. Their enthusiasm was so demonstrative that they stood up and shouted, demanding more. The band, however, segued into the Herman theme, "Blue Flame." Woody's recorded comment, "We dug it the most," sums up what happened at the Basin Street West. The Herman band, playing with unusual élan, had provided some of its most arm-pumping, hand-clapping, finger-snapping, foot-tapping big-band jazz ever!

Stan Kenton

I was so stunned when I first heard Stan Kenton's "Artistry in Rhythm," I immediately went out and bought three copies. Then, when I was discharged from the Army in August of 1946, the first thing I did—after seeing my folks—was to zip down to L.A. to catch the Stan Kenton Orchestra, which was really cookin' at the time.

When Stan asked me to write the liner notes for his album, *Live at Brigham Young University*, he instructed me before I started writing: "I want you to write copious notes and focus on education, on creativity, if you can."

He was obviously focusing on these areas. It's no accident that they called it "The Creative World of Stan Kenton," a label that meant more than mere promotion or an attempt to gain attention.

It's interesting to me how a man like Stan Kenton, whose music didn't bend as much as others, adopted a style that was more "crashing down" than bending. It seemed that a lot of his horn sounds, with their emphasis on brass, didn't have the flexibility it needed; at least that's what *I* felt they needed. If it had bent more, it would have swung more.

An illustration from an oft-told Kenton story: One day, when his guys were swinging their asses off, Stan walked in without the guys realizing that he had caught them really going at it. And he said, "Stop it, stop it! You guys are swinging so hard you're starting to sound like Woody!"

Stan Kenton and His Orchestra—*Live at Brigham Young University*
Crescendo / Creative World Records (ST 1039); 1971

Historian Arnold Toynbee declared, "Civilization is a movement ... and not a condition, a voyage and not a harbor." One of the fundamental ecological concepts dealing with the interface of man and his total environment is that the only constant in nature is change. These two statements are related to the observation made by author Peter Drucker regarding the daily changes that buffet our world in all directions threatening its safety; he indicates the process of innovating is the only way to remain relatively durable. The only stability attainable is stability in motion. The process of innovation has, indeed, been identified with a system of ongoing renewal for Stan Kenton. A quick review of the chronicle of Stan's thirty years as a creative, self-renewing individual vis-á-vis his innumerable accomplishments and contributions would bring his innovative consciousness into a focus.

Stan is an example of the creative being—inquisitive, sensitive, innovative—he is restlessly exploring new territories, trying out new strategies and seeking new insights. Innovation includes a new way of doing things and a new way of thinking about things, too.

Witness the plethora of ideas which have emerged in his music of three decades and the concepts which characterize his conduct in related activities and we arrive at another creative trait. Creative people are open to a host of stimuli of the external world that seem to be relevant to the individual's inner life. Stan displays selective awareness, offering him access to the rich spread of an individual's emotional, intellectual and spiritual experiences. Likewise, Stan has the capacity to be detached and independent regarding his creative work—an independence of creative people which carries the capacity to assume risks and to expose himself to criticism from his colleagues. Certainly Stan has been the center of controversies through the years. But Stan possesses the psychological safety and confidence to toy with concepts and ideas from numerous perspectives—changing directions, redefining the parts, etc. Stan seems to find comfort with flexibility with unresolved differences as he must "take one step at a time, examine it to see where it's taking me with no set formula in mind." And yet most people are immobilized by being caught in the circle of learned rigidities.

This Kenton band is one of the most cohesive, best balanced and driving units Stan has ever had. The selections are beautifully expressed on this recording and propulsive

John Von Ohlen's bass drum sounds like tympani. A real gas! Mike Vax leading the trumpets sounds like the head man of a blowing brigade on a charge! And the charts? Thousands of youngsters will be playing them on records, on tapes and in their own jazz bands. You better believe it.

The initial track by Bill Holman—"Malaga" was commissioned by the Millikin University Jazz Lab Band and is hereby dedicated to the band by Bill. The excitement generated by this opener is a strong cue for the rest of the album. Dig Von Ohlen! Bill's other chart in the session is "Rhapsody in Blue" featuring an impassioned baritone solo by Chuck Carter. Former Kenton reed player Hank Levy of Towson State College has contributed "Hank's Opener" (alternated in 7/4 and 14/8) a very funky, bright chart featuring brilliant altoist Quinn Davis and Gary Pack on trumpet—both are spotlighted through much of the LP; "A Step Beyond," also by Levy, finds Willie Maiden on baritone and Gary on engaging solos. Speaking of Maiden, here's a guy whose very competent writing injects a nice communicative swing ("Love Story" theme has tasteful Davis and Maiden work) and both "Kaleidoscope" and "April Fool" move with infectious lines that invite revisitation. Trombonist Shearer always delivers the goods with authority and Gary Todd is one of the strongest bass players in big bands.

Ken Hanna's own "Bogota" ... Ramon Lopez is a terribly fine percussionist and then incredible Vax tears it up! The more you hear Quinn's alto, the more impressed you become ... he plays with such command, taste and conception! Listen to him on Legrand's lovely tune ... for the rest of your life. Finally, Hanna who was inspired by a documentary film conjured his impressions into a four-part suite to close the album—"Macumba." Here is Ken's own narrative:

"Macumba" is deeply imbedded in the culture of Brazil; the cult of "Macumba" is a form of religious worship intertwined with musical sounds and rhythms, combined with dancing which reaches a frenetic savagery. The outside world knows little about this practice which is prevalent in the favelas (slums) and has wide influence in the life in that country.

"Twilight in the Favelas" describes the despair of its inhabitants as represented by the interweaving of plaintive and mournful instrumental voices.

The music in this album was recorded in Provo, Utah, by the Kenton band on the Brigham Young University campus on August 13, 1971.

"Procession to the Terreiro" calls the believers to the gathering place with the funereal-type march, swelling in numbers and anticipation, culminating in the arrival—musically represented by the trombone choir at the ritual site.

In "Omulu" the practice of the animal sacrifice is fulfilled, and the tortuous dancing begins with the accelerando and crescendo of the orchestra. Additional dancers (soloists) join in the mesmeric rhythms reaching a peak of fury, culminating in the collapse of the participants from the wildly expended energy of the dance.

"Cumprimento" suggests the fleeting and hysterical release of the ritualists from the realistic misery, drabness and utter hopelessness which surrounds them daily. The final sounds symbolize a distant shimmering image which falsely gleams with the hopes and promises of a more perfect future.

The jazz of Stanley Newcomb Kenton via this album of collective talents is another contribution from his creative world. It documents one of the most instantly explosive big bands ... reviving composer Roger Sessions' words, "Inspiration is the impulse which sets creation in movement; it is also the energy which keeps it going."

Louie Bellson

I became a full-time producer in the 1980s, but the first record I ever produced was in the '60s with Roy Eldridge and Louie Bellson.

The Basie Band was in town at Basin Street West and the guest soloist with them on the tour was trumpeter, Roy Eldridge. That, I thought, was exciting, as it had never happened before that tour. I don't know the reason behind it, but while I was there, Basie fired his drummer Sonny Payne. So I said to the Count, "What are you going to do about it Base?" And he said, "I don't know … I don't know where I'm going to get another drummer." I said, "Well, I do!" And Base responded, "Who's that?" I said, "Louie Bellson and here's his telephone number." And Base said, "Why don't you call him?"

So I called Louie and I said, "I got a gig for you; are you available? It's with some of the guys in the Basie Band." That's all Louie needed to hear. "I'm in!" he said.

Louie Bellson Big Band—*Dynamite!*
Concord Jazz (CCD 4105); 1979

The jubilant cheering, stomping and whistling might have led one to think it was the Super Bowl or World Series championship playoffs. But it was eruptive audience reaction to the dynamite performance of the Louie Bellson Big Band—the grand finale to the three evenings of the 1979 Concord Summer Jazz Festival. It was a night in which brisk winds whipped through the Concord Pavilion bandstand and music sheets were flying off the music stands. Bellson's spirited band played with a sizzling short fuse from the start, making way for frequent surprises heating up the cold evening air.

Like powerful sticks of dynamite, Louie Bellson's drumsticks are explosive. Under the control of his hands and feet, Bellson's distinctively arrayed drum kit and sounds have long become trademarks of his brand of jazz excitement. He has his own musical nitroglycerine equivalents soaked in emotions, bravura and an intuitive sixth sense of swing.

Predictably high anticipations occur whenever Bellson is scheduled to perform. Surefire gratification is attributable to his four decades of successful contributions as a professional jazz drummer and twenty-seven of those years leading a band.

A human detonator like Bellson, who swings in an incurably joyous tradition, enlivens his band and everyone within his musical outreach. The music on this album assuredly quickened heart rates and furnished good reasons for the ever growing respect he commands.

His overall tirelessness and dedication spills over to a wide variety of jazz educational activities on campuses. For instance, this winter he was the culminating inspirational and energy center for the Slingerland National Drum Contest. Thousands of ambitious young drummers competed. The shining example Louie sets as one of the world's finest drummers and as a personable and zestful person, is a living reward to the youthful aspirants.

Bellson and eighteen able colleagues … a large nucleus of key improvisers from the L.A. circle of jazz pros, kick off the colorful set with Don Menza's up tempo "Sambandrea Swing." Composer Menza's charging tenor solo leads off in front of Bobby Shew's trumpet and Al Kaplan's trombone solos. Dig the impressive long unison line beginning midway with a stop-time chorus. The exactitude of the ensemble's well-oiled negotiations gives the interpretation added sheen and drive. Menza was commissioned by Cal State University at Northridge to write this piece introducing it at the 1979 Pacific Coast Collegiate Jazzfest in Berkeley.

The alchemic blend of Bellson's pretty melody, Bill Holman's brilliant arrangement and Bobby Shew's elegant flugelhorn showcase makes "Deliverance" a special treat. Holman brings the tune to an enlightened life, giving it potential durability. Shew's soulful solo is approximated by his own enthusiasm for Holman: "Bill outdid himself. Everything is like a composition to him. The backgrounds are lines that are not pads of things to fill up. His lines behind my solos are incredible. I never tire of playing it or listening to it. The chart is such a masterpiece!" Incidentally, Shew's marvelous lead trumpet work throughout the album is simply awesome—especially his exceptional delivery of a natural, strong jazz feeling.

"Concord Blues for Blue" is dedicated to the late Blue Mitchell whose wonderful trumpet graced the band for several years. This minor blues features lead altoist Dick Spencer's inspiring idiomatic solo. Like Shew, he has spent about seven years with Bellson, straddled with five years playing lead for the Akiyoshi/Tabackin Big Band. Aside from his work with Doc Severinsen on *The Tonight Show*, Spencer's strengths include earlier tenures with Maynard Ferguson, Harry James and a bebop quintet in Barcelona led by the phenomenal Catalonian jazz pianist—Tete Montoliu. Note also the fine bass work of John Williams and Bellson's tasty earfuls.

"Cinderella's Waltz" was first arranged by Menza for the University of California at Santa Barbara Jazz Ensemble; it was debuted by the host band at its festival this past spring. Bobby Shew's horn is fiery and expressive. And pianist Frank Collett's excellence as a well-experienced vocal accompanist comes through in his splendid support.

Guitarist John Chiodini's exciting solo on Bellson's tune, "Where Did You Go?" evokes memories of Charlie Christian's epochal 1941 guitar solo on "Solo Flight" with Benny Goodman's orchestra and Jimmy Gourley's solo on "Flyin' the Coop" with Chubby Jackson's 1957 big band. Chiodini is a recent alumnus of Maynard Ferguson's band. Listen to the great buildup by the band! Prior to Peggy Lee's lyrics and new title, it was first called "Something for Joe" (Pass) and then "Something for John."

Talented young teenaged composer-arranger Matt Catingub wrote "Explosion" to reflect "Louie's style and my style all in one piece," he said. Catingub was selected outstanding young composer at the 1978 Monterey Jazzfest High School All-Star Competition. He uses close voicings and modal harmonic approaches. As for his alto playing, he subscribes to his influences—Phil Woods and Cannonball Adderley. Matt's straight ahead, burning solo offers unexpected conceptual shifts and consequent contrasts.

Lots of fills and horns you expect to hear are actually played by the drums, and toward the end, the big fanfare kind of ending chords push the band to a fitting volcanic climax to the festival. Louie Bellson uses the full scope of his instruments in his remarkable performance. Anything less need not be expected as Mr. "TNT" Bellson is simply DYNAMITE!

Buddy Rich

I happened to be helping out at the door when Buddy Rich was performing with his big band at Basin Street West on Montgomery Street in San Francisco. Soon after they started playing, I decided to go into the club to catch some of the band's first set.

That's when all hell broke loose.

The band had just started playing, when—all of a sudden—Buddy leapt up on his feet and started yelling: "YOU! YOU!" He was pointing at a young saxophone player who was brand new to the band. Buddy was saying something to him—obviously not something good—about his playing. And then Buddy started screaming, "YOU'RE FIRED, YOU'RE FIRED!"

All I can think is, "Jesus Christ, Buddy, you're scaring the shit out of him!"

So I went down to the dressing room during intermission and I said, "Jeez, Buddy, do you have to be so cruel? I mean, that kid, you shook him up like crazy." And Buddy says, "Nahh, I'm not worried about it. I'm just going to rehire him tomorrow, anyway."

The Buddy Rich Big Band—*Big Swing Face*
Pacific Jazz (ST 20117); 1967; Reissued by Blue Note Records

The mention of Buddy Rich and his new big band evokes enthusiastic reaction from both the young and the old, although the responses contain idiomatic differences. Buddy is a remaining and artistically productive survivor of that small, empyreal fraternity of swing era drummers—Chick Webb, Big Sid Catlett, Dave Tough, and Jo Jones; he has, therefore, on the one hand re-ignited and inflamed the sizeable communities of swing band-dance band fans. On the other hand, Buddy's philosophy of contemporaneity reflected in his driving and tastefully refreshing renditions of much of today's best pop material has undoubtedly elongated the listening antennae of the younger set. A case in point of this magnetic and perhaps somewhat hypnotic effect his music is having on the kids—I recall a girl just out of her teens dashing over to Buddy after his SRO, explosive opening set at San Francisco's Basin St. West a couple of months ago; noticeably unnerved, she told Buddy that the band's invigorating and entrancing music made her feel as if she was going through "a happening."

Accounting for his concept of playing the kind of music the kids can relate to and can dance to with the hope they might come into concerts and clubs, Buddy has observed, "The first reaction of kids is simply sheer amazement. They aren't used to the real big band sound. After the first half hour or so they choose not to dance but just to listen. At the Chez in Hollywood, the older audiences gave way to the young people with funny hair after the first week. They dig their music—the sound, the beat, the excitement." In reference to the discovery and identification syndrome of youth, Buddy adds, "They usually see a kid banging on a set of drums but rarely have they seen a bona fide jazz drummer per se. A common reaction I have encountered is the elation the kids express in their cry of … 'Look what and who we discovered!' Because most of these kids don't know me or ever heard of me, I'm literally a symbol of their discovery."

On this album there are several tunes of the youth genre. The Beatles' "Norwegian Wood" arranged by Bill Holman features a pair of young musicians—trombonist Jim Trimble and altoist Ernie Watts, a recent acquisition from Boston's Berklee School of Music via recommendation by Phil Wilson, ex–Woody Herman trombone star and currently a faculty member of the school. Trumpeter Shorty Rogers scored "Wack Wack," the pop chart mainstay by the former bassist and drummer of the Ramsey Lewis Trio—Eldee Young and Red Holt. Ernie Watts has room for his alto statements here. Rogers' arrangement translated by superb musicianship via Buddy and the band add color and spirit to "Wack Wack" without forsaking its inherent traits. Sonny and Cher's hit, "The Beat Goes On" introduces Buddy's 12-year-old daughter Cathy singing the lyrics about mini-skirts and teeny boppers et al.; her message was greeted with high enthusiasm by the audience at the Chez.

The other half dozen tunes will turn you on completely as you get trapped in the swirl of the roaring power of the cooking engines driven by Mr. Rich. The title selection, "Big Swing Face" introduces ex–Kentonite Ray Starling on piano, who also plays a sprinkling of charts using the mellophonium—the Kenton-designed hybrid brass instrument; the other soloist is trumpeter Bob Shew formerly with Woody Herman. Composer-arranger Bill Potts, who has charted tunes for numerous bands, possesses an awareness of several ingredients: a deep concern for voice leading, a strong effort to use a range of dynamic shadings, and definitive swing all the way, effecting an atmosphere of fiber and maturity.

"Monitor Theme" is literally the theme music for the NBC network Monitor broadcasts using Buddy's band. Shew gets another shot here on this Holman chart and tenor star Jay Corre is featured as he is on five other tunes on the set.

Cole Porter's "Love for Sale" has rarely received this kind of febricity-filled pitch. Dig the way it builds up a head of steam and seems to move everything and everyone out of its way as nineteen year-old Chuck Findley debuts impressively on trumpet and Corre swings hard. But there is no denying that it is the awesome, super-drummer ... even "superhuman" Buddy Rich whose blazing speed and deft command of the drums that sends the tune on its wildest ride ever! A skin-drenching performance no less.

Trombonist-composer Harry Betts contributed "Mexicali Nose" for one of the blowingest proboscises that has poked through a jazz chart. "Willowcrest" bears young Findley and Corre's sounds again. You hear Buddy's peerless fashion of juxtaposing the effects of the cymbals, tom toms and bass drum, and every conceivable intricacy and pattern he can or wishes to conjure—feeding into, underneath and above—enveloping the situation with fascinating improvisations. Would you believe "Bugle Call Rag"? Buddy relates amusingly, "When I first sounded Bill Holman out about writing the chart, he said, 'WHAT?!'" This old swing era hot tune gets re-tailored to fit the band's predilective abilities to handle a front burner like this. And I swear when my ears first copped the sounds of the chart in San Francisco I thought the trumpet section and Buddy would wake up and marshal all the troops in man's history so they could respond to the battle cry and CHARGE! It's a flag waver that doesn't quit—adrenalin is pumped a mile a second on this last track, and Buddy's drum solo is utterly fantastic. Listen and you can still hear the echo. WHEEEEE!

Retrenching for a moment, Buddy's concept of soloists is worthy of inclusion. Buddy explains: "We don't treat a soloist as a soloist—for a soloist is not really a soloist in the strict sense of the word. A big band is a whole unit and the band is not a vehicle for soloists ... if there are figures played behind the soloist, then he is never really by himself, is he? He becomes a part of a band without thinking; he has to fit his sound accordingly and become melded into the band. People lose sight of the fact that the sound, the intensity, and the excitement of a big band is unique." This may be why the guys groove so well.

Nearly every quarter of our jazzstream of life is enthralled with this exhilarating band. Whitney Balliett's beautiful profile of Buddy in *The New Yorker*, tours with Frank

Sinatra, TV appearances galore, his first LP (Pacific Jazz ST-20113/Pd-1 0113) scaling the sales charts, etc. And Buddy's figurative "Big Swing Face" reaches the eyes, ears and cognitive senses of a wide, diversified encampment of devotees. *Big Swing Face* indeed, for it's the biggest, swinginest jazz physiognomy in 1967—one that has a winning, irresistible countenance, so dig it hard *con passione*!

CHAPTER 2

Trumpet

One of the keys to a big band's success is the art of communication; it is the foundation upon which every great big band is built. And it is the trumpet that has traditionally taken the lead in that form of communication. Without communication as a top priority—without a great trumpet as a top priority—you won't have a great big band.

While the big band forms the foundation for jazz, it is the trumpet that sounds its clarion call as the next logical floor to explore. And it is Dizzy Gillespie's trumpet that sounds the clearest call of all.

Dizzy Gillespie

Dizzy Gillespie was the bebop king … the explorer … the discoverer. His curiosity and musical knowledge are legendary. He was also a generous man, a man with a heart as big as his cheeks, something I discovered when I introduced a young Jon Faddis to Diz at the Monterey Jazz Festival in 1968.

Jon (who was a giant talent when he was only 12 or 13) came into the Hunt Club (the festival's "Artist Bar") looking for Dizzy. "I know where he is," I said. To which Jon respectfully replied, "I would appreciate it, sir, if you would introduce me to Dizzy Gillespie."

Jon was holding a stack of LPs in his hands—I mean a *stack*—and I said, looking incredulously at the twenty or so albums he held in his arms, "You brought all those with you?" And Jon says, "Yes, sir, I'd like to see if I can get Mr. Gillespie to sign every one of these albums."

I got ahold of Dizzy and I said, "Dizzy there's this young man and he's a trumpet player and he'd like to have your autograph on all these albums he has." Without missing a beat, Dizzy says, "Yeah, I'll do it, man." He was always open like that.

Next thing I know, Dizzy and his quintet are on stage performing and, during the middle of that performance, Dizzy stops and says, "Where's that young man I was speaking to?" And so, Jon jumps up and joins Dizzy's group on the stage of the Monterey Jazz Festival to play "Night in Tunisia" … and that's how the two great trumpeters met.

Dizzy Gillespie—*Havin' a Good Time in Paris*
Vogue P.I.P.; 1952; Reissued by Inner City Records (IC 7010)

In jazz and other art forms there is a tendency, if not a practice, of classifying the performers and putting them into convenient categories. A long and impressive list of descriptors could be easily drafted in reference to Dizzy Gillespie and his towering artistic accomplishments. However, no category exists which amply accommodates Dizzy's uniqueness as a comprehensive jazz musician and master entertainer.

Dizzy's musical intelligence is broad and his curiosity is intense. There is little of the world's musical forms which he has not examined and considered for its potential rhythmic integration with jazz; this is particularly true of Latin American rhythms, the object of his successful experimentation beginning with patterns played with Chano Pozo and Machito. Norman Granz has commented on the intrepid attitude Dizzy brings to experimentation: "He's adventuresome. He takes chances ... I mean, he'll try everything."

Generosity is one of Dizzy's personal traits. He has consistently shared his fund of musical knowledge and values with historical jazz figures and new learner/players, literally teaching them and setting them in fresh directions he helped to develop. What was thought unorthodox and chaotic in the forties when Dizzy was playing "all those strange unheard of things" has emerged as vital classical aspects of modern music.

The Gillespie romping, bopping 1946 big band came into San Francisco for a couple of weeks to the old Barbary Coast. The area was pinpointed geographically on Pacific off Kearny Street—one block from Broadway in North Beach. A huge arched sign reading "International Settlement" stretched from one side of the street to the other, about three stories high, forming an ornate gateway to the area dominated by strip joints. Dizzy's blazing band played in one of these joints which was transformed into a night club. My memory of the gig is still vivid. I spent ten joyous nights in there getting blown away by the challenging music—Dizzy's own stimulating originals plus the compositions and arrangements of Gil Fuller, Ray Brown and Tadd Dameron. It was wild! And Dizzy's natural, dynamic leadership and showmanship was clear then, as it is now. Ironically, it has taken over a quarter century for this culture to hook into the solid, logical concepts of Diz and his fellow tide-turners—the ultimate justifications for the struggles on so many different kinds of fronts.

As one of the founding fathers of the music which altered the course of jazz and a pioneering trumpeter with an awesome grasp of the horn, Dizzy was heralded with fanfare and met with exultation on his trips to Europe, especially in the late forties and early fifties. At the time of this recording in Paris, Dizzy was struggling with the survival of his own Dee Gee record company, which was dissolved in 1953. The record shows how he stepped up the use of his own vocals to popularize his music without forsaking artistic quality.

Dizzy had gone to play at the Second International Jazz Salon at the Salle Pleyel. Two days prior to the concert, he recorded most of the music here with a quintet assembled for the date, including expatriate Don Byas on tenor. The three-man rhythm section—Arnold Ross, Joe Benjamin and Bill Clark—was with Lena Horne at the time. Except for "I Cover the Waterfront," the other tunes all have alternate takes from the session in March 1952. Dizzy's powerful treatment characterizes all of the selections.

Side B opens with the remaining three tunes recorded later in April. They were done with a different group, although Byas is present again. Trombonist Bill Tamper's sound and style, incidentally, is strongly reminiscent of Bill Harris. What is listed as "Cripple Crapple Crutch" is a meaningless title which, judging from the lyrics, may have resulted from an error in phonetic interpretation. The blues line goes like this: "I wouldn't give a blind sow an acorn, wouldn't give a cripple crab a crutch, 'cause I just found out, pretty mama, that you ain't so such a much." Then Diz follows up his vocal with words from Leonard Feather's classic "Salty Papa Blues," which Feather was responsible in getting Dinah Washington to record in 1943 with a half dozen men out of Lionel Hampton's orchestra. Diz sings and plays the blues with his gutsy authenticity.

Max Roach has said that Dizzy is without any peer and that "he's a cornerstone in the development and evolution of our music." Dizzy has continued to water his meadows of mind, keeping his inventiveness and facility going. He is well aware of his stature, placing him among the greatest in history. John Birks "Dizzy" Gillespie, who was born in October 1917, has been and *is* one of the world's greatest and most original trumpet players. Whether it be Gillespie of the forties, fifties, sixties, seventies or eighties—Dizzy Gillespie is a legend.

Pete Candoli / Conte Candoli

Dizzy Gillespie was not only a legend, he was a legendary influence on so many who followed—the talented players who became legends in their own right—perhaps no one more so than Conte Candoli. Conte's trademark was plainly Dizzy Gillespie. His solos had a shape and sound that smacked of Dizzy's approach and Conte was just a beautiful player.

His talents were identified early on by the efforts of his brother, Pete, who was a stellar member of Woody Herman's First Herd. Pete was promoting his brother, telling Woody how Conte was an amazing jazz trumpet player. So Woody hired Conte—at age 16!—and then he told him to go back and finish his high school education before coming back on the band.

Pete was called "Superman" and he would dress for gigs in a uniform, the same attire as the comic book Superman. When Woody had the band on the stage, he had it rigged up so that Pete could swing in the air from one end to the other end in front of the audience—just like Superman. He even looked like Superman; he had a similar musculature. And there was Pete, swinging from one end to the other, trumpet in hand; and then right there, in the air, he would play a solo!

Pete and Conte Candoli—*Two Brothers*
Hindsight Records (HCD 623); 1999

Brothers who are jazz musicians are a topic of more than casual interest. There are, in fact, over fifty sets of brothers who are or have been playing jazz. Jazz fans can recite a short list of jazz brothers (Heath, Jones, Marsalis, Dorsey, Montgomery, Brecker, and Adderley are examples). There is strong bonding among the majority set of brothers. Pete and Conte Candoli accentuate a powerful set of brothers with great mutual love and affection—a condition which is articulated in hearty and sensitive performances and human interrelationships with other musicians and fans. The Candolis are close as pages in a book and are each other's hero.

Both were destined to be trumpeters from their childhood days in Mishawaka, Indiana—with Pete (older of the two) serving as Conte's guiding influence and inspiration. Their dossiers are extensive and illuminated by significant experiences and high grade associations.

Briefly, Pete began playing lead and jazz for Sonny Dunham's Orchestra in 1941, followed by a long string of other name bands including Woody Herman's famed First Herd. At 16, Conte also joined Herman's crack trumpet section in 1944; he returned home to finish high school before rejoining the band in early 1945. Both brothers played key roles with Herman and Stan Kenton. Conte was with them at various times in a somewhat turn-style fashion between the '40s and the early '50s. He then opted to play bebop in smaller bands led by bassist Chubby Jackson and then with Charlie Ventura before his extended time with The Lighthouse All-Stars and other forays in L. A.—gaining prominence as an outstanding jazz player. Pete, on the other hand, had already settled into the L.A. studio scene after tenures with Herman, Tex Beneke, Jerry Gray and Kenton. Pete and Conte also co-led a band (1957–62); their omnipresence is reflected in the many bands they played with. As a preeminent lead trumpeter, Pete played for the orchestras of Axel Stordahl, Gordon Jenkins, Nelson Riddle, Don Costa, Michel Legrand and Henry Mancini. Conte's jazz exposure was heightened via Supersax with Shelly Manne's Men and the much extended gig on *The Tonight Show* big band led by Doc Severinsen. As a pronto update, during March this year I caught Conte in the Palm Springs area playing magnificently in different contexts—a post jazz celebrity golf tournament jam session, a Frank Sinatra Tribute big band revue and a quartet gig at Pasta Italia restaurant. Then two months later, Conte played notably in the four-day "Jazz West Coast II" event in Newport Beach. His fellow musicians proffered kudos for his impressive artistry.

A recent sampling of warm praise for the Candoli brothers by their peers is in order:

Louie Bellson who wrote/recorded a piece titled "Conte" on a 1998 Bellson CD (*The Art of the Chart*): "Whenever I can use Conte and Pete, I want them. They are dynamite players. I've heard people like Clark Terry voice the same opinion."

Clark Terry: "They're such beautiful cats! And, man, they are great players—both of them!"

Bud Shank: "Conte is the most inspiring and fun-to-play-with trumpeter. He's the finest on the scene—bar none!"

Bill Holman who was listening to Conte playing at Newport Beach: "Conte will be playing on this high level for the rest of his life."

George Graham: "Conte and Pete have been my heroes for years. Pete is the epitome of a lead trumpeter and he's left his mark all over the place. His jazz style is so different, not relying on high notes but always playful and interesting."

Jack Sheldon: "Conte plays all that great stuff and everything is on the beat—one of the great players of all time. And Pete can read anything—the top lead man in town for years. Just to be next to him was a great learning experience. And together the two are incredible!"

Bill Berry: "Besides his high notes, Pete can do anything and in style. He's done it all, from A to Z. He is Conte's hero and says that everything he does, he learned from Pete. And they really are the nicest people!"

Buddy Childers: "Pete and Conte have chemistry that's rarely matched."

Russ Freeman: "I love playing for and comping behind Conte. His time is as smooth as butter."

Moreover, for the record—high esteem for Conte was manifested early on via genuine requests by Charlie Parker to join his band (shortly before Parker's demise); by Max Roach to replace trumpet genius Clifford Brown—his co-leader (after Brown's fatal accident); and an invitation from Duke Ellington to join his orchestra. Clearly, Conte Candoli's validated artistic/creative stature deserves appropriate historical recognition.

Unanimity for Pete and Conte's personae speaks well through their music. Pete's exuberant premier lead work and dashing high note speciality is fueled with gratifying surprises. His sharp, peppered trumpet recalls the brilliance of Louis Armstrong and Roy Eldridge building peaks and climaxes. As for jazz, "I'm radical! I never play the same jazz thing twice!" asserts Pete. "I'm like a chameleon and I play what I feel although I may favor some patterns. Also, I'm a little staccato—on edge of my fiery type of playing."

Both brothers boldly reveal deep personal apperception and emotional immersion. Pete admires "Conte's soul, his feel and his sound." In regard to Conte's beautiful, extended long bebop phrases with a variety of shapes and turns—"they go somewhere in their development." Conte scripts the character of delivering his long lines as a unified essay: "I usually follow a long line with a shorter line—so it comes in bursts, with whatever I'm thinking." His well-reputed flair for exquisite taste—his judiciously chosen notes in his solos and his spicy fashion in shifting dynamics and merging colors are well marked on this CD. "Conte is so melodic and scary in his changes!" exclaimed Pete.

Playing in a big band limits a soloist to play something differently. "You get but one crack at it—usually 8 or 16 bars," Conte points out. He has never wavered about where his true feelings lie: "ad-libbing in a small band is most comfortable for me." Playing deeply together with simpatico, the two brothers detonate explosive jazz interpretations—inoculating themselves against the dryness of more restrictive routine choices: in essence, a combo setting is restorative.

This CD was recorded during a couple of weeks at Rick's Cafe—a Chicago jazz bistro housed in the Holiday Inn—during early March 1983 with a trio of first rate local rhythm section players. "On a date such as this, Pete would sketch out most of the music we play," explains Conte. "And I would dictate the pacing of the sets. Most often I would begin with a solo and Pete follows, and after the rhythm section plays, we play fours or eights, or feature someone. On voicings, Pete plays the lead—the upper part, and I'd be a third or fourth below ... and there's a lot of unison segments, too."

The program of eight tunes constitutes a wealth of material to revisit—underscored by interplay likened to an uninhibited five-way conversation. A balance of swing/bebop classics and standards make up the rich mix, played with verve and appeal. Except for Jimmy Rowles' chart for "Willow Weep for Me," all others were made up by Pete and Conte individually or in collaboration from Dizzy Gillespie's 6/8 bebop anthem "Night in Tunisia," swing staple "Stompin' at the Savoy" and Fats Waller's "Jitterbug Waltz"—to "Indiana"—"boptized" as "Donna Lee," Rodgers & Hart's "My Funny Valentine," the trumpet classic "I Can't Get Started with You," and Sonny Rollins' epic "St. Thomas." Despite familiarity with the melodies, the music enjoys new life with inspired, serious interpretive blowing.

The rhythm section sports three musicians who have been long term fixtures in the Chicago jazz scene. Pianist John Young whose history goes back to the great Andy Kirk Orchestra in earlier times, has worked with Coleman Hawkins, Louis Armstrong, Jimmie Lunceford, and Joe Williams among others. A fully-riped tone bassist, Danny Shapera was a member of drummer Barrett Deems' Trio, Bill Russo's Orchestra and various other local groups. Wilbur Campbell—an in-demand bebop modern drummer had developed a polyrhythmic approach recalling Elvin Jones and Philly Joe Jones, but forged his own voice; he has played and recorded with the likes of Johnny Griffin, Junior Mance, Ira

Sullivan, Charlie Parker, Sonny Rollins, Clifford Brown, Charlie Rouse and Dexter Gordon. "Each time I've played Chicago, I've been lucky to have Wilbur," says Conte enthusiastically. The intuitiveness and sense of unity melded well with the Candoli pair.

In tandem, the two superb trumpeters are a double-header event. Taking their combined experience quotients and the manner in which they have filtered out from those years, it adds up to collective authority and rapport. On this CD is the exhilaration of nice shifting juxtapositions and of their respective styles dissolving in the heat of creation. They are able to fuse individual lines of thought into unified statements. Pete and Conte propagate opportunities to play their music on their own terms. This "live date" allowed them to meet their objectives squarely. In sum, the two Candoli brothers define the jazz force at its best!

Freddie Hubbard

Freddie Hubbard was the one artist with whom I dealt over the years who rarely showed up for a gig on time. I remember when I was working on a television show in L.A. with Sarah Vaughan and everybody was waiting for Freddie to show up for the production to commence. Not only did he not show up *on time*, Freddie never showed up *at all*!

I eventually figured out a way around Freddie's "timing." When I produced five days and nights of the Palo Alto Jazz Festival in the early 1980s, Freddie was somebody I wanted in the show. I called to ask him to take part and he said, "When am I supposed to be there?" I gave him the date and time and I said, "Freddie, you have to be here on time!" To which he replied, "Well, I do what I do."

I thought for a minute and then it came to me. "Freddie," I said. "You don't want to miss the pre-festival party, do you?" And Freddie says, "What? There's going to be a party?" And I said, "Yeah, there's going to be a party!"

Sure enough, he shows up for the party and was on time for the gig.

Freddie Hubbard—*Back to Birdland*
Drive Archive (DE 2–41036); 1981

Shaw 'nuff! Freddie Hubbard's exuberant horn has came home to roost in bop!

Beginning more than thirty years ago, Hubbard started building his jazz career playing his trumpet with a string of groups led by celebrated modernists in New York—Philly Joe Jones, Sonny Rollins, Slide Hampton's Octet and Quincy Jones' big band. In 1961, his star began its ascent during his two and one-half year membership with Art Blakey's Jazz Messengers. Next, he was with Max Roach, followed by numerous other associations.

Before the decade was out, Hubbard had already amassed an impressive discography of his performances and compositions. Moreover, his recordings with Ornette Coleman, Eric Dolphy and John Coltrane in particular, rank as important contributions in the development of the music. In the seventies, he opted for some ventures which were broader-based and more commercial, embracing heavily produced electronics, fusion and rock. Through it all, he never compromised his criterion for musical excellence. His consistency calls for admiration. Departures from this general consumer orientation are clear indications of a shift of values. His public performances, particularly in jazz clubs and festivals, show he has negotiated a U-turn—returning to his strong, durable roots, from whence he first made his mark as one of the most exciting and brilliant players of his instruments and ultimately earning him a seat in the tight circle of reigning jazz trumpeters.

Hubbard's stylistic return to jazz mainstream is much like the homing instinct exhibited in bird behavior. Migration studies show the ability of birds to return to the same specific habitat year after year—the identical woodland, marsh, cliff or meadow. The faculty enabling birds to point their course accurately over vast expanses of land and water is regarded as a "sense of direction" or "magnetic sense." And, despite possible drifting by the winds which may alter direction, there exists an active, powerful striving to reach a particular direction. There is, then, a kinship between these avian impulses and the processes involved in Hubbard's round trip to "Birdland."

Hubbard's style is cast in a rich blend of Fats Navarro and Dizzy Gillespie's high technical dexterity to blow intricate improvised lines with blazing speed, and Clifford Brown and Miles Davis' deep and bold lyricism.

On this album, Hubbard is complemented on the front line by two horn players he had not worked with previously. First, the younger, thoroughly dedicated and likewise spectacular player—alto saxophonist Richie Cole. His territory and language are derived from the Charlie Parker–Sonny Stitt–Phil Woods mold—his chosen direction in jazz tradition. There is no mystery about his world-wide repute as a dominant force. His contributions here speak to that recognition.

Cole played with Ashley Alexander a good number of times and the two wanted to record together. I witnessed their forthright concepts and intuitive interplay at jazz events on college campuses and what Alexander says about their compatible musical thinking and instant rapport is accurate.

Alexander, a remarkable trombone soloist and a renowned jazz educator/band leader, fits securely into this niche. His work gained recognition via an alumni big band album tabbed as a Grammy nominated entry in the early 1980s. Likewise in another context, Alexander's euphonium was pivotal in the amazing Rich Matteson–Harvey Phillips Tubajazz Consort performances in the U.S. and abroad. He had indeed been paying his dues.

The rhythm team represents a stack of professional merits. George Cables was Hubbard's pianist for five years and was eagerly sought by the likes of Art Pepper and Joe Farrell. Andy Simpkins, whose bass was a ten-year fixture with Gene Harris as part of The Three Sounds, had been landing his supple, swinging sounds to a great variety of jazz groups and vocalists since 1968. Drummer John Dentz, very active in the L.A. area, is versed in Bird's idiom; his experiences with Supersax, Lanny Morgan and any number of other bop and swing bands help attend to the needs of this album.

The six upper echelon musicians achieve punctual unity, masking the fact they assembled strictly for this recording. The very demanding Gillespie/Parker bebop classic "Shaw 'Nuff" kicks off the album with a "head" that just flies at breakneck tempo. The band serves notice with fury, slashing and burning. "We were so excited, it was like getting levitated … walking on air!" says Alexander. The treatment echoes the elemental fire of the tune's heritage. The horns soar in solo work, revealing the bright plumage of their flight. This spirit is also on "Star Eyes," as Hubbard's long solo adds illumination and Cole's idiomatic statement enriches. Cables, too, provides fortification.

On "Lover Man," Hubbard opens the door with melodic splendor ushering in Richie

Cole, who demonstrates he is a truly great ballad player. The plaintive quality of his alto unfolds with a warmly gorgeous tone and lyrical appeal. Hubbard's golden-mellow flugelhorn has just the right touches to help frame Cole's showcase. Only one take was needed here; Bird would surely have applauded.

Hubbard's dedication to the late Bud Powell—pioneering genius of bop piano—is his original, "For B.P." It's a veritable skull-busting excursion loaded with inter-changes of cross-rhythms within different time signatures and frequent meter changes. Alexander's comments are incisive: "I love the way Freddie flows when he locks into an idea … it would just pour out of him. And he enjoys what he does so very much!" You can hear his joyfulness in his music.

Ashley Alexander is on intimate terms with "Stella by Starlight"; his blowing employs impressive facility and depth. Cole says "he plays the trombone like a saxophone. Ashley is one of the small handful of great trombonists around." He is regarded as the first and only double-trombone virtuoso. When the band was warming up on "Shaw 'Nuff," Hubbard stopped everything and asked Alexander, "Your slide isn't moving … what's that in your left hand?" Alexander relates: "Freddie hadn't realized what my horn was because he couldn't see from where he was standing and he asked me how it works. I did a few little things on the double-bone and he said: 'Whooeee! You're hired!'" On "Stella" a "head" arrangement was rigged up and Alexander gets to be free and loose at the bridge and gets a nice little vamp going.

The closer is another Hubbard composition which he curries with the hope of it becoming a jazz classic. It tumbles the walls as his horn crackles with vivacity and screams like an eagle's cry. Med Flory, leader of Supersax, zooms in on the first alto solo for a quickie. "I insisted he play on it," exhorts Cole, whose solo follows. Flory dashed out of the studio into the street and brought back his horn pronto. A nice bonus touch!

Freddie Hubbard disarmingly brings his rainbowed colorations, intense attack and full utilization of the resources of his horn back to Birdland. Axiomatically, this record underscores this restoration of values.

Richie Cole's words seem fitting in summation: "Freddie sounds great in any musical context. No matter what level or grade the music is, he will definitely upgrade any style of music and make it sound as great as it can possibly sound!"

Tom Harrell

Tom Harrell is, today, hailed as one of the great jazz trumpet players in recent history. He cut his teeth with Horace Silver and Woody Herman—very much with Woody—and was a stellar member and one of the chief improvisers in the Phil Woods Quintet. That was his jumping off gig into full time in New York City and, subsequently, his stock rose as a very creative, innovative trumpet player.

Tom has always been a different kind of trumpet player. As a teenager growing up here on the Peninsula (his mom and dad were on the faculty at Stanford), Tom exhibited proficiency and talent with his instrument from his mid-teens on. I knew his parents through my work in education and, as I was a resident of nearby Menlo Park, I knew Tom as a local teenager with extraordinary talent.

He was so talented, I decided to bring Tom to Keystone Korner in San Francisco's North Beach, where Cannonball Adderley was holding court as the organizer of Sunday afternoon jam sessions; this was while he was in town playing at night with his quintet at The Jazz Workshop on Broadway.

When I brought Tom in to see Cannonball during one of those jam sessions, I asked Cannonball, "Why don't you let Tom sit in?" And after Tom played on a tune, Cannonball turned to me and said, "Where in hell did this kid come from?"

Tom suffered from a psychological illness, but his marriage helped him compensate in a very positive way. He was cool with his illness … it didn't stop him from generating a solid series of recordings. In fact, his illness may have been a part of the reason why Tom Harrell was always something of a surprise.

Tom Harrell—*Play of Light*
Black-Hawk Records (BKH 50901–1 D); 1986

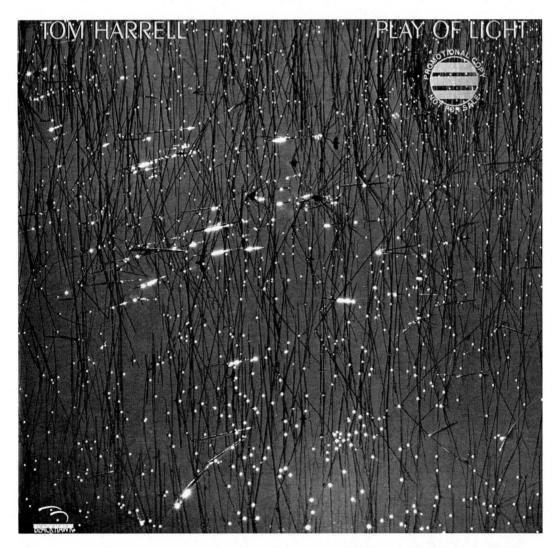

Album cover for Tom Harrell's 1986 *Play of Light* / Black-Hawk Records (BKH 50901–1 D) (album cover credits: photograph by Robert Holmgren; art direction by Zand Gee).

Phil Woods reports that Dizzy Gillespie has expressed how he'd like a whole set of music from Tom Harrell's trumpet and then write a feature article about him. "For Diz to even entertain such a notion is a true compliment. Dizzy and Tom had just recently played together in a concert for the benefit of the McDonald's Tri-State High School Jazz Program spearheaded by Lionel Hampton. It was a tremendous lift for both Tom and Diz."

Tom Harrell is simply one of the most demanded players in and beyond the New York jazz scene. His uplifting musical sound and fresh ideas are on nearly sixty albums to date—ranging from those led by Horace Silver, George Russell, Bill Evans, Gerry Mulligan, Woody Herman, Lenny White, Lee Konitz and George Gruntz to others by Ben Sidran, Mark Murphy, Sheila Jordan, Azteca, Bob Berg, and Pete & Sheila Escovedo among many others. While he maintains a spreading scope of varied activities, his current principal association is with the Phil Woods Quintet which actually began more than 2½ years ago; it is a highlight in his two decades of professional music. The re-chiseling effect his presence has had on the band is indicative of his persuasive talents.

Creating a magnetic field, he draws extraordinary respect from his fellow musicians. A trifle more than a year ago, jazz journalist Michael Bourne prepared a feature article on Tom Harrell for *DownBeat*. Phil Woods shared these cogencies with Bourne: "Tom is the best trumpet player in the world today. He writes. He's familiar with the classics. He can read a score. He's got perfect ears. He has total harmonic memory. He's the best. I've played with some great musicians, and I've never played with anyone better than Tom Harrell—and I'm not easily impressed. I think the whole group sounds better because of him. I'd been playing with a quartet for 11 years, so playing with Tom opens up the music, the sound. Tom has made music exciting for us again. I can say, 'Tom, I'm coming down off the plus five; you come off the plus nine behind Hal,' and he knows exactly what I'm saying. I guarantee that many of these hot-shot musicians can't do the same thing. Tom Harrell is the best musician I've ever encountered in 40 years of playing music. I can't put it any simpler."

More than a year later in April 1986, Phil just revealed to me with conviction: "Tom is like a new spark plug in my previous engine. In making the expansion from a quartet, I wanted an additional voice, not just another instrument. Tom is the most complete musician in my experience. I continue to be impressed with his total harmonic recall, his knowledge of tunes of the past and his compositions reflecting the future. He fits like a comfortable pair of slippers."

Drummer Bill Goodwin has been praising Tom for a long time, too, and before the Woods era. As another member of the Woods Quintet, Goodwin's observations are also close-up foci: "Tommy is the one trumpeter who is the sum of all that's happened before. Every night he plays, he plays the jazz styles—a true synthesist." Yet it is crystal clear Tom personifies his messages and tales, making music with highly oxygenated freshness likened to the ever newness of rushing river whitewaters. Imbedded in this personal communication is the real Tom Harrell—his beautiful, true inner self. He resists the tyranny of the formula and obviously finds the Quintet environment to be unpredictable, digressive and capricious. "I get bored easily," says Tom, "and I try not to repeat myself."

This fits into more of Goodwin's views: "Tom's sound is new stuff—what he plays is so immediate, so creative; he's brought a codifying effect on the group and is a tremendous influence on Phil because of his musicality."

Unavoidably, legendary trumpeter Clifford Brown comes into association with Tom, as an inspirational source. "Clifford was such a strong force and expressed so much warmth and joy," noted Tom, "that I try to play in a modern approach with respect to him, Dizzy, Blue Mitchell, Lee Morgan, Woody Shaw and others." Pianist Hal Galper of the Woods band adds his accolades: "Tom is a genius—it's the only answer. He's so authentic with incredible ears and sense of time! I feel I'm playing with Kenny Dorham and Clifford or one of the older giants ... certainly not a second generation trumpeter mimicking them and not a version of a historical model. Tom is unique."

I first heard Tom when he was a teenaged phenomenon at Monday night jams at the Jazz Workshop in San Francisco's North Beach in the mid sixties. He was living in Los Altos, next to Palo Alto. He learned much about articulation and intonation from Charles Bubb, a classical teacher at Stanford University who also played with the S.F. Symphony Orchestra. Besides his home support system with his parents' encouragement and their collection of jazz records (Goodman, Armstrong, Bird and Diz, etc.), Tom's Covington Jr. High big band director urged him to get into jazz; so through his time at Los Altos High, Foothill College and Stanford, he was actively involved.

Following his trail with Woody and then with Azteca in S.F., I saw him moving to NYC to join Horace Silver, spending four years and recording five albums with Horace. When the Silver Quintet came to Mandrake's in Berkeley, it was heartening to see him blowing so great with one of his dream bands. His destiny appeared more directed and satisfying.

As for the album at hand, I assembled this band for Tom to share his music; most of the musicians had prior inter-relationships which augured well for a rare date with Tom as leader. Everyone was eager. Ricky Ford had overcome time-distance problems as he was on tour with Lionel Hampton in the South; Ricky flew in to make the date at Van Gelder's in New Jersey and re-boarded a flight to rejoin Hamp after the date without missing a gig. And Bruce Forman zoomed in from S.F. The tight simpatico and spirited playing is all in the grooves of *Play of Light*. Incidentally, Tom titled the tune and the album as such, as he was musing about the interplay between light on water and the duality of what one sees and what one hears.

Four of the six tunes are Tom's. Bill Goodwin's comments about Tom's composing are apropos: "Tom's compositions have a recognizable sound, identifiable as Tom's music. They are very contemporary with deep roots—a description of the way he plays." "Play of Light" is a tune with a major/minor contrasting kind of sound with a jazz waltz feeling, harmonically sounding like Milton Nascimento. It's in 3/4 but feels like 6/8.... Dig the last 16 bars of Billy Hart and the late Albert Dailey going into a Latin-flavored 6/8 trip.

The 1941 lyrical ballad by Matt Dennis, "Everything Happens to Me," was a suggestion of mine. Tom plays a couple of choruses in a straight-ahead fashion exposing strong classicism, combined with poignancy and jazz feeling as he opens up the gates. Dailey, Eddie Gómez and Billy Hart add colors masterfully.

In fact, the rhythm section on this album, including Bruce Forman's guitar, is well meshed, playing with intensity and insightful strength. "The Boulevard" smacks strongly of Horace Silver's canopy and the band just boils. "Pictures of tree-lined streets in Barcelona and Dolores Street in San Francisco are associations with this tune," describes Tom.

Traces of Benny Golson's influence come through on "Mood Swings" as the melody moves into a major and minor line/undulating chords. "It's almost autobiographical," says Tom, "since I'm trying to experience balance in music and the way I live, and the repeated figure could be a symbol to apply in life."

And "Blue News" is a minor blues that swings from end to end with charging solos by Bruce, Ricky Ford's tenor, Tom and Albert, while Billy's cultivated ear leads him to brilliant rhythmic orchestrations. Closing the set is Andy LaVerne's "Where You Were" with a deceivingly simple and unusual form; the changes are more challenging.

"Music is a religion and it can structure your life and provide order in the universe," offered Tom. "If my music makes people feel better and hopeful, then it gives me meaning and hope." And all of it is here …

Terence Blanchard

Terence Blanchard represents the newer generation of jazz trumpet players. I think it's legitimate to say that, following the quick success of Wynton Marsalis—Wynton kind of opened the door for all other trumpet players—one of his most prominent disciples was Terence Blanchard.

Early on, Terence was identified as one of the worthy newcomers, someone whom people focused their attention on, because Terence was seen to be carrying the trumpet torch. He is rightly recognized as representing the return of the values of the tradition of the instrument. But, with the range and scope of his parallel career paths, Terence Blanchard represents so much more in music: film scores, education, soundtracks, compositions … along with his performances, of course.

"Joyful Jazz Journeys"
Jazz Educators Journal, September 2001

Prominent among jazz musicians who have successfully bridged two or more major parallel professional activity domains is standout trumpeter and muse figure Terence Blanchard, popping up here, there, and elsewhere. His omnipresence attracts due attention. Just how many Terence Blanchards are there?! You may notice his credits for film soundtracks and hear the music at a theater or television screen … or witness his band performing at a jazz venue … or conducting a master class … and, of course, you may listen to one of his outstanding jazz recordings.

During the past decade and more, Blanchard has been prolific, writing music for numerous film scores, placing him at the leading edge of the niche craft. The plurality of his career directions features his music as a superb and distinctive trumpeter, composer, arranger, and band helmsman—the latter a direction he maintains as his immutable primary perspective and creative tenet. Producing his acclaimed, straight-ahead jazz CDs with his band is a vital adjunct activity: his compositions are infused with effervescent harmonies and animated linear lines—altogether adding luster and blithesome spirit to his seductive palette of skills and body of musical works.

Recent affirmations have enlarged Blanchard's sphere of deserved recognition. Last year his captivating Sony Classical CD *Wandering Moon* featuring original compositions was cited for a Grammy nomination for "Best Instrumental Jazz Solo Performance." He was also the sweeping winner of DownBeat 2000's poll for "Jazz Album of the Year," "Jazz

Trumpeter of the Year," and "Jazz Artist of the Year." In the same year he was appointed Artistic Director for the Thelonious Monk Institute of Jazz Performance at USC. As an influential force in jazz education, he works with gifted young jazz musicians and other curricular programs.

Currently his quintet (tenor saxophonist Brice Winston, pianist Ed Simon, bassist Derek Nievergelt, and drummer Eric Harland) has been touring the U.S., performing in jazz bistros and jazzfests in support of his latest CD release *Let's Get Lost—The Songs of Jimmy McHugh* (an icon of American popular song). The music is a beautiful setting for four of the top-shelf women vocal jazz stylists on the scene today: Diana Krall, Dianne Reeves, Jane Monheit, and Cassandra Wilson.

Tracing Terence Blanchard's childhood foundation and evolvement as a jazz musician provides a window into his insights and the synergistic forces that influenced the shaping of his musical concepts and activity profile. To get closer to his strategic approaches in balancing the various planks on his musical platform, I have shared several dialogues with him over the last few years; excerpts follow. His responses to my queries serve well as sources for clues, notions, impressions and interpretations regarding his perceptions, attitudes, values and behavioral ethic. And seeing him in action with a High School All-Stars big band and the "Jazz in Film" Orchestra at the Monterey Jazz Festival and the Telluride Celebration in Colorado, plus his jazz quintet at Yoshi's jazz night club in Oakland, add to the total experience quotient.

Wong: You were born on March 13, 1962, in New Orleans, Louisiana and raised in a childhood home environment which cultivated a deep love for music. Your father, Joseph Oliver Blanchard, was a pivotal catalyst for your curiosity and fervent interest in music. How did the impact of his demeanor give you support?

Blanchard: My father listened to opera a lot in the house. He always challenged me to think about things—showing me mathematical games or tricks to get my brain working at an early age. Also, we'd go out on the street listening to music, experiencing our neighborhood, and then coming home to have our father say: "Look, this is Oscar Peterson. Sit down and listen to this!" Or for him to be listening to *Rigoletto* and telling me, "Look, man, you need to be listening to this, one of the greatest operas of all time." Yes, he was like the mother in *Mo' Better Blues*. He would sit on the couch listening to me practice my piano lesson and stop me and tell me to correct a mistake.

Wong: Were there other family members who enhanced your musical trip?

Blanchard: Yes, my aunt was a voice teacher and taught piano; she entered me at Loyola University's summer music program when I was a sixth grader. That was also when I met Wynton and Branford Marsalis.

Wong: Beyond the influence of your father's support and your exposure to jazz records around your home, how else were you turned on to jazz?

Blanchard: In New Orleans you always hear jazz bands playing in different functions and settings. I was interested in doing that because it seemed like a lot of fun playing jazz. But it wasn't until I got in high school that I began to learn about the bebop tradition and Bird, Miles Davis, Clifford Brown, Dizzy Gillespie, and others.

Wong: How and when did you begin playing the trumpet?

Blanchard: I started on piano at age five and practiced at my Grandma's house. My mom and dad then rented a piano so I could practice at home. But I came back from school one day after seeing a demonstration on New Orleans traditional music and said

I wanted to play a trumpet. My folks finally got me a trumpet the next year, but I didn't start lessons until my junior year in high school.

Wong: What particular recordings were most inspirational in those sunrise days?

Blanchard: One of the first was *Brown and Roach, Incorporated* with Clifford playing "Sweet Clifford"—it just blew my mind! The other was Miles Davis' *Someday My Prince Will Come* … oh yes, also *Clifford Brown with Strings*. I just wore out those records!

Wong: You attended The New Orleans Center for Creative Arts (NOCCA). What were the benefits or gains the school provided toward fulfilling your needs?

Blanchard: We had great teachers there. The school encouraged us to have private teachers, too. I studied composition and piano with Roger Dickerson—a major influence on my life; I also studied trumpet with George Jansen. At NOCCA Dr. Bert Braud taught me theory and analysis; and we did some composition and arranging, too. Ellis Marsalis taught sight reading; and other classes included voice, ensemble, and performance.

Wong: You had a wide-spectrum curriculum with tight interrelationships?

Blanchard: Oh, yes. That was the thing that was intriguing about the school: with Dr. Braud, we didn't think of a big division between jazz and classical music. We studied them as a representation of society and culture from which they were respectively created.

Wong: What are your notions on education regarding jazz?

Blanchard: First, I believe it's extremely important to give students a sense of the history of the music. Next, give them a sense of the time and effort it takes to accomplish objectives and reach goals. Third, make it seem it's all attainable to some degree. Though jazz musicians are often regarded as just somehow being born with the ability to instantly play jazz, we are actually like anyone else: working hard at it. Working hard reaps benefits. I always draw analogies between music and sports: it seems easier for kids to grasp.

Wong: Share an example.

Blanchard: Basketball fans have always heard how Magic Johnson or Michael Jordan would stay out on the court and dribble the ball all day or how they would keep the ball with them and dribble all day long. Those things are done for a reason, not because they love the game of basketball; it's to help develop their coordination between the hand and eye. And it is achieved only after a certain period of time and effort. The same thing applies to tonguing, fingering, breathing, and other skills needed to play a wind instrument.

Wong: When inculcating such values as you speak with young aspirants and students, are there other issues you address by way of analogies?

Blanchard: I use analogies in another key problem area for kids: getting over the challenge of speaking the jazz language when they play. They often come to the music with problems concerning phrasing or in understanding how to play in a jazz setting. They can surely learn some of the solos, but getting the phrasing down is hard. The analogy I use for that is any pop record, and I don't care who the artist is: most people walking down the street can sing some song's lyrics with the inflection of the performer. That comes only through repetition: they hear it on the radio everyday, and it becomes part of their subconscious. And though many instructors say you must listen to a lot of records I believe firmly you need to take only *one* record—I say *just one record*—and listen to it all the time: you'll absorb everything the record has to offer! That's how I learned, but suggesting focusing so much on *one* record is controversial with many people.

I had a couple of Miles Davis records that I listened to so much I could play all the drum parts, and I could sing the bass parts—because I was trying to figure out what jazz is! When it becomes part of your subconscious, you begin to understand how to speak the language.

Wong: Recall those special records for me.

Blanchard: The main one is the album *Four & More* with Miles' Quintet including Herbie Hancock, George Coleman, Ron Carter, and Tony Williams.

Wong: Oh, that's the live concert performance in Philharmonic Hall at Lincoln Center of Performing Arts. And you suggest total immersion?

Blanchard: Exactly, and through the subconscious. I tell kids: "Make a tape of the music, put it in your car, and let it run. Don't think about it wherever you go, just keep it on! Never mind turning on the radio: before long, you'll be singing all the melodies from your tape."

Wong: What do you perceive about people on the horizon helping youngsters, preparing them to sustain our jazz art form. What promise may the future hold?

Blanchard: The future can only be brighter with the infusion of so many younger artists in the business, and the information age we live in today provides a great many resources from which kids can draw. There's a whole new generation and crop of younger players who are coming along and want deeply to play the music. I had a simply amazing 19 year-old alto saxophonist in my band a few years ago: Aaron Fletcher. Yeah, you look around and "Wow!" A lot of young cats are on the scene. That's great!

Wong: Explain your listening process in pursuit of finding out about jazz.

Blanchard: The mystery was "What is jazz?" I used to listen to the trumpet solos, but I'd realize that wasn't the answer because the drummer was doing something different. So it's very elementary: listen. I listened to the records over and over again and just broke everything down. I would listen to Herbie and how he would comp. I mentioned how I dug Max Roach and Clifford Brown's record [Terence singing the "Sweet Clifford" solo]. I used to listen to that all of the time, trying to figure out what it is. The records confused me, since Miles and Clifford represented two different styles. Listening to them I finally discovered some common ground, and that's the thing I was telling my friends who weren't jazz lovers. I would sit them down and play records for them and point out: "Listen to the bass player keeping time, the drummer accenting the tunes with certain rhythms to give it punctuation, and the pianist giving color." I would also put on a John Coltrane record: it's different again, but the basic elements remain.

Wong: Did you diagnose why you prized these "model" recordings?

Blanchard: I started to notice the reason I picked those records: those were very well-established, working bands which had formed concepts and definite sounds as a group.

Wong: Ah, yes, those were bands that had etched a significant amount of high-quality history together, not bands with short-term relationships or ad hoc recording situations. You were with Art Blakey's Jazz Messengers from 1982–1986: one of jazz history's best-established, great bands, where you emerged as a young trumpet star. Blakey must have fulfilled your hopes that someone like him would provide guidance and inspiration as you were coming up.

Blanchard: That's the funny part of it, Herb. I guess guys in my band would probably be tired of me talking about Art Blakey because I'm *always* telling Art Blakey stories: the experience was very crucial and meant a lot to my development as a musician and as a person, too! Now I understand why Art told me those stories and things; at age 19 or 20, you think you know everything. He was very patient with us. I'm reminded of one of Wynton's analogies: it's like being a pilot. You've got to have "flight time."

Wong: Your philosophy and approach appear to be an effective template for teaching and learning.

Blanchard: That's what is challenging about education in the schools. I'm still struggling with how to teach effectively because at certain points you're telling kids to emulate artists in order to speak the language. At the same time, there are so many derivatives of the jazz language. This is when personal choices come into play: something they have to do on their own.

Wong: In forging individualism, are there ways you may suggest how one can help younger people release their creative powers?

Blanchard: I think it's through composition. I urge them to write a number of songs: they may not sound very good, but you have to write a bunch of corny songs before you get to one that's hip! There's something you have to work through within your soul.

Wong: Comment on how composing translates into playing and improvisation.

Blanchard: Art always said, "You find yourself through writing: you have to commit those notes to paper, and they take on a whole separate meaning." It's likened to writing a paper for a class. For example, many people don't realize how much they speak in slang until they write it down, and a lot of it doesn't make sense. In writing, you're conceiving things in your mind. You may play changes a certain way: committing it to paper will reveal what you like or don't like.

Wong: And since that process can train you to be selective, it should translate into potentials for improvisation.

Blanchard: Yes; it also opens your ears to another world.

Wong: Isn't the more immediate pressure in improvising another layer of challenge?

Blanchard: Yes, and a kind of escapism, too: because it's so immediate, some things will blow right by some younger musicians, such as the importance of every note. Sometimes they play notes that make no musical sense: notes go by so fast the players don't feel the effects of them. But you can sit down and try to make the notes last forever through composing.

Wong: Your already crowded activity schedule was jammed even more in September 2000 with your appointment at USC as Artistic Director for the Thelonious Monk Institute of Jazz Performance, giving artistic direction for the Institute's Jazz Ensemble. I note that the curricular components include "artistic development, arranging, composition, career counseling, and concert programming," plus master classes and campus community programs. With the breadth of student background, experience, abilities, needs, and other variables, your program must mandate a great deal of elbow room.

Blanchard: Absolutely. The program has to be flexible due to the artistic level of the latest group of students: that is, the students coming into the program now are so far ahead of the ones in the previous class, we won't need to deal with some musical issues that I addressed with the last class. Tailoring the program helps these students recognize their strengths and weaknesses, so that they can make an honest, intelligent choice about what they'll be working on to develop their styles.

At this point, it's not about learning the history of jazz; they have already done their homework. So we encourage them to accept certain parts of their musical personality and hopefully grow and expand those ideas which will help them to be unique.

Wong: As these students are more advanced, what are some processes you may expose them to that you deem are important?

Blanchard: For example, I plan to demonstrate how we're going to transcribe some solos. Then take a phrase from a solo, write a tune around the phrase, and show them how to do some contrapuntal things. Next, show how to add things to that phrase, how they can stretch that phrase and not necessarily use it the way it originally was, so that hopefully they can then take ideas that they hear in their heads and manipulate them.

Wong: What's the age range of the students, and what's your schedule of visitations to the Institute?

Blanchard: The age range is 22 to 29, and I'm there one week a month during the school year. I set the tone and direction of our activities; and when I'm away, another administrator facilitates other experiences. Jazz masters also visit and interact with students: there's an inundation of information.

Wong: Your scheduling pattern permits your personal contact via a progression of injections. You are able to combine the contests of student groups and your one-on-one interactions, sharing your strong, experienced-based convictions and values. It must be rewarding to manage these planks in your platform of objectives and logistics.

Blanchard: It's really workable and satisfying, and I like your use of "planks"!

Wong: How do you balance or merge your somewhat divisible career agendas of a working jazz band, scoring film music, and your educational programs?

Blanchard: Having several careers at the same time illustrates how influential my father was; he was a stickler for being on time and was a highly organized workaholic. I find myself walking in his shoes. The only way it can work is to keep things flowing on a schedule, like a well-oiled machine. If things back up, chaos will occur. I have Robin working for me, doing a fabulous job to ensure that my schedule runs smoothly.

As we speak, I'm working on a film score for a film due in August. I'm already mentally prepared for that. At the same time, I'm out on tour promoting my new jazz CD *Let's Get Lost*, but in the back of my mind I'm getting ideas for my film score when I'm away from the bandstand. So it's challenging but on the other hand fulfilling because it keeps you thinking and moving, never settling down on one area exclusively.

Wong: So you can switch on or off, or move to the left or to the right, by will or by motivation?

Blanchard: More by motivation: The need to accomplish something. Having only one career to deal with can lead you to a certain kind of discovery that occurs; but the way my life is structured now is different: discovery can be based on one discipline inspiring the other and vice-versa.

Wong: Synergism results in an economy of creative energies.

Blanchard: Definitely. Sometimes the inspired idea may not fit the other discipline. For example, while working on the movie *Original Sin* I came up with the theme that's too far in the other world: too hip! I was hearing compositions inspired by things I was seeing visually and so needed to try them out, jot them down, and store them in reserve. My mind then relaxed and went into another mode to help the movie along.

Wong: Compare the processes of composing material for a film with composing for a purely jazz purpose.

Blanchard: The basic difference lies in the intent. If I'm writing for a jazz CD, the intent is to write something very personal, reflecting my experiences up to that point in my life. What I wish to express is up to me. When I'm writing for a film or TV, the music is inspired visually and thus external to any personal experiences. The inspiration is totally different, and manipulating ideas that emerge is also totally different. In my mind, the music is serving another purpose.

Wong: What differences are there in the tools you use to write your music for film in contrast to writing jazz?

Blanchard: Another good question! For film I do a lot on the computer and print out the music, but for writing jazz I still prefer pencil and paper. There's simply a true connection, sitting down and writing the rhythms: it takes on another meaning. And I know you're aware I've been writing things in a notebook.

Also, writing at this point of my career is a different process. When I was younger, it seemed to come more easily, probably because I was writing music based on musical references, on ideas that might have been based on a record I had heard that influenced me. However, now I am not drawing from those references; and that's a scary thing! A blank piece of paper is really blank!

Wong: I presume whatever comes out is completely *you*!

Blanchard: That's the goal! When you make musical decisions which are not from references, you are forced to dig down deep to see if it all makes musical sense since some things may not relate to the past. I may ask myself, "Should this be here?" and answer with, "Not necessarily."

Wong: It's a declaration of a deep self-commitment when you do that.

Blanchard: Exactly. You have to be confident in conducting a weeding process.

Wong: Do you engage in re-tooling your skills or experimenting with new processes to enhance your percolation of ideas?

Blanchard: I've been going back to study composition with my teacher, Roger Dickerson. His suggestion is "write down everything and never throw it away. Those little kernels you fooled around with that you may think are meaningless may contain an impetus for something much bigger." Film scoring demands so much to do in such a short period of time; so when I get ideas as to what a score could be, I always jot them down on a script and keep them in a notebook. And I may never use these ideas. I may look back at them and say, "Damn, how did I think about that character that way?"

Sometimes these ideas do make sense and will spur new ideas for me to go in a particular direction. There's a large piece I've been wanting to write for a couple of years but haven't yet had the time and motivation to complete. But when I did have the original motivation, I wrote every aspect of what I wanted the piece to be. Those details have changed during the last two years; and, as I look through my notebook, it's interesting to see my comments. I love doing it and approached certain tunes that way for my CD *Wandering Moon*.

I wrote the tune "If I Could, I Would" based on an exercise my teacher gave me that I use in master classes and think is important. He took the phrase "If I could tell you, I would?" ending with a question mark, and asked me to write out a dialogue using only those words. The next lesson was to take those phrases and continue writing the dialogue—but to substitute exclamation points for the question marks. His point was that punctuation means a lot to those phrases. And the follow-up was to take those same words, change all the meanings, and still write a dialogue. So all of the periods, exclamation marks, and question marks are like dynamic markings, phrase markings, and other notations manipulating phrases of music.

Wong: And you used this process for the CD project? That is hot!

Blanchard: It's an eye-opening experience: You realize how vital everything is. It helped me a lot in my orchestral writing, too. In film writing, so much has to be *in* the music for the orchestra. It's not like a jazz band, where the musicians will get a hint of what's supposed to happen and then know what to do. You realize how important all the markings are: phrase markings, dynamic markings, rests, tempo markings, etc.

Wong: What does film writing offer you that may not be transparent to the casual observer?

Blanchard: It's all about inspiration to do something different—like you need a break occasionally—and to appreciate what you already have. That's what film does for me.

Wong: You're fortunate to have this extra valve that can give you a release and to afford you something fresh to turn to or focus.

Blanchard: I've come to understand that. There's always been this need to write for varied musical situations, not just jazz; and film allows me to do that, too. For instance, I had to write two piano concertos for the film *Caveman's Valentine*—something I would not have a chance to do on a jazz record. That experience affected me in terms of how I might write for a jazz ensemble; it relates to ideas I have been jotting down.

Wong: What might be your visionary or dream project?

Blanchard: That's a little difficult to say. It would probably be a project in which I would have the chance to play with some of the really great musicians I have yet to play with, such as Wayne Shorter, Herbie Hancock, Elvin Jones, and McCoy Tyner. I've played with McCoy on his gigs but not in some kind of formal situation wherein we could record. That would be the dream thing for me. I'm going to get an opportunity to write music for something special; and the biggest thing for me is to see if I could work with some of the great ones and gain a rich experience—and also to see what's like to be with them in the studio.

Wong: You spent much time in your youth listening to these musicians on recordings.

Blanchard: I feel fortunate to have had a chance to meet a lot of the greats before they passed on: Dizzy, Miles, and Art Blakey. So I'm encouraged that I may play with some of my heroes. I have had a chance to play with legends like Joe Henderson and Sonny Rollins.

Wong: Are you still chasing the "mystery of what is jazz"?

Blanchard: Jazz has become so broad, so vast in scope as the years go by, that it's harder and harder to actually define this thing. Just consider it as a language. It's like saying, "What is classical music?" I hate comparisons between jazz and classical music. In classical music, composers have taken folklore and then gone deeper into that folklore in their writing; and that process has been going on in jazz for years! In the jazz language, look at what Dizzy was doing with Latin music in jazz—or Coltrane with Middle Eastern music. That stuff has been around. So I'm still on the quest.

Wong: It's part of the magical allure of jazz. Keep chasin' it! Before moving on to your next jazz recording, your current edition, *Let's Get Lost*, welcomes your latest theme-based effort and invites comments from you as to its rationale and your perceptions regarding its message.

Blanchard: Since it consists of tunes written by Jimmy McHugh, let me say that this music speaks of Jimmy McHugh's genius as a composer. Many of the tunes are timeless, and they are beautiful. I feel it is healthy and important to experience certain types of music. I've always maintained the position of not cutting myself off from a variety of sources. And just because I have done this type of project at this time does not mean this is what I'm going to do the rest of my life!

Wong: There is such a wonderful fit between the four singers and the tunes they respectively selected to sing; perfect match-ups. How was this blending achieved?

Blanchard: First, I did not choose the songs. It's the other way around: The singers' styles set the tone for the songs. I know the vocal sound of all four singers well; Dianne Reeves, Diana Krall, Jane Monheit, and Cassandra Wilson. The record speaks to the very thing I love about jazz; the uniqueness of each sound and approach!

Wong: Agreed! It is utterly fascinating to listen to the idiosyncrasies in their styles and how they contribute to the common ground of the music. I also find the CD programmed with taste and attention given to the instrumentalists; the combination of instrumental outings on several McHugh jewels and the well-paced vocals makes *Let's Get Lost* a brilliant example of conception and interpretation. I might as well ask what your next poetic vision might lean on.

Blanchard: I want to develop those kernels and ideas I've put away. That's what I want to focus on next. By the way, this was stimulating for me: I love the questions.

There's no question Terence Blanchard has strategically resolved the traffic configurations of his constellation of careers. Anticipate more from his creative estate as his brilliant trumpet sings and rings in our multimedia turf. Don't be surprised if he carves another career niche into his wide world of joyful journeys!

CHAPTER 3

Drums

While the trumpet creates communication that is critical to every big band, it is the interplay between the lead trumpeter and the drummer that ultimately drives the band to success. The role of the drummer is to internalize the breathing that gives life to every ensemble. The beat of the drum is the heartbeat of the band; without a key drummer, without a heartbeat, the band will lack life. Without a key drummer, it's simply not going to happen.

Buddy Rich was probably the best drummer I ever encountered. After Buddy, there is a list of drummers who are the crowning performers in their field, the top drummers who were available in their day. Art Blakey, Elvin Jones, Shelly Manne ... and, of course, my friend of many years, Max Roach. Every one of those guys was a giant. But it was Max who changed the whole world of drumming. There wasn't a drummer who wasn't influenced by Max Roach.

— ·· — ·· — ·· — ·· — ·· — ·· — ·· — ·· — ·· — ·· — ·· — ·· —

Max Roach

Max Roach is the jazz world's renaissance man in the true sense of the word and the world: Brilliant percussionist, creative composer, proven genius via his work in theater, in education, in choral and more.

More than that, Max has been a true friend for life to Marilyn and me.

One day, I received a call from Max, who said, cryptically, "I'm out here." "What do you mean, *out here*," I said. Max continued, seemingly ignoring my question: "You know, Herb, I've never been to San Francisco. Now, I have a person guiding me ... Chinatown in particular." More mystery was afoot. I asked Max, "What are you doing in town?" To which he replied, "I'm doing a duo recording with Jon Jang."

At that point, it all became clear, as I recalled an evening at the Holiday Inn in Emeryville, across the bay from San Francisco, where Jon had approached Max about a possible collaboration. I guessed that this was the gig that they had discussed at the hotel.

"Jon is a great composer, and we're tying to work on something significant. So I decided to come out here to see if we have something that's viable for a recording."

The recording was to take place in a studio that was contracted by Asian Improv Records and there was a lot of preparation that took place before the sessions began. During the course of that time, the album's executive producer, Steve Hom, brought Jiebing Chen to the studio with him. When they came into the studio, the producer said that Jiebing would like to meet Max Roach. Jiebing, he explained, was the most prominent of musicians in China specializing in playing native instruments. Max met her and, almost immediately, invited her to bring her instrument in.

It turned out to be an *erhu*: a Chinese two-string violin. And when he heard what she was shakin' up with her instrument, Max decided to include her in the recording.

And so the Jon Jang/Max Roach duo evolved in an ad hoc way into the Beijing Trio. That's how Max's ear worked. He knows what he will do with whatever situation is presented. And, as it turned out, he was very happy with the situation.

That was all part of his persona. He instinctively knew that it would work. As Max says on the CD cover, this was "one of the most refreshing and enjoyable experiences in my career. In this cross-cultural artistry, I heard and did things musically I had never done before."

Max Roach with Jon Jang and Jiebing Chen—*Beijing Trio*
Asian Improv Records (AIR 0044); 1999

This is music that must not be regarded off-handedly with nonchalance. Featuring a dynamic triumvirate of Max Roach, Jon Jang and Jiebing Chen, it merits being viewed as a landmark singular statement. A world renowned iconic percussionist of contemporary American music, Roach is simply sublime. An inveterate seeker of new experiences and discoveries, he is never at a standstill. With irreproachable artistic integrity, his obsessive quest has led him to this highly unusual recording project. "I'm always looking for new ideas and this was an elegantly fresh, new one for me. Because I've been involved with creative music for a long, long time, it is rare to do some things I haven't done before," says Roach. "So it was an opportunity to deal with completely new ideas with the brilliant Jon Jang and the wonderful *erhu* artist Jiebing Chen."

The spirited group gestalt infectiously pulls the listener into their conversations. All three are master storytellers taking advantage of an intimate conversational approach, ignoring any formal regularity. Tightly attuned to the nuances of each other's feelings, personalities and inner souls, the trio illustrates how simpatico players can relieve tension and allow passage for individuality and spontaneous imaginations. It's micro-democracy at work and play.

Beyond these dynamics lies the crux and fulcrum of the experience of this recording that celebrates diversity and juxtaposition of cultures and people. Jang believes "We are making music that is constantly and culturally translocating itself—from North Carolina (Roach) to North China (Chen)." And, of course, the intervallic connection between the two is Jang in North California. What is also intriguing stems from the confluence of cross-cultural pollination—as it embodies the holism of music cast in a contemporary complexion and context. Together the trio evolved a novel, tenaciously new musical dialect.

So how did this project emerge among the three principals representing different ethnic/musical backgrounds, and achieve an inter-idiomatic summit recording? First, it's apropos to thumbnail a sketch of each of them in order to bring the rightful level of esteem to this interactivity.

Max Roach's rich odyssey ushered earlier in his historically important and phenomenal work with the likes of Charlie Parker, Thelonious Monk, Sonny Rollins and Clifford Brown, exploded later on—expanding his creative thrusts with a broad terrain of musics, individuals and groups. Reflecting his interfacial span, his diverse collaborative projects have included those with Cecil Taylor, Dizzy Gillespie, the Kodo Drummers of Japan, Anthony Braxton, the Boston Pops, Spike Lee, the Alvin Ailey and Bill T. Jones dance companies, writers Amiri Baraka, Toni Morrison, Maya Angelou, and playwrights Shakespeare, Eugene O'Neill, and Sam Shepard.

A prolific composer, Roach has created works for soloists, choruses, orchestras, television, film, theater and dance ... and for his own constellation of groups (Max Roach Quartet, the Double Quartet, the Uptown String Quartet, the percussion ensemble M'Boom and the So What Brass Quintet).

Surely one of the most celebrated artists of our time, Roach is recipient of a fellowship from the MacArthur Foundation in recognition of his distinguished contributions to American cultural life. Among numerous other international awards, Hall of Fame inductions and honorary doctorates in Music and Fine Arts, he has an extensive discography. Easily one of the most recorded artists of this century, he is a two-time winner of the French *Grand Prix du Disque*.

A Chinese-American, Jon Jang was born in Los Angeles. An alumnus of the Oberlin Conservatory of Music, Jang has been active on the scene for the past decade as a pianist, composer, and a leader of a variety of ensembles. During this time frame, he has been acclaimed with many distinguished awards, honors, grants and commissions via a wide spectrum of national/international media, institutions, special performance events, and international polls.

These modes of recognition are comprehensible accompaniments to the path-finding artistic peaks and strides he has made as a gifted complete musician. His notable original works are rich admixtures of cultural influences and sounds. Specifically, he has integrated traditional Chinese folk songs into varied contemporary music. Indeed, Jang is critically hailed as a pioneer, an innovator and a worldly leader in his fields of endeavors. Earning gainful audience respect and enthusiasm, he has performed in Europe, South Africa, China, Canada and the U.S. His latest of three Beijing visits was an invitation to perform his works at the Beijing International Jazz Festival in 1997. Jang was a focus of interest because of his model blending of the traditions of Chinese and African American musics. Jon Jang was the perfect catalyst to precipitate this recording project of the Beijing Trio.

Jiebing Chen is recognized as the world's foremost virtuosic exponent of the *erhu*. Shanghai born, she began performing at age 6 and graduated from the Shanghai Conservatory of Music with high honors. In 1988, the highest honor given by the Chinese government was presented to her—as a "National First Rank Performing Artist." She was soloist with Shanghai's Symphony Orchestra, Chamber Orchestra and Dance Theater Company. On a scholarship, she finished at the State University of New York in Buffalo where she earned her M.A. degree. Since then, she has performed with symphony orchestras in Moscow, Hungary and Taipei among a multitude of other venues.

As for recordings, she has recorded with banjoist Béla Fleck and flutist James Newton; she has also performed with the prominent trio of pianist Dr. Billy Taylor and the Jon Jang Sextet. During the course of the past fifteen years, she has produced the largest catalogue of *erhu* recordings extant in China and the U.S. In 1996 she had a Grammy Award nomination for "Best World Music Album" (with Béla Fleck and Vishwa Bhatt). Currently she resides in the San Francisco Bay Area.

Through most of the first eight years of the 1990s, Jang and Roach crossed paths a number of times. In May 1998, when Jang and James Newton were researching *When*

Sorrow Turns to Joy in New York City, "I spoke about doing a recording with him and he was ready to do it in June in San Francisco. Beijing was very much in the air and we spoke a lot about Beijing," Jang recounts. "And Max had never been to China and he was intensely interested and curious about things Chinese."

Roach explains: "When I heard Jon Jang perform in NYC, I heard something original, attracting me to want to do something with him. As our friendship grew, I began to see how this duet project could be done. We didn't need to rehearse—literally. The 'rehearsals' were already in place when I heard him perform in New York.

"Even though I had come to San Francisco with Benny Carter in 1943, I didn't know much about San Francisco's Chinatown or the Chinese community."

Roach told Jang he wanted to delve into Chinatown. He wanted to partake of everything. Staying at a hotel nearby, he walked the streets with lanterned street lights—the streets flanked with seemingly interminable numbers of restaurants, apothecaries, produce markets, shops and businesses of all sorts in the Chinatown environs ... checking out the smells, the music and the food. "I loved feasting my eyes and all my senses, and listening to the stories about the culture," say Roach.

"Steve Hom (Producer) is a fountain of knowledge, but you, Herb, are the one who first whetted my appetite years ago."

Jang arranged an array of people and activities for Roach to experience. The capstone experience for Roach was to go to a rehearsal and performance of Cantonese opera. "Wow! The sounds really turned me on—the sound of the percussion, the acting, and the music itself. I just fell in love with it! And the stamina to keep up with demands of these long operas is just amazing."

As an aside, "being a percussionist, the Chinese gongs have a sound that fascinates me," describes Roach. "It's a sound unlike any other gong sound. The colors are just astounding. I had not used the Chinese gong before. Jon Jang has given me three to use." Clearly Roach brought joys and discoveries from that experience to the studio recording.

Roach's large thirst for new ideas was given expression again by way of Steve Hom's arrival (at engineer Cookie Marenco's studios) with Jiebing Chen who had brought her instrument with her. She was merely making a visit to meet Roach and she had no inkling she would wind up performing and ultimately recording with Jang and Roach. Roach was impressed by her consummate artistry and the deep human vocal character of the *erhu* sound. Hom declares this was not just another recording for her by any means.

Chen had been pre-conditioned for this ground-breaking setting since she had been performing with Jang during the last few years; e.g., she performed in his sextet at the 1996 Monterey Jazz Festival in company with David Murray, Santi Debriano, James Newton and Billy Hart. Likewise, Chen was at the Beijing International Jazz Festival with the Jon Jang Sextet in 1997.

Of recent, she stretches to create different things—improvising with ease. Hom also notes that her duets with Roach showed strong adventuresomeness. A world class musician, Chen was able to flow smoothly into this context sharing her unique *erhu* voice. "I learned a lot about different kinds of music performing with Jon," she says. "I actually composed new music when I was performing with Jon and Max. Usually, drums for me is to maintain the tempo. But Max Roach is different—every note he designs feels so melodic and not just on the beat."

Roach was warmly impressed by the wide range of the 2000 year-old, two-string *erhu* and with Jang's knowledge of Western and Chinese systems—rhythmically, melodically and scale-wise, making it all work out successfully. He adds: "Jon is creating Chinese scales and motifs, and that to me is swing! And, of course the Black American systems of improvisation are very flexible and can fit whatever situation."

In response to how he and Jang approach wholly fresh tunes, Roach referred to totally improvising melodically—"developing what's logical that has form, content and style, and also tell a story. We were looking for something that mingles cultures and expressing one's view about the world of sound." Gratified it was an inspirational and educational experience, Roach summarizes: "We all feel pain and joy, expressing feelings in our own ways and translating the feelings into sounds."

Unquestionably the duos/trio navigate quite comfortably through the series of songs. The assured sense of invention was a quintessential quality which distinguishes their performance. Innate excitement fueled the music's melodrama. And there are times where the silent notes are as vital as those actually created. The nuances and lyrical subtleties are woven into the tapestries of sounds. The group is an omnivorous ensemble species of its own.

And the songs ... a basic rationale for the predominantly floral titles is derived from the inspired symbolism of flowers in Chinese culture. Jang volunteered some annotations:

"Moon Over the Great Wall"

The recording was made at night and the moon conveys an evening ambiance. "Max represents the Great Wall."

"Sweet Whisper of a Flower"

Inspired by Chinese poetry, flowers symbolizing beauty, it evokes Jang's own elegant "Two Flowers on a Stem" composition as well as composer Billy Strayhorn's pronounced penchant for naming tunes associated with flowers ("Passion Flower," "A Flower Is a Lovesome Thing," "Lotus Blossom"). "For me," says Jang, "it comes off first from China. It's a kind of intersection with Strayhorn."

"Heart in a Different Place"

"I just felt we were all in different places." Obviously they were in the perfect "places" opening up new possibilities for heart and soul.

"Fallen Petals"

"I knew Jiebing's father had passed away last year and her brother the year before, so I came out with the expression of change in Chinese culture by way of the changing seasons."

"Now's the Time!"

This is naturally in reference to Charlie Parker's seminal bebop classic "Now's the Time." But here there is a different inflection emphasizing TIME! Its meaningfulness points to the special opportunity to introduce Max Roach to some new things and music, so now IS the time!

"When the Blossoms Bloom"

Jang wished to pay tribute to Michelle Kwan—one of the world's greatest figure ice skaters. As *Time* magazine called her "Soul on Ice," the song here relates to how she unfolds so gracefully and beautifully on the ice.

"THE FLOWING STREAM"

"This is dedicated to Bruce Lee and his depth of feeling and Max is always like a flowing stream, always doing something about now," Jang explains. My take on it is that Roach did "Now's the Time" with Charlie Parker. Now's the time with Jon Jang and Jiebing Chen!

Max Roach has carved new vistas and new perspectives for the trap set, percussion art pieces, inter-media projects and creative new musical settings and ensembles. His summary remarks about this recording—from genesis to completion—bear serious consideration: "This is one of the most refreshing and enjoyable experiences in my career. For me, everything has to have a true meaning. In this cross-cultural artistry, I heard and did things musically I had never done before."

The Beijing Trio matters and it will continue to matter. Perhaps it will lead to a special progeny of this organic, amazingly intuitive approach. Clearly this was a triumph and an enticing preview of things to come.

Max Roach passed away on August 15, 2007. Shortly thereafter, the *Jazz Education Journal*, a publication of the International Association for Jazz Education, re-published this article and conversation I had with Max in 1991.

"Max Roach—Master Statesman of Jazz"
Jazz Education Journal, Spring 1991

Max Roach is a complete world musician and legendary drummer. This embracing umbrella is, however, short in covering the whole of Roach's renaissance stature. His reigning role in musical history is promptly revealed when considering the long term and abundant international respect accorded him.

His place in modern jazz as a pioneer was etched in 1945 when Charlie Parker formed bebop's most significant jazz combo—a quintet which included Dizzy Gillespie, Bud Powell, and Charles Mingus in addition to Max Roach—carving new territory and altering the traditional perspectives of jazz. "I've been blessed in so many ways for so many years," says Roach.

A review of his brilliant artistic career paths emphasizes his innovative breakthroughs and mutations in the lexicon of percussion. Over forty-some years he has been the illuminating dean of the drums—leading the way in the exploration and reshaping of its functions, honing its expressive power as a solo instrument, and building new musical architecture. As a premier courageous change-master, Roach's influential contributions and creativity have been duly recognized and acclaimed. His numerous awards include: the MacArthur Fellowship "genius grant" in 1988 (first jazz artist recipient); Command of the Order of Arts and Letters (highest cultural honor in France); twice-winner of the French *Grand Prix du Disque*; Hall of Fame, International Percussion Arts Society; Obie Award; composing music for three Sam Shepard plays plus five honorary doctorates.

As a prolific recording artist, Roach's rich, cross-cutting discography is beyond the scope of most musicians' compass. With such luminaries as Bird, Dizzy, Monk and Miles to Rollins, Ellington, Braxton, Clifford Brown and Cecil Taylor ... to name a few ... his recording resume can be likened to a pocket documentary of the history of jazz greats and the development of the art of jazz percussion. And on the horizon are many more projects of diverse contexts he will be addressing in the coming months.

Roach continues to teach part-time at the University of Massachusetts at Amherst where he is an adjunct professor in the Department of Music and Dance. His teaching also takes him abroad as well as to domestic campuses for residencies. He has invoked fresh epistemological concepts and systems and devised archetypes in the percussive arts.

At age 66 his crowded life continues with full throttle, illustrated in part by any thin slice of his activities. Just recently, in January, he spent a month-long period in San Diego's Repertory Theater rehearsing the underscored music (which he composed and orchestrated) for Amiri Baraka's theatrical bopera *The Life and Life of Bumpy Johnson*. Also during January he appeared at the International Association for Jazz Education's International Conference in Washington, D.C., for an evening's performance. He brought his impressive Double Quartet—the sum of his own working quartet (Cecil Bridgewater—trumpet, Odean Pope—tenor sax, Tyrone Brown—bass) and the Uptown String Quartet (which includes his daughter Maxine on viola). After his appearance in Washington, he returned to San Diego to complete preparations for the musical's premiere at month's end. A couple of days later he rejoined his quartet for a road tour and looked toward yet another tour with M'Boom—an eight-piece percussion ensemble and an unconventional polyglottal group Roach founded in 1972.

In my conversations with Max, he spoke at length on a variety of topics with deep conviction and sincerity. The following excerpts seem most germane to share herein:

Wong: What are your retrospective impressions of your own brand of jazz education?

Roach: I learned the hard way. We all learned the music on the job, exposed to hard life, exploited by record companies, club owners, etc. But it's all right as evidenced by what came out of it—Pops, Bechet, Tatum and Charlie Parker. And the great composers—Duke, Benny Carter, Noble Sissle and the resident composer at the Cotton Club, Harold Arlen, who wrote many beautiful songs. My education came from the environment of 52nd Street in New York, working with Charlie Parker, Bud and the others. Bird often expressed what it might be like if his musical thinking were to be involved in larger areas of music—orchestral works and the like, to take advantage of what's available. We would check out people like Segovia, Casals, and Ravi Shankar who came to Carnegie and Town Hall—just to say to ourselves, this is possible with playing solo on instruments. My solo work on the drums: the instrument is supposed to be a time-keeper but to make it into a whole instrument had much to do with my listening to Tatum, Segovia, the solo piano of Fats Waller. I'd say "Damn! You could do this with any instrument." It's simply language—not necessarily expressed in words but through sound. I knew it when I first heard Ravi and Chatur Lal's tabla.

We would consort with these people when possible. Fifty-Second Street was a fertile ground where people came to hear us. It was a good time for us to be around. Our education came out of the joints and speakeasies. The clubs were our classrooms and our "profs" were Duke, Chick Webb and Louis—standing close to them, breathing the same air. They spoke through their instruments. My peers going to school with me were Diz, Bird, Miles and that crowd; we were students doing the same thing as others were in other cities, be they Detroit, L.A. or wherever the club/classrooms were to be found, and there were plenty of them in those days.

Many say it's the environment that influences learning. Louis Armstrong's was a very harsh environment. They indeed set up the routes for us to follow. Fletcher Henderson, Don Redman and Benny Carter, for instance were great arrangers who established the styles and modes that big bands today are still modeling. Of course, today we also reflect Gil Evans' leadership and newer approaches, expanding the virtuosity of the legends—virtuosity involved with making people *feel* something and not just how fast one can play or how technically super you are. Armstrong used to say, "You got to learn how to play the lead."

Wong: Without person to person access to these pioneers, what is involved in the transmission of these original jazz cultural models?

Roach: Mingus used to say it's passed on mouth to mouth. Institutions of higher learning have opened their doors to the Dewey Redmans and others—thereby learning from person to person (who had heard it from others) and passing it on to young people. A whole new breed is discovering Tatum, for example. We're witnessing a genuine resurgence of interest and respect for jazz. But today, the school campus environment is providing the vehicle for communication. Most clubs who have weathered inflation and economic forces must charge very high prices to cover their overhead; e.g., the Blue Note in New York—its prices are prohibitive!

Wong: Jazz education has been in the milieu of high schools and colleges/universities for several decades now, and increasingly so; what's your perception as to problems, needs for change, and ways and means to facilitate progress?

Roach: A major issue is a matter of appropriate faculty staffing. My example is from my experience at the University of Massachusetts. Auditions there relied on what students knew about classical European music and their competency in reading this music. Of course, these very students have had training at or before high school. But that's not necessarily all of music. There's music and there's *musics*—all kinds of genres of music.

(Max Roach believes that in essence, the term "music" is wholly antiquated in its connotation, that it is archaic nomenclature and does not fulfill the full meaning and substance of its contemporary scope and concept.)

Music today must include the great composers and instrumentalists who have come out of the U.S. The music department formerly had to adhere to narrowly viewed rules. Before, when a student auditioned who could really play, making music creatively, but not within the classical European tradition, they weren't assessed with proper criteria. But these students *were* musicians! They came in already playing jazz. What we did to enhance the jazz program was change the audition rules. For instance, how would you handle an Erroll Garner (who was not reputed to be a reader)? A battle royal occurred to remove prejudices against students wishing to attend an institution of higher learning. Existing classical music faculty are not capable of teaching these students, so we had to consider new faculty who could manage these assignments successfully, taking these kids on to the next levels.

I firmly believe IAJE is important. When I looked around the conference in Washington, D.C., it made my heart feel so encouraged and good to see so many qualified people involved in education of this particular genre of the world's music. I sensed that you didn't have to testify if and where you earned a doctorate, where you went to school in order to contribute to the teaching and learning of jazz. During the Vietnam war period there was a big cry for black faculty; as a result we could say we went to Juilliard or Manhattan, not necessarily for a doctorate, but we just went there and that was it! I think IAJE is the tonic we need to restore what has been missing for too many years.

Wong: Describe your programs for elementary and high school students as part of the Thelonious Monk Institute of Jazz.

Roach: The MacArthur Foundation fellowship has given me the opportunity to invest time to share the things I have learned. I am doing this by word of mouth to young people, retelling how I got into the music, repaying my dues. I'm involved with two programs, The Lester Young Program in Brooklyn—the Bed-Stuy section where I grew up; it's housed in the old Brooklyn Boys High School, which is now a condemned old building, and we have been given a space. This program was initiated by a group of musicians I grew up with; they put it together and I'm simply in it because of my roots there.

The second thing I'm involved with is my recent association with Jazzmobile in Harlem. Again, the MacArthur grant allowed me to buy equipment and materials for an International School of Percussion and I don't need to travel on the road as much as I used to. In this manner the tradition can be passed on, as you said earlier, but in a way dealing with this world of organized sound with instruments and voices you hear all over the world. People are becoming more conscious that this music interacts with the musics of many parts of the world and the U.S. is part of the totality. And I can't tell you how good it is to know Lincoln Center is instituting a program that will include much more American music (in a jazz format as a part of the Center's regular schedule). I only hope that other U.S. cities will take note and follow the lead.

If any progress for this music occurs, you can be sure Max Roach will be somewhere in its forefront, lending his energies, insights and wherewithal to assist in its maturation. It appears to me Max Roach's time is filled with events that endure and overlap in dialectical succession, and we are all blessed with his living legacy.

—·—·—·—·—·—·—·—·—·—·—·—·—·—·—·—·—·—·—

Shelly Manne

Shelly Manne was a pioneer of "West Coast jazz." He created and managed one of the best jazz bistros in the history of Los Angeles: Shelly's Manne-Hole. As owner and house drummer—and as a human being—Shelly was such an unselfish person. It showed in everything he did, in every performance of his, and with every performer he hosted ... and the fans knew it. Whether at its original location on Cahuenga in L.A. or after they moved, Shelly's Manne-Hole always had a trail of advocates and fans. They always knew that whatever the show, whoever performed, it was always going to be a good one.

For a great many years, Shelly was house drummer for the Monterey Jazz Festival. In 1984, when Marilyn and I were visiting with him at the festival, he had a long break coming up between performances, so we all decided to eat, and went across the street for dinner at a Chinese restaurant, Chef Lee's Mandarin House.

Several months before that, Shelly had suffered a heart attack while playing golf. But during dinner, Shelly kept adding soy sauce to whatever food he had on his plate. I said to him, "Shelly, you know it's not healthy for you to have all that soy sauce after your heart attack." And Shelly paused, pouring still more sauce on his entrée, telling me, "I have no problems, Herb. All I have to do to control my blood pressure is to think real hard and positive and it will come down." I couldn't believe what he was saying. "Come on, Shelly, it's not a magic thing, you know." And Shelly says, "No, really, if you were to take my blood pressure right now … and I'm thinking real hard that it's going to be low … it will be low."

Three days after that, I had to fly to New York for a *JazzTimes* convention, where I got a call from Marilyn. "I know you don't want to hear this, but Shelly Manne just died."

Shelly Manne—*Perk Up*
Concord Records (CCD 4021); 1976

This is one of the most head-clearing, heartening Shelly Manne records you'll hear. Anyone hobbled by stagnation of some sort may indeed "perk up" with optimism and creative new values. Isn't this kind of prospect a little too lofty to realize? Soberly speaking, it isn't exotic at all for good jazz to be possessed of regenerative powers in relation to a variety of human affairs. I submit that the soundscape of this recording issues a good measure of that kind of exultant vigor.

Shelly Manne is one of jazzdom's drummers *cum laude*, a true omni-percussionist. His long-held philosophy of drums as another instrumental voice—especially in texture and timbre—can be experienced immediately as the design of this recording begins to take shape with the title selection: "Perk Up" is a lovely Trinidadian tune composed and charted by pianist Jimmy Rowles. A resourceful use of dynamics contributes to the West Indian flavor. Shelly comments "The melodic line on piano was overdubbed with steel drums to give a quarter tone feeling, creating an attractive kind of dissonance." It is more of an ensemble mood piece than a "blowing" piece.

Richard Rodgers' beautiful staple "I Married an Angel" is a tune Shelly's group had been playing when pianist Russ Freeman was still part of the quintet, sometime before Mike Wofford joined the group. Shelly recounted "I think Conte and Frank's playing are great! Especially exciting is the last ensemble: Conte's inimitable big band trumpet playing in the upper range offers a good example of his full expressive style." Conte and Shelly's playing together goes back to the bands of Woody Herman and Stan Kenton during their respective earlier years. And Frank Strozier was recruited from New York after Shelly had heard him with Roy Haynes' group, playing opposite Shelly's own group at Shelly's old club—the Mann-Hole on Cahuenga Boulevard in Hollywood.

Speaking of Frank, he is a very different kind of player with an individual sound and approach. Along with his marvelous technique, he is also happily a player infused with unpredictabilities. "Frank always surprises—it's truly fun to play with him," waxes Shelly. On "Seer (Crystal Ball Gazer)," a mood piece by Strozier, a straight eight, soft jazz-rock feeling prevails. "Comeback" is a boppish tune written up-tempo all the way. Shelly's editorial acumen is illustrated as he institutes the noticeably tasteful change-of-pace idea "because of the way the figure is built and accelerated until it reached a tempo in four bars. The rhythmic line lent itself to acceleration with logic and ease. It makes the tune more creatively interpreted so that it falls out of being just another tune." The level of refreshing interest is clearly heightened and, in essence, is consistent with my premise of Shelly's music offering a bright potential for personal reintegration.

Mike Wofford is an arrestingly gifted musician and has impressed me over the years since his advent on the Los Angeles scene in the early sixties. Although his appearances on records have been somewhat sporadic, they strongly show him to be extremely creative harmonically and as a player with fire and lyricism. Enthusiastically endorsing Mike, Shelly said "Mike is outstanding—marvelous, a musician's pianist. Many 'in' musicians regard him as a genius. He comps so well behind soloists—and knows just when to, and when not to. He inspires as he plays," (this is abundantly evident on this record) "and he is so easy to play with." Check out Mike's uncanny sense of time on "Yesterdays." It's beautiful. Frank and Conte again maneuver and zero in on target like falcons. And Shelly's work is so utterly melodic, radar-like in sensitivity and just damn exciting!

Monty Budwig has been with Shelly off and on for some twelve years. He is a very flexible bassist with a simply beautiful sound and I have personally been attracted to his in-person live sound for some eighteen years. Shelly loves Monty for his nearly instinctual, symbiotic ability to collaborate. "Monty is easy for a drummer to play with. His time is impeccable and literally takes the burden off of me. He listens and gives and takes with me so naturally. There are, by the way, great solos by everyone on 'Yesterdays'!"

"Drinkin' and Drivin'" is a gorgeous ballad with an appealing line. Belonging in the genre of late night urban atmospheres, musically it emulates the effect of drinkin' and drivin'. Listen to the bent notes in the ensemble and the loosely played feeling. Conte's magnificent solo and Frank's alto solo are veritable improvisation models for study. This Jimmy Rowles tune is also dubbed as 502 Blues—502 is, of course, the police code for an arrest for drinking and driving. (A 1967 recording by Wayne Shorter with Herbie Hancock, Reggie Workman and Joe Chambers used the "502 Blues" alternative title.)

Audition Mike Wofford's "Bleep" and you might think that Thelonious Monk is walkin' and swingin', "Bleep" is a wonderful jazz caricature of T. Monk—explored first by the composer, then taken for a mellow Monkish trip by the whole band. And everyone really cooks on this. Mike's treatment is imbued by the inspiration of Monk. Another highlight is Monty's imaginative solo.

The capper is another Wofford original, "Bird of Paradise," sporting a jazz–Latin feeling. However, this piece is not to be mistaken for Charlie Parker's own line with the identical title.

After hearing these contemporary jazz sounds, it may be of parenthetical interest to note that the music on this recording was recorded in 1967. It had lain dormant as a result of a change of record company ownership plus being an object of neglect, but everyone on the date remembered the session fondly. Ultimately it found its resurrected way to Concord Jazz via the perseverance of Shelly and the receptivity of Carl Jefferson. The point is that it is as fresh as the other side of today and this side of tomorrow.

What's happened to the musicians on the date since its recording? Well, Conte has emigrated to Doc Severinsen's band on *The Tonight Show* and also has been a regular with Supersax. Conte was with Shelly's group from 1961–1968 and made his move to a trumpet chair with Doc thereafter.

Since his departure from Shelly's enclave, Frank has returned to New York, playing part time in a variety of groups and special projects by night, and teaching elementary school during the day.

Mike has been busy as a journeyman in a spread of contexts in Southern California. Following an aborted start as a recording artist in the latter sixties (they were superb albums!), he is continuing his tenure in the studios, having recently etched an emphatic mark of attention with an album of his exquisite personalized interpretations of the works of Scott Joplin. Shelly and bassist Chuck Domanico are on the session, too. Hopefully, we'll hear a great deal more from the enlightenment of Mike Wofford.

Monty has continued to work with "everyone," blazing an incredibly extensive trail of associative credits. His professional worth is so respected, it seems he is always occupied.

Shelly's own activities are wide ranging—from his umpteen years as an ace studio habitué to working and recording as part of the L.A. Four (with Bud Shank, Laurindo Almeida and Ray Brown on Concord Jazz), doing jazz records for labels here and abroad … and the list goes on.

Shelly is rightfully proud of this quintet on *Perk Up*. He singles out the constant empathy—the front line with the rhythm section and vice versa. The fact that this group had worked together for some time shows in the prevailing cohesiveness. Dig how they listen to each other, ensemble and solo-wise. Empathetic interaction occurs on a prominent level.

Throughout the record, there is the beguiling, mystical work of Shelly who surprises, even startles with his phenomenal qualities. As a powerful advocate of the need to feel one's fellow players' vibrations physically, Shelly asserts that physical proximity is essential to bring about both physical and aural vibrations. "This record has some of the best Conte Candoli on record," exhorts Shelly. "Mike is sensational and I feel it contains some of the best playing I've done. It's good jazz which improves with age."

Articulating Shelly's conviction, this record therefore has a good nine years of vintage to begin with. *Perk Up* may possibly be your tonic, as it does meet the expressive and aesthetic needs of the contemporary psyche.

Elvin Jones

I went to the studio early one morning to set up a recording session for Palo Alto Records with the drummer, Elvin Jones. I mean this was very, very early in the morning. I walked into the studio and there was Elvin with one foot on a stool, a cigarette between his fingers, puffing away. I said, "Elvin! What are you doing here? Why are you here so early? The recording session doesn't start until 2:00 this afternoon!"

His reply: "Herb, I *am* a professional." To which I responded with deep admiration, "Elvin," I said, "I wish *everyone* were as professional as you."

Elvin Jones—*Brother John*
Palo Alto Records (PA 8039 N); 1984

Just coming off Elvin's first outing on Palo Alto Records (*Earth Jones* / PA 8016) with David Liebman, Terumasa Hino, George Mraz and Kenny Kirkland, a quartet date was an appealing contrast for a second album. Although I had heard Pat LaBarbera with Elvin numerous times during the past nine years and quite frequently with Buddy Rich's big band much earlier, I zeroed in on Pat for about eight months prior to this recording. The scope and ripe maturity of his playing with Elvin and the uninhibited purity of his sound wiped me out … at the University of California festival in Berkeley, at the Village Vanguard and at the jazzfest in Edmonton (sans Elvin's band).

Elvin's immutable approval was instant. "Our standards are high and not easy to reach and keep. Pat has tremendous musical ability beyond technical facility. He has been broadening his horizon with more composing and is functioning as a complete pro. He has great power of concentration to detail and is totally committed with body and soul. So he is more than a good friend, colleague and soul mate; I am extremely proud of Pat LaBarbera!" Pat's diligence and musical mindedness came through during the prep period and at the session. And man, he played magnificently!

"Reggie has great ears!" Elvin describes bassist Reggie Workman. "It's not easy to hear subtleties but he can, with keen alertness!" Reggie and Elvin worked together with John Coltrane one-and-a-half years ahead of Jimmy Garrison's five-year tenure as Coltrane's bassist, who in turn left J.C. in mid–1966.

As for the impressive Kenny Kirkland, his worthiness was so large on *Earth Jones* that it was natural to recall him for this new venture. Elvin echoes the excitement: "I can't get enough of Kenny. He has so many layers upon layers of new ideas, he's like a new person each time!" And there's plenty of quiet, rock solid confidence in his selfless support and tasteful choice of surprising notes.

Sharing some of Elvin's perceptions is apropos. Together with Dan Morgenstern's commentary [included on the original Palo Alto Records LP], these notes should carry

Album cover for Elvin Jones' 1982 *Brother John* / Palo Alto Jazz Records (PA 8039 N) (album cover credits: photograph by Darryl Pitt; design by Brian Collentine).

understanding a mite closer to the music and its makers—a strong effort deserving enthusiasm.

--·--·--·--·--·--·--·--·--·--·--·--·--·--·--·--·--·--·--

Art Blakey

Art Blakey had one outstanding characteristic that comes to mind whenever I envision him in front of a band: He was a leader's leader. Whenever I saw him, whatever the situation, wherever his band played, there was never a question about it, Art Blakey was the consummate leader.

He "vocalized" with the band—not singing, but saying things and saying them all the time. He would constantly make comments about each band member's playing. It was always encouraging, always in support of his players ... and sometimes it went to their heads.

I recall when Wynton Marsalis—still a teen-age player back then—was a part of Art's horn section, one of the band's featured horn soloists.

I remember speaking to Wynton during an intermission when the band was playing the Keystone Korner. I wanted to make sure Wynton appreciated Art's encouragement for what it was and didn't take it the wrong way. I called him aside and said to him, "Wynton, don't let Art's comments go to your head ... don't be a Columbia Records hot head."

A few months after that, we ran into each other in Geneva while Art's band was playing the Montreux Jazz Festival. I approached Wynton with a smile, asking "So how are you doing with your leader?" Wynton smiled in return. "I remembered what you said. I'm cool.... I'm cool." And cool, he was.

Art Blakey—*In This Korner*
Concord Records (CCD 4068); 1978

Don't let go of this record if you just picked it up!

Hundreds of people packed into San Francisco's Keystone Korner the evening of this "live" recording could not willingly let go of the music. The excitement of the music emanated from the walls of the jazz club into the night air in May and like a giant magnet, it pulled in crowds which spilled onto the sidewalks trying to get a share of the memorable event.

The idea of the record came from Blakey during an earlier gig at Keystone because he knew this band was on fire. Keystone's Todd Barkan helped to set up the date via his fervent encouragement and facilitation. The title selection "In This Korner," a wonderful shuffle—is Blakey's update of the spirit of famed Birdland in NYC, reborn and re-expressed in Keystone Korner. Art feels that few jazz clubs today retain the aura of 52nd Street of the late '40s, early '50s and the late '60s; Keystone in its sixth year, as a rarity, exemplifies the capture of the spirit.

To state that The Jazz Messengers is a vibrant hot group is redundant. Art Blakey himself is a key energy figure in the history of jazz—a veteran of marking new trails alongside of drummer Max Roach. In no uncertain terms Blakey and the Messengers have followed a modern straight ahead road exerting creative energies in hard swinging, incisively enunciated music. Since its inception as a co-op group in 1954 with Horace

Silver, Hank Mobley, Kenny Dorham and Doug Watkins, the Messengers have uncompromisingly carried the tradition of jazz in their compelling music. Through the years, "the message my men have tried to deliver, no matter which personnel we had, was always jazz. When you get away from swinging, get away from developing along the lines that were started by Diz and Bird and Max, you may be in danger of losing the essence of jazz."

This record reinforces Art's virile musical language—keyed with instinctual rhythmic fluency and vivid melodic colors, played with inner drive, commitment and fire. Following Art's own authoritative drum intro, the group roars into altoist Bobby Watson's samba, "Pamela"—grabbing your ears with no pause or mercy. And this tenacity is gnashingly sustained from start to finish on the record. The amazing caliber of musicians carry through Blakey's record as one of the foremost promoters of young, fresh talent. All editions of the Messengers have been successful laboratories for incubating and developing gifted players. The long roll call of Blakey alumni reads like an all-star jazz billing. The album at hand shows he has jelled another band of unusually impressive individuals.

As per the tradition of Blakey's pianists doubling as fertile composers vis-à-vis Horace Silver, Bobby Timmons, Cedar Walton and Walter Davis, his current pianist James Williams is a first rate writer and a magnificent pianist. Red Garland, who hung out at the session, praised Williams, "I think he's definitely ready to be heard! He's beautiful—very versatile." What a pair of great ears and hands bassist Dennis Irwin has! The lofty precedent of Blakey frontlinesmen is matched by the horn players—Valery Ponomarev, the brilliant Russian import on trumpet; Bob Watson, the mean altoist from Kansas City and David Schnitter from Newark, a four-year veteran with Art and a major voice—a rightful heir to the line of driving tenor saxists. Hell, just listen to their burning solos! "The Song Is You" is as fine an example as any tune on the record for gauging the quality of the group. I recall vividly how it wiped out everyone that night.

"Blakey should be the barometer for all young drummers," said Louie Bellson. "When he plays, he opens up the doors. He has honesty with humility. When someone mentions Art's name, they smile and say, 'Oh, man, that's the poppa!' Shelly Manne, Buddy Rich, Billy Cobham all admire him ... and as drummers say: 'Art Blakey is still swinging everybody into bad health!' ... he gets better all the time, losing no vitality."

Or, take Tony Williams' comment: "Blakey's ability to swing is dominant. There's a certain way he uses his high hat I love. His power, his drive and his swing turn me on." And Eddie Gladden who has been drumming for Richie Cole and for Dexter Gordon recently, considered Blakey and Roach as his idols: "Art is a master of what he's doing: I'm especially impressed with his brushwork and his press rolls."

In the forties, Max and Art took the new playing approaches unearthed by Jo Jones and Kenny Clarke and brought them to fruition, fitting them to the more open contemporary character of jazz. Notice Art's intelligent manner of embroidering, of tightening up the group's sound and giving direction to the soloists for fresh venues of expression.

Art's prominent place in jazz noted by Todd Barkan is an apt summary: "Art Blakey is one of the few living schools of this music, one of the primary forces that keeps the true spirit and direction of jazz alive. When he comes to town, everyone at Keystone Korner including the bartenders, waitresses and managers feel the promise and purpose of the club is fulfilled and we realize why we knock ourselves out week after week."

Every night Art Blakey plays is an event ... in any corner of the world, including "the jazz corner"—*IN THIS KORNER*!

CHAPTER 4

Tenor Saxophone

With its warm and sexy tonal quality, the tenor sax has always been romanticized by listeners and players alike. Maybe that's the reason so many musicians have chosen the tenor saxophone as their instrument, outnumbering players of all other jazz instruments by far.

When it comes to a role model for tenor sax players, nobody can approach "Mr. Sound," Stan Getz. He was *the* tenor sax player, *the* model for countless saxophonists who followed.

Stan Getz

Stan and I were very close. He was a neighbor and a frequent visitor to our house. On one occasion—my 50th birthday—the doorbell rang and there was Stan, holding a brand new tenor saxophone. Stan says to me, "Happy birthday, Herb," quickly followed by "I've decided that you don't need anything." He walked into the house, proffering the sax, saying, "This is for your daughter, Kira."

Stan knew that Kira had been planning to switch from the flute to the sax and was thinking of using Richie Cole's alto sax to audition for her high school jazz ensemble. But Stan, tenor in hand, said, "Where is Kira? I want to show her a few things." So we sat on the couch, while Stan taught Kira how to play tenor sax. He was so kind, he wrote her the following note to accompany his presentation of the gifted saxophone:

> On Feb. 16, 1940, my Father gave me my first saxophone. It was my Mother's birthday on that day. So, as everything one receives in this world, one gives back, as an offering of Thanks to Providence, I present you with this horn. To make music is a privilege and a challenge. To make others happy, as well as ourselves, with music, is a very special honor bestowed upon us by God. Very few are chosen for this by Him. Therefore it is also a responsibility. Good Luck, Chosen One.

"Stan Getz—A Memorial by Dr. Herb Wong"
Jazz Educators Journal, Fall 1991

The world of music and jazz in particular suffered an irreparable loss on June 6, 1991, when super-star tenor saxophonist Stan Getz died in his home in Zuma Beach in Malibu, California, after a lengthy bout with cancer. Getz was a musical genius whose hauntingly lyrical, sensuous and intensely personal sound and style created an irresistible aura of enchantment triggering one's imagination to roam, invent and find aural imageries. His warmth and singular beauty—his unexpected epigrams—literally pulled at the heartstrings of witnesses who willingly allowed Getz to spellbind them. Hearing just a few notes of his horn was more than ample to identify him instantly; one of his distinctive badges was his uncanny ability to improvise richly and to synthesize skeins of poetic phrases.

Most frequently it seemed magical, even mysterious, that his intuitive grasp of structure balanced with open freedom and a keen sense of dynamics and melody, empowered him to blend all the elements into mature compositions of ecstatic beauty. In particular, ballads by Getz easily illustrated why he was the jazz world's greatest balladic weaver—a creator of treasured new memories and unforgettable dreams. Lest we ignore or forget, Getz was also a sinewy hard swinger on tunes that were interpreted with front burners turned up high and hot. His extensive discography is replete with premium examples.

In my presence, Getz made serious references to his respectful allegiance to the philosophy of Tao and we had occasion to discuss this behavioral path conceived by Confucians. Getz's son, Steve, shared observations toward what I surmise as a Taoist kind of practice of unassertive action devoted to self-removal, enhancing Getz's transcendent quality of excellence: "When Dad had several nights in a row at a club (Steve has managed many a top flight jazz bistro in New York and on the West Coast), he could actually top himself. He always knocked me out as he did it repeatedly ... and so effortlessly. (This refers to territory exploited beyond the obvious attributes of tone and technique.) One night after one of these amazing experiences, I asked Dad, 'What are you thinking about when you're deep in concentration?' The reply was 'I'm thinking about the music and psyching myself into letting notes come out naturally.'" Anyone who has watched Getz's eyes during these moments of translocation will promptly relate to this commentary. He was, indeed, a master of the art of relaxation. Steve Getz hastened to add that this phenomenon is not exclusive to Stan Getz and cited Wayne Shorter and Phil Woods as examples of others who also subscribe to comparable manifestations and practices.

Professor Nathan Oliveira of Stanford University—an illustrious figurative painter of international repute and a champion/friend of Getz—feels that "Stan thought more like a painter creatively than most painters I know. Beautiful artists like Stan color the world. Like visual artists who respond to the challenge of inventing within the same structure numerous times, Stan did it with freshness each time; structure becomes a platform for something else. Somehow he just did it!" It is my belief that Getz was perhaps endowed genetically with an internal compass because time and again he showed how a "map" would be extra luggage.

Getz was born in Philadelphia on February 2, 1927. At age 6, his immigrant family moved to the Bronx. His long, remarkable career stemmed from the time he joined Jack Teagarden at 16 and then joined more big bands—Jimmy Dorsey, Buddy Morrow, Benny Goodman and Stan Kenton among others. His most notable alliance was with Woody Herman's Second Herd as Getz became one of the key members of the famous "Four Brothers" saxophone section. It was with this Herd that Getz's magnificent 7 bar solo on "Early Autumn" catapulted him into prominence and launched his role as leader of his own groups. ("Early Autumn" was the epilogue of Ralph Burns' programmatic *Summer Sequence* recorded on December 27, 1947.) The arch of his stretch across decades landed on several phases with historical peaks and valleys, leading numerous outstanding quartets—his most favored and successful format in the main—but including varied sized groups and special projects attaining artistic and also popular triumphs.

He is documented on more than 200 recordings; he continued to record: witness the release of several discs these past 12 months. And what is predicted as one of his most rewarding efforts is the most recent one, featuring just him and pianist Kenny Barron. He admired Barron immensely! It was recorded at Montmartre in Copenhagen during four days this past March during a 6-week tour with the entourage of musicians who contributed to the A&M 1990 disc *Apasionado*. Jane Walsh, a close friend of Getz for many years, reports this final project was one he was strongly determined and motivated to complete. Titled *People Time*, it has not been released at the time of this writing in July. Barron recalled vividly: "During the last two days of playing and taping, Stan's stomach was on fire. It was taxing for him as he had to play more and harder without a full rhythm section. He couldn't coast and it really took its toll, but you would never sense the pressure by listening to the tapes. He was, as usual, incredible and beautiful."

As most of the biographical/discographical information and details are more than less familiar to Getz followers, I have elected to forego any further recapitulation in favor of devoting attention to illustrations of his blend of leadership and empathic persona.

Pianist Lou Levy, who had known and played with him for some 44 years, beginning with their time with Woody Herman, noted their closeness and Getz's impact as an inspiring leader. "We roomed together, shared things Yiddish as well as tastes in food. He was

Herb Wong working with Stan Getz on *Voyage*, a 1986 release for Black-Hawk Records, at Music Annex Recording Studios in Menlo Park, California (photograph by Veryl Oakland; courtesy Veryl Oakland).

a great leader. He surely made me get on my toes every second, motivated me to pay close attention and as a result, everyone on whatever band he led would play better just because of him. I know I reached a higher, different level. And no matter where we were playing—in a club, a cellar, festival stage, hall or whatever—every moment was like Carnegie Hall quality. When I played with others, however, it was simply a jam session—nothing necessarily special. Every gig with Stan was like Sinatra standing on stage with his unbelievable magic." Levy's perspectives and experiences simply amplify the charismatic power Getz exerted on his musicians and audiences alike. Little wonder that he was a musical giant.

Among a slate of leadership assets, Getz had an acute ability to identify emergent talent and to permit vital germination of latent potentials of his musicians, and he deliberately nurtured growth in his own style of support. Pianist Andy LaVerne, who was in his quartet 1977–1980, relates his first meeting with Getz. After LaVerne had departed from the Herman big band

and was subbing for Joanne Brackeen in Washington, D.C., he sat in at one of Getz's gigs at Blues Alley, without the benefit of rehearsals. "In the afternoon the first thing Stan asked me was 'Do you have any original music?' I said that I did."

LaVerne had expected Getz to open the handbook and conduct an audition. Instead, "he immediately tapped my own music and put me at ease. I shared my 'Pretty City' (a reference to Jerusalem) with Stan and he sight read and dug right into it playing chorus after chorus after chorus … grooving with it. He gave me incentive to write more for him. It was a period when he was doing mainly originals. He opened up my writing confidence and energies and I'm indebted to him for his support in many ways as I also am to Woody." This was the band when Getz had Mike Richmond on bass and Billy Hart on drums. LaVerne has subsequently demonstrated how widely open his creative floodgates have become: witness his grants, awards and numerous excellent recordings/performances, educational activities and strong compositions. Getz had observed "Andy's writing literally flowed out of him" while praising him for his impeccable musical taste and integrity.

Noted pianist Horace Silver is another of a long line of major talents identified and introduced by Getz. Silver's career was given impetus by Getz who heard him with Walter Bolden and Joe Calloway at the Sundown in Hartford, Connecticut when Getz was a featured attraction. Silver said, "I had been saving my money to go to New York and I tried to do this two times but without enough gumption to make the move. I was apprehensive about the prospects. Stan said he liked my playing and followed through with his promise to hire the entire trio. I dearly owe it to him for leading me into the jazz world. I was and always have been impressed with how deeply Stan loved the music. Master musicians like Stan, Diz and Miles love it so intensely they are like children when they get together and share energies about the music."

Turning to more of his generous assistance to young musicians, no part of his life stream had provided him more stability, happiness and fulfillment than his recent years associated with Stanford University in Palo Alto, California. Professor Oliveira says, "Quiet, solace and a warm, friendly support system were here for him. Stan was definitely at peace with himself. He related to people he normally didn't relate to and he fitted in so well … he was so very bright and the large circles of university community people were sources of comfort and interest for him whenever he got off the road and came home here." Getz's connection here was initiated via participation in his first Stanford Summer Jazz Workshop in 1983, on his 40th anniversary in jazz, and, appropriately, discussed his 40 years in music. He brought his rhythm section which had just come off tour—Jim McNeely, Marc Johnson and Victor Lewis.

Shortly after he moved from a San Francisco residency to the Menlo Park/Atherton/Woodside environs, with its upscale neighborhoods close to campus, he became an integral part of the community fabric while he maintained a touring schedule with good blocks of time at home. In January 1986, he began his several official years of Artist-in-Residency status with the jazz department, allowing him maximum freedom to come and go; so Stanford essentially adapted its schedule to Getz's availability.

During one of my chats with him (I lived less than 10 minutes from him), he shared enthusiastically, "I'm seeing it's possible to motivate bright young people just by being around them and I look forward to working with them. I rehearse the big band on occasion, coach about 7 combos and speak about my theory of music in the music theory classes—and sometimes the American Music History class. I try to give them confidence by just blowing my sax in their ears and telling them 'Let's have fun with it!'"

Ted Gioia of Stanford added, "Stan taught the students best with his horn in his hands, taking standards and trading fours in a way similar to how a Stanford Nobel laureate might teach with chalk and board. At his most effective, he taught intuitively, compatible with his natural approach. He made some wonderful things happen as students would transform their own approach as a result." As a jazz educator, Getz managed and adapted well in his relationships with a wide range of student abilities, experience and backgrounds—the more advanced combos (which garnered national awards at competitive festivals) as well as the most rudimentary groups vis-à-vis "a classical player with no jazz experience, a blues sax player who couldn't read a note, a marching band saxophonist, and a new-age player who could only play a few pretty notes" reports Jim Nadel, Director of the Summer Jazz Workshop. "At one point Stan dropped into this beginning combo when they were all working on Freddie Hubbard's "Straight Life"—they all played around the 2 chord vamp; they traded fours around the room and Stan heard and understood everyone's specific musical personality in the circle of horns. They each traded fours with Stan and he was able to answer one person and then make a stylistically fitting comment to the next person—much like talking to two people at once with each saxophone comment, completing this process with everyone. Simply awesome."

Nadel further indicated how Getz would go out of his way to help someone he thought had high potential. His enormous efforts toward jazz scholarship support was most notably significant in the case of bassist Larry Grenadier (who most recently was a member of Gary Burton's band); he was enabled to matriculate and graduate from Stanford. Getz recruited the likes of Bob Brookmeyer, Art Farmer, Victor Feldman and The Manhattan Transfer to join his quartet in concert performances and clinics, generating scholarship funds. Four major concerts with such artists were organized by Getz each year.

Getz told me an anecdote and Nadel confirmed that on one occasion he stepped into the music theory class when it was discussing jazz education's adoption of nomenclature drawn from early Gregorian chants and 12th century church modes to describe contemporary jazz organization of harmonies. Stan was asked what he thought of the Dorian mode among others. Getz's reply has become a classic response—"It's not the mode. It's the mood!" Getz remarked to me, "I don't care much for chords or modes— my area is feeling."

Speaking of feelings, Getz's quiet reputation as a very compassionate person is fraught with examples and his humanism was a large piece of the emotions in his musical and life equation. Let me share a few instances dealing with others' plights, futures and destinies wherein he would exert efforts to comfort, abet, nurture, finance, celebrate or whatever was needed to make things better. One poignant happenstance was when he played outside of the window of the wheelchair-bound daughter of a Stanford professor after she had been nearly killed by an auto. Kenny Barron revealed a time when he had to leave a Getz European tour to return to NYC to care for his wife who was ill with a worsened battle with cancer and had planned to rejoin the band after the weekend flight. Suddenly while he was home, his mother-in-law died. Upon learning of Barron's tragic situation, Getz told Kenny "it would be a drag for your wife to be alone after the funeral so I'm flying both you and her to Europe."

My own daughter, Kira, was a recipient of Getz's kindnesses. When he learned that she had been playing flute for several years and wanted to learn the alto to audition for a chair in the high school jazz ensemble, he gifted her with a brand new saxophone at one of my birthday fetes. He said as he brought the horn into the house, "This is not for you, Herb. It's for Kira and I want to show her some things on this horn." It was accompanied by a spiritually written message to her [reproduced above] which built self-esteem. We were overwhelmed with this lovely act. And it goes on ... he was charitable and caring to friends, band roadies, budding musicians and vocalists like Diane Schuur and other citizens here and abroad.

In October 1990, a special tribute to Getz was held at A&M Studios in L.A.; musicians such as Conte Candoli, Lou Levy, Bob Cooper, Monty Budwig, Pete Jolly, Shorty Rogers and Johnny Mandel were present and Getz played several selections. The A&M sound stage was also where one of two memorial services was held for Getz on July 1, 1991. Herb Alpert, Horace Silver, Steve Allen, Lou Levy and others shared their sentiments. On the East Coast in NYC at St. Peter's Church at about the same time on the same day, services included music by Kenny Barron, David Williams, Victor Jones, Andy LaVerne, Ray Drummond, Steve Kuhn, George Mraz, Helen Merrill, Mel Martin and Lee Konitz.

I have been a near lifetime fan of Getz ever since I met him more than 40 years ago when he was a rising star with Woody's bebop Herd, playing in Sweet's Ballroom in Oakland, California. I cherish the occasions we have had to chat, to walk and run, to listen to music, to drive, to dine, and the privilege of working with him at festivals and in the recording studio.

Herb Alpert's support system in the past couple of years gave Getz even more pleasures to savor and more music to create. Alpert relates how Getz's insightful perceptions about jazz were worthy returns for producing Getz's *Apasionado* recording. Getz described, "Jazz is not about flashy licks. It's a story with a beginning, middle and end. You must first learn the vocabulary—scales, chords, etc. ... then let it fly. And be sure to listen inside the rhythm section—that's the motor."

Apropos then, is the Stan Getz Memorial Fund with a start up donation of $25,000 from Alpert designed to benefit talented high school jazz musicians; it is being administered via IAJE and the National Foundation for Advancement in the Arts.

In closing I think another classic guiding concept bears serious application and appreciation for Stan Getz's primacy of values: "If it sounds good and if you like it—it doesn't matter if it breaks the rules—the ear is the last court of appeal!" No wonder Herb Alpert refers to Getz as "a conduit from a much higher and deeper source." Thank you, Stanley, for the millions of gorgeous, magical star-dusted notes and moments. They will outlast all of us.

God bless you.

David Liebman

David Liebman is a super brilliant individual, not only as a musician, but in other modes of expression. He has composed music, he's composed written material, he's a bright light who can play all those horns—but soprano and tenor seem to be his features. He's a very prominent musician as well as an inspirational clinician.

David is an expert on John Coltrane, an authority on the ins and outs of Trane's music. I think it's because he finds that Coltrane's music has an affinity with his own values.

It was somewhat unusual for David to farm out liner notes for one of his CDs—

David is so versatile and he does things in such depth, he usually does liner notes for himself—so I was especially pleased to get the liner notes assignment for David Liebman's *Joy: The Music of John Coltrane.*

David Liebman—*Joy: The Music of John Coltrane*
Candid Records (CCD 79531); 1993

My initiation into this disc was a turn on! It occurred when driving my auto on a rainy evening. The first tune, "After the Rain," began with the sound of rain drops which were in amazing coincidence with the sounds of rainfall on my windshield. Discriminating the two sources was a momentary challenge.

David Liebman's music promptly conjures a special aura of emotionally charged excitement much like a child's bubbling anticipation of an assured, satisfying experience. The most intense aesthetic experiences of improvised music are likely to catch one by surprise. Beauty is felt in the abrupt contact with an aspect of creative music that one has not known previously; it's an antithesis of the acquired tastes for certain musiscapes or the warm feelings for very familiar places and experiences.

Some twenty odd years ago, by way of his remarkable messages and essays on recordings, in-person performances, and his written words, Liebman entered my mindscape with penetrating power and generous influence. His capacity to share compassioned music was recruited into the bands of Elvin Jones (*Merry-Go-Round*, 1971 and *Live at The Lighthouse*, 1972) and Miles Davis (*On the Corner* and *Get Up with It*, 1973); also impressive were current recordings by The Open Sky Trio and the bold *Lookout Farm* band. In sum, Liebman's permanence was anchored in the international jazz echelons of reputation. His music has been a carrier of major improvisatory energies which strike a just right balance of binary oppositions and of the notion of primal unity and harmony.

Liebman's music is his private language abbreviated to its communicative essence. And there is a strong conviction that the John Coltrane environment and body of music is the single most embracing conceptual and inspirational source of truths for Liebman's expression. He achieves this objective through his own filtered interpretations while immersed in Coltrane's full circle of energy and impact.

The disc at hand illuminates Coltrane's fruitful seeds of joy through the freshness of Liebman's vocabulary—providing nutritives to the process and resulting in the big band orchestrations played by the superb James Madison University Jazz Ensemble, guest artists, and the colorful, cogent soprano saxophone statements. There are points of departures, but not necessarily ends, which pose as musical challenges that carry no anonymous solutions but rather, a multi-layered deeply personal research articulation. The arrangements are for him evocative, suggesting a mood, often positive and sunny but provocative and discordant, too.

Liebman's strong, mature music pulls attention easily via its emotional force and sometimes mystical essence. A witness would be hard pressed to allow an unaffected, unmoved response; i.e., his is an art of a really forbidding awesomeness. "Musical sound is realized in shapes," Liebman says in his book, *Self Portrait of a Jazz Artist,* "consisting of all types of lines: straight, broken, curved, wave-like, figure eight, etc." The varietal range heard on this disc is remindful of his rich employment of line configurations. He incessantly searches for better ways to unleash his artistry and to dig deeper and press forward explorations of the untreaded musical wilderness and into himself for new strata of expressiveness. Clearly, he does not coast on his past achievements.

Early on, the Coltrane quartet made an indelible impression on the then teenaged David Liebman. His knowledge of Coltrane's music is wide and his love for it is sincere and deep. The many meanings and truths of Coltrane's music are kept alive or realigned by plural crowds of players around the globe. As an heir to the magic carpet legacy of Coltrane, Liebman's intense admiration and respect is seamless. His ritualistic practice to record Coltrane anniversary tribute projects in five year increments are marked as special homage and inspirational events. "I did a Coltrane homage record in 1987 for Owl Records, changing the sound using both acoustic and electric situations and I rearranged his music." Then came the *Live Under the Sky* recording in Japan with Wayne Shorter, Richie Beirach, Eddie Gómez and Jack DeJohnette—a straight ahead blowing session. This 1992 project grew out of a situation originally suggested in Helsinki by Esko Linnavalli, leader of the UMO Band.

Insight on Liebman's perspectives concerning Coltrane is germane. He described: "For me, Coltrane will forever be the top of the line. When I was younger I wasn't together enough with my own sound to say these things or to make recordings of Coltrane. Secondly, critics are likely to and *will* link someone like me to the Coltrane tradition; however, I am actually more of a *wing* of the Coltrane school of players. As you grow older, your credits rise, just by the fact you've lasted."

From this aspect of maturation, Liebman outwardly manifests his acknowledgment to Coltrane in many ways—technically, musically, and most of all spiritually and the commitment to playing. "That's what really inspired me to play the music—seeing him, hearing him play so many times." So it is a continuing homage.

"Each of the tunes on the disc is a special kind of tune. While Coltrane wrote many, I wouldn't say he was a sophisticated composer like Monk or certainly Ellington or even Horace Silver whose tunes are simple but sophisticated. But Coltrane was a composer like Charlie Parker was, or like Miles was in the sense the tunes are perfect vehicles for what he wanted to say improvisationally. It's how I also write. I write a tune because I'm interested in that particular compositional challenge, that improvisational framework. Also, I truly don't expect anyone else to play it. That's why when you take a Coltrane tune, it's incumbent upon you in this day and age to not change the tune, but rather make it contemporary—make something out of it different than what he did. And it's OK, as it does not tarnish or detract from his music—that's the challenge! In my case, playing the soprano on *all* the tunes changes the colors right away because it's not the tenor, so that's an advantage I enjoy."

Liebman's personal program notes enhance the listeners experience. Herein are a few more comments. "After the Rain" is a prime candidate as Coltrane's most lyrical piece. The "Untitled Original" was never recorded and is one of his nice lines that Liebman reports came out of a bootleg tape that people used to pass around. Liebman was buoyed by hearing "Alabama" in the film *Malcolm X* as it bears significance to the Civil Rights Movement; also, the small group version on this disc rounds out the record with contextual balance. Liebman's signature tune is "India," with a twelve-bar melody, which Liebman "plays every night with my group—any group I have." Indian music is important to jazz musicians as it inherently has such a heavy improvisational tradition. An historical jazz anthem is the gorgeous "Naima," probably the most well known Coltrane tune. Finally, two brief melodies Coltrane played near the end of his career—"Joy/Selflessness" close the ambitious, brightly successful program fired by David Liebman's authoritative horn, the exceptional young JMU musicians, the tangible, relevant guest artists, and Gunnar Mossblad's web of contributions. *Joy* is a celebratory experience!

— — —·— —·— —·— —·— —·— —·— —·— —·— —·— —·— —·— —·— —·— —

Wayne Shorter

Wayne Shorter's evolution from membership with Miles Davis skyrocketed in the last decade, with Wayne playing his own music with his own group to critical acclaim and audience appreciation.

He is one of jazz's most gifted composers, inventive beyond bounds and unbounded by convention. He's a magnetic personality in jazz who comes up with unpredictable material, and his jazz relationships—with Herbie Hancock, in particular—have delivered a good measure of new music now etched in jazz history.

Wayne Shorter—*Super Nova*
Blue Note Records (BST 84332); 1969

"*Super Nova*"?!! The album title conjures analogous relationships of Wayne Shorter and his music with the astronomical interpretations of super novae in our galaxy of about 100 billion stars. Although the word nova means "new," the term is applied to stars that are not actually new in the strict sense. Novae are "new stars" that blaze up into great splendor and then become faint again; these stars are classed as variable stars of no determined period. Some novae burst into a brilliance thousands of times greater than they formerly possessed such as the super nova, Tycho's Star, in the constellation Cassiopeia near the end of the year 1572. Wayne Shorter, in the strict sense, is not a "new star" either; but he is, indeed, assuming greater star-like luminosity.

Another analogy finds its basis in astronomer Johann Bayer's *Uranometria*, a star atlas of early 17th century which first designated the relative brightness of stars in the community of constellations via letters of the Greek alphabet. Wayne Shorter's star magnitude could, therefore, be regarded as one of the alpha or brightest stars. However, we don't need any system devised by astronomers of the likes of Bayer, Ptolemy, Hipparchus, Flamsteed or Norton to help us realize that Wayne is a musician of the first magnitude. Just as a shell of exceedingly hot gas is blown out from a nova at the time of intense brightness, jazz musicians approximate this phenomenon in their supreme outbursts of creativity. Moreover, it is exciting to observe how the jazz man continues the inventing process—for what he invents is of the moment and for the moment.

Wayne Shorter is nearing his sixth anniversary with the Miles Davis quintet. And like Miles, Wayne is extremely self-challenging and exploratory; he is uninhibited by conventional attitudes. In his evolution as a notable composer and improvisor, the all-viable Miles Davis laboratory has provided Wayne with a rare combination of equipment, processes, awareness, and opportunity to develop his own concepts. To all of these, the inspired leadership model of Miles and the stimulating aura of the quintet add to the formulation of Wayne's own ethic for music and life.

Despite his being cited by the 1968 *DownBeat* Critics Poll for Talent Deserving of Wider Recognition as a jazz composer, Wayne remains underrated. Pianist-composer Herbie Hancock, who spent over four years playing with Wayne as a fellow member of the Davis unit and as the pianist on Wayne's four most recent Blue Note albums, bemoans the fact that Wayne is an unsung jazz composer of great worth. As Herbie remarked, "Miles does Wayne's tunes, why don't others do his tunes? I'm going to do some of his things in my own recordings. I get a big kick out of doing Wayne's tunes. I like his conception and personal style—there are enough elements in his tunes to consistently identify them as his creations. He has a keen sense of chordal relationships. You can detect his special way of moving from one point to the next, vertically speaking; horizontally speaking, all his tunes are lyrical. Wayne is a great composer."

Another thought expressed by Herbie Hancock, which goes back a couple of years when we were discussing Miles' ways of providing creative encouragement and when Herbie was still with Miles, offers more clues to the Davis philosophy which is reflected in the musicians in his group. Miles had apparently told Wayne, Herbie, Ron Carter and Tony Williams, "I pay you guys to practice on the bandstand." Hancock explained, "This concept recognizes that there is really no way to practice certain ideas at home and that they occur only on the bandstand, since ideas come from being stimulated by the atmosphere, the audience and the other players, whether in a studio or club. It's like playing a set of drums without a bass drum—the bass drum being the audience, et al. It's the only real situation for improvising."

About five years ago, Wayne strived to relate his music to the manner in which he responded to the life and times surrounding him. He then enlarged his outlook to relating himself to the universe. Reflecting his passion for increased involvement toward "total involvement," Wayne has composed, played and recorded an enormous amount of music featuring his tenor saxophone and, of late, the soprano saxophone, to express his involvement. On this latest album, the music represents a transect of contemporary music.

There is an exciting collaboration of some of the best elements of the idiom effecting a fascinating collage of sounds that evoke impressions of space and the universe. And like the recent Miles Davis epochal recording, *In a Silent Way*, the Shorter album sets up movement for new directions with consummate power. There are correlations between the two albums in the use of polyrhythms, polytonalities, openness and the personnel on the sessions. Wayne, Chick Corea, and John McLaughlin performed on Miles' date; Jack DeJohnette who replaced Tony Williams as Miles' drummer is on Wayne's album here. Their combined musical perspectives on the album bear extra advantages.

Wayne has obviously found the soprano a very compatible instrument for his explorations. His individual stylistic approach and quality of sound come through on the horn beautifully. Note, for example, how his performances on "Water Babies," "Capricorn" or "Swee-Pea" (a tribute to the late Billy Strayhorn) serve as excellent initial objects of study. Jobim's "Dindi," the only tune not composed by Wayne, deserves special attention. It features a very compassioned debut performance by Maria Booker, wife of Walter Booker who plays classical guitar on the track. Maria had never sung on a recording and was greatly concerned with her involvement. As producer Duke Pearson commented, "Maria and I are old friends. She's Portuguese and hails from Lisbon. Maria was very emotional about the whole thing. She put everything she had into it. She started to cry as she sang with joy. As you can hear, I left it all in there." Hancock who heard it added, "I cried when I heard it. Wayne was like a giant to Maria and she wanted to contribute something special."

Like "Dindi," the entire album is one of deep sincerity. Pearson believes it is Wayne's most sincere album he has ever heard. It was a very loose date with no rehearsal. Wayne had the music in mind and told the musicians what he desired and expected and to take it from there with their imagination and wherewithal. Near the close of 1968 in *DownBeat*, Wayne wrote, "While recording, I'd like to create the atmosphere that we're not just at a recording studio. I've written something down, but we'll have a jam session spirit." And about where the new music is heading he stated, "I don't know if that's as important as where did it come from, because if you know where it came from, it's going anyway. I don't like labels, but I'll say "new music" anyway—total involvement. From soul to universe."

Musicians today are thinking very much in terms of the cosmic sphere rather than just musical feeling of the "true" sense. That is, there are leanings in terms of not just earthbound music you might expect to hear traveling around the globe in the traditional sense, but rather what impulsive music might go on in our heads and what it might sound like if music could be heard from the stars and the celestial environment. Therefore, we hear a wide panorama of sounds, colors and movement in Wayne Shorter's music—some mystically dark and introspective, some wildly slashing and throbbingly incandescent and others floatingly evanescent and ethereal. This recycles us to super novae and their figurative implications of youthful "newness" and the super, indeterminate flashes of creative glory that Wayne Shorter's music represents on this planet, enlightening our lives and internal spirit with fresh experiences.

Zoot Sims

Zoot Sims—the eternal swinger—was another of the richly expressed disciples of Lester Young. Because of the way he interpreted elements of Lester, Zoot had a tremendous influence on many other players.

His tonality and his continuation of Lester Young's concepts substantiated his importance as one of the four saxophone players—the famed "Four Brothers"—who were the leaders of Woody Herman's Second Herd. The "brotherhood" originally included Herbie Steward, Stan Getz, and Zoot Sims on tenor, joined by the band's baritone saxophonist, Serge Chaloff. In the '40s, Al Cohn replaced Herbie Steward as a "brother" and Zoot's partnership with Al became undeniable, as "Al and Zoot" became a familiar trademark in the jazz world.

Zoot Sims—*One to Blow On*
Biograph Records (BLP 12062); 1979; Reissued by Shout Factory

Zoot Sims is synonymous with genuine, classic swing. Everything he plays inherently carries this unalterable, satisfying quality. You can actually take it for granted—a rare phenomenon today at the close of the seventies. It's a warranty clearly felt and heard but somehow eludes precipitation of definition within literal parameters.

Sims is marvelously superior in light, swinging tunes wherein the buoyancy of his swing remains at its crest without teetering. He consistently retains the feeling of fresh inspiration. You can't truly tell when he is NOT inspired. Conversely, you surely can tell when he's super-inspired. He doesn't seem to pick up the horn WITHOUT the feeling of inspiration.

It is transparent Sims enjoys playing and is very serious about it. This loop between satisfaction and insatiable hunger to play/swing implies an inner space of variable fulfillment. It is articulated by Sims in very positive ways for there is a relationship to his air of calmness and serenity. He IS serene and composed. He obviously uses his feelings in his playing and commands excellent control of his musical feelings which, incidentally, seem to be more available to him than to many other jazz musicians. Moreover, he has that feeling of lift and swing with him at all times ... strongly reminiscent of Phil Woods who also has that constant feeling when he's playing and when he's not playing.

One way to accentuate the elusiveness of Sims' pervasive sense of swing and vitality is to consider its impossibility of being interpreted a la Sims from the notation of his playing. That is, in the first place, you just can't notate the swing in Zoot Sims' solos ... they wouldn't sound the same if you wrote them out and tried to play them. Whereas, for instance, you can transcribe Charlie Parker's solos and play them with relatively close approximation to the way Bird sounded.

There is a sizable bundle of subtle elements in the sum of Sims sound and swing. Central to this is what pianist-composer George Handy said in reference to that incredible album featuring Zoot Sims in quadruplicate. Handy commented on the extreme difficulties in his attempts to transcribe Sims' first solo as a basis for harmonization by three more multiple-taped solos by Sims. "I found myself faced with more than notes. There were slurs, slides, slitherings, spacious soarings, false notes, blue notes, whisperings of notes, non-existent notes, grace notes, millions of pieces of notes—Zoot Sims notes."

Sims was forging his saxophone voice early on when I first heard him with Woody Herman's Second Herd on a one-nighter at Sweet's Ballroom in Oakland, California. I remember hurrying through a tough final exam on endocrinology at the University of California in Berkeley and rushing off campus to get in front of the bandstand in order to zero in on the heralded "Four Brothers" saxophone section. I was literally bowled over by the entire band's charging spirit and the dynamics and phrasing of Stan Getz and Zoot Sims in particular. Like a number of other tenors of the same stylistic school, their work was basically and heavily indebted to Lester Young, embodying tangents of Parker's influence. The fermentation of their respective individual styles was manifested in the vocabulary of their roots which were, of course, derivative. But each of them was clearly developing his own distinguishable sound.

In the subsequent fifties, Sims was actively playing with a broad variety of jazz luminaries. He was featured with Stan Kenton's road band and likewise toured Europe with the Benny Goodman and Gerry Mulligan bands before teaming up with Al Cohn, his tenor compatriot, for a lengthy alliance. Speaking of Cohn, he expressed unsurprisingly: "Zoot has always been remarkable. In spite of the millions of hours we've played together, he's still one of my favorite players."

Sims was recording frequently and jamming regularly in New York ... accelerating his arrival as a key jazz musician who knocked out everyone with his mature, inspired, hard driving playing. Leafing the pages back to late 1956 when this record was made, Sims consistently demonstrated how his emotions remained uncloaked and how they were infused into every tune (he's ever played). He literally breathes passion into his horn and lights up everyone playing with him or listening to him. Without hesitation, he boots the others to play over their heads. Sadly, there is but a small cadre of musicians who are dependably effective this way.

Valve trombonist Bob Brookmeyer has had numerous associations with Sims. Bob has ranged widely in Europe and the U.S. in the club and festival circuit with Mulligan, covering every major one in their transcontinental pathways. For Brookmeyer, this record preceded his union with Jimmy Giuffre and Jim Hall in their very intriguing context— The Jimmy Giuffre 3—which created much excitement during its existence. Like Sims, Brookmeyer was much in demand, garnering a healthy reputation for his forthright creativeness and professional skills.

Brookmeyer's sound and style are immediately recognizable, but defy prompt categorization. It is a rich meld of traditional and contemporary concepts suffused with warmth and a liberal amount of wit and humor. I've always enjoyed his attack and his articulateness in telling a story with his instrument. His eloquence in the language arts, I believe, is a good clue to the thoughtfully intelligent structure of his improvisations and compositions. The presence of Bob Brookmeyer on this record is a royal bonus.

The fat, lush blend of tenor and trombone which are in approximately the same register, offers one of the classic sounds in jazz. It's the closest register to the human voice and is, therefore, very natural.

The evergreen, "September in the Rain," is the spirited opener. Sims' instant improvising powers swing out with a seemingly endless stream of finger poppin' ideas. His tête-à-têtes with Brookmeyer indicates further joyful interplays on the album.

The pianist on the record is Vermont born John Williams who claims composer rights to "Down at the Loft." His jazz career is most notably connected with his tenure with Stan Getz. Dipping behind the Getz experience, Williams played with the energetic, driving New England band of Mal Hallett followed by stints with the orchestras of altoist Johnny Bothwell and Charlie Barnet. There are some good examples of his recorded work with Getz just in front of the mid-fifties. Bearing relevance to his playing with Sims, Williams had expressed a leaning toward Al Cohn and Sims prior to the making of this record: "I have been feeling lately as if I must want to be a Zoot Sims–Al Cohn piano player, to do on the piano what they do with their horns. I find, in my rare good moments, that my rhythmic freedom will allow me to open up and widen out and damn near soar, as they do so easily. Anyway, that's the happiest kind of feeling I can ever get in blowing." Well, Williams captures the quality he speaks of via his work on this record. His original line here is a very infectious one.

"Ghost of a Chance" is a ballad Sims often uses as a point of departure. His pretty solo is devoid of amendments of throw-away frills and wafer-thin non-essentials. Sims is one of the truthful players. Note Brookmeyer's lovely timbres and beautifully fluid segues, his humorous incorporations and personal approach.

The Sims-Brookmeyer duality is enlivened with a vibrantly rhythmic quality which seems to humanize their open blowing. On the kind of hang loose air of Sims' original tune, "Not So Deep," the rhythm section is well fused within itself and with the continuity of the horns. Williams' percussive approach shows great compatibility; no wonder he counted Hank Jones, Horace Silver and Bud Powell as his models. Gus Johnson's sure-fire tasty and lively drums moves the band with flawless time and control. Milt Hinton's bass just soars with the greatest finesse a bassist could engender.

You never lose your hold on the melody, regardless of Zoot Sims' variations and transformations of the line. "Them There Eyes" gets a marvelously swinging treatment. Once again, Brookmeyer's humor is used in an appropriate way and the general shape of his solos is a gas to perceive and listen to. Johnson's neat and strategic drum breaks shows his impressive versatility with cymbals and sticks … what a beautiful sound!

Just lean back and let everything in your system flow naturally as "Our Pad" is filled with nicely woven lines that stimulate wonderful feelings with no strain. Hinton does his "perfection act" without flinches and is solid as Gibraltar. Johnson's drums are perfect on this tune he and Brookmeyer conjugated as composers.

When I first heard the mellow melody and the light feathery swing of "Dark Clouds" in the late fifties, I was hooked on it. I found myself gravitating to it often as I selected it for frequent plays on my jazz radio broadcasts on KJAZ-FM. "Bob Brookmeyer is a circus!" said trombonist Frank Rehak. "Bobby can make you cry and he can make you laugh. He can bring every emotion out of you because he is a tremendously emotional player. And he knows all about taste and he sure has it. Some of the best fun I ever had was sitting next to him in various settings. He's very inventive … you never know what's going to come out of his horn and he never repeats himself. There's always new stuff flowing from Bob." Brookmeyer's lettuce-crisp solo and burry tones are delightful on this track and Sims is so comfortably great on this kind of groove!

The final tune is the title selection "One to Blow On" and it is literally just that. Both hornmen swing their heads off and unleash their high geared blowing to drive it home. A carefree spirit undergirds the band's blanket approval as everyone has a ball blowing on this one to close the session.

Sims and Brookmeyer are true musical spirits. They began that way, were that way in 1956 and remain that way as we move into the 1980s. They are both playing better than ever, surviving with artistic splendor and integrity. "I think Zoot is a national monument," said Brookmeyer, "He was born one!"

Joshua Redman

I first bumped into Joshua Redman when he was in kindergarten and I was working as a school administrator. His teacher called me, saying, "I have a problem and I need your help. There's this little boy in our kindergarten class with whom I've had some difficulties." I said, "I'll be on campus soon. I'll come down and check it out and try to help you out."

I went to the teacher's room and asked, "Where is this young man, this problematic kindergartner? What's his name?" The teacher then introduced me to Joshua Redman, to whom I said, "Joshua, why don't you come with me … we're going to go out for a few minutes." A worried looking Joshua asked, "Are we going to your office?" I responded as gently as I could, "No, I don't see children in my office. We're just going to take a little walk and sit down on a bench."

Then I had a chat with him and brought him back to the teacher, who happened to be an ace educator, one of the most reputed kindergarten teachers in the country. I said to her, "You are so lucky. This little boy has his own mind and he's going to be very creative." And that was my introduction to Joshua Redman.

"The Heart and Soul of Joshua Redman's Music"
Jazz Educators Journal, November 2000

Joshua Redman is one of the best known, popular, and celebrated jazz musicians in the world today, earning an avalanche of acclaim. His many musical triumphs have catapulted him into the limelight, veering toward the apex of the tenor saxophone suprastructure.

Ever since the rapid rush of success and recognition arrived in 1991 (when, at age 22, he was awarded first place in the prestigious Thelonious Monk Institute of Jazz Saxophone Competition and captured a Warner Brothers recording agreement), Redman has been scaling a ladder of artistic milestones. His first recordings promptly gained significant attention from the media, normally inaccessible to young jazz players. A dominating poll-winner, he has also been honored with first-place awards in major music magazines. Impressive, heavy record sales have been part of the mix, too. Moreover, this year Redman's seventh and latest recording, *Beyond,* reaches a high watermark of growth and excellence. It reflects his consistent explorations in seeking challenging opportunities for creativity and adventure; the wherewithal to take risks is a given in such enterprises.

It is not surprising Redman is a resourceful, intrepid risk-taker in music and in life in general. This values-laden behavior was evident very early on when Redman was enrolled in a special, demonstration-model primary school in Berkeley—specifically, Washington Elementary—one of three University of California Laboratory Schools dedicated to curriculum research and development of innovative frontier concepts and experimental educational practices. As the administrator, yours truly had launched a school-wide jazz education curriculum beginning in 1965 (at a time when such curricula were not a part of elementary school programs); I was able to enlist the participation of Oscar Peterson's Trio, Rahsaan Roland Kirk's Quintet, and the Duke Ellington Orchestra. Redman revealed incipient, divergent thinking as well as much curiosity and a sense of search and discovery.

Risk-taking was a natural part of young Redman's improvisatory character from kindergarten onward. Given his first tenor sax at age ten, he became involved with instrumental music in the Longfellow Middle School Jazz Band and ultimately the Berkeley High School Jazz Ensemble, wherein his uncommon level of discipline and creative talent emerged and blossomed. Redman's jazz band director (and my jazz education co-conspirator/recruit) was the late Phil Hardyman, who carried the jazz torch from Washington and Longfellow Schools to the High School.

In the process of adjudicating the Berkeley High jazz bands led by Hardyman and his successor Charles Hamilton at competitive festivals, I noted Redman as a superior soloist who showed an unfoldment of risk-involved rewards in his solos. So in his teens, his inspired convictions were articulated in making daring trade-offs pay off! All the while he pursued his studies with peak academic successes.

Redman's mother, Renee Shedroff, a dancer and librarian, was solely responsible for his upbringing in Berkeley after she and his father, Dewey Redman, separated. The elder Redman is the noted tenor saxophonist who was associated with Ornette Coleman's innovative quartet in the late '60s and early '70s, Charlie Haden's Liberation Music Orchestra, and the Keith Jarrett Quintet.

Key circumstances framing the backdrop of Redman's dramatic leap into the frontal niche of the jazz world are certainly not unfamiliar to many, but a re-orientation should be useful. He went to Harvard University on a full scholarship, graduating *summa cum laude* in 1991. Before his planned entry to Yale University law school, he took the summer off to visit New York and to check in with his father. This decision became a pivotal point in the new shape of his life.

He picked up his horn again and assumed the mantle of a jazz musician: He gigged on tour and recorded with his father and he enlarged his circle of activity with top-shelf musicians such as Jack DeJohnette, Charlie Haden, Paul Motian, and Elvin Jones. Saxophonist Joe Lovano recalls: "I had met Josh in Boston but had not heard him play. Then I did hear him play with his father, Dewey, with whom he recorded at that time. I was happy to hear him play! Josh played his butt off: He plays with energy, imagination, and execution on his horn."

Encouraged to enter the Thelonious Monk Institute of Jazz Saxophone Competition in the fall of 1991, his conquest in taking first place amidst very talented contenders became the linchpin for a battery of strategic career thrusts and advances. Taking a risk, he then gambled to pursue his musical targets, forsaking his law-school ambitions. A post-competition perk to the winner of the Monk event was a special appearance at the Telluride (Colorado) Jazzfest, where we had a chance to chat—at which point he expressed to me his heartfelt gratitude as a beneficiary of good fortune and timing from his earliest Berkeley days forward. His warm glow was likewise in regard to his first chances to play overseas and to the anticipation of recording his own albums.

The victorious overnight ascent of his brilliant career in the 1990s is common information. The year 2000 has already been marked by pinnacle achievements, reinforcing his atypical profile as a youthful jazz musician. The aforementioned forward stretch in his recording, *Beyond,* is just cause for his pride. The record precipitates a signature sound of his band. Redman contends that the most praiseworthy records are not made by bands assembled in ad hoc fashion but are the fruits of bands with musicians "who become well-acquainted and comfortable with one another on and off stage, playing the music comfortably and naturally enough to enjoy the freeness of the music." The slate of ten originals solidifies his role as a compelling composer. His music discloses a rich palette of infectious grooves and memorable lines plus a network of odd time-signatures and polymetric structures.

Infused with a deep passion and a patent joy of playing, his quartet's powerful improvised commentaries exude virility, telepathy, and a balance between skin-tightness and a relaxed, open, fluid, interactive approach—and as Redman describes, "a balance between complexity and simplicity, between formal sophistication and emotional directness." The quartet meeting Redman's requisites features pianist Aaron Goldberg, bassist Reuben Rogers, and drummer Greg Hutchinson. Evident in the music is the rationale that "all of the songs are musical explorations of a search for meaning" in a world offering no pat answers. Redman says: "We found a common ground to express ourselves as individuals within a group. It's all about camaraderie, chemistry, creativity, and commitment. You can have the four greatest players on the planet come together; but if there's no empathy or sense of community, the music will sound uninspired. It was my goal to make this album a statement of our collective identity. I conceived all these songs with Aaron, Reuben, and Greg in mind." *Beyond* unifies the give-and-take process contributed to the liquidity and spontaneity of the music: that is, a communal sensibility of improvisation is achieved via the band playing beyond just a support role during a solo by one of the other musicians.

The plentiful highlights on the CD include the irresistibly gorgeous "Neverend," written by Redman for his wife Gabrielle and recorded originally in 1995 on his album recorded live at the Village Vanguard. It enjoys a welcome reprise here. Ballads that blow you away with staying power are scarce. The magnetic appeal and masterful intrigue occur with "Neverend," an elegantly lyrical ballad destined for sustainability. "This is the best ballad I've ever played on record," declares Redman. "I'm really happy with this one." Rightfully so!

Another sparkling performance illustration is "Leap of Faith," on which Redman's long-term friend from his Boston days, tenor saxophonist Mark Turner, joins Redman as a guest. A departure from the usual classic tenor battle milieu, the pair's focus is on communication in their organic dialogues and not on a competitive mode.

Redman's very early experience with Indian drums and playing in a gamelan orchestra is reflected in the nuances and flavors of Eastern music. His strong advocacy for melting walls between musical genres allows the merger of varied musics. *Beyond* represents a fresh milestone in his journey of adventure. He asserts: "It's deeper, more patient, more mature, more personal, more substantive than the other records." Indeed, it contributes to his quest for the spirituality of life.

In tandem with the release of his CD, Redman was immersed in assuming brand new responsibilities as the Artistic Director/Artist-in-Residence of the San Francisco Jazz Festival's debut of "SF Jazz Spring Season 2000." He contributed an organizing theme, "Traditions in Transition," knitting a series of five weekends of jazz in "Baghdad by the Bay" beginning logically with the saxophone as the initial sub-theme expressed in four events. It was followed by topical weekends on "The Guitar," "World Fusion," "The Drums," and "Latin Jazz."

THE TENOR TRADITION

The tenor jazz saxophone was celebrated with Redman's solo saxophone performance at the beautiful French Gothic–styled Grace Cathedral. Before the concert, he told me: "I'll be playing pieces of music that were strongly associated with great tenor saxophone innovators. I don't plan to give a history lesson, nor am I going to try to play in the styles of the saxophonists; but I am going to interpret their approaches, which span a wide range of time. I'll try to interpret their music, performing in my own way. I have no agenda other than to express myself in my horn. I'm not one who is going to teach the music when I play. If there are lessons in history and a style and an idiom that people can gain from, I'm happy; but when I play, I just want to play and hopefully create something inspiring. It's a terrific challenge!" And Redman met the challenge.

With enhanceful acoustics at the Cathedral, Redman played his tenor from the recesses of the inner halls at the onset and subsequently strolled through the entire perimeter of the seated audience while playing a program of tributes to various iconic legends of the instrument. His program began with Coleman Hawkins' "Body and Soul"; Lester Young's "Lester Leaps In"; verbal mentions of Ben Webster, Don Byas, and Chu Berry; Stan Getz's "Desafinado"; and Dexter Gordon's "Homecoming." His second half featured more vital source material: Sonny Rollins' "St. Thomas"; John Coltrane's "Alabama"; Joe Henderson's "Inner Urge"; and Wayne Shorter's "Footprints." Surely this was a rare performance in Redman's own vocabulary and language! It brought back memories for me of the Duke Ellington Orchestra's rare performance in the same venue on September 16, 1965—naturally in Ellington's own language—as the first of the Sacred Concerts.

THE MUSIC OF WAYNE SHORTER

A two-part concert at the Masonic Auditorium celebrated Wayne Shorter and his music. His band, which featured trumpeter Shunzo Ohno, pianist Helen Sung, and drummer Brian Blade with Shorter, performed mostly pieces he wrote when he was with Miles Davis' quintet of the late '60s; and more strength came through on his tenor than on soprano. Tunes included "Fall," "Water Babies," "Juju," and others of that vintage. The second half boasted the all-star tenor masters—Redman, Joe Lovano, and Branford Marsalis—with the rhythm section of Brad Mehldau on piano, Robert Hurst on bass, and Greg Hutchinson on drums. The set, driven by charging emotions, included titles such as "Speak No Evil," "The Soothsayer," "Lost," "Children of the Night," "Nefertiti," "Black Nile," and "Infant Eyes"; then Shorter joined in on "Footprints" and "Yes or No." Wow, what a night!

Joe Lovano shared his impressions: "Josh did an amazing job of organizing the whole thing. The way he put the concert together—it was beautiful, very free and loose. We just talked about the repertoire. Josh has really made a scene for others." Likewise, Redman programmed Lovano's own group for a family matinee concert featuring Lovano's enormous talents and profound music.

Jazz on Film

To wrap up the spotlight on the tenor saxophone canon, Redman hosted a "Tenor Sax on Film" program: a veritable parade on film of some of the greatest performers on the instrument, offering another dimension of media delivery on the theme—which engendered more esteem from those in the audience who have not lived long enough to experience the music of the legends.

Jazz Masters Mini-Concert & Workshop

A very pertinent component of Redman's activity schedule at the SF Jazz Weekend was manifested on the day after the concentrated programs on the saxophone. As part of a series of learning experiences for selected Bay Area schools, jazz masters conduct interactive demonstrations of history and performance practices of jazz. Redman and the Marcus Shelby Trio visited San Francisco's Urban School to carry out the mission. His band performed; then Redman answered questions from the multi-ethnic crowd of 300 secondary school students in the school gymnasium. The manner in which he handled questions was warmly empathic and sensitively responsive—much like his playing. In sum, he's cool! Tunes like "Billie's Bounce," "Monk's Dream," and "Juju" were introduced. A sampling of questions and Redman's answers should be useful in typifying the nature and values of the exchanges between Redman and the students at hand:

Student Question: How much of the music is improvised?

Redman: Almost all of it is. Melodies take place on certain harmonic structures, and there's a form to each tune. We improvise over the chords with our own melodies. I've never seen the music on paper before. I learned only through playing with musicians and through listening to records. It's improvisation that attracts me to jazz. There's freedom to play anything at anytime—but it has to tell a story! The excitement for me comes from the interaction. The rhythm section members have opportunities to interact with each other and my solos are influenced by rhythm sections. Generally, many of my ideas come from rhythm sections giving me inspiration. That's why they are so important to me.

Student Question: How long has the group been playing together?

Redman: About 15 minutes! We're not afraid to play with each other because there's common knowledge between musicians about certain phrases and about harmony.

Student Question: What are you thinking about when you're playing?

Redman: We're not thinking too hard—it's mainly intuitive; I don't have to think about the rhythm section. There's so much to learn intellectually, like the vocabulary! You can forget it as it becomes a part of it all. You don't have to think consciously about it.

After the above mini-concert/Q&A session, Redman adjourned to a large practice room for a workshop critiquing a student trio. There he made handy suggestions, gave approval and encouragement, and duly emphasized the crucial importance of time and the spirit of expression.

An Interview with Redman

Wong: What are your ideas on the prospects of "jazz education" as per your perspectives on inculcating people with a better informed comprehension of the nature of jazz?

Redman: There is jazz education that is a kind of academic form which is essential, which we need to teach to not only musicians but to people in general about the history, values, and structure of the music. What is improvisation? How is it different from other forms of music we listen to? That's an important kind of jazz education: teaching what this music is, exposing kids to jazz by simply bringing the music into the schools so they can hear it—because ultimately jazz is a language as English is a language. We don't just learn English from a course: we learn it from hearing it spoken at school, in the playground, and at home. We can start to understand the complexity of the music, the formal elements of the music, and we can intellectualize them. We must develop an intuitive understanding in people when they're young.

Wong: You must really recall your own childhood foundation at Washington Elementary School in Berkeley, where jazz legends shared their music at a time that kind of curriculum didn't otherwise exist in elementary schools. How did that set of circumstances hark back to your own early experiences, and how have you gleaned the rewards for your current programs?

Redman: I was terribly spoiled by it all: coming up in the Berkeley Public Schools with the University of California connection, your pioneering efforts, and those of Phil Hardymon, Charles Hamilton, and others that helped make the program happen. We had an exposure through the visitors' performances but were also able to learn the instruments and music to play in the jazz ensemble—an exposure very few public school students have; and that has shaped my perspective. I had close to an ideal experience, one unlike any other. It's not available in the schools now, but it's an ideal for which we should strive.

Wong: I still view it as a period when jazz in schools was literally a subversive activity: there were hurdles to jump over, corners to curve around, and things to elude or camouflage. It's gratifying that it now serves as a source for your agenda-making within your programs here in San Francisco and elsewhere.

Redman: Yes. By presenting the series program formats to a great variety of listeners, we can try to turn people on to the music and hopefully provide some sort of contextual basis from which they can appreciate it.

Wong: Intuitive aspects of your playing are key. Where and/or how do you get your creative juices?

Redman: I don't think anyone can explain where creativity comes from. We are all creative. Human beings are creative animals by necessity. Creativity isn't like going to a juice bar and buying 10 ounces of creativity. It's just there. It's a matter of tapping into it. I think it's a combination of great focus and great relaxation: a combination of being very focused on yourself and everyone else, being very focused "in the moment," but also being relaxed and accepting of the moment so as not to force things, allowing things to come to you and accepting them. That's what creativity is to me!

Wong: Back in Berkeley High, your solos were strongly intuitive.

Redman: Yes, there's a sense that my initial talent had been based more on intuition than formal understanding. I don't wish to dismiss formal understanding; in fact, in recent years, I've tried to build up my analytical understanding of harmony in particular and build up a stronger technical foundation from which to play, just because I felt I was reaching a point where I was hitting my head against the brick wall. There were obstacles getting in my way; so I needed to take a more methodical approach to learn some of the things I had ignored or postponed. I believe creativity, intuition, and inspiration are things that cannot be taught; but there are other things in music that can be taught and are valid—and in some cases essential to learn at some point in your development.

Wong: What is an example?

Redman: One of the things defining jazz is harmonic language, a lot of which you can learn intuitively based on how good your ears are. Some people have incredible ears, with all types of perfect pitch and recall and perfect relative pitch. They could probably go through life never having learned what a C major scale is or $C7^{(-9, -13, +11)}$ is; but they can play it when they hear it. I have good ears but not that good. I've found that if I start to learn what some harmonic things are right when I'm on the cusp of hearing those things—if something clicks as I develop an intellectual understanding of it—I'll develop a greater intuitive sense of it. So that is one example.

Wong: How does the creative process fuel your work in improvisations versus the content and process in composing?

Redman: Obviously there is a big difference between the two acts: with improvisation what is played can't be changed; it's gone when the moments are gone; but in composition, you can continually make changes with as many drafts as needed. Composing is a continuing work in progress. We just changed something in a composition I wrote one and one-half years ago. We changed a chord. In another sense, as an improviser I have a very compositional approach coming from listening to improvisers like Sonny Rollins, Thelonious Monk, Herbie Hancock, or Lester Young: the sense of motivic development, having a sense of where you've been, where you are, and where you're going—trying to tell a story. As a composer, the initial inspiration or composition is improvised; but I don't sit down and say: "OK, I'm going to write a song about 'X' or I'm going to write a song with these formal requirements." Initial inspiration for composition is the same initial inspiration for improvisation. From that I can start to bring my knowledge, flesh it out, try to dig it out, and put things around it.

Wong: Do you recall any breakthroughs you've experienced?

Redman: That's difficult to say. It's generally not my experience—or I might have had it and don't remember. Recently I have felt I had a breakthrough: I finally was able to let go of any sort of expectation with regard to my playing before or while I'm playing. I've gotten rid of too much intentionality, meaning thinking "I expect or need to do this." I've gotten rid of an agenda behind the music and now just let the music flow for what it is. That is a breakthrough of an attitude that has really helped my music—that, combined with much more rigorous, intensive study and practice. I don't mean to simply say: "Well, I don't care how I sound and let the music play itself." I've been practicing for the first time seriously in my life. But doing that and then leaving it as a separate world so that I come to music without any agenda except just playing: ahh … that's a breakthrough!

Wong: I remember you were a very sociable and joyous person when you were in the Berkeley school bands. You seem to have modeled yourself after your happy, satisfying years in school.

Redman: Yes, yes! The Berkeley High School experience taught me about the fun in playing music and the importance of strong social bonding and setting up relationships. Music is relationships. Music is personality. Music is communication. Berkeley High taught me you had to have that kind of rapport with fellow musicians on and off the bandstand.

Joshua Redman appreciates and regards jazz as high art and that it is also the music of the heart and soul. You need only to be an attentive eye-and-ear-witness to his music and to his deeds and presence to realize he personifies the language and spirit of jazz. Joe Lovano's observations summarize this backdrop to Redman's healthy, powerful influence on the future of jazz: "Josh is one of the most assured cats on the scene today. He has a passion for the music and for communicating with the people. He has opened doors. And it's all about love … and he loves to play … and that's the story."

Chapter 5

Alto Saxophone

While the tenor saxophone revels in its romantic expression, the alto saxophone has its own particular appeal; alto saxophonists seem to have their own private fraternity—an unspoken brotherhood—and altoists seem to listen to each other more intently than any other musicians I know.

There is a unique pronouncement in the tonality of the alto—a departure from the tenor—which generates a much softer sound. Given its own pronouncements, the alto saxophone demands a sure grasp of the instrument in order for it to be played to its fullest potential, and no one grasped that concept—or the alto sax—like Phil Woods.

Phil Woods

Phil Woods is the king of the altos. Nobody can touch him. He's the most accurate reflection of Charlie "Bird" Parker on the alto saxophone *ever*, the number one alto player in my view. His fluid mind is such a quick one and he has these phrases that are just gorgeous. Each note melts in your brain. And the notes all *sing*. This isn't just a technical situation; it's warm ... it's human ... and the notes ... they simply sing.

Phil Woods has been the model for countless altoists ... his sound and musical attitude are clearly distinctive ... listen to just a few notes and you know it's Phil.

"Phil Woods, King of the Alto"
Jazz Magazine, Summer 1978

Things have finally come together for Phil Woods. He is a success in his own country after years of struggle and more years of exile. He leads a highly successful quartet that plays gigs more than forty weeks a year. He automatically wins every poll as best alto player. He is able to refuse studio work unless he knows that he will be able to play his own, uncompromising music.

In short, he has formed his life so that it is devoted to jazz without compromise. As Bill Watrous said to me recently, "Phil Woods is the number one complete jazz musician in the world today."

Ten years ago, Phil Woods was a top altoist, a mainstay in the studios, a widely respected player, leader and teacher. But he was a troubled man, unhappy with the studio scene and deeply uncomfortable with the direction of American politics after the assassination of John F. Kennedy.

His five years in Europe, Woods says, allowed him to reestablish his identity as a jazz musician. During that time he led a hard-swinging group known as the European Rhythm Machine, and after returning to the States in 1972 he put together an adventurous but short-lived group in Los Angeles. Since then, the pieces have fallen together.

His present band, a cooperative group known simply as the Phil Woods Quartet, has for almost five years grown artistically as its stable membership grows musically closer.

In 1975, at the age of 43, he started winning the *DownBeat* readers poll as best alto player; this year he also won the magazine's international critics' poll. After his first win he gave a rather uncomfortable interview to a *DownBeat* writer in which he put little meaning on polls and winning them. His personal musical ethos does not allow him to sit outside the jazz scene and meditate on his Grammy Award or any other of the many laurels he has received.

He has managed to stay out of the studios except in situations he accepts—like playing hot alto improvisations behind Billy Joel's vocal on Joel's excellent pop tune "Just the Way You Are." The record is one of the biggest-selling pop tunes of the year, and because of Phil Woods—and a sensitive producer—millions of pop listeners have heard beautiful jazz despite the usual efforts of the commercial music world.

"It's a gas to fulfill a dream of mine, and that is to work in my own country after living in Paris for years and traveling extensively abroad," Woods said in one of a series of interviews in recent months. "Took me a long path to figure this out for myself—I'm a part of America and it seems a logical challenge to make it in my own land. I'm happy to say it's going very well for all of us. We're very busy with gigs filling up more than 40 weeks a year and trying to get some new tunes written."

The Phil Woods Quartet was born in 1973 in the Pocono Mountains of Pennsylvania, where Woods settled down after leaving the West Coast. The other members—pianist Mike Melillo, bassist Steve Gilmore and drummer Bill Goodwin—all live nearby. The band flows easily in and out of different musical territories but with no detours from the central core of jazz that swings with compassion and lyricism. The group's hefty repertoire of more than 100 songs testifies to the fulfillment of its quests, from Tadd Dameron's "The Scene Is Clean" or Dizzy Gillespie's "Shaw 'Nuff" and the timeless literature of Harold Arlen, Irving Berlin and Cole Porter, to captivating originals by Woods and Melillo.

"The guys in the band are all monsters," Woods went on. "Everyone knows precisely where they are all of the time; we function within the classic form of changes and within a structure. Being together for five years provides us with a kind of reflex action that can usually come from a long duration of interplay. We all take chances all of the time and we discover new dimensions unexpectedly. I learned that from the greats of jazz—Charlie Parker and Coleman Hawkins didn't rely on comfortable, secure choruses, man."

There is an urgent elegance to the music of the band. In the last year, I have caught it at the Keystone Korner in San Francisco and at Storytowne in New York, and at this writing it is only a matter of days until I hear it again at the Concord Jazz Festival. The following freewheeling conversation took place in meetings on both coasts:

Wong: Your music has apparently shifted to another milieu from your European Rhythm Machine concept. It is a reaffirmation?

Woods: It's a reinforcement of my strongest suit—melodies and changes. Many people say this group is not as far out as the ERM; I think they're talking about the material more than a different style. It was a different group; e.g., Daniel Humair was different than Bill Goodwin as a drummer. Daniel was more out-front and Bill is valuably considered more of a group player—more sensitive and meshing, much tighter than ERM, which had its own brand of excitement and heat. We played things like "Freedom Jazz Dance." It was a sort of soaring period for me, after being in the studios and confused in the U.S., not having played for a long time; I just wanted to get out there and whoooooooooeee! And let it all out. That period permitted me to reestablish my identity—that I *am* a jazz musician. Then I came back to the States and got into that group with Pete Robinson at Donte's in L.A. and that was *really* an "out" group, doing totally "out" stuff, blowing everyone's mind out! You were there, Herb.

Wong: Yes, I remember those nights at Donte's in 1972. So is your current musical association a natural extension?

Woods: Seems logical as a next step. The current group, a co-op group, began at a jam session when no one was working. When I left L.A. and went back East, I stayed with Bill and I had met Mike many years ago at the Clifton Tap Room in the early sixties. We started out playing tunes in the jams, so we carried it over to the working group. There's a tape of our present group playing extremely "out" music, but the group evolved into what I consider my strong beliefs and approach—playing songs and playing changes and the meshing of the delicacy and nuances of the group. We've been together four and a half years, so we should be tight. It's an encapsulated version of our evolution so far. And since it's continuously evolving, I don't know what the next step is. Perhaps overcoming economic problems, we might have an augmented group but it is difficult to keep a steady group together. So adding pieces is hard; for instance, we're working as a quartet and not a quintet now, even though we added Harry Leahey one-and-a-half years ago.

Wong: Tell me more about the genesis of the group.

Woods: We all lived in the Pocono Mountains in Pennsylvania. I got a call for a gig and it seemed logical to use the cats from the jams. Steve had played with Thad and Mel, Al Cohn and others. Bill is the veteran of the group and has worked and traveled more with more people than the others. Mike was with Maynard Ferguson and Sonny Rollins, he's been around. None of the cats are fresh young kids by any means. Mike is a complete musician, any music he gets into he's got it covered. He's really deep into Charles Ives, always searching. Great to have a cat like that in the band.

Wong: Have you found the emphasis on songs being a catalyst for more response from the audiences?

Woods: Probably … gives them something to hang their ears on. I've done my share of experimentation—throwing away all the changes and rhythm and getting out there. It's great fun doing it, but I find that listening to it is not. I actually found it more boring than dealing with changes. The epitome of freedom for me was Charlie Parker, Louis Armstrong or Ben Webster—those are the *great* soloists—they're so free. They're not playing the chord changes bar to bar. The freedom is in getting away from what other cats find as restrictions. The great artist uses a plan of departure so he's not hung up with changes. A lot of young people who don't have the chops say: "Oh, man, playing the changes—oh, that's a drag…." Maybe it's the way they do it is a drag because they're playing *changes* and they're not playing *melodies* on the changes. That soaring over the established conventional harmony … you can go anywhere over it and then you have a real symbiosis, as it were, of disparate elements. It's more exciting to me than just, "O.K. fellas, it's freedom time…. Let's just blow!" You can only go so far without much control.

I like working within a form rather than abandoning the past entirely. And I don't think you can.

Wong: Do you hold a sense of responsibility not to abandon the past?

Woods: I feel strongly about it. It's peculiarly American, you know, the ash tray is full, get another one. Or the new car routine. It's like neglecting the older cats unless they're big, gigantic, real big-money stars. Not like Dizzy, who will be around and loved forever, but I'm talking about Ben Webster, who died in Europe, and all the transplanted musicians—all that sad stuff. People don't listen to the past. It's always the sense of now—now we've got loft jazz. Every five to seven years we've got to call jazz something else and that to me is divisive. There's not that many jazz artists *per se* and we're important artists; we should present a united front and be a strong cultural force. This divisiveness is unhealthy for the artists, like when the moldy figs didn't dig the beboppers. Perfectly natural within human terms, but we've moved—the whole society has moved and I think the jazz mentality, however, has perhaps not moved … at least not enough. The jazz artist is kind of quiet, not bitchin' and screaming or being outrageous anymore. He's sober and educated but not colorful, not speaking out. There's a caution to waiting for a messiah to lead us out of the morass and where are we? Disco, cross-over, fusion—that's just horseshit, man! The American musicians *can* work together. Don't put me down because I play an old song and I'm not going to put you down for playing a non-song. It could be more valid if we communicated instead of looking down our noses at various stylistic periods—like, "Oh, he's an older cat. He ain't doin' it no more." That's bad for the art.

Wong: The band gives clinics along with concerts. Obviously young players in the jazz education movement are aware of your roots and the connection to Bird.

Woods: I'm historically perched at a very convenient time. I went to New York in 1947 and I was part of it, taking lessons there and caught the tail end of Fifty-Second Street. Also I was a young musician catching the end of the big band era, the first generation of bebop. The absolute madness of the post-war period—I didn't understand it at the time but now I'm starting to realize the hysteria and how bop was a natural thing, not only musically. It just had to be historically right for it to happen—small groups opposed to the big band machine. So, yes, I always get questions about Charlie Parker, but I always say I first tuned into Johnny Hodges and Duke's band playing "Mood to Be Wooed." Bird was the strongest. You couldn't be a young musician and not be touched by Bird no matter what you played—even the tuba. But if you were a young alto player those days, Bird's shadow was just too much.

Wong: Any other folks provided stimuli to your evolution?

Woods: A whole bunch of folks—Bud Powell, Fats Navarro, all those beboppers. I was really into it!

Wong: How about the last five to ten years?

Woods: I listen to everyone else: Keith Jarrett, Johnny Coates, Tom Harrell, Randy and Mike Brecker—all exciting soloists weaving a little different kind of thing, so I keep my ears open. Let me clarify myself: I don't find myself influenced so much; I'm really too old to change. I've spent my whole life trying to find out who I am—started playing when I was twelve years old. I guess I have a style; as I said, my experimental stuff is over. I'm just going to be me now. I like to think I'm getting better and I'm learning all the time. I'm not saying: "Hey, that's it." I've got to keep moving within my point of reference. I can't suddenly get turned on by another musician and say, "Yeah, that's what I'm going to do." I want to utilize the elements that include my own identity.

Wong: Do you find any tie into the three levels of creativity in jazz—from the baseline first level, to the bulk of jazz musicians on the second, and on up to the top tier, earmarked by rare moments of sheer creativity? Do you feel you have moved into that third level at times?

Woods: I'm really interested in this! Yes, I can tell when it's magic time. All of a sudden, from the first note you know it's going to be a super-special night. Can't pin it down specifically. Some say it's the alpha state. I'm curious, too, about the fact that sometimes when I go to work—and it may be because I've been doing it so long—but I just don't feel it, man. I don't like my career summed up in one set. Why are some nights so good! It has nothing to do with how you live … you could be totally beat and haven't eaten or slept yet and feel terribly rotten—and it sounds great! Other times, you take care of yourself, absolutely clean and you eat well and get plenty of rest and splaaaat! Zero!! There's no sure-fire approach—absolutely no consistency in the creativity on the bandstand although I think our group reaches a pretty high level most of the time. Of course, I'm interested in getting to that third level more often. I've been trying to figure it out and researched it with my own life patterns. If I had a good day yesterday, I'll try to do the same thing today. Every group I've had has felt this. The best example of this was the Frankfurt Jazz Festival. It was a great night. I don't know why, but I'm glad it was recorded [*Phil Woods and the European Rhythm Machine at the Frankfurt Jazz Festival*; Embryo SD 530, 1971]. Some other "live" performances, I have wished they had recorded it the next night!

Wong: You have a focus on "live" performances for records. Apparently you have a bias; does magic time happen much less frequently in a comparatively more bland environment, such as a recording studio?

Woods: I don't spend any time to speak of anymore in a recording studio—thank God!

Wong: Considering the lofty status you occupy in the jazz scene, do you find a challenge and a feeling of responsibility as a front-ranked altoist?

Woods: I look out there into audiences and frequently see a house full of young sax players. Occasionally I wonder if they're listening to the music or watching my fingers; the latter annoys me. I wish they'd get more into the music and not worry about the mouthpiece and the reeds. Anyway, I'm thankful for the many nights of work we have now. The more we work and have more days of the year to jack up our average of magic nights, the more love we're going to have into it. I always love going to work—I look forward to it more than ever. When it feels like a chore, I shrug it off and say, "C'mon, man, you're lucky to be on this bandstand, so let's get it on!"

Wong: What's your self-evaluation of your writing?

Woods: I'm still a novice writer. I'm still learning even though I've been writing for many years. I've got to learn how to prune; I put too much energy into my charts. Perhaps I do that in my playing, too—I'm an aggressive player and my charts may be too aggressive sometimes. I should back off some of the colors.

Wong: What's the big band chart you're writing for Buddy?

Woods: He wants a chart of my theme music: "How's Your Mama"—you know, the bluesy thing we play … should be fun.

Wong: Where does your inspiration for composition come from?

Woods: Same as improvisation. Composition for me *is* improvisation. I'll write when I don't have an assignment. I'll noodle at the piano and jot things down that please me and I'll refer to these notes and notions for stimuli when I do have an assignment.

Wong: When do you do this when you're on the road nearly forty weeks a year now?

Woods: I do it whenever I can snitch time to do it. Right now I'm writing an arrange-ment for Buddy Rich and I'm working on material for an expanded version of this band, as we're going to Japan this coming year. I hope to get a tenor, baritone, trumpet and bone to augment us and do a couple of albums, too. I don't intend to stay with the quartet make-up forever. It's logical to add horns as you can get into more compositional areas and it opens up all kinds of educational avenues. If horns were represented, you could have some dynamite clinics and hopefully they would be cats who could write too.

Wong: Speaking of clinics, what is your best advice to aspiring young players you meet in that context?

Woods: Listen—that's what I tell them. When they get too involved with the playing thing, they don't realize jazz is the only group art we have. I'm leaving out improvisational theater here. You can't really play jazz by yourself. Art Tatum was an exception. Jazz is essentially the byplay between musicians. If you have two players, you can play jazz. Rar-ities like Sonny Rollins can play unaccompanied solos well but the foundation is the dia-logue and the interplay from the beginnings of Dixieland—the meeting of the lines. The tendency for young players is that they don't often get asked to play—so they spill it all out with youthful energy when they are finally invited. I tell them to slow down and leave some holes so you can listen to what's going on around you. To tell them how to do it is impossible. Just do it! Do you know what the piano is doing at this point? Or do you know the alternate chord he just laid on you, etc.? I just point out the improvisational devices, which are nothing more than compositional devices you can get out of any book. There are so many ways to go up and down, and contrary motion. By listening you can clarify it. Music isn't as hard as people make it out to be, but there's no shortcut. When the young players dig something they hear, they shouldn't go to the store and buy the written music. Take if off the record. The accessibility is incredible today. You can get books on Trane and Bird solos—all the homework is done. Take it from the record, and go to the keyboard. Instead of learning fifteen Bird solos, study one great one thoroughly to get the essence of his style. You'll get a glimpse of the offshoots of the man's other works. It's like you don't have to look at all of Picasso's paintings to dig Picasso.

Wong: What's your latest project for records?

Woods: As I got into other people's songs, the album concept evolved into my writing a jazz ballad LP doing songs representing people I respect and love. It's called *Remem-brances* and it was done in England. Included are: "Charles Christopher" for Bird; "Paul" for Desmond, using a string quartet; "Ollie" for Oliver Nelson; "Sweet Willie" for Willie Dennis; "O.P." for Oscar Pettiford, featuring Steve Gilmore; "Flat Jack Willie" for Willie Rodriguez, "the precursor of all percussionists"; and "Gary" for Gary McFarland, featuring pianist Gordon Beck as guest keyboardist with trumpets, French horns and woodwinds. The music will be published through Kendor to serve as appropriate material for campus dates—a miniature suite with our quartet as the integral core.

Wong: What could we be doing with the college graduate musicians?

Woods: We don't nurture the young in the period after leaving college. There should be a government thing, a loan or some kind of repertory orchestra in America. Shameful we don't have a Voice of America jazz program for America! Here we're disseminating jazz all over the world, educating the world about jazz, but we are not doing it for our own people. Does the government assume we're all hip? Bullshit! They just know jazz is a good propaganda weapon. But if it's a good weapon, it must be strong; if it's strong, why don't we tell *our* people about it! A dedicated young musician who wants to make it will need some help; he's not going to hone his craft by being a dishwasher. Socially we'll be the poorer if he doesn't get help.

Wong: Can you mention some key upcoming jazz alto players?

Woods: Yeah, there's Richie Cole, Bob Mover and Eric Kloss. I'm close to all those cats and know their work well.

Wong: Your band has been recycling a good many tunes and thereby advancing their validity and lots of messages come across to the young or new ears.

Woods: There are so many great tunes: "Stella by Starlight," "All Blues," "Milestones," Shearing's "Conception," so many, many more—early Bud Powell, like "Dance of the Infidels"—all terrific stuff to play. They all hold up. As Bach is to fugal music, bop is to improvisation; you can't get any more involved harmonically—can't move the eighth notes any more. Bop has all the ingredients. It's classic American jazz. It isn't the only music, but it's a distilled version of all the elements. The epitome of improvisation is still: Do it well. I don't think young kids should play it exactly like that, but they must get into this body of music.

Wong: Your jazz on alto is heard by millions of people who hear Billy Joel's commercial record of "Just the Way You Are."

Woods: Yes, I'm on that. Phil Ramone thought the tune might suit me and called me in for the session—it's a basic song and it's not really weird. The sales on that album is triple platinum or something!

Wong: Another point is that you played what you wanted to play.

Woods: Yes, I'm in a lot of living rooms and car radios. Lots of young sax players come up to me and ask, "Hey, are you the guy on the Billy Joel record?" And I say "Yes, and what do you do?" And they say: "I'm an alto sax player." "And have you done anything on your own?" "Ha, ha, ha," they laugh, and I say, "And you're an alto sax player!" I wish program directors of radio stations would include soloists in the announcements for DJs and make it a practice to give credit. Many times my fans would call up radio stations and inquire about the soloist and the DJ would say: "I dunno who it is. Let's see, we don't have the album here. It's on tape…" But it doesn't really matter; perhaps things will change so jazz soloists will get their due. Maybe we're bullshitting young musicians in a way … not telling them the truth. You've got all those Coltrane and Bird solos written out and you carry around all these books and you "major" in jazz? Be careful, sir. It's really street music; it's an aural tradition. It's not meant to have mass appeal. If everyone started poppin' their fingers at 2 and 4, then jazz is removed to something else. I'm really not worried about jazz becoming a popular art form.

Richie Cole

I first heard Richie Cole when he was with the Buddy Rich Big Band. Richie had been recruited by Phil Wilson—the trombonist with Woody Herman—while Richie was still a student at Berklee College of Music, where Phil taught. Phil recommended Richie to Buddy as a candidate for his lead alto saxophone and soloist … and Richie just took off!

He became so popular, the license plate on his van read "ALTO 1." At one point, Richie and Eddie Jefferson, the scat singer, decided to take that van and their act out on the road. Eddie's vocal partnership with Richie Cole's alto sax was a difficult combination to beat and they combed the byways of the country, performing in towns you never heard of. They would perform in just about any environment, be it haystacks on a farm or a club in the city. Traveling together, they performed as a regular act, all the way across the country and overseas.

It was a tour that was to have a tragic end.

The minute he heard they were scheduled to perform in Detroit, Eddie expressed concern. He was visiting with us at the promoter's office in Berkeley and, all through our meeting, Eddie kept saying, "I don't want to go to Detroit. I don't like the city and I've got bad vibes about it." We kept egging him on and he eventually agreed, saying, "Well, I'll do it one more time and that's it."

His premonition of "one more time" turned out to be too true. On that trip—as Eddie and Richie were walking out of Baker's Keyboard Lounge following their gig—Eddie was gunned down in a drive-by shooting in the city he didn't want to visit on a trip he didn't want to make.

Richie, apparently not the shooter's target, escaped injury and "alto madness" lived on.

Richie Cole w/Brass—*Kush / The Music of Dizzy Gillespie*
Heads Up International (HUCD 3032); 1995; Reissued by Concord Records

Bow! Bam! Look Out! Richie Cole the bebop buckaroo is really back in bebop city and he's having a ball with his voluble alto sax. Back in the spring of 1993 he emerged from a four year recording sabbatical cocoon with an eclectic wide spread of music (*Profile*—Heads Up International Ltd. HUCD 3022). The unarguably strong thematic concept of "KUSH" enables Cole to center on his most natural and unabashed idiom; indeed, bebop is his stylistic heritage and musical sustenance. An appetizing banquet of Dizzy Gillespie's music is a sumptuous menu that stimulates, satisfies and fits Cole's jazz palate.

His focal interest in Gillespie's and Charlie Parker's path finding harmonic and rhythm concepts were sparked from age eleven onward. "I stayed up all night listening to jazz radio stations secretly up in my attic bedroom in Trenton, New Jersey—WHAT in Philadelphia, WRVR in New York and the station from Princeton. That's how I got acquainted with bebop—the music I love," says Cole. "I started alto at ten and bebop fascinated me. Wow! I like this. I want to play this!"

Among other big bands he enjoyed—Glenn Miller, Count Basie, and Woody Herman, he was enraptured by Dizzy Gillespie's big band. "I was about seventeen and took a train from Trenton to New York, and showed up at The Town Hall concert where Dizzy's big band did 'Manteca' and other big bebop tunes like 'Things to Come' and 'Emanon,'" recalls Cole. "Also Leo Wright and Jerry Dodgion were on alto and Leo played a marvelous 'Skylark.' 'Twas my first in-person contact with Dizzy and I was blown away!"

As for influential forces, he describes: "Bird and Diz as a team were my greatest influence and after them, Cannonball Adderley and Sonny Rollins." Cole admired the unrestrained, lively manner Gillespie and Adderley conducted themselves—with their fellow musicians and audiences alike. These values of rapport and communion, and the hang loose fun of making music contribute to the humor, surprises, and drama Cole offers. Mirroring his idols' demeanor, Cole's raw enthusiasm and antics are often comically zany as cartoon characters.

For years after Buddy Rich's big band, Cole hit the road as a peripatetic ambassador of jazz joys and good will with his Dodge van bearing the license plate "ALTO 1." Also, a pseudonym "alto madness" was hung on him during his tenure with Rich on account of "my strange and crazy alto madness." A distillate of these hijinks and spirits in his M.O. and bebop is infused into this program of Dizzyland.

The genesis of the concept for this disc rests initially with Heads Up label chief Dave Love inviting arranger-producer Bob Belden to brainstorm a special project for Richie Cole (Love and Belden had been fellow students at North Texas State in the late seventies to early eighties). Subsequently one of Belden's inspired cache of ideas hit the green light nerve to score a slate of Gillespie chestnuts. Belden's burgeoning career as one of the most gifted arrangers on the scene is remarkable for his gilt-lined imagination and striking resourcefulness. His admirable set of niche skills is heated by his postulate to humanize the playing experience with pure joy. "Knowing Cole is really into bebop, it would be natural to cover Bird or Sonny Stitt's music, but why can't an alto player do Dizzy," Belden asserts, "and everyone knows the tunes and they're fun to play."

Belden built in a complement of brass in a quasi Gillespie tradition for about half the charts. Beside a couple of tunes which included Paquito D'Rivera on alto and clarinet respectively, "any sax you hear would be the artist—Richie Cole—the main soloist. Timbre-wise it sets it off. Dizzy's forte was always the brass, an extension of himself, so I thought the brass could be that extension again and without cluttering it with saxes or woodwinds," notes Belden. "Writing for brass essentially simplifies matters, omitting the need to deal with many contrapuntal things. On practical terms, you mostly try to support the groove, to keep things going," Belden adds.

In accommodating Cole with generous windows of space to improvise and interpret, Belden explains: "The idea was to set it up so Richie could just step in and play and wouldn't have to look at the chart. I just wanted his music, and to expose him with a brass backing ... ideally to make him feel comfortable and unforced. My goal was for him to really enjoy himself. I think he was a happy camper!" Cole was effusive about Belden: "Bob did a phenomenal job. He knows just how to arrange for me, making it simple for me. Basically he wrote out the melody and the parts I needed to play, and pointed and signaled to me to 'play' and 'don't play' or 'don't stop'—go, go, go. And the band parts didn't have to concern me. It worked out great and I appreciate Dave Love for this grand project and its values."

"The aim was to ensure it worked on a musical level, regardless of arrangement or choices of notes. With a rhythm section like this one, there was no worry about swinging!" says Belden. "As for Richie, everyone knew about him. When I was in college, he was known as the cat in the van traveling on one-nighters spreading the gospel of bebop."

With no messing around or uncertainties about its thrust, the disc opens with Gillespie's original "Be-Bop," first recorded fifty years ago. The spectacular brassy sound is punctuated by Cole's fiery solo and Jack Walrath's trumpet solo soaring over the swinging rhythm section. Kevin Hays' piano makes your ears perk up, and Vic Juris' statement is fluid smooth. Dig Roger Ingram's cloud-reaching lead trumpet adding to the mad excitement and energy. "Be-Bop" is the perfect opener and harbinger of this recording.

The standard "You Go to My Head" is, of course, not composed by Dizzy Gillespie; it is rightfully credited to J. Fred Coots with lyrics by Haven Gillespie, vintage 1938. It was not meant to be part of this program, but as there was so much enthusiasm for its quality performance and at least someone with the surname Gillespie was involved, there was a consensus it should be included and not be relegated to a future anthology of Heads Up artists.

Walrath, Sam Burtis, Juris and Ray Mantilla are long term associates of Cole. The latter two have played and recorded with Cole off and on during the past fifteen years. Walrath and Burtis join Cole as the only horns attacking "Birk's Works," with precision (premiered in a 1951 recording session). "I was hoping to have my buddies Jack and Sam on the date, as we went to Berklee College together years ago," says Cole. Psychological support came from the presence of these friends. "Familiar faces reduced tensions immediately and I wished Richie to be around cats he's comfortable with," offers Belden. Take note of Burtis' nimble trombone solo, and Walrath's muted trumpet is amazingly Dizzy-like in flavor with articulated nuances.

"I Waited for You" is a heavy contender for first place among Gillespie's prettiest melodies. Is this beautiful or what! Suggested for inclusion by songwriter Carroll Coates, the tune's inherent attractive assets represent the model vehicle for Cole's lovely ballad interpretation. The quintet setting is well suited to its poignant delivery.

Gillespie's African rhythm and tone poem, the title selection "Kush" features two gladiators of the alto saxophone—Richie Cole and Paquito D'Rivera—and how this dynamic duo can build a pyramid of excitement and musical splendor. The synchronicity of their respective styles and tones is so close. Cole points out, "People say that Paquito and I sound quite alike. When we were playing 'Kush,' he said he didn't know if he was playing or I was playing. We come from the same bebop mold." On the "Salt Peanuts" racetrack, D'Rivera switches to his high flying clarinet as the band reformed as a sextet. Built on a riff set by Gillespie in the early forties, Juris and Cole also board the bebop jet with some fleet-fingered lines.

Although D'Rivera and Cole have jammed together at jazz festivals, this was their first official joint recording experience. D'Rivera who had worked closely with Gillespie's The United Nations Orchestra (and now its leader), is wrapped snugly in Gillespiana. "It's a lot of fun playing with Richie and we have many personal and musical affinities. He integrates Dizzy's music very well. Hey, Richie's a bebop man! And Bob Belden is a magnificent arranger," says D'Rivera.

He adds accolades to the unanimity about Kevin Hays, Peter Washington, Carl Allen and Ray Mantilla. Sharing more pleasures with the session, D'Rivera explains, "Playing Dizzy's music, I feel Dizzy was there with us playing with a bunch of new friends. When I'm having a good time with a good band, it's like Dizzy's playing with the trumpet section, making jokes and saying 'Go, Baby!'"

"Con Alma" means "with soul," and the selection reveals openly the deep soulful passion the band communicates. The blend of French horn, trombone, bass trombone and tuba evokes a warm golden-brown burnished brass merger and leads to comments by Belden on the brass coloration's, "John Clark's French horn gives you an instrument between trombone and trumpet," filling a niche, "it has the fluidity trombones do not have, but has the attack. My focus in arranging is that it's a soloists' date and the horns are there to add to it, as opposed to arranging big band music with few solos, wherein people want to hear the shout chorus and how great the trombone section sounds together. But to me, if the rhythm section and the soloists aren't burnin', you haven't got it!" Belden draws from the Miles Davis/Gil Evans and Don Sebesky schools of thinking.

"I try to stay out of everyone's way and let things flow. On 'Con Alma' I was reflecting Sebesky's way of voicing trombones, placing them in the context of the ensemble." And Belden does write in a way allowing individual freedom to the soloists which stimulates and buttresses them with a solid floor of rhythmic and harmonic substance. Key to "Con Alma," too, is Hays' strong sense of form and keen ear for beauty. Washington knows exactly what to do. Weaving Fareed Haque's guitar is another vital addition to the sum of the feeling at large.

"A Night in Tunisia," the Gillespie classic was born out of Fifty-Second Street in 1942 at which time he played it in Benny Carter's band. Cole and Walrath illustrate the renewed life they can breathe into the tune's exotic atmosphere with its heavily syncopated bass line. Cole gets inside of Gillespie's solo space including the wonderful, historic break, staking a personal claim as a sure-fire alto interpreter. Walrath's authority and verve are impressive. Mantilla, by the way simply magnifies the Latin beat which gave rise later, historically speaking, to "Manteca."

Gillespie stated in his memoirs that "This Is the Way" was a ballad "I wrote to show my sense of chord progressions and that I was sticking to fundamentals." He wrote this beautiful song as a Leo Wright alto feature, and Wright can be heard playing it on Gillespie's big band recording of March 4, 1961, "live" at Carnegie Hall. When Belden asked Cole about Wright, Cole replied, "I love Leo Wright! I have a bunch of his records. Only a few cats know about him." Belden's acumen as a bright alchemist is demonstrated again by his format for this tune, using only Haque and Juris' acoustic guitars with Cole.

Ending with "Manteca" was another judicious move. The inevitable choice was seconded by Cole, "I've always wanted to record 'Manteca.' In my earlier days working at The Tin Palace, we played it regularly in a band with Eddie Jefferson, Vic Juris, Mickey Tucker, Eddie Gladden, and Ray Mantilla. And I just love the bridge!" Cole's uninhibited alto reinforces Belden's claim that a high caliber saxophonist can illuminate the usual trumpet obligations successfully. "Manteca" recalls Chano Pozo's pioneering work of multi-rhythms with Gillespie in 1948. The blistering admixture of Afro-Cuban and jazz idioms in "Manteca" is so hot, it could scorch the paint off the walls.

Richie Cole says gleefully, "I go where no man has gone before to play jazz," like a bona fide, free spirited jazz musician stretching across the planet. Likewise, Bob Belden's crowded itinerary across continents makes his ready availability a tall challenge. So it is providential that at the top of their careers, their paths have finally crossed. This is a convivial project celebrating the genius and legacy of Dizzy Gillespie—one that makes it easy to smile, bob your head, prance around and say Yeah!!

Charles McPherson

Charles McPherson is another disciple of Charlie Parker. Before he came out on his own to San Diego with his own band, he was the alto player with Charles Mingus. He was also a very popular player in Japan; so much so, that I booked him several times on tours in Japan, knowing that every venue would—and did—sell-out because he's such a tremendous draw with Japanese jazz fans.

Charles McPherson is one of the few Charlie Parker–type players who has his own voice, a voice discernable as an influence from Bird. When the Monterey Jazz Festival decided to do a Charlie Parker tribute, they called on Sonny Stitt, Richie Cole and, of course, Charles McPherson, to carry the tribute torch.

Charles McPherson Quartet—*It that It? No, But ...*
Vega Records (ART 1005); 2001

Charles McPherson represents what an artistically flourishing jazz musician should manifest. His extraordinary musicianship and personal assets flow with emotional heat and glowing joyousness. His soulful expressiveness illuminates the special brand of his spirited connection with band mates and audiences alike. McPherson's brilliance and vivid imagination infuse fruitful creativity in his authoritative saxophone vocabulary. He has developed his own stylistic treatments filtered from his assimilation of Charlie Parker's harmonic and rhythmic notions. Spurred by his dialogue with Parker's language, some measure of transfusion is fundamental to much of what McPherson does. Dig his motivic development of the source material and his breathtaking melodicism, power, tone and speed.

This CD was recorded in Tokyo culminating a tour in Japan. Opening with the gorgeous "But Beautiful," McPherson and his laudable trio of Don Friedman, Earl May and Akira Tana promptly announce the strong appeal of the music and the band's imprint. McPherson's huge, wonderfully lyrical sound resounds in an impassioned fresh treatment. "The phrases and the way Charles plays gives you goose bumps!" says Friedman. And all of the soloists play with vitality; they are consistently driven by inspired interplay. Their communion becomes a worthy signature process for managing the balanced program of originals, standards and jazz classics.

All of the players on hand have a long notable string of performing/recording experiences with numerous jazz luminaries. Besides "Bird" (Charlie Parker) roots, McPherson counts mentor Barry Harris and his lengthy tenure with Charles Mingus as germane to his jazz life stream.

Drummer Akira Tana relates the enthusiastic reception for McPherson in Japan; "Charles had not been in Japan for years and people came out of the woodwork to see him. He's one of the last living embodiments of Bird, and he's open to all kinds of music." McPherson's fluency, clarity and fullness of every note stand out. Tana adds, "His sound is so big and unreal! In small halls, we didn't need a P.A. system."

A crest of this CD is the duo of McPherson and Friedman on "Old Folks"—a veritable paragon of synthesizing two musical streams and free flowing exchanges, dissolving in the heat of creation. Friedman comments on its specialness, "The way Charles played the melody with soulfulness, I really got into it. It's an incredible tune; Bird recorded it, too. I felt I was almost playing with Bird. It was an inspirational moment. As we finished, everyone applauded!"

A fixture on the jazz scene for years, bassist Earl May says, "I've been around a long time and have heard the best—the duo of Charles and Don is among the best. Don listened to Charles well and complemented him well."

The band wanted to feature Friedman in a trio on "Almost Everything"—a tasty line on "All the Things You Are"—a truly rewarding performance. And dig how McPherson re-harmonized "Spring Is Here"—interesting! His focus on the blues is illustrated by his original music. How uplifting "Like Someone in Love" is with its bossa beat! While McPherson got into Bird's feeling on "Old Folks" and "Visa," he also played brilliantly with a magnificent sound in his personal manner—which generated much drama on the other tunes.

Pianist Friedman's extensive jazz journey has included Dexter Gordon, Shorty Rogers, Buddy DeFranco. Chet Baker and Ornette Coleman to Pepper Adams, Booker Little and others here and abroad. Currently he has been with Clark Terry for several years. "I hold Don with great esteem on and off the bandstand," says May. "Don has a breadth of knowledge and experience in different contexts," Tana points out. "He plays in a stream of consciousness but still in the tradition of the music and very much inside the changes." Whatever Friedman plays, he is subservient to the music and he prides himself as an accompanist and team member: "I try to make my voicings fit in with the solos by listening closely and tuning in. I can often anticipate where a player is going to go via substitute changes that people play."

Earl May, the selfless bassist whose rich background with Billy Taylor's Trio, as Gloria Lynne's musical director, and recorded with Chet Baker, John Coltrane, Herbie Mann, Dizzy Gillespie and is playing again with Frank Foster—is a superb accompanist who plays in the tradition of Oscar Pettiford, Percy Heath and Paul Chambers. Friedman observes: "Earl knows just the right notes to play, he's a consummate professional." Tana reminds us that May is a left-handed bassist, "and he is so melodic.... Charles requested Earl specifically." McPherson places much value on May ... "I like Earl's concept of the basic beat—his time feel. I enjoy his rhythmic attitude—the quarter notes. How he functions allows a horn player like me the right kind of cushion for my notes to float. He's got a floating quality but is still sturdy and dependable. It's a little oxymoronic! Somehow May blends a free approach with energetic, youthful abandon and spirit." Articulating his own objective, May asserts: "I strive to play some great notes and background support so musicians and audiences can experience their joy." As Friedman says, "Earl knows exactly the perfect notes and his tone is perfect, though he understates his solo."

Drummer Akira Tana's credits are impressive. He has played and recorded with a very long list of heavy jazz artists; it boggles the mind. A partial list would not do him justice. An in-demand drummer/producer, his strengths are clearly known entities. Check him out on any tune ... he provides continuous stimulation for the band and cinches things together on any tempo and setting with the shape of the music in mind. Tana intuitively coordinates his footwork and strokes with balance between fierce, rapid-fire and inner quietude. "Akira plays great swing," says May. "Wherever you want to go, he's there." Friedman offers: "Akira plays the way I like—conversational style. Finally, McPherson sums it up: "Akira is energetically responsive and listens with great ears!"

Everyone contributed to the simpatico engendered in the group. This cohesion and altruistic carriage makes for the artistic triumphs on this recording.

—··—··—··—··—··—··—··—··—··—··—··—··—··—··—

Art Pepper

Art Pepper had been in prison—San Quentin—more than once. I was very aware that he was there. One night, during one of my KJAZ broadcasts, a fellow came by the station and said, "I'm a guard at San Quentin and I want you to know that the radios at Quentin are all tuned to your show every Monday night when you play the music of Art Pepper..." adding, in a rather respectful manner, "...who is with us."

The guard continued, "I thought you would be interested in this," and he proceeded to pull out the front page of the *San Quentin News*—the inmate produced newspaper—and there on the front page was a photo of the Art Pepper Big Band!

I sat there thinking ... Art went from playing with Stan Kenton to playing in San Quentin ... and *that* certainly was interesting! And then I thought, I had no idea they were listening to my show in San Quentin every time I featured Art Pepper.

I featured Art Pepper a lot. I loved his sound and what he did when improvising. Many times on my radio show, I showcased Art playing clarinet, always stating that had he selected it as his chosen instrument, he would have wiped everyone else out.

When he was released from prison, I actually presented him with a clarinet, telling him that's what I had pulled out from his recordings ... samplings of him playing the clarinet ... and I was looking forward to his playing the clarinet when he got out.

Some time after that, I arranged a gig for Art, featuring him on the clarinet. And the first thing he says is "I can't make it." When I asked him why not, Art said, "I sold the clarinet."

This stayed on my mind for a long time; I had bought the instrument on an installment plan and I had to keep making payments on it long after he sold the clarinet ... long after he died. But every time I paid, I felt it was an expression of my admiration of what Art Pepper could do with that instrument.

"Art Pepper, 1925–1982—A Memoriam"
JazzTimes, September 1982

Notes from a Jazz Survivor has been hailed as a brilliant documentary of Art Pepper, and, ironically, this fresh new film began its international circuit of screenings just shortly before Pepper's death on June 15 of this year.

Legendary archetypes are often created out of struggles that pit people against incredible odds, only to see them burst through successfully. Pepper the survivor had resuscitated his career and lifted it to a starbright status in the last few years. He had been strapped to about a 30-year losing battle with himself—for he was his own most fearsome enemy. His ultimate victory and rebirth were capped by the long-sought wide recognition of his greatness in the jazz world. At age 56 he was clearly one of a small handful of alto saxophonists occupying the top rung of the ladder.

Art's powerful individuality and daring emotional expressiveness coupled with his uncompromising resiliency for success helped him to wrestle with his bewildering life, always playing his heart out. His autobiography, *Straight Life*, published three years ago, amplified in broad daylight his severe hang-ups and losses in life. Beset with a parade and thick web of problems from alcoholism to drug addiction and "boosting," with round trips to prisons and intermissions in mental institutions—Art's extraordinary clinging to life (actually many lives) was connected musically to his goal to play ... to scratch and claw his way up to the peak and be regarded as a creative, major artist and the unique jazz voice he knew he owned some 40 years ago.

In retrospect, the binding element was an irreducible inner compulsion to be identified with his musical genius. "I feel my whole musical life is on the line with each performance," he once said. And he was not one to say that playing jazz was not difficult; it was always a challenge—the context or his condition not withstanding. "If you don't play yourself, you're nothing ... I've been playing what I felt, what *I* felt, regardless of what those around me were playing or how they thought I should sound."

I first met Art in December of 1943, when he was in his first tenure with Stan Kenton. He definitely sounded like Art and no one else, and he was impressive with his natural drive and buoyant swing. Somewhat shy as a person, his flowing solos, in contrast, were boldly exciting, and I was promptly hooked on his playing. As good friends through the years, our paths crossed intermittently, as I would seek him out whenever his gigs were accessible and whenever I could help him with work. He telephoned frequently, especially during the sixties and seventies, often complaining about someone not paying him enough after a gig where he had attracted a full house.

During the sixties, when Art was imprisoned in San Quentin, I consistently programmed about a solid half hour of his music on radio KJAZ to open my 9 p.m. show. One day a prison guard dropped into the studio in Berkeley to tell me Art and a lot of the guys tuned in religiously to the show, as Art was leading a San Quentin big band and had become an admired celebrity, headlining the front page of the San Quentin newspaper with photos on a number of occasions.

In my opinion, Art Pepper was also one the greatest jazz clarinetists. One of the best earlier examples is "Anthropology" from the 1959 album *Art Pepper Plus Eleven* (Contemporary M 3568). His clarinet work showed the same imaginative improvisation, rhythmic sinew and lyrical eloquence he expressed on the alto. (He started on clarinet at age 9, three years before the alto—his true love.) I have teased out every note of his clarinet available on records and have frequently showcased this aspect for the last 23 years on KJAZ.

This passionate belief led to my buying a clarinet for him upon his 1964 release from Quentin—not only as a welcome back gesture but to encourage his pursuit of the instrument. He was deeply into Coltrane's music then—something that surprised most of his fans. When Don Mupo, whose love for Art's music was likewise very deep, hired him to play at his popular jazz watering hole in Oakland—the Gold Nugget—Art roared with unbelievably powerful overtones of Coltrane's prevailing influence. (The L.A. rhythm section was Frank Strazzeri on piano, Hersh Hamel on bass and Bill Goodwin on drums.) I can't remember when Mupo's club was ever more crowded, flowing out into the street. People were frenetic, cheering and rallying for Art! Mupo featured Art there frequently for months. "I also put together a Maynard Ferguson reunion band when Ferguson was hanging out in Los Altos with Tim Leary," recalls Mupo. "Maynard flipped out when he spotted Art in the 12-piece band along with guys like Al Porcine, Don Rader and Med Flory."

A film clip of the 1964 Pepper Quartet and his adventuresome playing was captured as a segment of the old public TV series *Jazz Casuals*; it was shown in Art's memory during the 1982 New York Kool Jazz Festival "Alto Summit" concert at Carnegie Hall on June 28. Art and his quartet had been scheduled to appear opposite Phil Woods' group. Richie Cole and Sonny Stitt played in place of Art, and ironically, Sonny passed away July 21, three weeks after the performance.

A postscript to my clarinet gift to Art: he hocked it shortly before his final trip back to San Quentin (and I was still paying installment payments on it)!

After he got out of prison in 1966, he was scuffling again. His brief episodic musical reprieve via membership in Buddy Rich's big band is a familiar one, riddled with physical problems he couldn't resolve without hospitalization and surgery. I remember the particular evening when the band was playing in San Francisco's Basin Street West very well—he and his friend Christine had an early dinner at my home, during which he drank heavily even though he complained of stomach pains. Then he spent two hours at KJAZ studios where we chatted on the air, shared his records and drank some more before going to his gig, where he had been playing with all the vigor he could muster. His intolerable pain prompted Buddy to zip him into St. Luke's Hospital where his ruptured spleen was removed. My brother Woody (who was Art's last dentist and a devout admirer of Art's) and I visited him often. Art was dejected and declared: "Man, I don't see how I'm going to ever play again … and I was just getting back into the groove with Buddy!" His subsequent self-imposed exile in Synanon in L.A. offered him a new lease on life. He and Laurie Miller, his last wife, met there and together they staged this eventual comeback. He was elated about "finally finding my best friend—Laurie."

Later, I introduced him to a number of campus jazz clinics and educational jazz festivals—an environment in which he was intrinsically valuable and warmly received. But it wasn't until later that his recording career was renewed, mainly through his long time faithful supporter, Les Koenig of Contemporary Records, and lastly with Galaxy Records after Koenig died. And there were numerous other records with a garden variety of labels in between, too. His eminent success at the Village Vanguard during his debut visits to New York City was yet another triumph.

His esteem in Japan was of the highest; he was literally revered by the Japanese and by European fans as one of jazz history's greatest. Art Pepper reissue albums and newly "discovered" tapes were coming out of everywhere. Moreover, he was particularly happy about his book finally being published.

Last fall, when he had arrived at Davies Hall for the San Francisco KJAZ Festival, I spent a good hunk of time with Laurie and Art in his dressing room. Sick as he was with liver problems, he remained jubilant about the "live" date at Maiden Voyage in L.A. last August. He moved jauntily, playing different segments of a cassette tape for me, exclaiming how fresh and rich the improvisations were and how great his band played (it was released on Galaxy 5142 as *Roadgame* with George Cables, David Williams and Carl Burnett).

Al Evers of The Berkeley Agency should be credited for a role in helping Art to appear in a range of venues here and abroad. Things were clearly being integrated into a perceptible whole—one which thrived on a lively support system.

Art's last performances at San Francisco's Great American Music Hall, with his working band and a string quartet, highlighted music from another cherished wish of his—recording (and performing) with a string quartet. *Winter Moon* on Galaxy was the reference, and, as Laurie says, "He really loved this record."

Art spoke effusively about the film *Notes from a Jazz Survivor* and how satisfying it was to him. He shared, too, his feelings about how he had not ever played any better than in recent months. The occasion was in February during his recording on Palo Alto Records with Richie Cole for the first (and only) time.

Finally, he and "my favorite pianist—George Cables" recorded a duet disc in April at Fantasy Studios. It's planned to be titled *Goin' Home* and scheduled for fall release.

When Laurie was by his deathbed he told her "how satisfied he had been in the last several years—particularly (with) the book, the film, and the string album." Before he slipped into a coma due to cerebral hemorrhage at Kaiser Hospital, he was aware he was slurring his speech and had movement control only on the right side of his body. He declared: "If this is a stroke, I don't want to play anymore."

Art's funeral was held in the Chapel in Hollywood Memorial Cemetery on June 21.

The services started and ended with music from *Goin' Home*—"The Sweetest Sounds" and then "Goin' Home" from Dvorak's *New World Symphony*.

The epitaph on Arthur Edward Pepper, Jr.'s crypt includes: "The winner always in the fatal game. Love Forever."

Lanny Morgan

Lanny Morgan cut his teeth with Maynard Ferguson as Maynard's chief alto soloist. After that, Lanny led—and continues to lead—his own quartet in L.A., where he became a mainstay with occasional journeys to Europe, where he is very popular.

A top bebop soloist, Lanny lacked the national attention that New York–based musicians enjoy; so, for many critics and audiences with an East Coast focus, he's an undiscovered talent.

Like all great altoists, Lanny's music reflects the sound—or, rather, the influence—of Charlie Parker. All of these great players were influenced by Charlie Parker; in fact, I don't think I could name a single alto player who didn't have Bird as an influence. Given his early exposure to the bebop world via his dad's swing orchestra, Lanny Morgan would certainly be included amongst those under Bird's wing.

Lanny Morgan—*It's About Time*
Palo Alto Records (PA 8007); 1981

Far too many years have elapsed since Lanny Morgan, one of the handful of the great jazz alto saxophonists, has recorded his own music with his own group. You'll see what I mean when your eardrums leap with joy hearing the opening moments of Morgan's explosive bebop alto sharply cutting contours of swinging long lines.

As with Phil Woods, Cannonball Adderley, Jackie McLean and many others, Morgan was under the influential weight of Charlie "Bird" Parker. But his route to Bird was circuitous. Like the others, he has forged his distinctiveness with a collective background of several cloths of inspiration. "I've never considered myself a 'Birdwatcher'" although his concepts have, of course.

Morgan's first chief model was, in fact, not Bird, but alto saxophonist Art Pepper. "I love the feeling of Art as much as I like Zoot, Prez, Getz and Bird too. Brubeck was in vogue when I was going to college and everyone was listening to Paul Desmond's alto. Paul had such command of the horn and was so lyrical." Morgan summarizes an assimilation process: "By way of osmosis you collect all these things and they eventually become part of your musical personality."

Born into a family of musical parents, Morgan remained in Des Moines, Iowa, until 1944 when he was ten. The family then moved to Los Angeles. "My Dad had a band of the '30s in the swing age and my mother was a semi-classical singer." He played classical violin for a few years and by the time he graduated from high school in 1952, he had also played clarinet for nearly six years. "I started my father's clarinet in junior high and didn't study the alto until I was out of high school."

Lanny Morgan's jazz life has been nurtured on bebop. "It was the first music that turned me on to setting my goal to be a jazz player." He went to Los Angeles City College and after some private woodshedding, he got on Bob MacDonald's notable college jazz

Album cover for Lanny Morgan's 1981 *It's About Time* / Palo Alto Records (PA 8007) (album cover credits: photograph by Giuseppe Pino; design by Joan Ingoldsby Brown).

band. After one and a half years on campus he joined Charlie Barnet's road band in '54 playing tenor, followed by two years of military regimen with the 7th Army Symphony. In the service he also blew his alto with such fellow draftees as saxophonist Eddie Harris, pianist Cedar Walton and the late Don Ellis.

Morgan's musical fortunes were on the rise in 1960 when he became a key member of the talent-laden Maynard Ferguson Big Band. Lanny settled in New York where he became part of the jazz and studio scene leading his own sextet whenever Ferguson was not on the road. During his six years with Ferguson, his impressive alto solos were featured on numerous Ferguson albums and they represent my own introduction to Lanny Morgan's superb playing. Back in L.A. to begin the decade of the '70s, Morgan immersed himself in studio gigs mixed with a tonic of workshops, jazz clubs and festivals. He also had a lion's share of involvement in the lineup of various chat and variety show bands.

The attempt to gain some measure of jazz-art equilibrium has come from Morgan's identification with the excellent big bands of Bill Holman, Bill Berry and Bob Florence. And of course, his Birdflights with other Birds of a feather in the fleet fingered sax section of the Supersax Band.

This album is representative of Lanny Morgan in the 1980s. The rhythm section of Lou Levy, Monty Budwig and Nick Ceroli is his most valued back-burning support. "Lou is almost a legend—a master of subtlety and good taste. He can burn on the fast ones and turn around and play a ballad with such beautiful lyricism, harmony and inventiveness. For me he's a rock—so comforting to know he's there." Morgan adds, "Speaking of rocks, Monty is as solid as they'll ever make them. He's always there with perfect time and perfect notes ... he's a marvelous soloist at any tempo."

If you have ever experienced the Nick Ceroli sound you know he is one of the most resourceful, selfless drummers around. He's oriented acoustically: He uses wood instead of plastic-tipped sticks. "I don't dig in and play real hard, I play off the drums rather than into them," says Ceroli. "My influences were Philly Joe, Max and Shelly—a light bright sound." As Morgan says, "Nick Ceroli is one of the best big band drummers in the world. If you can't play with Nick in the band, you just can't play—he does everything for you except breathe." He's also one of the best small jazz band drummers in the world. As the role of drummer changes from big band to small group, he must keep the same vitality—maintain the energy, yet with much more subtlety in most cases.

Guitarist Bruce Forman is most closely associated with altoist Richie Cole. Young Forman is an anomaly as he is not stylistically descended from the usual lineage of Charlie Christian; but rather with the line of development of such saxophonists as Parker, Adderley, John Coltrane and Johnny Griffin which accounts for his emphatically powerful hornlike lines and melodic continuity. As for his responsive rhythmic comping it is derived from the work of master jazz pianists like Tyner, Corea, Jones, Hancock and Garland.

Both Morgan and I independently decided Forman should be appointed guitarist. Morgan first played with him on October 6, 1980, when they were both on a jam session I was presiding at the Great American Music Hall in San Francisco. Morgan recalls colorfully, "There were seven of us on the stand—rhythmic section, tenor player and trumpet, myself, and a guitar player. We played 'Ornithology' and when it was this 'kid's' turn to play a guitar solo, he knocked me flat!"

Don Rader is on but one track—the title selection "It's About Time." His presence is a musical plus because of his blending with Morgan's finely tuned drive and brilliance. Lanny notes, "I've been a fan of Don's since we played together on Maynard's band. He's an exciting, fiery player on up tempos and thoughtful and lyrical on ballads. When we play together the empathy is usually magical."

It's apropos to glean from Morgan's own comments about the tunes included:

"Friends Again"

This is based on the chord changes to "Just Friends," and was written about four years ago, during the period that Dick Spencer (alto saxophone) and I had a quintet together. Once I got the spark, the tune almost wrote itself. The "Tristano-ish" out chorus came much later—I wanted to add more body and structure to the chart. I always liked Lennie's lines (and Lee Konitz') but never thought they were real "toe-tappers." So, I wrote this second line with Tristano in mind—but with swinging also in mind.

"Jitterbug Waltz"

I first played this Fats Waller tune about a year ago and instantly fell in love with it. Some tunes feel natural and are fun to play … the first time you play them. I felt the first half of the "in" chorus rubato and that's what we did—leading into a very relaxed second half—in tempo. I feel this tune is slower and more relaxed than a "jazz waltz." I think Monty's solo is gorgeous!

"Koko"

I first played this with Supersax. When I got the idea for the alto/guitar quintet, I immediately thought of "Koko" as a flag waver and a showcase for guitar—if for no other reason than just reading the part. I used Bird's intro and first chorus and his ending. The kind of guitar player I needed to play this is virtually nonexistent. Someone who could read notes, for starters (Bird lines do not particularly lend themselves to guitar), could play the notes with conviction stemming from deep roots in Bird, and could solo at that tempo. I found him! Bruce Forman is an incredible player. He played everything as if he had written it himself. He's a monster!

"It's About Time"

This was written for the album. I was originally shooting for something based on the blues or rhythm changes. I wanted something light, happy and rhythmic. This melody kept recurring, so I forgot about "I Got Rhythm" and the blues and went with it.

"Easy Living"

I've always loved this tune and never played it. I wanted a real ballad on the album— where the melody was strong and even over stated—not just a chord base from which we could all double and triple time, as so often happens with ballads. It turned out simple and pretty, which is what I had in mind.

"Bagatelle"

This was written for a sextet I had in New York—about 1964—with Mike Abene, Ron McClure, Tony Inzalaco, Frank Vicari and Richard Hurwitz. It's reminiscent of "Milestones." Frankly, I don't remember if it was intentional or not. Probably, yes. The Miles Davis sextet was very hot at that time. It's almost a 24-bar minor blues, but not quite. Lends itself to modal playing.

"Acapulco Hot"

I fooled around with this melody at the piano for months before I finally wrote it down. Definite Mexican flavor, although we decided to go into straight 4 for the solos. The ensemble passage after the piano solo is extremely difficult for guitar—lots of 4ths. The title came from a canned preparation called "Acapulco Hots" that you melt with Velveeta cheese to make a dynamite party dip.

The band feels so good it smiles and even laughs when it plays—because it swings. Nick Ceroli notes, "I played with Lanny for better than ten years off and on. As sidemen we've landed in a lot of bands together. I always look forward to playing with Lanny's group—it's a chance to clean the carbon off my valves—to get my engine roaring. At the end of a Lanny Morgan gig I always feel I've accomplished something—not just the speed with which he can play, but he's so musical and he takes chances so it's like running a track with him." "Lanny is an unsung hero," says Bruce Forman. "He has a firm rhythmic hold—so easy to play with. His concept of bebop is my music and we worked well together. I dug his extremely challenging material."

Everyone locks in easily to Lanny. You play behind Lanny Morgan, Zoot Sims, or Al Cohn and you've got it made because they'll put it right in your lap. "I think I'm a time player," says Morgan. "I would sacrifice notes for time. I think jazz or bebop or whatever, is all fun—it's a happy music even when it's sad. To me, having fun with it is playing it with a good time feeling.

"In New York, I was a great admirer of Coltrane and incorporated many of his things and dug it. I realized back in L.A. that I'm really a bebop player—that's where I came from, that's what I feel, that's what I do best."

Lanny's music never delays bringing abundant pleasures as it promptly invites and provides renewal … he's a total gas! If you haven't dug into Lanny Morgan…. IT IS ABOUT TIME!

Bud Shank

I did the liner notes for a Bud Shank recording for World Pacific Jazz early on. Dick Bock was the label's owner and producer (he started the label with the Gerry Mulligan Quartet). Both Dick Bock and the World Pacific Jazz label were very much a part of West Coast jazz history.

The project was for a recording Bud was doing with Michel Legrand, an orchestral thing based on Michel's score for the film, *Umbrellas of Cherbourg*. Michel had a lot of respect for the musicians in Southern California. "These guys here," Michel once told me, "could read *anything* and read it right away. I would always come to Southern California to record with Hollywood musicians because it guarantees quality."

So it was a natural that he brought in Bud, who worked as "chief horn soloist" in the L.A. area. As an almost-every-day studio musician, Bud had a lot of work and made a lot of money working in Hollywood. Anybody who had the right ears for music could detect Bud's playing in most of the motion picture sound tracks of the day. If you heard an alto sax in just about any movie during his time, a lot of that sound was Bud Shank.

When he switched to a small group, The L.A. Four, with Shelly Manne, Ray Brown and Laurindo Almeida, Bud demonstrated that he was able to switch from one musical environment to the next. He was extremely adaptable, yet he never lost his identity.

There was a transformation by Bud in his last twelve years. He decided that he didn't want to play tenor sax any longer as a part of his battery of instruments and to concentrate just on the alto. Once he made that decision, he focused on music that was likened to the East Coast modern jazz material. He said he was very happy about switching because he was really able to express himself—like he had ever expressed himself in all the previous environments!

Bud felt more comfortable in that small setting; it liberated him to feel more creative, with more latitude. The series of albums Bud recorded since that decision are outstanding. He continued to produce outstanding material until he passed away in 2009.

The Bud Shank Sextet—*New Gold!*
Candid (CCD 79707); 1994

Hang on to this recording! It is definitely not a disc to regard with nonchalance or ennui, or to assume the ingredients would be easily predictable. Instead, it is one which finds this new band interpreting music replete with surprises from one tune to the next, resulting in a high shouting quotient of diversity and excitement. *New Gold!* is a disc your hot hands will not want to relinquish—it is a flat out irresistible grabber!

The ideational birth of this rewarding new Bud Shank Sextet occurred in Shank's Port Townsend home in Washington in July 1993 following its annual jazzfest: he shared his notion of a sextet without a piano, with Bill Perkins and the others. Besides the comparative ease of portability, lighter economic pressures, and a refreshing concept, it plainly offers a different kind of flexibility. And it is not a concept foreign to Shank's varied experiences, and certainly not historically, vis-à-vis numerous examples ranging from the 1952–53 Gerry Mulligan Quartet hailed for its seminal instrumentation of two horns, bass and drums—unorthodox at the time—and among later editions, the Max Roach Quartet has been unassisted by piano.

Some may even believe it to be a harmonic hazard, but with these premium players, the mesh is perfect. Shank says "I was searching for a way to make the most amount of music out of six people. I figured the four horns would give us the harmony and the soloists … and bass and drums are sufficient for a rhythm section." Perkins adds: "You don't have any piano constantly feeding you chords, so it's between you and the bass, and we have the right bassist for that—John Clayton." In reference to the inherent increase of freedom as an integral feature, Conte Candoli says, "Because you don't need to stay with the basic chords, you can deviate somewhat into something new." "The four horns sound so big," says Jack Nimitz, "it's fuller than a smaller group." Sherman Ferguson says, "We have new liberties."

Prior to the recording date, the band spent five nights in L.A.'s Catalina Bar & Grill getting its book together on the gig. "By the second night the guys were all saying 'Wow! We love it!'" reports Shank. "You can explore the whole range of extensions of chords without clashing with anybody. You can go up and play around at those extensions and not come out sounding like you're wrong." There is, then, a demand to sharpen attention since there's no crutch to rely on all the time. "Pianists are always telling you where you are, so maybe you don't want to know where you are at times, but they're telling you anyway, with all due respect to my pianist-friends. I love playing with piano, but this approach provides a special freedom and mode of concentration. And it's actually improved everyone's playing!"

Shank's wide open attitude was expressed in the process of recruiting music of uncommon variety and quality. "When I hired the guys to write the music, I told them this is it! But write anything you want to. I gave no guidance to writing as far as tempo, style, or whatever. And it all worked! You see, I had already gone through that very process myself and assumed no one would reach for those extremes—'Linda' (strongly melodic) at one end, and 'Perkolator' (out there!) at the other end."

A case in point is John Clayton's five generous open-door contributions written with no restrictions, stepping into relatively un-treaded territories. As Clayton notes, "It's seldom someone invites you to write that many pieces and gives you carte blanche all the way. Unaccustomed to no piano or guitar (although they may lay out when I'm playing an ensemble, they're there at some point), I then imagined how it would sound from beginning to end, song after song without those instruments." The challenge was lessened by the musicians on the band. "It was easier for me to write because I could imagine their voices which automatically made the music sound better."

The band was enthralled with Clayton's formidably creative writing; words are inadequate to describe the consensual adulation for his acute sixth sense intuition and taste. "I think John's writing reminds me of Thad Jones," says Perkins, "and I'm a tremendous admirer of Thad, and it's Dukish, too, but John's his own man. I like the way he puts a lot of crunches in the music." Candoli explains his warmth, "When you first play John's music, you try to figure out what it is, but after playing it over and over—Wow! You get the feel of it and it makes sense, similar to Thad's stuff." All of the writers' music comes alive and thrive in process through the galaxy of exceptional players. The sound of the horns is great and as Perkins observes, "Between the four horns themselves, we have well over 200 years of collective experience."

"Port Townsend": The chart is written by trombonist Mike Barone (he moved to Vancouver, Washington) who contributed charts to many bands here and abroad such as *The Tonight Show* band when he lived in Southern California. "Mike's a killer writer," says Candoli, "and they always come off. This small band material is great. It's 'I Got Rhythm' … but what he did on it … the line is fabulous!" Barone recalls asking Bud Shank: "Do you want it straight ahead?" And he told me I could stretch out so I gave them some rhythm changes to play on, even though it's in F, and do some other things with it, as I knew in the blowin' they'd get into it easily, so I added some bars, a little vamp, and some stop time. They interpreted it beyond my expectations."

"Alternate Root": A funky trip for Candoli's trumpet. Clayton remembers: "First, I was trying to write five pieces in five different styles and second, I wanted things that would feature everyone. So I wrote one that's blues-like and dirty for Conte to come in on, for not only can he play bebop—Dizzy's style, but he can also play bluesy, greasy things." Candoli remarks, "It's great fun playing this strong composition." Notice the special sequence after Clayton's melodic bass solo as the horns play an ascending thing, and then they descend in the same fashion, with Candoli playing cupped mute. Dig Nimitz's baritone roar—both a treat and a surprise. In truth Nimitz is not a tenor man thinking as a baritone; he *is* a pure baritone.

"Let Me Tell You Why": Bud Shank is featured on a strong, seductive suit of his musicality—bossa nova. Clayton's lovely melodic tune uncorks another unguarded piece of fine writing. "It's a tune I'd written recently with lyrics and Bud just popped into my mind as I recalled his gorgeous bossa novas in the past," Clayton explains, "I tried to free the band from sounding like horns plus rhythm section, so at the onset I changed my role, took out my bow and stuck myself into the horn ensemble." It's a judicious change of pace to hear Clayton merged into the horns. "This is 180 degrees different from John's other charts," adds Candoli. Clayton's unusual voicings and range of moods illustrate his elastic perspectives. And Shank rose to the occasion with his exquisite ballad playing.

"Straight No Chaser": This version of Thelonious Monk's classic is a head turning departure from the norm. Perkins had written out just the line with no arrangement. A suggestion was made to make it a round like "Row, Row, Row Your Boat" after someone had come in too soon. So Shank asked Perkins and Nimitz to start with the melody and then two measures later Candoli and Shank came in, and they finished two bars after the first pair of players stopped playing—in all, an engaging off-the-cuff idea. Candoli's crisp, peppery trumpet retrieves the brilliance of Clifford Brown.

"Perkolator": Drawn from Shank's suite *The Lost Cathedral*, it spotlights Perkins' fluid, superb soprano saxophone. It's transparent why Shank picked it for Perkins whose soprano sounds so apart from his tenor work, playing different notes, employing more movement, betraying his solid command and instinctual comprehension of the horn. Candoli says, "I like where Perk goes—it's unexpected. He'll jump in and wonder where he's to go and then he finds the spot." Noting Candoli's incandescent solo, Perkins states. "Bud had Count (Candoli) in mind, too, just like he turns on the gas and he cooks!"

"Grizzly": John Clayton's musical intelligence partners well with his radiant imagination pool, and "Grizzly" allowed him to set in motion another blueprint. "I wanted a kind of Monkish bebop head—influences that spurred me. Actually the tune is based on the chords to 'Just in Time,' tho' I tried to mask that. And I thought this would be something we would open to feature whoever wants to play. Also I hadn't really written a long ensemble so I used this one to do contrapuntal writing and ensemble work. These guys are such great ensemble players they can read anything. They put a lot of effort on dynamics, what notes should be long or short, etc. It's real pros like them that make the music sound good."

"Finger Therapy": Sherman Ferguson is a percussionist never to be taken for granted. Aside from his trademarked excellence on dozens of varied recordings, his inventive, spirited artistry on "Finger Therapy" and filling the role in this piano-less band evoke high esteem. His spicy way of blending colors of a hybrid mouth percussive form or "mouth-poppin" with percussion via hands and fingers is truly a focal ear-pleaser. "I tried to create a totally open sounding melody that embellishes what Sherman does and to give him something to play around, so the melody services the drum solo completely," Clayton says. "It's an oddball way to write a melody but I had two goals—first, provide holes for Sherman to take over where the melody ended and then the band would pick it up again, like an exchange between band and Sherman; second, create a joyous calypso street carnival type of melody. I had Sherman's sound, his style and his groove in mind." Ferguson offers, "I had to musically incorporate the 'mouth-poppin' into my solo without being gimmicky or hampering the soloists, and it's one of the best things I've ever done. I had a ball!" Perkins asserts, "No matter what we played, weird or not, Sherman was alert to it and was right there!"

"Linda": "I sat down to write something nice and pretty for my Linda," says Bud. Indeed, it is a testament to the quality writing Shank consistently demonstrates; his tone clusters and ideas arouse excitement. Like other extraordinary players, not as much time is devoted to composing; when Shank does write, tunes like this are events. His sensitive playing shows intense, personal apperception and emotional involvement with his beautiful piece. Candoli's attractive solo lines are like rushes of fresh air.

"Killer Joe": Perkins' clever arrangement of Benny Golson's classic is an incisive example of adaptation to no piano. Clayton bows the theme with horns and Ferguson, and after the in chorus, it's just Shank and Nimitz for a chorus without rhythm section, then the section comes in and after a chorus, different moods flow in. Towards the end Candoli's quick Harmon mute is on the melody then back to open horn resurrecting the original Art Farmer/Benny Golson Jazztet 1960 approach. Perkins nailed it: "Be faithful to Golson's tune and you can't lose." Ferguson's input on the rhythmic part is a resourceful contribution.

"Funcused Blues": John Clayton's final chart is a daring medium. Named as a flip flop of the word "confused," it's a fun piece. As Clayton reports, "The title says it all. It's not a melody you expect your mom or dad to whistle. Written eight years ago, I dusted it off and worked it over for this band as it was prime for something more adventuresome, and it's thrilling to hear them going out on the limbs as they did. As a writer I listen carefully to what they do and pick up things that strike you as memorable." These musical memos obviously load up Clayton's creative capacity with a reserve of critical data.

"Little Rootie Tootie": There are moments when the band sounds so full-bodied it is deceivingly like a big band. Perkins' little voicings are appealing, especially going into the first bridge. He encouraged Candoli to play an octave higher. "It really changed it completely, responds Candoli. "Taking it out I played something an octave up, too. It really fits." Perkins sums up the inherent strengths of Monk's classic: "It plays itself."

New Gold! is an apt, literal cue to this lodestone disc. "The music is uncontrived," says Jack Nimitz. "When you're playing you want to get into the flow and just let it happen, and it happened on this one. Everything was so different, every tune has its own flavors—a different kind of album with no 'West Coast' stigma." And Ferguson's pointed reaction: "This record doesn't get stale—sticks to you. It's exceptional and my opinion has nothing to do with me being on the date." Bud Shank's New Sextet edition armed with a renewed temperament and direction never forsakes its immutable commitment to the values of swing. Small wonder that Shank declared: "I love it! Mission accomplished!"

CHAPTER 6

Baritone Saxophone

The baritone saxophone is the basement of the reeds section; it anchors the section with certainty. With its full, deep sound, the baritone sax generates a hugeness of an impression, causing a deep, visceral feeling within the listener, a feeling no other instrument can quite convey.

It was a deep, visceral feeling that drove a baritone saxophone into the hands of Gary Smulyan, a well known alto player who suddenly found himself in need of a bari during his audition for the Woody Herman band.

Gary Smulyan

Gary Smulyan's desire to be a member of the Woody Herman Band was well known. He made no secret of it and other musicians in the band were well acquainted with his wishes. One of them urged him to try out, suggesting that you had to be an alto player in order to make the band. So Gary followed his advice and came into the audition with his alto in hand, only to discover that Woody was looking for a baritone saxophonist.

Never having even *picked up* a baritone saxophone before, Gary auditioned for Woody on a borrowed instrument. He just got into it and played so well in front of Woody that Woody's thinking, "This guy's really got it!" And he got the gig, with Woody hiring him on the spot; and this was absolutely the first time Gary had ever laid his hands on the baritone saxophone!

Gary Smulyan Nonet—*Saxophone Mosaic*
Criss Cross Jazz (Criss 1092); 1994

Strong advocacy is rapidly gaining ground for baritone saxophonist Gary Smulyan as the deserving heir to the mantle of the most outstanding player on his instrument in jazz. He is assuredly an eloquent exponent on the scene, his youthfulness notwithstanding. The affirming evidence is readily available in person and on recordings.

Modeled mainly after the superb Pepper Adams—whose chair Smulyan inherited when he joined the Mel Lewis Orchestra in 1980—promptly following precisely two years of impressive playing with Woody Herman's band, Smulyan has nurtured the seeds of his own originality producing a powerfully personal stylistic voice and approach. It is not surprising Smulyan's matured style is likened to attributes in common with Adams. Whereas Smulyan began with the alto and was duly touched by Charlie Parker, "it was

Pepper's harmonic and rhythmic ingenuity and the ease he showed in handling challenging hurdles that inspired me most of all. He was my idol!"

Smulyan blisters with an enormous, ferocious sound, without vibrato; he articulates notes with uncompromising clarity and facility, giving each note its full value. Also he savors harmonic challenges and translates this into a peculiarly Smulyan harmonic vocabulary. His pin point focus allows him to mediate perfect balance between speed, tone, and accuracy. You won't hear a skein of 16th notes that border on muddiness out of his horn, even when he is downright aggressive—roaring and speeding like a bullet express train. Another asset is his ability to internalize and codify all he hears and retrieve it at will. It's not just uncanny cognitive processing—it's a feat he uses as a musical support system.

It was a providential happenstance that Smulyan arrived at playing the baritone. He describes: "Glenn Drewes and I had a quintet in Long Island and he joined Woody's band and in turn got me on. But I played alto and Woody needed a bari. So I managed to get a bari, but I was scared to death for six months waiting to be fired. Woody was patient and had faith in me." True. Woody Herman told me in 1979 that Gary was among a handful of the best baritonists passing through his bands in the last four decades.

The original root concept of this disc came from the allure of the remarkable sax section in Mel Lewis' band during the days of Joe Lovano, Ralph Lalama, Ted Nash, Dick Oatts and Gary Smulyan. In time, Lovano and Nash were replaced by Rich Perry and Billy Drewes, but the idea remained pregnant and developed into having Smulyan stand in front as the primary soloist, cushioned behind by the saxes. Arranger Bob Belden suggested to Smulyan about doing a sax record on this basis. Admittedly it is not a novel idea as Jimmy Heath had written music for Nat Adderley and the Big Sax Section on *That's Right*—a 1960 Riverside record featuring the saxes of Heath, Yusef Lateef, Charlie Rouse, Cannonball Adderley, and Tate Houston on baritone with Wynton Kelly, Sam Jones and Jimmy Cobb.

"The idea was not having a Supersax thing emphasizing soli but a sax section background of sound enveloping the band, and knowing these guys well, I knew just what they would sound like. These charts were not meant to be tight but to swing and to allow Gary breathing space," explained Belden whose long association with Smulyan began when playing side by side on Herman's Thundering Herd. Smulyan added. "I wanted a rhythm section familiar with everyone's style and who have played together a lot in a variety of bands. It was logical that Mike, Dennis and Kenny were the given choices. So the music jelled quickly; it was like old friends playing in a studio session!"

Regarding his fellow saxophonists, Smulyan noted: "Dick Oatts is the best lead altoist I've ever played under. Musically strong improvisor, when he gets up to play he just knocks me out! I've known Billy Drewes since we were kids and we were in Woody's band together. Billy forges a style you can spot after a couple of notes. Ralph Lalama is probably one of the swingin'est tenors around. The groove he plays with is very strong and he'll swing you into bad health. We have a grand time sitting next to each other at the Vanguard. Scott Robinson who is my main sub in the Vanguard band does everything well. There's no instrument he hasn't played. And Richie Perry is a unique player who is creative and really interesting to listen to." Belden adds, "Every phrase Perry plays means something—nothing extraneous, and he's been that way since age 19 when I first heard him."

Opinions from one's peers and colleagues are generally worthy as a result of frequent, long term interactions close-up. Here's a sampling of their insights on Gary and the session.

Bob Belden: "The first night I was with Woody, Gary just nailed everything—just ridiculous! He's a definitive player, and my respect for him is unflagging."

Dick Oatts: "Thank God for all us alto players Gary switched to bari! A wonderful soloist, he's such a support in the section. It's a real treat to put Gary out front with saxes weaving around him. I couldn't believe his stamina at the session. And Bob wrote just great, giving Gary the ball so he could run—beautiful icing on the cake."

Billy Drewes: "Gary was an incredible child prodigy. Coming out of a certain school but taking it to just his place—a place he owns—that is very special! Everyone has his own voice in improvising in the section, and I was just digging playing the part, groovin' on the sound and unity."

Rich Perry: "What charisma! Gary is comfortably amazing."

Ralph Lalama: "Gary stacks chords on top of chords. With a gifted musical mind and a photographic memory, he can play anything he can hear. It was a fun, positive and hip session."

Scott Robinson: "Gary's the torch-bearer. He's the baritone cat! When the saxes solo left to right and then it's Gary's turn—suddenly everything's inventively different."

Mike LeDonne: "Gary's my absolute favorite. He plays the bari like an alto. Wow, the way he gets around that huge horn and really plays the changes fast and clear. He never skirts over them. Gary's harmonic concept puts him in front. On the date the sax section knocked me out, playing the solo on 'Fingers,' I could feel it on the floor."

And also from former section mate Joe Lovano: "We've been in some great bands together—Woody's and Mel's bands. Gary is one of my all-time favorite musicians to listen to and to play with. A giant on the baritone, he has total command of it and an amazing comprehension of the music. I love him."

Belden arranged all of the music except the anchor tune "Fingers" by Thad Jones. Plainly it was a tall assignment to locate material which met the requisites of a chart for five saxophones.

"Smoke Signal" is Gigi Gryce's irrepressible tune based on "Lover" and was recorded in 1956 on Oscar Pettiford's *Orchestra in Hi-Fi, Volume One*. Likewise Horace Silver's infectious theme "Speculation" is from the same record, now reissued on an Impulse CD. Both are virtuoso kinds of tunes; they essentially have a harmonic sound prevalent in the post Charlie Parker era, basically influenced by Parker's harmonic modulations. "These songs are very detailed in themselves so it didn't take much to draw out things. But you can't overwork them or it takes away from the solo efforts," said Belden. "It's a problem when writing for a sax section; there's a tendency to write only solis and ensembles—all the excitement will be in the last 8 bars of the chart or just before the last head, and it should rightfully be the soloists' domain."

"Speculation" is a bright, effervescent tune and a fine launch for the blues mood even though Silver's melody doesn't sound like a standard 12 bar blues, except for the improvising. I am impressed how it sounds like a band far larger than nine musicians. Significant support and fire come through the inspired drums of Kenny Washington. "I used to listen to Kenny Clarke play it and also Osie Johnson's drums on Oscar Pettiford's records," said Kenny.

Smulyan picked "The Wind," pianist Russ Freeman's obscure tune for its particular harmonic content. "It's one of the tunes we concentrated on the sound of woodwinds,"

Belden commented, "and not the sound of saxophones." Smulyan's warm, private dialect of serenity is simply exquisite.

Dig the arresting solo Smulyan tears off with Nijinsky-like nimbleness on George Coleman's "Apache Dance." "I re-harmonized it and put some substitute changes for more improvisatory interest," Smulyan said. It features all the saxes, each with their respective styles as they emerge and then retreat into the section, achieving a beautiful blend.

"Stockholm Sweetnin'," the Quincy Jones classic for trumpeters Art Farmer and Clifford Brown written nearly forty years ago, is a lovely melody with great changes to play on. "Gary knows the meaning of the notes he plays and somehow finds the prettiest ones," Belden offered, "and the hippest notes that swing." Similarly LeDonne and bassist Dennis Irwin thread tasty notes into the groove.

Belden transcribed the keystone orchestration of Gil Evans' treatment of Johnny Carisi's "Springsville" which was included on the Miles Davis 1957 recording *Miles Ahead*, reducing it to accommodate the saxophone section. It's not an easy tune, but Smulyan enjoys provocative harmonic progressions.

"Fingers" is a perfect closer featuring all the players in a sax summit. They know it like the back of their hands, after playing it for years with Thad and Mel. Everyone had a ball with it. Beyond the exemplary soli, all the saxes traded a gigantic storm of solos, and the heroic rhythm section had bottomless drive. These fireworks say it all. What a gas!

Small wonder the demand for Smulyan is kicking dust. In recent times he has been heard in a variety of bands including big bands besides the Vanguard Orchestra—the Philip Morris Superband, Mingus Epitaph Orchestra, Carnegie Hall Jazz Orchestra and the Smithsonian Masterworks Orchestra among others, he has also been playing in a rainbow of small groups, plus he has recorded two prior Criss Cross Jazz discs under his own leadership—*The Lure of Beauty* (Criss 1049), in 1990, and *Homage* (Criss 1068), in 1991. And now this powerhouse date adds even more sparkle to his ascent.

"I love playing the baritone and I'm now trying to aim at a deeper musical level to forge a strong individual style that is uniquely mine," Smulyan said with sincerity. Gary Smulyan has indeed arrived as his own sourcebook and architect.

Pepper Adams

Pepper Adams is a model for all other bari players; he has amazing facility with the horn, a sound that is clearly his alone. Pepper is well respected by the jazz community; he's an asset to any musical project. His small group playing is sufficiently elastic to have included Pepper Adams in key roles as a prominent player participating in many big bands, mainly with the Thad Jones/Mel Lewis Orchestra.

Pepper Adams with Don Friedman—*Don Friedman:*
Hot Knepper and Pepper
Progressive Records (PCD 7036); 1980

Friedman was born in San Francisco in 1935 and, until he deferred wholly to jazz in 1954, he was immersed in classical piano for a solid ten years. This writer recalls catching him in the late fifties playing at S.F.'s Blackhawk with Terry Gibbs' quartet, playing a lot like Red Garland and much bebop. Currently he plays at the Knickerbocker in New York in a duo with bassist Bob Bodley; when he's not confined to straight-ahead music, he plays often with Zoller, Eliot Zigmund and Harvie Swartz.

In retrospect, "basically what people heard on my early records in the sixties was the actual formulation of my playing," says Friedman. "Many of the newer things have influenced me; namely, the younger pianists—Richie Beirach, Joanne Brackeen, Andy LaVerne et al. They're doing things differently. Actually if I hear substantial music, it doesn't matter who it is, I unconsciously incorporate things into my own."

Pianist Lou Levy who alternates with Friedman at the Knickerbocker when he flies into N.Y. from L.A. observes: "I love to listen to a pianist who practices. Players like Chick and Bill Evans are examples and Don Friedman is another who has equal strength in all his fingers and you can hear it. Mix that with good taste, knowledge, experience and an individual sound … and you have a helluva player, and I think Don is a great player. I remember him from the early Chet Baker days on the Coast and until recently when I heard him again, I had forgotten how beautiful he is!"

Certain facets of Friedman's approach are illuminated on this album. There is the lucid, inviolable respect for the integrity of the tune, even as he infuses fresh dimensions. "I take the notion that the structure of a standard time must remain intact. And I have incorporated some freer aspects—some from Keith Jarrett which I like to call 'pedal point music' … opens up a lot of color things: I'm using it in a limited way but it's part of my current direction."

Another attribute is the personal sound Friedman gets from the piano, especially on ballads. As a tangent of Bill Evans, there is similarity in their expressive feeling and the creation of a mood, but upon closer inspection there are great contrasts in lines, harmony and technique.

"Classical music evokes strong emotions. I started playing it at about 4 years old," says Friedman. Obviously he has never lost that derivative feeling which may account for the wonderful sound he captures. His flair for a lilting looser concept, breaking up the rhythm and crossing bar lines convey a floating feeling. "Ballads offer a lot of time to produce dynamic levels and the slowness per se creates a 'down' mood," he adds. Friedman's softer, romantic playing is simply pretty and meaningful.

This album is likened to an impromptu jam session with minimal preparation. Since everyone on the date is a superb individual and team player of renown with much to say, the challenge is met with a blend of dexterous technique and fertile intuitiveness. Friedman's date benefits from the excellence of two self-styled, imaginative horn men in Pepper Adams and Jimmy Knepper and, two powerful, ubiquitous rhythm mates—George Mraz and Billy Hart. All five play with finesse and sensitive authority.

Adams' aggressive incisiveness reflects the deep throated sound of pre-boppers Chu Berry, Coleman Hawkins and Harry Carney although he also pays homage to Barry Harris' modernity. He cuts through lard and reaches the heart of musical messages. Adams has been freelancing since 1977, after 12 years with Thad Jones and Mel Lewis' Orchestra, and is finally topping some jazz polls. He and Friedman worked with Chet Baker twenty years ago and have touched bases intermittently.

Jimmy Knepper's fame as a member of Charles Mingus' Jazz Workshop Quintet 1957–61 precedes his gigs with notable interest, and it has come full circle since he rejoined other Mingus associates in the Mingus Dynasty tour group. Justifiably so, as his solos were veritable works of art, architecture and music on the classic Mingus records. His depth of imagination is expressed thru daring surprises and held by warm tonal textures and lithesomeness. He lights up with Adams, boiling with excitement ... especially when he hits the ceiling register while he plays intricate multi-noted phrases.

Czech-born bassist George Mraz was classically-trained at Prague Conservatory ere coming to the Berklee jazz academy. Like Adams and Knepper, he, too, was with Jones-Lewis. His chops are impressive—dig his clean, round notes. Likewise, drummer Billy Hart is in great demand attesting to his assertive, disciplined dependability and adaptability, to his great time, tasty ideas and encouraging energies.

The album bursts forth with "Audubon" in bustling fashion. Then trombonist Tommy Dorsey's theme "I'm Getting Sentimental Over You" is tackled by Knepper with understanding; it's a natural for his human-like singing quality. Hart impresses with his lightning responses—a meld of artistic and athletic assets. On Adams' own "Hellure," he is exuberant, showing relish for good chords to blow on. Then there's Friedman's voicings, Knepper's humor and with Mraz's colorful lacings and Hart's cyclotronic peaks.

Gillespie's solid "Groovin' High" combines the conventional lines with some unfamiliar horn improvisations, stoked by a burning rhythm section. Friedman's comping deserves notice throughout the album. "Groovin'" illustrates how he voices chords to support horn players without intrusion—at the same time as part of the rhythm section, obligated to create a valid rhythmic pulse.

The spontaneity of the medley is equal to any other selection. Friedman's gorgeous solo on the beguiling minor "Alfie" is impassioned. Knepper's "Laura" is remindful of the stylistic impact of Lawrence Brown and J.C. Higginbotham. Mraz's booming timbre and appealing lyricism holds melding power on "Prelude to a Kiss." Adams' discography reveals great love for Ellingtonia; "I Got It Bad" gets a crying, peppery Carney call.

"I learned Victor Young's 'Beautiful Love' years ago with Scott LaFaro when we worked for singer Dick Haymes around 1959–60 in New York," notes Friedman. It is a fitting closer as everyone's swinging vitality leaves the album with uplifted fulfillment.

Nick Brignola

Nick Brignola is a gift of upstate New York, where he was born in 1936 and spent much of the rest of his lifetime. I first caught him sitting in with Cal Tjader at the old Blackhawk in San Francisco, with Nick blowing an impressive baritone sax.

Nick Brignola was a major force as a baritone saxophonist, widely known to stretch the limits of the instrument. Lauded as a teen-age phenomenon, Nick held the baritone chair for Woody Herman's Band—and that was a very important chair in the world of jazz. As Woody said of Nick, "He was one of the dynamite baritone players I have really dug over forty years of Herman's Herds."

Nick Brignola Quintet—*L.A. Bound*
Night Life / Sea Breeze Records (NLR 3007); 1980

Good hot blowing jam sessions are earmarked with plenty of freedom and serendipity. The musicians correspondingly revel with a party in their minds and music, swinging at a moment's notice. Horace Silver's challenging piece, "Quicksilver" swings open the doors to this album, roaring with a powerful version by the Nick Brignola quintet. The burners are switched on to maximum as the raging spirit of a jam session atmosphere pervades.

Baritone saxophonist Brignola's impressive talents have long vaulted into maturity. He can be readily accounted as a forerunner on stretching the range of the instrument. His particular contributions add to the lively potential of the baritone.

By no means a sophomore to the jazz scene, Brignola, who was born in 1936 in Troy, New York, gained early attention when he was awarded the first scholarship to the Berklee College of Music in Boston; he was touted as a teen-age phenomenon. It was in 1958 when I first caught him sitting in with Cal Tjader (along with Vince Guaraldi, Al McKibbon and Willie Bobo) at San Francisco's old Blackhawk. It was here, too, drummer Dick Berk and Brignola met as aspiring young players.

As a sideman and leader, Brignola's associates make up a long roster of jazz luminaries—Clark Terry, Wes Montgomery, Woody Herman, Elvin Jones, Buddy Rich, Chet Baker, among many others. However, it has been his alliance with trumpeter Ted Curson beginning in 1967 which has provided him with the most effective exposure.

Although the baritone is his instant identification, Brignola has masterful command of a veritable arsenal of a dozen different woodwind instruments. Aside from leading his own quartet around his home base in Troy, unsurprisingly he is an active clinician and teacher; he serves on the jazz education faculties of Albany State University, Russell Sage College, Union College and the Creative Music Studio in Woodstock.

"When I start playing, swinging is automatic," Brignola notes, "and I like playing long interesting lines utilizing substitute chord changes." Brignola's solos are fiery and animated; his rich ideas pour out fluidly. "Nick's ideas are unending," Bill Watrous said. The character of his playing includes personalizing every note—whether the notes are part of a brief comment or of an elongated musical essay.

Reflecting his direct transference of Gerry Mulligan and Paul Desmond's tenet of emphatically strong melodic lines, Brignola is also a gifted melody player. Consequently, if you freeze a Brignola solo and review the pattern of notes, they are all essentially strings of melodies. Add to this, another Brignola asset—his strong rhythmic trademark, and we arrive at a communicative brand of swing.

"I get a well-rounded sound," volunteered Brignola. There are times on this album, for instance, when the combination of Brignola and Watrous' trombone achieves "a two trombone sound." "I take the edge off my sound when I play. There's a certain way to make the reed vibrate, so I take the vibration off so it'll blend a bit more."

Gary Smulyan—Woody Herman's current baritone player—made a descriptive comment: "Nick doesn't just blow into his horn—he screams into it! And he should have been out front on the scene ten years ago." Physically, the baritone is, of course, a large, imposing horn. Brignola has forged a resilient psyche allowing him to transcend this contest. "Every time I pick up that horn, I'm challenging it as it challenges me. I have to conquer it and prove that I can play it with force and conviction," Brignola says. This is precisely the way he plays it. This album represents as boldly fine an example of Nick Brignola's unraveling strengths as anything else he has on record.

This record is also Brignola's reunion with Watrous and Berk—relationships which go back some years. "Bill Watrous and I both play modern music in a more traditional jazz sense," Brignola observes. "We are locked into each other's playing. We hooked up several years age in my neck of New York state called the 'Tri-City Area,' playing in spots like the Ramada Inn in Schenectady and Shaker's Pen and Pencil—places where there was a steady jazz policy. Bill was also riding high with his Manhattan Wildlife Refuge big band. No matter what tune either of us would call, we'd jump right in—it was really smooth." A comparable quality of rapport is captured on this album. Likewise, their deep roots in bebop are clear. In reference to Brignola's musical determination and energy, Watrous described: "Nick is unflagging and his thrust is unbending. The record date was fun for us as we've had our act together for years."

Berk and Brignola have been acquainted for half of their lives and have played together in a variety of contexts. "Dick is one of the last of a dying breed—content to sit back and just swing! Some drummers run hot and cold, but Dick is absolutely dependable … you just know he's going to lay it right in there," Brignola commented enthusiastically about Berk's consistency. "Musically, Dick has the traits I admire in Jimmy Cobb—good time and no fancy frills or ego trips. His solos make sense, and with the right bassist—like John Heard, there is just no better swinging time!"

The very hip opening track, "Quicksilver," will take some ears out! Watrous and Brignola's straight ahead direction is knitted with intuitiveness and technical competencies. They play with awesome intensity and tasty, meaningful flair.

Billy Strayhorn's "Smada" (Adams spelled backward) was a completely new tune to the band. It was a tune suggested by producer John Brechler. I recall Ellington recording it at the end of 1959 for the *Blues in Orbit* album featuring Johnny Hodges and Ray Nance. "We gave it a little modern Ellingtonian jungle-like flavor," Brignola offered. The rhythm section rejoices in improvisation. Dig Berk's swinging drums lending just the right colors or propulsion at the right times. And Dwight Dickerson's piano is prominently crisp and musical.

"Groovin' on Uranus," an original Brignola blues in A flat is a relaxing finger-snapper. "I'm thinking Oscar Peterson on it," said Brignola, "because it has that hip groove he reaches so often." Ted Curson has said that "Nick is a natural player. And lots of people can get into what he's doing, but he doesn't sound like any other musician."

Ellington's "In a Mellow Tone" illustrates Brignola's expansive range—from the bowels of the horn to the upper register. And Watrous re-affirms why he is a poll-winning, world class player. The rhythm section cooks … simmering, bubbling and boiling, never losing touch of its ubiquitous sensitivity. Dickerson's piano has been called on by such fastidious players as Sérgio Mendes, Bobby Hutcherson, Bola Sete and James Moody simply because he can deliver the messages. With Berk and Heard, the three show unvarying rhythmic sense.

Brignola's ability to be astutely effective in being laid back, shatters the image of his being pegged only as a high energy player. His excellent control and melodic values are featured on a beautiful duet with Dickerson on "Spring Is Here." Little wonder, by the way, that Anita O'Day, Damita Jo and other vocalists have used Dickerson as their accompanist.

Kenny Dorham's familiar and attractive melodic contour of "Blue Bossa" carries out the closing tune. Brignola's baritone and liquid soprano plus Watrous' trombone, "rewrite" and freshen the tune via their rich and lively conversational interplay.

A value judgment from Woody Herman adds a summary of interest. He has said on several occasions that besides the late Serge Chaloff (the vanguard bop baritonist of the early Herman "Herds" of the forties) he would cite Nick Brignola as "the other dynamite baritone player" he has really dug in the bands he has led the last forty some odd years.

As a super player of a super big horn, Nick Brignola has well earned his admittance to the "House of Jazz."

And as for the band on this album, Dick Berk's words capture its essence: "I have never heard Bill and Nick play so inspiringly. We just ate up this session! Man, this band ought to play together and go on the road!"

CHAPTER 7

Bass

The bass is a hugely important instrument. It governs the pulse of the band; as the bass breathes, so does the band. It has such a warm tone and trajectory. Given the number of different techniques that can be used to vary the ways in which the instrument can be played, the bass serves a very versatile role in the band. Sometimes it's hard to discern the subtleties that come from the instrument; but the subtle sounds of the bass are as vital to the whole as any other part of the ensemble.

Of all the players I've ever known, Milt Hinton is *the* top of mind bassist for me—and also for most of the jazz artists I know.

—·—··—··—··—··—··—··—··—··—··—··—··—··—·—

Milt Hinton

Milt Hinton has been on more recordings than just about anyone else in the jazz world; everybody and his brother wanted Milt to play in their recording sessions. He was so dependable; you could always count on him. You would always know that whatever Milt played would be not only essential ... it would be perfect. You didn't have to tell him anything; he knew, intuitively, what to play.

Milt is equally well known for his exquisite and extensive work in the field of photography. He is the visual historian of jazz. I've been in his home near Queens, where he had file cabinet after file cabinet filled with photos. And then he would point to a bed nearby and say, "That's where Ben Webster would hang out and sleep." They were obviously very tight friends. Nearby was Count Basie's home, just down the street. It was quite a neighborhood and it was a privilege for me to visit and be a part of his digs.

"Grandmaster of Jazz"
Jazz Educators Journal, Winter 1993

Grandmaster of the jazz bass Milt Hinton is a 1993 recipient of the National Endowment for the Arts "American Jazz Masters" Award. A 1991 honoree of the same award and M.C. of this year's award ceremonies, Dr. Billy Taylor describes Hinton: "Milt Hinton is really the walking history of jazz—one of the people I respect the utmost both as a musician and as a rare living repository of information of the first person. Milt is irreplaceable!"

Indeed, Taylor is keenly on target with this recent prompt response to my invitation for an ad hoc assessment of Hinton. Rare and extraordinary, Milton J. Hinton is one of the most charitable, charmingly charismatic, warmly humorous, witty, and caring human beings on the planet. Pushing toward his 83rd birthday midyear, Hinton has played his instrument—the acoustic bass—in coincidence with the whole of jazzdom's growth and development with an immeasurable majority of the key musicians involved with the art-form; he has played on hundreds upon hundreds of recordings and in performances, embracing a broad plain of styles, contexts, and vintages—from Louis Armstrong to Branford Marsalis, Charles Mingus and John Coltrane, from Billie Holiday and Pearl Bailey to Barbra Streisand and Frank Sinatra, and from Frankie Avalon and Paul McCartney to symphony orchestras.

During his more than six decades on the scene and appropriately esteemed as the Dean of Jazz Bassists, Hinton defined the art and craft of bass playing far longer with far more eminent success and in far more diverse situations than anyone. Moreover, Hinton is affectionately nicknamed "The Judge," a response to the insightful, helpful counsel, and compassionate mentoring he has tended to musicians of all stripes through the years.

Illustrative of the deep heartfelt appreciative feelings musicians have for him are hereby a string of samplings of the dozens of tributes to him by jazz bassists on the occasion of Hinton's 80th birthday in 1990 … here are some thoughtful judgments on "The Judge" via Chiaroscuro Records and Hank O'Neal:

"Milt is the standard that all of us try to measure up to."—**Ron Carter**

"Milt is a sterling example to all bassists, both musically and personally. His playing has always personified the very best jazz music has to offer: warmth, joy, the blues, humor, love, and of course, indefatigable swing! He has always inspired me to give 110% and always has a kind and encouraging word. I hope that his legacy will always be a part of my musical being. Thanks, Judge, for being you."—**Todd Coolman**

"I met Milt 'Judge' Hinton in 1942 when I was in the U.S. Navy, and we have been in contact with each other since. I feel that Milt has been the inspiration of all bass players to 'play the bass' in all respects, whether jazz, classics, movie soundtracks, gospel, chamber groups, Latin, bass choirs etc.—He did it. He's doing it, and is still competing for future horizons. 'The Judge' has touched all the basses."—**Major Holley**

"Milt Hinton, in short, possesses integrity, vitality, sincerity, a love for others, and is a beacon of light for all of us to be guided by. He is a great role model for me in every way. As a musician, I can't say enough. As a bassist, he is a rock of Gibraltar."—**Rufus Reid**

"Milt Hinton plays in a style that never goes out of style. In his long career, he has been a positive role model for all musicians, and has earned the title of 'The Judge.' We are fortunate to have such a person in the forefront of the jazz scene."—**Harvie Swartz**

"Milt Hinton is one of the most wonderful human beings that I have ever met. He is always willing to help or give advice to channel whichever direction his peer or fellow bassist wants to go. And Oh! can he play that bass, with his various techniques. He is certainly one of the major founders of the jazz bass violin, and an inspiration to all who play or listen to music."—**J.J. Wiggins**

"Milt Hinton is the source from which many of us have derived concept, style, ideas and inspiration. His musicianship and humanity have touched us all. Thank you, Milt."—**Eddie Gómez**

Born in Vicksburg, Mississippi, on June 23, 1910, he was raised and schooled in Chicago beginning at age nine. In his school bands and music education, he learned to play several instruments—tuba, bass horn, cello, and, of course, the bass violin. While he was attending Northwestern University, he opted to leave to perform with such pioneering jazz figures as Art Tatum, Zutty Singleton, Jabbo Smith, Erskine Tate, and Eddie South among others during the late 1920s and early 1930s. Beginning in 1936, he spent fifteen years in Cab Calloway's band which afforded him opportunities to play with the likes of Ben Webster, Chu Berry, Dizzy Gillespie, Jonah Jones, Illinois Jacquet, and Ike Quebec. In my own record collection, Hinton is easily found resplendently on numerous classics accompanying Teddy Wilson, Billie Holiday, Benny Carter, Lionel Hampton, Pee Wee Russell, and Coleman Hawkins, as examples—concurrent with his Calloway experience.

After his Calloway period, Hinton became an active freelance habitué in NYC radio/ television recording studios, and performed at countless jazz concerts, parties, festivals and other settings around the globe. Currently he resides in Queens, NYC, and has been there over four decades.

It is clear that jazz education is precious to the sharing of his resources and spirit. His enthusiasm for working with students is unbounded as he spoke glowingly about his active, ongoing streams of jazz workshops, first at Manhattan's Hunter College and now at Baruch College. "There are no written exams as such but every student writes something and presents it in concert to the people. Then once a year, I play at a Children's Concert at Temple with their combos; students are between the ages of twelve to twenty. I try to instill in them the art of listening whether in a performing role or as listener/ observers." Hinton promotes his best students on his personally created record label named Exposure Records.

It is purely axiomatic that his ears are always open to the ranks of the new, exceptional, youthful musicians just as he is alertly curious about fresh music. He likewise pointed out his positive perspectives in teaching a master class in summer at Skidmore College. "The future is very bright for the music. Young, eager bass students come from all over to study with me, jazz history, the bass, and to participate in combo work. We are like a family; we lunch together and play at faculty/student concerts together."

Speaking of Skidmore, the college awarded Hinton an honorary doctorate. Also, he has received three other doctoral degrees conferred by William Paterson College of New Jersey, Hamilton College in New York, and DePaul University in Chicago. His impressive, tall stack of honors include highlights such as membership in the Duke Ellington Fellowship at Yale, the "Eubie" award for the New York Chapter of NARAS, the "Benny Carter Award" from the American Federation of Jazz Societies, Newport Festival Hall of Fame, and his expertise and quality service have had significant impact on other organization roles—Bass Chairman for the International Association of Jazz Educators, Panel member for the National Endowment for the Arts, and Board member of the International Society of Bassists. In 1990, the latter honored him by establishing the Milton J. Hinton Scholarship Fund to assist advanced jazz students of the acoustic bass and to pursue private bass instruction.

The ISB dedicated its New York Convention to Hinton's 80th birthday. "One hundred bassists played Happy Birthday to me at Lincoln Center. Dick Hyman orchestrated 'The Judge Meets the Section'; I played the cadenza arco, the bassists answered me and I went into my slap bass and they played pizzicato. The symphony orchestra was spirited too. Ron Carter, Richard Davis, Major Holley, Ray Brown, Bob Haggart, Jack Kesberg, Eddie Gómez, John Clayton, Charnett Moffett, and Lonnie Plaxico (one of our scholarship holders) all played with Rufus Reid conducting."

Hinton's eventful lifetime of creative work as a superb musician, accomplished photo and oral historian, and dedicated educator has included the founding of his elephant portfolio of photographs of jazz artists which has culminated in recent years in the form of several milestone books. *Bass Line: The Stories and Photographs of Milt Hinton* is a true work of art about his life and the subculture of the eras of the jazz life and jazz musicians—an insider's views of a special genre of substance preserved in 186 photos chosen from more than 25,000 Hinton photographs—mainly informal, candid snaps and his acute remembrances. This autobiographical volume was written in collaboration with David G. Berger, Professor of Sociology, Temple University who at fifteen met Hinton— seeking bass lessons in 1956—who befriended Berger and, subsequently, their near life-long friendship blossomed into a devotion to organizing Hinton's photos through the years. Without competition, it is one of the most flowing and stimulating real life documents which, like the sequel publication *Overtime: The Jazz Photographs of Milt Hinton*, should be required references for all jazz history curricular courses. *Bass Line* is published by Temple University Press, Philadelphia 1988. And *Overtime* is published by Pomegranate Art Books, Box 808022, Petaluma, CA 91975 and includes collaborators Berger—Director of Hinton's Photographic Collection—and Holly Maxson, the archivist/ conservator.

Joe Williams summarizes: "For me, Milt's pictures are a slice of history of very happy times, of making music and harmonies together." And Hinton tells me he is in the process of preparing a third volume from his collection of over 60,000 photos. Wow! Another artful treasure to look forward to! Milt, you are a gas! The worlds of music are grateful to you!

Red Mitchell

In his day, Red Mitchell was one of the most in-demand bass players in the Hollywood/L.A. scene. He was constantly in and out of the studios—until he got turned off by all the political crap that was going on. He left the States and moved to Stockholm, where he lived for many years, to focus on playing jazz. He started coming back when his wife, Diane, assuming the role of his manager, began to generate stateside performance opportunities for him.

I knew that Red favored the context of a bassist and guitarist playing together. So when I met with Joe Beck, who was a known factor in the New York scene at the time, we had a long conversation about the possibility of Joe working with Red … and the recording *Live at Salishan* was the result.

Red Mitchell was one of most intelligent musicians I have ever met. He was a worldly individual … you could not let go of him, because he had so much to contribute. He left this world on November 8, 1992, not long after he and Diane had settled into their Oregon home.

Red Mitchell with Joe Beck—*Live at Salishan*
Capri Records (74033–2); 1994

Uncounted precious, artful moments of jazz occur without being recorded for retrieval. This is, of course, not uncommon. But when in-person performances are made rare by virtue of the musicians involved, a documentation of the event is, indeed, a choice decision and ensures high potential for very special and rewarding results.

The illuminating experiences of master jazz bassist Red Mitchell and guitarist Joe Beck demonstrate how greatly fulfilling their close synergy and instrumental conversations can be. About a dozen years ago the pair had recorded "live" at Bradley's in New York—promptly after their first meeting each other. Precisely the same fundamental ground rule of complete spontaneity was applied to their approach on this disc as it likewise informs their ad hoc duo performances.

Placing this March 1992 event historically, Mitchell had recently returned with his wife Diane to live on U.S. turf in Salem, Oregon after he had chosen to expatriate to Stockholm in 1968. His trips to the States had been more frequent in recent years coinciding with enlarging interest in jazz in America.

In 1991, at Jim and Mary Brown's highly reputed annual jazz party weekend at Otter Crest on the Oregon coast, Mitchell contemplated doing an encore to the 1980 New York recording with Beck, entitled *Empathy*. As fortune will influence at times, the Browns relocated their event this year to the beautiful Salishan Lodge, south of Lincoln City and this disc was made in the intimate lounge of the Lodge with an audience of around 200. It also marked the start of their tour through Just Jazz in St. Louis and the Sweet Basil in New York.

The reprise celebrates the magnificent tapestries of their improvisations, making up a living moment to moment musical portfolio, laced by creative flows of eloquence— what a joy to eavesdrop to savor a private, vivid stimulating conversation, riding freely between meshes of their candid texts and unvoiced spaces. Mitchell and Beck are playful colorists who paint with peaked passions and precise discipline.

"The duo format is the smallest possible society as it's not a solo but a group effort," explains Mitchell. "But there's more freedom while there are more demands on both players. I love it! It's definitely my favorite format." About the keen intuitiveness between him and Beck: "We do best when we're playing a tune we haven't played together—it's a tight rope with no safety net except that we care for each other, and this could be interpreted as an unspoken safety net; I could make a mistake and Joe would make a minor symphony out of it ... he's that quick!"

Reciprocal assent is expressed by Beck, "Red makes a mistake sound good. He's so fast in reacting to a musical direction in our solos, they sound like they're planned. We prime ourselves to react to improvisation and actually the more we plan things, the more we enjoy the unplanned ones—things we do for the first time. At times we'll play a club and agree not to play anything we've played in the past months; Red will suddenly pull something out of the hat we've never ever mentioned. He is unpredictable as he is so spontaneous, and I can't ever lose Red because he always has an appropriate response."

Both Mitchell and Beck are so musical and possess such gigantic ears! Their large palettes of affluent assets are reflected in their performances. Sunny dispositions light up the music. They make Ellington's "In a Mellow Tone" sound like his orchestra. Beck's own tender ballad "What Would I Do Without You" is a reference to his wife, Marsi. "Blues for Gremlins" memorializes the multiple nagging problems and gremlins they experienced during their closing number—e. g., the pick guard fell off, and Red acquired a buzz in his bass plus numerous other disturbing occurrences and hang-ups.

The alluring combination of Joe Beck's pianistic melody-harmony-bass line approach to the guitar and Red Mitchell's celebrated innovation of tuning his string bass in fifths literally creates a unique conjugation of notes. And Mitchell gets the "longest and slowest crescendos I've ever gotten," surpassing the sonic quality of most horn players. "Salishan," explains Mitchell, "comes from a native American Indian concept meaning a coming together from diverse points to communicate in harmony." Indeed this gorgeous music at Salishan is simply not to be missed.

Ray Brown

What a concept! All bass, all the time, without a single other instrument present. And what a lineup! Bass masters Ray Brown, John Clayton and Christian McBride ... all together ... all on one disc ... no wonder they called it "super."

Ray was responsible for bringing *SuperBass 2* about. He had been recording for Telarc Records and, prior to this release, Ray had been experimenting with musicians playing their own instruments exclusively—no other instruments appeared on the recordings. It was a part of a series of about a dozen CDs Ray was doing, each with an emphasis on a particular instrument: saxophones, pianos, trumpets. *SuperBass 2* was the highlight of the venture.

Ray judiciously selected two of very best bass players in the business—John Clayton and Christian McBride—who looked to Ray as the guru, which he was. With all three playing at once, they slayed their appreciative Blue Note audience!

Ray Brown with John Clayton and Christian McBride—
SuperBass 2
Telarc Jazz (CD 83483); 2001; Reissued by Concord Records

SuperBass 2 is a natural sequel to the 1996 debut CD recorded live at Scullers in Boston. An overdue reprise project, this souvenir of the final three nights at the Blue Note jazz club caps a twelve-night performance stream which began in Seattle's Jazz Alley and culminated in New York City.

SuperBass (the band name *and* the title of the first CD) was born seven years ago. The episodic occasions on which SuperBass gets together every year or so are veritable rare treats. A jazz group consisting of just three jazz bassists is easily a mind-boggler for the uninitiated with no experience with the SuperBass plurality of spirited music. There may also be a shadow of dubiousness cast on its prospects. Curiosity, however, is satisfied, as the challenges are in the remarkable hands of three world-class jazz bass players who also bring a classical backdrop to the performance credentials. Considering the formidable summit of Ray Brown, John Clayton, and Christian McBride in one breath is nothing short of "wow!" enthusiasm and interest despite their departure from a fixed, conventional norm and context. And their reunions are infrequent simply because each one of them is crammed to capacity with many projects, recordings, and playing with his own cluster of bands.

Useful to the understanding and esteem for SuperBass is a sharp reorientation of values; i.e., there is the commonly perceived role of the bass as a traditional part of the rhythm section or "back line." Seeing the three premier bassists appearing alone on stage may seem like an incomplete band. But SuperBass is internally-externally complete because it is also the "front line" achieving the fluency and flavors of horns. Also, "we got 'em covered musically and entertainment-wise—a complete package," notes Ray Brown. "People don't realize how much music you can get out of three bassists." Serving as color multipliers, they bind their interwoven voices and subtleties of tone. Each bassist is an extension of his own personality—traits coming through their prismatic temperament, nuances, and rhythmic attitude—peppered with deep passion and wit.

A living legend of Olympian stature, Ray Brown is one of the original creators of bebop. His long, illustrious career is replete with historical associations and events, recordings and highlights. "Ray is so important to so many musicians on the scene—besides bass players," says McBride. "A man of great depth and wisdom—it's a privilege to spend time with him even if it's not musical. Hang with him! Get some of that energy from him!" Brown was Clayton's mentor from the time he was a budding aspirant. "Ray's the master of the bass—a pivotal player. He bridged the gap between swing and bebop. He was a young man playing with Charlie Parker, Dizzy Gillespie, Bud Powell," says Clayton. "Ray is one of few bassists of this generation who has gotten progressively better by leaps and bounds. He practices all the time."

The warm camaraderie among the trio is powerful. Their genuine mutual admiration includes embracing their respective strengths. About McBride, Clayton points out, "Standing next to him, you can really understand how phenomenal he is. He does things—feel-wise, groove-wise, and note-choice-wise that you cannot teach." Brown adds, "McBride is eatin' the bass alive! He's going up and down like a banjo! He and John have all the ingredients—swing, good sound, ferocious chops, a sense of great time, and they can bow. John is a consummate bass player; his forte is bowing. This band—it's just a delight, we just had a ball on the bandstand every night."

Of prime importance is Brown's strong stand on how very serious their playing is. "Everyone in SuperBass is a serious player, but we want to have fun with it, especially with the two vocals." There is excitement in feeling the unleashed energy amidst the seriousness and energies. "It's great to have guys like John and Christian around to keep my juices flowing and to keep me on my toes. I've led them down a path for years—they're taking over now. They've blossomed as major league players."

The music for the live recording is a balance between new pieces of work or arrangements and the impromptu jam tunes. Brown had all three of them contribute an equal number of new pieces to the group. As a warm-up, "we rehearsed the material and started playing it on the Seattle gig," recants Brown. "We began recording on the last gig weekend at the Blue Note." The parity of the material was reflective of an insistent perspective of Brown. Clayton recaps, "Ray told Christian and me that he wanted us to understand SuperBass is a co-op of three bass players—not one guy with two side bass players."

Clayton's observation of the Blue Note during the nights of recording is valuable input. "The air was thick with the oeuvre and this total energy—everybody loved the trio. A lot of jazz artists were in the audience; e.g., Regina Carter, Benny Green, Diana Krall, Monty Alexander, and a crowd of bassists like Bob Cranshaw and Jay Leonhart."

Brown's savoir faire as a presenter sets up the shows with taste, sensitivity, and rapport. The sets began with SuperBass' signature theme. On this CD, there's a transition into McBride's arrangement of "Get Happy," followed by one of Thelonious Monk's blues—"Mysterioso," a Clayton arrangement.

The first of two audience vocal participation selections—"Papa Was a Rolling Stone"—is the old Temptations hit tune. What a crowd grabber this dancin', prancin' McBride entry is. McBride recalls, "Ray is quite a 'fun-meister.' He said he'd like me to be the instigator for SuperBass—to bring in something to get everyone all riled up. So I searched in my mind for a novelty vehicle and 'Papa' came up." No wonder Clayton says, "McBride often ends up doing something greasy and flashy."

Deeply serious, lustrous bass playing is articulated in its varied subtexts in the creative musings of Brown's arrangement of Gershwin's *Porgy and Bess* music. Dig the superb bowing, the horn-like voicings, wonderfully stitched bass lines, propulsive bass patterns stretched over the terrain of "Summertime," "Porgy," and "It Ain't Necessarily So." "We gave it much respect in how we played it," reminds Brown.

The format of a pair of showcase jam duos finds Brown featuring the nimble McBride on the 1950 Dizzy Gillespie bebop classic "Birks' Works" and the brilliant arco playing of Clayton on "My Funny Valentine." Deep!

Clayton's melodically tenacious and appealing "Three by Four" is gleefully infectious with a rhythmic attitude that resists going away.

If you're not ready for Brown's funky Latin show-stopper "Taco with a Pork Chop," then be alert! Its surprising buoyancy will snag your attention. "I snuck up on those guys with it. I get these little whims about every twenty years. The last time I had one of these whims, it became a hit song—'Gravy Waltz.' This is whim number 2. It's a social statement on reality (without a lyric)," explains Brown. It's a lot deeper than the song title at face value. It points to the Los Angeles populace—that if blacks and Mexican-Americans were to unite, they would constitute a strong political entity. So Brown is saying, "Let's combine the two groups to gain powerful clout vis-à-vis 'Taco with a Pork Chop' (using ethnic food symbols)."

It feels so good to surrender to the lively interchanges between artist and artist and between artists and audience, making this *SuperBass 2* snapshot a hip, durably rewarding event.

CHAPTER 8

Trombone

The trombone is somewhat of an awkward instrument to play, unless you have consummate facility with it. The instrument promotes a range of very different, very distinctive sounds—and I have found most trombonists have a certain distinctiveness about themselves as well.

Guys like Phil Wilson, who used to be with Woody's band, made a name for themselves on trombone. In those days, nobody played the trombone like Phil did. He, in turn, was influenced by Vic Dickenson, a trombonist from another, earlier era, who played with Count Basie. But Phil turned the trombone into a very personal, different instrument. Phil was in Woody's band on the *Live at Lake Tahoe* album and, with his trombone, he created a sound you'll never forget ... a big, swooping sound unlike any other.

When I think of today's trombonists, Robin Eubanks immediately comes to mind.

Robin Eubanks

Robin Eubanks sounds like no one else on the trombone. His concepts—and his ability to translate those concepts into a sound—are like nothing else. He takes a concept and, through his horn, he creates a sentence; and then he makes the sentence complete, fitting it perfectly into the larger paragraph of music.

Robin is one of a number of well known brothers—Kevin Eubanks is his younger brother—and he has a great personality; he's such a nice guy, always open, and always willing to be flexible ... he is just a nice cat.

For all those reasons, Robin is an in-demand trombonist who has played with a number of different groups and remains one of the very best.

A Conversation with Robin Eubanks
Oakland, California; March 1999

> **Wong:** Let's review a little about your home situation. Were there recordings?
> **Eubanks:** Yes, plenty of records around.
> **Wong:** Is that how you first got interested in this creative music?
> **Eubanks:** In jazz, you mean?
> **Wong:** Yes ...
> **Eubanks:** No, I didn't get into jazz really until I was about 20.

Wong: Were you playing the instrument prior to that?

Eubanks: Yes, I started playing when I was 8. I was playing mostly funk and rock music. All those horn bands they had in the '70s. So we were playing that kind of music.

Wong: Were your parents in some kind of musical relationship at all?

Eubanks: My mom was a music teacher. She taught in the school system and taught privately at home, so I would hear the piano all the time.

Wong: And your dad?

Eubanks: Not musically inclined per se. He was an amateur kind of guy. Harmonica and an old flute.

Wong: Did you have private lessons?

Eubanks: Yes, the first 6 years I played, it was all private lessons.

Wong: Did you play a lot of classical or chamber music?

Eubanks: Yes, the first 6 years I played, it was all classical.

Wong: How long did you play classical?

Eubanks: All the way through high school and college. Mostly it was through high school. In college I concentrated more on jazz. I went to Temple University for a few years and then I graduated from what is now known as The University of the Arts. When I first went there it was Philadelphia Music Academy, then it was called Philadelphia College of Performing Arts. Now it's University of the Arts.

Wong: Would you describe how you became infected with jazz?

Eubanks: I just started listening to it. First to try and understand improvisation better, because my solos were so sad that I wanted to improve. Some of my friends and I would play some recordings and things and I would check that out and listen to it. It got to be very interesting. I heard Dizzy and Bird play "Shaw 'Nuff" and couldn't believe that two people could think that quickly and play together like that. Then I started studying a little bit and I quickly realized that in jazz, they had one of the best documentations of African American history. By studying the history of jazz, you were also studying the history of black people in this country. So I got into it from that perspective. That's what really hooked me a lot.

Wong: You said you had done some studies. Was that course work or private?

Eubanks: Mostly reading. Just trying to study, because they didn't have a curriculum … there wasn't any "jazz studies" at school. Then around my junior year, they started a jazz program at University Arts.

Wong: Was there any particular person or persons that turned you on, other than the recordings you just mentioned to me? Was there some person or mentor?

Eubanks: Not in the beginning. I was hearing the music a lot. My uncle, Ray Bryant, used to come by the house and I used to hear him play. He used to bring Papa Jo Jones around sometimes. There was plenty of contact, but I wasn't really into the music at that point. I guess the first mentor I'd say I had was Slide Hampton, when I finally met him. That was after I graduated from University Arts. He had just come back from Europe. His *Sophisticated Giant* album, the one he arranged for Dexter Gordon, was out and Slide came to town to play. I sat in with him one night and he asked me to join his trombone choir, the World of Trombones. That's when I first met Slide and then I started going to New York every weekend rehearsing and staying at his place. He gave me keys to his apartment, so I used to stay there and we used to practice together for hours and hours and hours.

Wong: Would you be able to describe stylistically how you play jazz on your instrument? I can identify you when I hear you play. There is just a certain quality of your sound and that gives me the biggest cue; and then I try to listen to how you're attacking the assignments. It's hard to nail down any specific style, per se. You are just you. That's it.

Eubanks: It's hard for me to define. I just know what I try to convey, and the sound is the most important thing to me—and articulation. Making sure things are clean, clear and precise. As precise as I can make it. And lots of rhythmic kinds of things. Rhythmic ideas. I like to approach trombone like a percussion instrument—rhythmically. I would think those are the main three things. I'm trying to develop more harmonic stuff. It comes out from time to time, but not to the degree that I want it to yet.

Wong: What do you consider to be your most important or memorable recordings of your own? You've done quite a number now.

Eubanks: Well, of my own, which I led, *Mental Images* is my favorite. I like that the best because it incorporates a lot of the things that I'm working on now. A lot of the odd meter funk type stuff. We tried to incorporate some of the electronics I'm using with the trombone and African rhythms and things like that.

Wong: What other ones do you have esteem about?

Eubanks: I like the albums I did with Kevin.

Wong: Which one is that?

Eubanks: *Spirit Talk*. We did two of those. I like the album we just did with Dave.

Wong: *Points of View*?

Eubanks: Actually the one we recorded in December, that hasn't come out yet, I like even more.

Wong: You told me about that today. You said "Wait 'til you hear this one!"

Eubanks: Yeah, it is better I think.

Wong: It's carrying through what you guys have done on *Points of View* and forward?

Eubanks: Well, we hadn't really played together on *Points of View*. This one we played together for over a year, so we knew the songs we'd been playing for a long time. We got the chance to record them. So, they were developed; but it's usually the other way around—you record and then go out on tour.

Wong: What do you consider some of your most historical associations?

Eubanks: Obviously, Art Blakey and Elvin Jones. I'm working with Elvin Jones' band now.

Wong: Are you going to come into town with him?

Eubanks: No ... and it's the *second* West Coast tour that I have missed. It's the same one as last year, because I had a conflict with Dave's dates. Fortunately, both band leaders are flexible enough that they allow me to miss some gigs with their bands. It's interesting, that when I don't make it, they don't replace me with a trombone player.

Wong: What does that tell you ... you're irreplaceable? ... by virtue, that is, of their behavior, in a sense.

Eubanks: Well, I try not to read into it. I just appreciate that I'm able to make the other gigs.

Wong: Tell me something about the one with Elvin. He's a pretty inspiring guy, isn't he?

Eubanks: Oh, amazing! I think he's the greatest jazz drummer ever, for a number of reasons. He's really incredible; I've never heard anybody that has his sense of time and rhythm and space. I used to study it on record a lot. Now that I get to see him on stage for extended periods of time, I *still* don't know what he's doing. I'm watching him like a hawk. When I'm not playing, I'm watching him—and I still don't have any clue what he's doing. I'm starting to see into a little of it, but it's really amazing. Also, the fact that he's able to play better than ever at 71 is whole other testament as to where he's coming from.

Wong: His deep intuitiveness has always amazed me. It's just instant. He's where he has to be.

Eubanks: We had an instant lock-up when we played together. It was really, really nice. I've always loved his playing. The Trane Quartet is my favorite band of all time. I got a chance to play with McCoy and, of course, I'm playing with Elvin now. I'm getting to play with half of my favorite band. I can't even imagine what it was really like when all four of them were together. I got to play with two segments of it. Not even at the same time, but he's really something.

I used to see him play at the Vanguard a lot when I first came to New York, around 1980. I'd tape record him and listen to him and wish I'd get a chance to play with him. Then, in February of '98, I had a gig in Boston at the Regattabar; they needed to get a horn player and Sonny Fortune recommended me. I did those couple of gigs and he said he wanted me to join the band.

Wong: That must have thrilled you to death. It was quite a compliment.

Eubanks: Oh yeah, it was amazing! And it's continuing now. I told him, like I just told you, I like to approach the trombone like a percussion instrument. He said "I can tell."

Wong: Who else is in the band?

Eubanks: Sonny Fortune, of course. Carlos McKinney and the bass chair has been changing a little bit, but the last gigs it was Cecil McBee. There's another young bass player, named Greg Williams who does it sometimes.

Wong: You know Elvin was on my label for awhile … amazing!

Eubanks: He's a very incredible person. He's one of the very unique people I've had an opportunity to play with and get to know a little bit. He's very distinctive.

Wong: Do you get creative juices from playing with him? Obviously, he stimulates you and inspires you. How do you get that from him? He doesn't tell you?

Eubanks: No. Just the way he responds to what I do.

Wong: And you can feel that?

Eubanks: Oh, yes. He listens very, very well to what you're doing.

Wong: And that helps to pump you?

Eubanks: Definitely. He can deal with whatever I throw out.

Wong: So has the relationship with Elvin spurred you into areas you might not have explored? They help to open the gates?

Eubanks: I don't think it's put me into things I haven't explored, but it's helped to strengthen and reinforce what I was trying to do. A friend of mine, who hadn't heard me play in about a year and used to play in my band … Michael Kay … he was up in Boston last week when I was playing with Elvin. He told me, "You and Elvin have really got the connection. I can hear all the stuff you were trying a year or two ago really getting crystalized." So, I was happy to hear that. You know, it's so gradual for me, I don't really notice it. I think I'm playing better than I've ever played.

Wong: What are a couple of these things that he's referring to as being "crystalized?"

Eubanks: Just the freedom and the rhythmic concept as far as just being able to do whatever I wanted to do. Like I play the same way with Art Blakey, but Art would say, "That's my job." All the rhythm stuff.

Wong: He told you that?

Eubanks: He said, "Get out of there, don't be playing my stuff." He was half way joking, but only half way; half serious, half not. But Elvin welcomes it and he loves it; that's what he's into. His wife, Kieko, told me, "You make Elvin very, very happy. When you play with Elvin, you play whatever you want." So that's exactly what I do.

Wong: You were with Art Blakey at what period?

Eubanks: I was with him at two periods. The first time was in 1980; he had the big band together. It's when they added the two sets of brothers. Kevin and me, Wynton and Branford Marsalis. We went to Europe and did a recording and did a tour. Then I joined the sextet in '87 and '88.

Wong: Was there any difference between the two periods?

Eubanks: Only that it was just the personnel and the smaller group and getting to play more. I was music director. The other thing is, I really feel fortunate. I've been able to play with five or six of my favorite drummers. Since I've tried to approach trombone like a percussion instrument, I have a strong affinity to drummers and percussion. Playing with Art and Elvin and Philly Joe Jones—another one of my favorites. I got to play with him when I was like 20. Another one was Roy Haynes. The other two I haven't gotten to play with are Max and I never got a chance to play with Tony Williams. So to me, they were the best drummers in the era … that I've been alive, anyway.

Wong: It seems your ambitions have been fulfilled quite a bit with these associations.

Eubanks: I'm very fortunate. I'm in a good space right now, working more than I've ever worked in my life. '98 was the busiest I ever had and '99 is continuing more of the same.

Wong: And does that permit you spend time composing as well? I know you write.

Eubanks: It doesn't give me a lot of time. Also, February of '98, the same time I got Elvin's gig, I got another job where I teach at Oberlin. So between Elvin and Dave and Oberlin, I'm moving non-stop pretty much.

Wong: How do you maintain that schedule? It has to be irregular.

Eubanks: I go there between tours. I was there before this started. Before we came *here*, I was *there*. When I was in Boston last week, I flew straight to Cleveland to teach. And then, when I finish this two weeks with Dave, we finish in Chicago. The day after that, I go back to Oberlin. I fit it in at the beginning or end of gigs.

Wong: And the students do maintain some sense of continuum?

Eubanks: Oh yes, definitely. I have a page on my website for them so they can stay in touch while I'm on the road.

Wong: Tell me, in your opinion, what are some of the most meaningful albums in jazz … ones that are important to you.

Eubanks: Several of the albums with the "Trane" quartet. *A Love Supreme*. A whole lot of those. *Live at Birdland* I like a lot. That band and the Miles quintet band, with Wayne, Tony and Ron. *Live at the Plugged Nickel*. Those are my favorite ones of that. Art Blakey's sextet is one of my favorite bands also. I like a lot of stuff. Things that got me into listening to odd meters and that kind of thing, which I'm really, really into now. The Mahavishnu Orchestra *The Inner Mounting Flame* was very, very influential.

Wong: How do you improvise? Don't you have to have some inspiration to do that?

Eubanks: The first class, I just talked for the first 15 minutes and just asked people questions. I'd ask them a question and have them answer me. Like … if I asked you your name, you say "Wong." If I asked you what do you do and why you do it? And you tell me and I say, well we were just improvising. You didn't know what I was going to say. I didn't know what you were going to say, and you were just responding. Telling them this, it's the most natural thing. People do it all day every day, their whole lives. Right now we're improvising using English. If you want to use music, you have to develop your vocabulary and syntax and sentence structure just as you do to communicate in a language. So you are just using music as a language, but it's very, very natural.

Wong: Quality of improvisations I distinguish by something that may be harder to pin down. Those of you who come up with an improvisation that's, oh … precious … how did you come up with that? I guess a lot of it has to do with imagination as well?

Eubanks: For me, it's a very spiritual kind of thing also. I've been a Buddhist now for 15 years. Every day, chanting and studying it, and I think it's really given me a strong foundation and a strong vantage point, too. A strong perspective to draw upon and to view things from, where I am able to channel a lot of influences into myself and have them come out of me as opposed to sounding like somebody else.

Wong: Is that where most of your creative ideas come from?

Eubanks: Basically, it's just channeling. I just throw things into a funnel and let them all come out of me. I grab aspects of this over here and little bit of that over there. Instead of it sounding like this person over here and that person over there that I may have been influenced by, I blend in whatever influences are more prevalent at the time and use myself as the common denominator to try to get my perspective and my inflection.

Wong: Are there any typical or special conditions that you require? Or those that seem to enhance your process more.

Eubanks: I think a good drummer and a good rhythm section. Amazingly enough, a good audience. People don't realize how important they are to the process. They seem to think that they are just observing from the outside; but every time we finish playing and we are getting all the accolades, I'd say, "Thank you for coming, because if you weren't here, it wouldn't sound the same." Which is true. It's like the difference between a rehearsal and a gig. Or, another obvious comparison would be the difference between a gig and the studio. One of the main differences is that there is no audience. There's other differences, the way you set up and everything; still, the biggest difference is that you don't have anybody to interact with.

Wong: It's rhetorical to even say this, but the interplay that you have with your fellow musicians is critical. Somebody that has an attitude can dampen things.

Eubanks: For when I'm playing, they just need to be open rhythmically and harmonically to let me go where I want to go and be able to complement, which is what the word "comp" is short for. A lot of musicians don't "comp" me a solo. A good rhythm section is sensitive and actually becomes very integral because it becomes a part of a group improvisation. It's not like me playing with a Jamey Aebersold record or anything. They're listening to me and I'm listening to them and the song is greater than the parts.

Wong: When you create a jazz composition, are there any constraining factors involved with that? Do you need certain things to be able to usher in the creative process?

Eubanks: Not for me.

Wong: Whatever you're writing … for instance, on the record *Points of View* you did "Metamorphos"; we'll take that as an example. How did you do that?

Eubanks: It was one kind of sense of the rhythm that I've been studying for a while; about hearing the same rhythm and the same bass line from a lot of different angles. You can hear a beat, not to get too technical, but basically you could divide the beats into an infinite number of sub-divisions. I like to deal with the sub-divisions a lot. In "Metamorphos," for instance, there's the beat bass line cycle. First bar 4/4 then there's a bar 6/4. The 6/4 I sub-divide and make it into a whole lot of other things. The baseline stays the same, but everything changes around it. So that's how I started getting the title for the song.

Wong: Was it a sketch or a full blown composition?

Eubanks: It was almost an exercise to continue to try and develop this rhythmic concept that I'm working on. I just flesh things out. I write very fragmented, then I put pieces together. On my computer I have fragments of lots of things. I hear something now, but I may hear something tomorrow that may connect with something that I wrote last year. Then I try to find a way to put them together. To me it's a different thing composing and having the muse strike, so to speak. Whereas, it's something that's just coming like a flash of insight. I just try to document the flashes of insight then I use the craft of composition to weave them together in an interesting way.

Wong: You mentioned something about Steve Turre. How do you regard Slide and Steve and these other people—how are they important to you?

Eubanks: Oh, very important to me. The last CD that I put out was called *4: JJ / Slide / Curtis and Al*—my four biggest influences on trombone. It was to Al, Al Grey, and then I dedicated it to all of them. I'm very close with Jay. He has a website with a mailing list I post on and we stay in close contact. I've been calling him every year on his birthday for 10 years or so. We're very close now. Closer now than we've ever been. And Slide just took me under his wing and took very good care of me when I first came to New York. Curtis was one of the first trombone players that really inspired me. Al Grey was in Philadelphia, and he used to tutor me on certain things. So I had great examples of trombonists to aspire to. And when I see people like Elvin and a lot of really great musicians in their 70s, it's really inspirational to me. It gives me a lot to look forward to. Playing with Elvin and Art and J.J. My dad's about to be 70.

Wong: You're lucky. The younger kids don't know them.

Eubanks: They don't know these people. They don't have any interaction with them. I've been extremely fortunate that I've been able to spend as much time as I have and had those kinds of examples to look up to.

Wong: Fantastic models that won't come along again.

Eubanks: They may never come along. The thing is the music is changing so much.

Wong: Have you had to give up any particular things in life to pursue this career?

Eubanks: Well, there's a lot of sacrifice in being a musician, playing jazz. You know, family life. I haven't had to give it up, but it's something I haven't dealt with yet. But, hopefully, I'm going to deal with it soon. There's just a lot of sacrifice, when you compare your life to other people's lives. Just the fact that I've never had a "job" in my life. It's a whole different thing. My whole life I see as alternative, which I like actually. The music I play, the instrument I play, the religion I practice, my whole life style is completely off the norm. Ninety percent of the population works from 9 to 5. And does it for 10 … 20

... or 30 years. I've never done it once. The closest I had is when I worked on Broadway for two years. I hated it.

Wong: When was this?

Eubanks: It was in the '80s that I did Broadway. I make my living improvising—doing things differently—and down there, if you do something different, it's wrong.

Wong: But you were stuck with it because you needed it at the time?

Eubanks: It was the first steady paycheck I ever had in my life, because I never had a "job." So it was interesting. I saw a lot of people do it.

Wong: I wanted to ask you, what is this thing called jazz? It's a loaded question, but what is it for you?

Eubanks: Well, for me I see it as a continuum and I see it starting from the roots of Africa and our two cultures, merged over here. Basically, it reflects back to what I told you in the beginning of why I started getting into the music. I saw it as a great documentation of African American life in this country. It's transcended that to a large degree, where people are playing music all over the world.

I remember when I was playing with Art Blakey and we went to a jam session in Paris. One of the guys in Art Blakey's band said, "Man this guy can't play ... listen to the Parisian play," he said. "He sounds like a French guy trying to play jazz." And I said, "But he *is* French. You want him to sound like he's from Detroit—some black guy from Detroit? What's wrong with him being who he is?"

I thought that was one of the things that has really stunted the development of jazz, is that people are trying to emulate eras that have passed. So I see it as a continuum, I see it as reflecting the time you're living in. You know, bebop was revolutionary and incredibly amazing because it was created as a post World War II art form that developed here and was new and exciting. The guys that had been to Europe and seen things they had never seen before were being treated like they had never been treated before. So it was very liberating and it was all reflected in the music.

In the '60s, we had all the civil rights stuff and all kinds of other stuff and there was a lot of upheaval. We had the avant-garde developing. It was reflecting the time we were living in. We're going to be in 2000 next year and people are still playing the music like it's 1950. To me that's a problem. I like the fact that people are still doing that, because I wouldn't want that tradition to die.

At the same time, the people that are upholding that are the same ones that are really putting down people who are trying to do something else. It's the same kind of criticism that Bird and Duke got. Not to say the parallel, musically, is the same; but it's the same principle. They're saying something that's new and different—they're saying, "What is this? This it isn't jazz." To me it's a continuum. My stuff, based on the people that I've played with, is rooted in the tradition of the music; but I don't want to play the traditional music, I want to play stuff that represents my life span. I just want to add my little two cents to the branch on the tree. Hopefully, generations after me will add their branch. It just continues to develop and mirror society as opposed to being like a museum piece. Which some people are trying to do, and it has validity too, but don't be restrictive. What you're going to wind up doing is alienating the people that are coming up.

Wong: And then, also, the investment that people need to make doing this music is part of the continuum that is the future. There are things that should be happening now.

Eubanks: That's one of the reasons that I'm trying to use electronics and stuff. I'm on the computer every day. Why shouldn't I make that a part of my music? Everybody's on computers every day whether they know it or not, and to negate that, you know, as I said before, you have to have your own personal concept broad enough and strong enough to encompass other influences. As I said, I channel everything through me. I use myself as the conduit and the common denominator. I may grab something out of a hip-hop thing, but it won't necessarily sound hip-hop; but I hear an aspect of that that I may want to use in my music, but it'll come out the way I want it to come out.

Wong: Are you looking forward toward a recording project of your own to express some of these ideas?

Eubanks: Definitely. The closest one I've gotten to now is *Mental Images*. The next thing I'm going to do, I think, will definitely incorporate a lot of the stuff I'm doing now.

Wong: Are you tied to a label?

Eubanks: No, not really. I'm like an in-house producer for an independent label in London now call Sirocco Jazz. Of the last two records I did, I did one on Sirocco and one on TCB. They were mostly straight-ahead records, because that's what they wanted. I have nothing against that, but it's just not a growth thing. Almost 90 percent of the music I play is straight-ahead.

Wong: What about the growth factor or factors that are involved, hopefully, in your association right now with Dave Holland?

Eubanks: There's a whole lot of room for growth there, because the band is very, very open. I can bring in something like "Metamorphos," which is basically a funk tune, an odd metered thing, and play it. We go there and it sounds authentic. That was my whole concept. On my first record I had a Stevie Wonder song … I was playing straight-ahead on there … I was playing funk … I was playing odd meters. To me, the common denominator is that it's good music and it's coming through me. I like to check out all the directions and not just one.

Wong: So this particular environment is satisfying to you? You've got great players.

Eubanks: It's a great band. It's wide open. Dave's not as open to me using my electronics with his band … yet, anyway! I use other outlets for that, but everything else has been more than I could have hoped for.

Wong: What strikes you the most about Dave Holland's playing?

Eubanks: I guess the thing about him is his time. He's the best bass player for odd meters that I've ever played with. He's very good at it and he's like a rock on it. You can lean on him. Like I said before, the two main things that are most important for me or my thing, is sound and articulation. Those are two of the things that he's definitely very good at. He has lots of facility. You can hear every note. It's all clear. His sound is full. He has it all as far as I'm concerned.

Wong: Let me ask you one last thing. Do you have any reactions to my rationale for this project about creativity?

Eubanks: I think it's good. My whole thing is that people *can* be creative. As I was saying, improvisation is the most natural thing that people do. Everybody does it all day long when they're walking down the street. Any conversation is improvisation. It's good that the whole creative process is seen beyond the scope of music. People can be creative in their office job. They can be creative behind their desk in whatever they do. Not to just see it as a musical thing, but you can draw parallels by *you* asking these questions. People can draw parallels to other disciplines.

Wong: The reason I'm focusing on it is that I have a bias that jazz is a personification of the creative process. It is inherently a part of it. It has to be.

Eubanks: I think it's good. Personally, I'd love to hear the answers. I know my answers, but I'd love to hear everybody else's.

Wong: They're all different. There are some commonalities, but everybody has a very fresh kind of thing. You've had some things that no one else has mentioned. I really appreciate it.

Steve Turre

Steve Turre is a highly unusual musician, the only jazz musician extant who plays the sea shells—an entire range of sea shells that he uses to compose and improvise along with his trombone. He is a unique, supremely talented, and uncompromising musician. He displays a multitude of idiosyncrasies in his approach, eccentricities that characterize his range of ideas and expand that range—literally creating a battery of sounds.

He's a very creative trombonist who has demonstrated multiple extensions in his talent over the years, offering up more sounds than one would ever expect, sounds that greatly widen the potential of his instrument.

His idiosyncratic approach might be best exemplified by his use of those sea shells in his performances. If you need evidence of Steve Turre's uniqueness, just listen to him blow those shells!

Steve Turre—*Fire and Ice*
Stash Records (ST-CD-7); 1988

The re-surfacing of the jazz trombone has been dubious for a couple of decades, but pushing toward the 1990s there are perceivable signs of support for the movement. One indicator is clearly in the music of Steve Turre who has paid his dues on the trombone for many years.

When he was in high school in the mid-sixties, I caught him playing in varied situations in the San Francisco Bay Area, and later, more regularly at the Both/And—a yesteryear jazz club on Divisadero where Steve played with Rahsaan Roland Kirk, Prince Lasha, Charles Moffett and a host of other visiting stalwarts. His credits began piling up on tour with Ray Charles and then he was recruited by Art Blakey for the Jazz Messengers. Roosting in New York City in 1973, Steve played in the Thad Jones/Mel Lewis Orchestra, then joined Chico Hamilton and spent a significant five years with trumpeter Woody Shaw participating on ten Shaw recordings. Concurrent with his Shaw experience and hence, Steve affirmed his uniqueness as an instrumentalist/improviser through associations with dozens of leading cadre of modern jazz. In recent years his work included McCoy Tyner's big band, Lester Bowie's Brass Fantasy, Dizzy Gillespie's big band, his own shell choir, plus so many others.

For all his central virtues—fertile imagination, resourceful design of notes, distinctive sound, and deep emotional colors—Turre is a trombonist who conspicuously carries the integrity of tradition while peering into the future. It wasn't until 1987 that Steve recorded his first leader-credited album: *Viewpoint* (Stash ST-270, ST-C-270, ST-CD-2).

It is an auspicious album deserving keen attention. And, not incidentally, Steve blows various seashells with their humanized tones—a skill he picked up from Rahsaan back in the early sixties. Steve has over thirty shells representing a two octave plus range. He is phenomenal.

This second project, *Fire and Ice*, speaks eloquently to his growing stature as one of the most inspired and talented trombonists who has forged the best elements of his antecedents. An uncompromising musician, Steve has invested his values and insights into the undisputedly high quality of this recording, vaulting him to the top turf of trombonists extant. "The main thrust is the quartet—a sound that should be heard more in public," Steve describes. "I am awed, humbled and excited by the company of three of my favorite musicians—Cedar Walton, Buster Williams and Billy Higgins. And I want to fuel the trombone sound to be accessible—to re-awaken the consciousness of the jazz trombone."

Steve's impressive blowing opens up Steve's brisk composition, "Fire and Ice" … the concept is a blues with a bridge featuring the Quartet. Cedar and Buster steam with passion and swelled fullness.

A gorgeous ballad with strings, Steve's composition, "Juanita," utilizes the strings not by convention as background only. Check out the violin/trombone melody on the bridge and interplay at the end of Steve's solo. And dig Billy Higgins' dancing brushes. Resplendent music from the heart!

Ushered in by strings with John Blake soloing, Benny Carter's swinging classic, "When Lights Are Low," features Steve's rainbow colors on Harmon mute—an uncommon sound indeed for this genre, although it's routine to hear trumpets with Harmons. "I'm trying to develop this as a new sound for trombone jazz." Solos also flower from Cedar and Buster.

"Shorty" is another vivid Turre composition. It features his sensational seashells over the montuno. A deep Latin groove, there is strong melodic fiber and … energetic, creative spirit. Yeah!

"Andromeda" is an extraordinary piece featuring the Quartette Indigo alone. Named after Akua and Steve's daughter, it serves as an illustration of Steve's ability as a "serious" composer. A demanding, challenging piece of music, it offers the Quartette a display of their rhythmic riches. "All solos are improvised, yet the piece is highly structured and complex," summarizes Steve.

Stevie Wonder's "You Are the Sunshine of My Life" welcomes Jerry González's congas and güiro on a Latin groove. The strings swing with the rhythm and John Blake wails on his violin. Steve adds his irresistible shells. "You could dance (cha-cha) to this one," says Steve. "A funky feeling."

Thelonious Monk's infectious "Well, You Needn't" is akin to Steve's admiration for Monk's compositional prowess. The Quartet swings through and through.

"I Thought About You" ranks as one of Steve's favorite standard tunes. He says, "It captures my sound the way I like it." Steve unfurls a warm, personalized tapestry of tonal splendor and inviting excursions. And Cedar's and Buster's solos are full of new melodies.

"'Mood Indigo' is my tribute to Duke and the plunger." Sitting beside Quentin "Butter" Jackson, Ellington alumnus (who specialized in plunger-mute solos a la Tricky Sam Nanton) in Thad and Mel's big band, taught Steve about the speech-like "wahs" plunger effects. Solos are by Akua's cello, Melvin's viola, Steve, Cedar, and Billy's brushes. The Quartette Indigo is refreshing and brilliant.

Rahsaan's influence on Steve continues with "E.D."—a vehicle for Steve's speedway trips. "I played fast and had great fun doing it!"

"The recent comeback of the grand master of the jazz trombone, J.J. Johnson, my major influence" is a powerful lead to restore the trombone to its rightful place. Referring to the fresher trombone voices, J.J. in *DownBeat* (March 1988) cited Steve Turre as one of these deserving voices. Amen!

CHAPTER 9

Clarinet

The clarinet is not a common instrument in a jazz musician's world. It's personified by the facility of both Benny Goodman and Artie Shaw. Artie enjoyed a tremendous reputation with an historically poor ending. At the height of his orchestra's popularity, playing in all the posh places, he dropped the clarinet. And the world of jazz was saddened.

The clarinet's position in jazz—in particular, in modern jazz—is rooted in the 1920s and '30s, when the clarinet was one of the principal front line instruments. In the history of the clarinet, it was a much more popular instrument during the swing band era, because the sound augmented the tonal impression, such as you heard with the Glenn Miller Orchestra and the Benny Goodman Orchestra.

Fascination for the tenor saxophone has overtaken the clarinet for most reed musicians. There are clarinet soloists that we don't hear that much about, but we do hear them playing their principal instrument. Phil Woods, for instance, is a wonderful clarinet player, but he's known for his alto.

There are today, in modern jazz circles, very few musicians who enjoy the seniority and reputation needed to play the clarinet. So when someone like Eddie Daniels emerges, there's a lot of attention to be paid.

Eddie Daniels

Eddie Daniels was one of the front running tenor saxophonists who sat in the reed section of the Thad Jones/Mel Lewis Orchestra. Eddie was one of the spearhead soloists, a master of the tenor. Then he started to explore beyond the tenor and he chose to examine the clarinet. As a result, since he left Thad and Mel's band, Eddie Daniels has carved a niche in the current spectrum of jazz as *the* jazz clarinetist in the industry. It's amazing how his facility was so smoothly transferred from the tenor sax to the clarinet.

Ever since he dropped the tenor, I encouraged him to pick it up again and add it to his arsenal, because he was such a wonderful tenor player. I hated to see him just drop the whole thing. Since then, Eddie has included the soprano saxophone in his repertoire as well; his versatility is very impressive.

"Eddie Daniels: Clarinetist Supreme"
Jazz Educators Journal, Summer 1992

Eddie Daniels' sunny *vivre de joie* pours and sings out of his clarinet, fired with the curious passion that drives the creation of his music. Daniels has clearly ascended to the contemporary pantheon of the clarinet and occupies it with aplomb and elegance. His strong versatility makes him a *raris avis* whose consummate excellence embraces both classical and jazz worlds from Charlie Parker to Brahms, drawing much acclaim from all echelons—jazz buffs, peers and critics alike. The diversity of his performance activities and recordings testifies to the breadth and quality of his abilities, training and persuasions. Surely he has rekindled serious interest in the appeal and strength of the clarinet per se, exemplified by his supple technique and amazing range.

My own eyewitness experiences of the last year, for example, compound my earwitness esteem for Daniels' recordings which stem from his tenor saxophone prowess initially in 1966 when he was with the Thad Jones/Mel Lewis Jazz Orchestra and subsequently his clarinet, back in 1973 on a disc with Bucky Pizzarelli—*A Flower for All Seasons* on Choice Records, followed by those on the Marlin, Columbia and Muse labels—all prior to his GRP series. Some ten years ago, Bob Brookmeyer urged that Daniels should be recognized as the premier jazz clarinetist. It has been keenly rewarding to experience his contributions during campus clinics and in recent concerts at the Telluride Jazzfest and at the IAJE Conference in Miami.

Although Daniels is an outstanding tenorist and plays the flutes, alto and soprano saxophones and bass clarinet, the clarinet is now his exclusive instrument. "My dad, who studied with Rudy Wiedoeft, played alto and turned me on to my first jazz record 'Tenors Wild and Mild' with Eddie 'Lockjaw' Davis and Morris Lane, but the clarinet became the instrument I studied on—like going to the gym and working out. I was first inspired by Benny Goodman's famous 1938 Carnegie Hall Concert recording," reviews Daniels, "and I started imitating Benny when I was about 12 years old as I admired his sound. Then I led my own band at 13 in the Catskills."

It all comes full circle as Daniels' latest disc is titled *Benny Rides Again*, co-led with vibraphonist Gary Burton and a rhythm section of Mulgrew Miller, Marc Johnson and Peter Erskine in a tribute to Benny Goodman and Lionel Hampton. Bear in mind this is not a reprise of the swing era sound and approach but rather, it reflects the group's own persona in an impressive contemporary palette.

My recent chats with Eddie Daniels (who has migrated from New York to Santa Fe, New Mexico) yielded perceptions and values of sharp interest … selected portions follow:

Wong: Eddie, within the mosaic of your sounds and approaches, how do you celebrate and proliferate alternatives?

Daniels: In direct reference to Benny, I don't play anything like him as I do contrasting and not imitative things; likewise, Gary avoids anything that sounds like Lionel. Often you get a student who latches on to a Mike Brecker model who never finds his own way. I hate repeating projects, which is why every GRP record of mine is different and each is a new learning experience of varied environments, revealing more of how the clarinet works. And I don't care to rehearse much as I would rather sink or swim in the recording studio. Billy Childs, Dave Grusin, Roger Kellaway and Mulgrew Miller are all different pianists and affect me differently, coaxing me to learn from them. It's like going out to different restaurants. I'm not enslaved to any one kind of recording concept.

Wong: Describe what might be among your most pleasurable memories related to learning.

Daniels: I had great fun when I was part of Marshall Brown's Newport Youth Band; Marshall was a crusading jazz educator from Farmingdale, Long Island. His own high school big band played at the Newport Jazz Festival in 1957. We were his first guinea pigs in an experiment of a school-out-of-school, different from a jazz course study.

He put an ad in *DownBeat* and solicited the best kids and auditioned them, and I got the second alto chair, and guys like Herb Mickman, Ronnie Cuber, Eddie Gómez and Larry Rosen were all in the band, and this special band worked the Newport Jazz Festival and Europe in 1959. It was "live" and wasn't "school"—it was totally extracurricular and did we learn!

Wong: The brand of jazz studies during your early developing years must have been very personalized.

Daniels: In the old days there was no jazz band in schools, and the charts were Glenn Miller arrangements. Today the charts are those of the quality of Thad Jones. All of the jazz study I got was from friends like Herb Mickman, the bassist. We'd get together and he would show me chords and other stuff, and I struggled with it to succeed. The motivation was different. Today 25–30 students come into a classroom, and there's a curriculum they have to learn, whereas I was a hungry kid and learned by bits and pieces … slowly.

Much of today's curriculum has little to do with reality and is like learning to drive a car without the teacher. Jazz education must reflect the culture and personality of jazz history. Joe Henderson, for instance, one of the best jazz players in the world today, comes from a heritage of the jazz tradition that is so deep! The great players express an evolution of the living past Prez, Hawk, and Getz."

Wong: Your own playing reveals a rich, loamy lineage and legacy.

Daniels: My own playing includes Bird, Getz, Rollins and Coltrane as pieces of influence I picked up. Lineage of a player doesn't suddenly pop up in my past. It's part of a tradition of historical values and of a larger spectrum in society. The truly great ones—Coltrane, Getz, Evans and Miles studied and lived in its constantly evolving culture; e.g., on one of Mike Brecker's first records, he used my tenor solo (an exemplary one!) from "Mean What You Say" with Thad and Mel's band, absorbing me and others and generated what is his own transmutation.

Wong: You had taught some instrumental music in a formal school setting?

Daniels: After getting my music ed degree from Brooklyn College and a teaching certificate, I taught high school concert band at Ft. Hamilton High in Brooklyn for a year and in a tough George Washington vocational high school near Manhattan. Then I received my M.A. from Juilliard in 1966.

Wong: As you know, there is a good number of outstanding colleges and universities with time-proven programs in jazz education, spawning many illustrious artists into the jazz life-stream who, in turn, recycle their worthiness to propagate the music in our world culture.

Daniels: I agree. Eastman in Rochester, University of North Texas, and University of Northern Colorado are a few examples. Gary Burton whose duties as Dean of Curriculum at Berklee College of Music illustrates a teacher who shares his life in jazz as an active performing musician. For students, it's not enough to just be in a jazz course. They need the real pressures of learning a wide range of music to become involved in making a living as a reality of the musical life. They need a true teacher and not just the fingering of the Dorian mode. We need elders who have wisdom. Education must go toward creativity but not without knowledge. Students must learn and copy in the beginning and then hone the required skills. There are some wonderful results emerging from jazz education, and I'm eager to share my gains to help. I personally still have a lot of growing to do—it's never ending.

Eddie Daniels is obviously a perpetual learner / teacher / learner who subscribes to a total synergic kind of power and loves to savor the fruits and euphoria of discovery.

Buddy DeFranco

Buddy DeFranco is, exclusively, the leading Charlie Parker–influenced clarinetist of all time. He's a bebop clarinetist and nobody can play the instrument in that style as well as Buddy. Buddy DeFranco is incredible, really. He's played with everybody; an historic clarinetist with historic credentials.

Buddy DeFranco with Dave McKenna—*You Must Believe in Swing*
Concord Records (CCD-4756-2); 1997

Though rare up until some 25 years ago, duos now occupy a pivotal niche in jazz. Their interest stretches beyond mere curiosity; two-instrument bands face the challenge of creating musical moments germane to their special environment which neither solo musicians nor conventional small combos can furnish.

Most duos highlight the beauty of musicians of similar styles and schools of thought playing with a preferred consonant sound. On the surface, therefore, the pairing of Dave McKenna and Buddy DeFranco might seem unlikely. "At first thought, Dave and Buddy may not be a perfect fit, since they come from somewhat different directions," recalls Dr. Dave Seiler, Director of the University of New Hampshire Jazz Band. "But we watched them rehearse—the way they communicated was incredible!"

The background trail leading to this unusual pairing is of interest. Born in the vision of one Joe Stellmach, a devout fan and good friend of both McKenna and DeFranco, this recording was inspired by the spectacular match-ups of DeFranco with super piano icons Art Tatum and Oscar Peterson back in the 1950s. The prospect of DeFranco's thorough mastery of the instrument (with his modern harmonic vocabulary and improvisational skills) brought together with the extraordinary pianism of McKenna (one of the most triumphant post–Tatum pianists) was Stellmach's dream.

"I was inspired to bring Dave and Buddy together—specifically Dave as the third prodigious jazz pianist to be coupled with Buddy," said Stellmach, who was the catalyst in gaining the enthusiasm of Concord Jazz to make this recording. Less than a week after the teaming was agreed to, a debut concert was organized by local piano great Tom Gallant and the aforementioned Dr. Seiler for October 9, 1996, at Portsmouth, New Hampshire as part of the Harry W. Jones, Jr. Jazz Concert. Prior to this venue, McKenna and DeFranco hadn't really played together other than brief jams at parties. A week later, they were in New York recording this CD.

DeFranco's esteem for McKenna is markedly illustrated by this anecdote: "Two summers ago in New England, a friend of Dave's asked me if I'd like to go hear him play solo in a hotel by the coast. I had a plane to catch later on, so I decided to catch one set and then fly home. I wound up listening to the entire three sets."

McKenna is an anomaly in the world of jazz pianists; his two-handed style is so rhythmically powerful that he's essentially self-sufficient. Ace trombonist Carl Fontana, who has played with McKenna many times, simply said, "Dave *is* a band. You don't really need one when he's around!" Pianist Dick Hyman agrees, "He's his own rhythm section. The left hand plays a 4/4 bass line, the right hand plays the melody, and there's that occasional 'strum' in between—like three hands." Check his right hand off-beat single notes, and unpredictable spaces promoting accents that create ear-tugging reactions. Reminiscent of Tatum, McKenna's arpeggios at times seem like they're 50 feet long.

"Dave plays a different way—an orchestral way," DeFranco elaborates. "Of course, Erroll Garner and Oscar Peterson had it too, but Dave has a bass line going on *all* the time. He has the orchestral melodic part, and those exciting chord progressions, but somewhere he sneaks in what might be 'brass figures,' and it's fascinating to wonder how he gets them in. He inserts these figures while everything else is going on."

McKenna explains it quite simply: "I like to play a long line—like a horn player's single notes, which also equate to single notes on a bass. Well, sometimes I'll pause—take a breather in that line, and on occasion just throw in a chord or two." His predilection for single note lines suggests that he has listened a great deal more to horn players than he has to pianists.

Buddy DeFranco is the titan of the modern jazz clarinet who had taken his instrument to the peak of mastery decades ago and has maintained this preeminence internationally since the forties. He has pushed his digital precision to its technical boundaries, and early on merged his blazing, flawless execution with the vital force of Charlie Parker's harmonic approach. With his devastating speed and gorgeous, fluid tone, he improvises with emotional candor and blows nuclear ideas that explode with surprising hues and shapes.

An accomplished clarinetist himself, Seiler says simply "Buddy is a clarinet player's clarinet player."

DeFranco also serves as a dedicated jazz educator on countless campuses. He promotes the improvement of clarinet techniques and improvisation skills—adding expertise through his newly available *Hand in Hand with Hanon*, a distinguished contribution to pedagogical literature for clarinet. DeFranco is indeed ubiquitous. In a span of ten months, this writer witnessed him in Long Beach featured with the Terry Gibbs Big Band; in New York as guest soloist at a recording session with the Woody Herman Legacy Band; in Chicago conducting a clinic at the IAJE (International Association of Jazz Educators) Conference; and in San Francisco's Grace Cathedral playing at a memorial service for the San Francisco Chronicle's beloved columnist, Herb Caen.

Speaking about DeFranco, McKenna said firmly, "It was a real pleasure working with him. Man, he's got it all! In a duo you have to be busy all the time. It's one of the hardest things to do, but with a great horn player like Buddy—that's something else! I really enjoy his musicality."

You Must Believe in Swing was a liberating experience for both players. You know McKenna and DeFranco will play a strong swinging solo each time; their individual power is such that you can almost leave either of them out there without accompaniment.

"Both of us are left naked because there isn't interference or overlap by other instruments," said DeFranco. "Everything can be heard clearly. It felt so good!"

Besides the DeFranco original—the bluesy, opening title tune—all others are standards. Both players expressed their love for the American songbook—a few even became objects of rekindled interest. All of the songs betray the nice, warm feeling the musicians produce, proving themselves as expressive romanticists as well as hard driving swingers.

Possessed of the blinding fast facility of Olympic gold medalists, Dave and Buddy turn "The Song Is You" and especially the Parker-Gillespie bebop anthem "Anthropology" into adrenaline-pumping *tours de force*. And what jazz clarinetist hasn't included "Poor Butterfly" in his song cache! DeFranco's imprint is lovely. Likewise, McKenna's signature is in open relief on his wonderfully sensitive solo piano performance on the closer— "Detour Ahead." "Oh, I just love the blues quality of it, and I knew the writers of this tune—Lou Carter, Herb Ellis, and Johnny Frigo [joint composers and members of The Soft Winds Trio of 1947–52]."

In a duo, each musician is truly half of what happens. It's a matter of the freedom to express and letting things happen with complete confidence—a process which shows the music is worthy of risk. There's an enchanting aura about the numeral "two." This duo reflects that mystifying magnificence. There is something pristine about combining a piano note and a clarinet note. Dave McKenna and Buddy DeFranco share in tandem a striking set of properties of integrity and musical character only mature creative players experience. Their sophisticated knowledge and simpatico are self-evident.

DeFranco said it well: "If it doesn't swing, it isn't happening!"

Benny Goodman

It will come as no surprise to any musician who knew him: Benny Goodman was a perfectionist, but a perfectionist with an attitude.

I was asked to attend a direct-to-disc recording session with Benny; this was sometime in the late '70s or early '80s. They flew me down to L.A. for the session, which involved a small group—a sextet, I recall—including, of course, Benny on clarinet.

Direct-to-disc is a very different and demanding method of recording. If you "goof" you have to start from scratch and begin the recording all over again.

So, the recording session begins and then, about half way through, the engineer stops the session. Benny growled, "Why are we stopping?" The engineer answered deferentially, "Oh, pardon me, sir, but I didn't expect the trumpet player to have notes as high as he had when we were recording. So we'll have to do it again." "Do it again?" Benny said. "But *I* was perfect!" Still, he was told, they had to repeat it. And Benny growled once more, *sotto voce*, "And I will be perfect again!"

They re-recorded and it was successful; they went all the way through without a glitch. At the end of the recording, the engineer says, "Everything's fine and it worked out! We don't have to do it again." Benny's retort: "Of course it was fine. And *I* was perfect *again*!"

After the session, I approached Benny and asked if he wanted to come into the studio to listen to what the group had just recorded. And Benny, being Benny, said: "I don't need to. I know *I* was perfect. Now somebody get me a limousine!" And he walked out.

Benny Goodman—*Ain't Misbehavin'*
Hindsight Records (HD 619); 1978

Several bold facts promptly come into focus when Benny Goodman comes to mind. Benny, "The King of Swing," has been an unchallenged household name in jazz for over forty years. His familiarity to the public had already approached nation-wide dimensions prior to his famous Carnegie Hall Concert in 1938. His explosive powerhouse band was studded with star players in the making—Harry James, Teddy Wilson, Gene Krupa, Ziggy Elman and Lionel Hampton for example.

BG was, indeed, a pioneer in popularizing the music, opening the way for a large new wave in the music business—records, radio, dance concerts, etc. I recall as a kid I had my ears glued to the radio on Saturday nights listening to *Let's Dance*, the three-hour NBC slot featuring Benny's band. And the BG worshipers who serpentined around the block trying to get into Sweet's Ballroom in Oakland, California—my hometown—there just wasn't enough space to accommodate everyone. On that same week Jimmy Dorsey was playing at the T & D Theater, Count Basie at the Orpheum and Lucky Millinder and his orchestra was on a one-nighter at the Oakland Civic Auditorium, but it was Benny who really drew the crowds.

More than any other living musician, he is a public figure synonymous with jazz. Little wonder that a major credit card company has used him extensively in its multimedia advertising; the message has carried implications of Benny's worldliness via the international scope of his appearances. Then there's the ad for an insurance company which pictures him with his clarinet—an associative cue rooting his identification. A minority of his followers is also intrigued with his involvement with classical music although his long association with the classical vein is and has been secondary to jazz.

Benny is a remarkable clarinetist with consummate command of the instrument. He is extremely hard on himself, pressuring and expecting himself to be adept as possible at all times. This value of perfection has always been something he clearly expects his musicians to share; therefore, they must respond with utmost proficiency. BG's notable virtuosity and flawless technique comes from being always close to the horn. He practices several hours a day religiously. At age 69, he exhibits no signs of relinquishing rigor and self discipline to keep his chops up and ready at once. What has become a ritual began over a half century ago when he was one of the early and most demanded studio musicians in New York City. At 17 he was embroiled in recordings, radio work, and playing in show orchestras. Musicians who have played with him at one time or another attest to the virtues of his mode of "working out."

Keeping in excellent shape and maintaining a certain operation level is something a crack musician has to do to survive in the music profession. BG's longevity in jazz as an active, super musician speaks for the validity of his agenda. It's like a champion in any endeavor. The human condition seems to dictate requisites toward keeping the imposing, rapier-like edge of a winner's equipment or instruments intact.

Insightfulness emerging from unclear sources operates the Goodman psyche. Any good jazz player worth his/her salt better have a good amount of instinctual sense for many things; this is especially true for band leaders per se. Primary among these factors is an instinct for correct tempos. Pianist Hank Jones, who has spent several years with the Goodman troupe, emphasized how BG has an unusual instinct for correct tempos. "I got a chance to do a date with Basie and Illinois Jacquet and we were having a helluva time trying to find the right tempo. Basie was slated to play organ and I was to play piano, but he was late getting there. When Basie finally arrived and sat down at the organ and got into a tempo, the thing immediately started to swing. This is precisely what Benny does—he can get into the correct tempo immediately. I don't know how he does this. Sometimes it's a little tricky to get the right tempo for any particular tune. However, he uncannily does it very well and does it consistently."

Another attribute is the pure jazz sound of BG's music and the Vesuvius-like flow of rich improvisations articulated with customary eloquence. Instant new melodies pop out of his improvisations. Moreover, his solos have taken on a warmer, mellower tone. Warren Vaché is a very talented young cornet and flugelhorn player who joins BG on his East Coast performances. Warren said enthusiastically, "Benny always plays great. When he is on top, he is on top! He can't be topped by anyone. He is stimulating because he likes to be challenged. I think he must view the other guys somewhat like they were in a cutting contest. He definitely gets you to play over your head. I'm thankful to be associated with such a giant of the music." Their alliance has reached the four year mark already. Benny knows how to pick the best, mind you. For there's no denying, Vachè is an outstanding jazzman. Likewise, the sensational young tenor saxophonist Scott Hamilton is from the Goodman circle, becoming a recent alumni member after a good period of time. Scott was quick to offer, "Benny is the hottest player we have when he's hot. He is absolutely full of fire! Not that many jazz musicians have that genuine high heat."

In *The New Yorker* last December, writer Whitney Balliett also hovered and elaborated on this same point of Benny's fiery approach: "Goodman was also a 'hot' player, of which there have been surprisingly few (Ben Webster, Wild Bill Davison, and Dave McKenna come to mind.)" And Balliett recounted several other BG earmarks: "He used a 'dirty' tone and intense on-the-beat and staccato phrasing, and he frequently sank into the chalumeau, or low register, which endows the clarinet with great intimacy and lyricism. He favored tremendously fast tempos—the high winds of jazz playing, which invariably give the effect, even when the musicians are being blown galley-west, that everyone is swinging like crazy. But above all, there was a light-some ease about his playing that is rare in jazz."

All of these Goodman traits were magnified at his first contemporary direct-to-disc record. He and Glen Glancy of Century Records had been discussing the making of a record over a year's time. Suddenly, early in the third week of June, BG called in from Sacramento about the full ripeness of his band for recording and the convenient geographical proximity and the right time to record. Glen flew up from Hollywood to catch BG's group and agreed it was indeed appropriate. BG was playing in concert at the state capital and Governor Jerry Brown had presented him with California's first Jazz Award.

Although it was more than 90 degrees outside of the studios, the session was musically hot inside. Benny whistled a phrase, noodled a bit on the clarinet and after a few minutes' hold while Glancy finished his directions to his technical crew, the session opened up for cutting the disc. BG was eager, started playing at the sight of the amber light going on but was told to wait until the red light lit up. This peek into the prelude of the session reveals the anticipation and absolute gestalt of readiness.

As for the music at hand, it begins auspiciously with Cal Collins' beautiful acoustic guitar, announcing the bright, happy and familiar opener, "Lady Be Good"—long connected with BG. It is essentially a preview of the premium quality of the remainder of the record. Cal had been holed up in Cincinnati, and not known to too many outside the inner grapevine until Jack Sheldon recommended him to BG after playing a gig with Cal. I personally had heard about Cal through jazz vocalist Mark Murphy who had also hung out in Cincinnati in the past.

Listening to Cal, you might wonder if it is 1938 or 1978. Although Cal has a wider realm going for him, his sound is wonderfully reminiscent of the late Django Reinhardt. Yes, it's really timeless music. How perfectly congruent with Goodman it is! Dig BG's instant wizardry in his choice of musical phrases and sentences. Major Holley's characteristic bowed bass solo accompanied by his own humming/singing on the same notes lends refreshing colors to the overall sound of the octet. The tasty work of Connie Kay's drums and John Bunch's piano along with Cal and Major feed into making the rhythm section one big swinging heart of the group, providing a selfless, supportive yet vigorous foundation.

Benny's philosophy on playing ballads is expressed magnificently and yet very simply via Jimmy Van Heusen's lovely "Here's That Rainy Day." He has a rare ability to establish or get into the soul of the tune he's playing. Thus, not as strange as it may seem, BG plays the ballad the way the composer intended it to be played. You're left with the impression that's the way the composer would like to have heard it. For years Johnny Bunch has been one of the most keenly antennaed jazz pianists on the scene. His multi-faceted career has included a key role as accompanist for Tony Bennett for six years, among other singers. Of course, Benny makes his instrument sing, too. Bunch is used to accompanying and his playing here is attractive and satisfying.

"Makin' Whoopee" shows Holley's warm full thumping bass is like Gibraltar in its solidarity … and what a great sense of time he has. Veteran tenor man Buddy Tate makes a contribution toward carrying on the tradition of the jazz tenor saxophone. And Jack Sheldon's first horn solo of the session is a well-shaped melodic solo. From the Ellington songbook comes "I've Got It Bad," virtually a showcase for Cal, getting more space to demonstrate his swinging prowess and sonority. He draws sounds from the guitar you're not supposed to! Connie Kay's subtle work on brushes and cymbals recalls his marvelous playing as a member of the famed Modern Jazz Quartet for so many years. BG had recorded this Webster/Ellington classic featuring Peggy Lee on an Eddie Sauter arrangement in 1941.

In a relaxed groove, Fats Waller's "Ain't Misbehavin'" ushers in a second side of the disc with a charming Goodman solo. This is also the title of the smash Broadway award-winning musical at the Longacre Theatre in NYC devoted to thirty songs associated with Fats. For my money, Sheldon plays his most appealing and well constructed solo of the date; it is likewise typical of his sound and approach at its best … the kind of solo Jack has gassed me on so many occasions in the past twenty years. Ex-Basie star, Buddy Tate's big, warm-toned solo takes us back to the jazz roots and virility of the tenor. Benny wraps it up in the elegant way only he has the first class wherewithal to wrap up music. Somehow he does it with more justice than one would conjure the music inherently demands.

Speaking of Buddy, "All of Me" is all of Buddy who features his Texas horn thoughtfully on this favorite, evoking joyous images of Herschel Evans and Coleman Hawkins. His strong authoritatively firm sound perks up your ears. His style communicates with a direct, straight and conclusive shot, shorn of filigree of any sort, swinging forthrightly with an unusually fat sounding rhythm and loads of melodic imagination. When Buddy blows, he brings forth unexpected melodic adventures and a sense of urgency through alterations in texture, by accents and by a battery of other means in his total expression. Benny regards him with much respect: "Buddy's one of the great ones!"

Another Van Heusen gem is "Darn That Dream" which BG introduced in the 1939 musical *Swingin' the Dream*—a hip version of Shakespeare's *A Midsummer Night's Dream*. Benny drops out on this song to allow trombonist Wayne Andre some space to stretch out. Busy as he is in the N.Y. studios, Andre made this trip to the Coast with BG. Andre's expressive trombone solo is excellent, triggering the mind to link him to Urbie Green and the late Bill Harris vis-à-vis the deep burry personal sound and control of the horn. In 1932, "Alone Together" was a new song with lyrics by Howard Dietz and the music by Arthur Schwartz. It was introduced by Clifton Webb and Tamara Geva in the musical *Flying Colors* the same year. This tune is all Benny.

Finally, the rideout tune is another fixture in the Goodman repertory—"Limehouse Blues"; it flashes back to another up tempo rendition by a BG Sextet 37 years ago, featuring Lou McGarity on trombone with Mel Powell on piano, Tom Morgan on guitar, Sid Weiss on bass and drummer Ralph Collier. The rhythm section here on this newest version cooks with all burners turned on high. The exquisite interplay of Cal and Benny constitutes a highlight of the record. "We've been using the classical guitar almost exclusively the last two years because it blends so well with Benny's clarinet," Cal explained. "I can play a very good rhythm sound plus the single-line through a microphone. We both love the sound via the mic to our respective instruments. Put them together and you've got something more than just nice" and about Benny, Cal was adulatory: "Benny's been an idol of mine since I was a kid of 12. Playing with him is an unusual experience—absolutely the high point of my career. And even though we may play many of BG's favorite old items, they are wonderful tunes and he plays them different every time. He's out of sight!"

The entire session was completed in short order, attesting at least partially to the perfection level BG's groups normally attain. Shortly after it was all over, Benny and I had a chat in the control room. His first post-recording reactions were positive, "I love doing this. This is the way we always used to do it forty years ago. It wasn't as long as 18 minutes but the 78s were challenging too; we had to get everything out within pretty strict time limits. I have a fine cohesive group and they know what they're doing. Don't they sound great! I love those guys. Like Buddy Tate, they're real players ... real pros. Yes, I thought the band was really ready for direct-to-disc, and believe me, it was an ideal time to make this record. You can hear it!"

From the height of the swing era to 1978, Benny has somehow consistently captured the essence of his past, retreaded what he deemed judiciously appropriate or downright necessary, and selected contemporary music that connects with his values orientation. Goodman's combos have exemplified the finest in chamber music jazz. This marvelous edition is another cluster of master musicians held together by the peerless pied piper, Benny Goodman. "The King of Swing" has banded together another majestic court playing regal, swinging music. Benny Goodman is one of a kind—a living legend.

CHAPTER 10

Piano

The harmonic contribution of the piano to the overall impression of the band cannot be overstated. The piano is *the* instrument that galvanizes the rest of the band's ideas and sound; and then it throws those ideas and sound back to the band for elaboration. The piano serves as the central nerve center for the band; without the piano, the band lacks a directional core.

The ultimate impact of the piano involves more than just the mobility of the pianist's fingers; it's what the pianist creates, improvises, supports and elongates that allows the piano to go anywhere, from anger to soft sexiness.

Two greats tie for my top-of-mind pianist in the world of jazz: Oscar Peterson and Herbie Hancock; Oscar for his mastery of swing, Herbie for his ongoing exploration with the instrument.

Oscar Peterson

Swing master Oscar Peterson's talent is never ending—it just never stops! His facility with the piano is mindboggling. As a testament to his uncanny playing abilities, when Oscar had a stroke, he continued playing with only one hand; but he sounded exactly like he was using both hands. It was unbelievable.

Oscar enlivens every tune that he plays; it has a lot to do with the sunny personality and smiling disposition that he brings to everything he does. And he brought both to the birth of my career in jazz education.

In addition to being a wrist watch fan ("Hey, check this one out," he would say whenever we met, displaying yet another nutty timepiece on his wrist), Oscar was also a "duck" fan—the Peking variety. So whenever Oscar came to town, in keeping with our long-standing tradition, Marilyn and I would take him out for a Chinese dinner.

At one of those dinners, while discussing my jazz education endeavors—then in the nascent stage—Oscar expressed interest in learning how to teach jazz to children. During one of our phone conversations that followed, he asked me to help him get involved. "I don't know anything about it," Oscar said to me, "and I would appreciate it if you could help me with that, Herb."

Sometime later, on his next extended visit to San Francisco, I called Oscar and told him I would like to introduce him to the jazz education environment. Little did he know how big the introduction would be. I suggested that he and his trio visit us at Washington

Elementary School in Berkeley with the aim of performing for the students and learning how they learn.

Unbeknownst to him, I had been prepping the students for this potential visit. I approached my friends at Mercury Records, who generously donated some of Oscar's albums. While I played Oscar's records, I had the kids painting a surprise for Oscar and his trio.

When Oscar arrived at our school, I brought him to the auditorium, where I had previously placed the results of my surreptitious sessions with the kids. There, facing him on the stage, were three twelve-foot high murals the students had painted. Each of the three panels depicted a member of the Oscar Peterson Trio: Oscar on piano, Sam Jones on bass, Louis Hayes on drums. Oscar—who had no idea of the artwork's existence—was stunned into silence.

When he had a chance to regroup, Oscar Peterson became the first "guest performer" in my budding jazz education programs. At my behest, he and his trio played back-to-back concerts at the school—in reality, clinics for the students—showcasing Oscar's inventive talents, first to the kindergarten through 3rd grade students, and then to the 4th through 6th grade classes.

In each of the concert/clinics, I suggested to Oscar that he interact with the children. "Ask them for different notes," I said, "then compose a tune with the notes they give you." So Oscar solicited notes from the students ... and created tunes on the spot. But he didn't stop there. He said to the students, "OK, now that we have a tune, let's see what we can do with it." At which point Oscar launched into multiple variations, improvising new and different tunes, all based on the original, and all to fascination and understanding on the part of the kids.

It was magical, not only for the children, but for the executives from the school district I had invited to the concerts—for I had ulterior motives in arranging Oscar's visit. One of those executives happened to be in charge of setting the curriculum for the district; she also happened to have an affinity for Oscar Peterson's music. So, by inviting the school district execs to the concerts, I paved the way for my pursuit of this new idea of teaching kids about jazz, thanks to the help of the ever-eloquent Oscar Peterson.

The Oscar Peterson Trio—*Eloquence*
Limelight (LM 82023); 1965; Reissued by Blue Note

> *el' o-quence (ĕl'-ō-kwĕns), n. Discourse characterized by force and persuasiveness; also, the art, action, or power of using such discourse.*

Oscar Peterson is to me the personification of ELOQUENCE. Off and on stage he's the quintessence of sartorial eloquence. From an epicurean standpoint his discriminating palate strongly smacks of an eloquent taste for fine foods ... (and man, does he dig Peking Duck with all the groovy, ancient and exotic trimmings—Oscar is a gustatory gas!). More familiar and zeroed in jazzwise are his impressively articulate abilities of elocution, and his dynamic eloquence as a jazz pianist of fantastic performing prowess. (Yeah, as an aside, his growing obsession with nutty wristwatches may turn him into jazzdom's most eloquent timepiece collecting freak. I just spoke with Oscar on the phone and for a birthday goody he was presented with ... you got it ... a nutty wristwatch!)

Ingredients making up Oscar's pianistic eloquence have been dissected, examined, analyzed, evaluated, argued, expounded and speculated innumerable times in the past decade and a half and the exigency to recapitulate these exfoliations would seem to be minimal. Ergo, a talus slope of adjectival accumulation will be withdrawn on the somewhat comfortable assumption that Oscar's gifts and wide reputation for consummate beauty and taste, fiery gusto, devastating command of the instrument, etc., is common knowledge to most jazz aficionados.

Appearing currently at the London House in Chicago at this August writing, Oscar's contemporary views are reflected in his comments and by the music in this album on Limelight; all of this indicates to me that he is in the midst of a period of reassessment. His outlook has always included a couple of principal components. He points out that "for one thing, my trios have tried to sound mutually compatible ... it is a basis to expand on our ideas. Basically the three men can at times do much more than larger groups. The process does involve a certain amount of pre-conception on which to work; otherwise, if individuality takes over completely then what we're striving to achieve will come apart and be destroyed. However, this is not to say we have the key to these nebulous areas."

Oscar adds, "Another thing is that we are striving for proximity and sensitivity in our playing and I think we achieve it regularly," Presumably, then, if anyone scans the discographical history of the Peterson trios, he'll subsequently discover pertinent examples of this achievement. The trio of Peterson, Brown and Thigpen exemplifies a tight, eloquent community of ideas and concepts translated into propelling, swinging performances.

Evaluating his own work on the piano, Oscar asserts that he expresses himself within only a few bands of confinement and that he really doesn't play "800 choruses and 17,000 notes in each chorus!!" In reality he is trying to move in a different direction. He recognizes the individual viewpoints and approaches of Bill Evans, Phineas Newborn, and the late Art Tatum, all of whom are held in high respect by Oscar. Patently with a strong focus on the piano as a solo vehicle, Oscar says, "The instrument should come out on its own. Not too far in the future we will be attending concerts to hear a jazz solo pianist rather than just to hear groups—not that Tatum was the only one who could have accomplished this successfully, but perhaps we who are jazz pianists and jazz enthusiasts have not pressed it hard enough."

Turning to the subject of Ray Brown, Oscar's poll-winning bassist of long standing, Oscar rhapsodizes with profound sincerity, "We will never see another bass player like Ray Brown. Not too many guys are so musically unselfish. He has expanded his talents beyond anyone I've ever heard of. Ray has extended the basic meaning of the use of the instrument—his harmonic and rhythmic concept when playing for someone is out of sight! There are so few who possess the feeling he has when he plays. In effect, Ray is saying 'I am playing *with* you!'—not in a musically subservient way but in a creative, definitively personal way. Many mistake the intensity of his artistry; that is, they hear profound strength in his notes but miss the relativity of the notes or the interrelationship of harmonics to what's going on. Ray has never really disputed the numerous possibilities of the instrument. I have never heard him say that he couldn't play this or that on the bass, or that this cannot be made; instead, he would remark 'You cannot get that *today!*' implying that 'X' time later I'll have it for you but not right now. I think this whole process is a mark of genius. Someday I'd like to write a book on Ray Brown from a pianistic standpoint."

Now about this album recorded live at the Tivoli Gardens in Copenhagen ... Oscar was very desirous of having current performances recorded in Europe especially since the 1958 Concertgebouw Verve recording in Amsterdam, Holland was the most recent previous European session of this nature. He felt it was warmly ripe for another set of performances and he had the added wish to play for the younger set in Europe.

"Children's Tune"

This is just prefatory music to the afternoon concert ... a sort of scene setter. A lovely tune of just two choruses which can fruitfully develop into fuller explorations; (I heard the trio blossoming out with extensions and new elements at the London House) although here it ends all too quickly, but I think you'll get hooked on it just as rapidly. I can project and hear youngsters humming it immediately upon the first audition. Oscar's inspiration for the tune garnished with a little bit of triangle work is based on his observations of children in the Tivoli Gardens during the day ... kids watching puppet shows, riding the Ferris wheel and the like, but mainly he spent a good deal of time noticing boys and girls running and romping through the park. The tune documents his impressions delightfully.

"Younger Than Springtime"

The only pre-structuring here is Ray Brown playing the melody. Ed Thigpen provides tasteful percussive accompaniment. There is some exciting tension building with Oscar's cascades. Albeit, the whole affair is left comparatively light and springy. Ray Brown is a gas!

"Misty"

Erroll Garner's tune has been done, re-done, and will be re-done ad infinitum. Oscar feels that the real essence of the tune has usually been lost—subterfuged by the emphasis on its lyrics and that the tune has much instrumental depth and innate beauty so often not capitalized adequately. On this version Ray Brown steps forward and states his own conception without accompaniment instead of just playing a bass accompaniment resulting in a magnificent display of Ray's powerful array of talents.

Oscar's approach here hints at his new pianistic direction, an approach ultimately to be used when he is divested of a rhythm section. He attempts to draw out of the natural resources of the tune all that he could. As Oscar says, "I'm trying to bring back what's been sorely missing of late; that is, to reintroduce and reuse the bottom end of the keyboard so effectively implemented by Teddy Wilson and Art Tatum, especially on ballads with deep chords and clusters in the left hand."

In detailing this re-emphasis or revivification, Oscar accuses himself of overlooking the lower spectrum of the piano, for he admits how complacency sets in at the bottom end when he functions within a group's context and relegates the role to the bass or guitar.

"Django"

John Lewis, the composer, urged O.P. to record it when he first heard it in Zagreb. Not done exactly the way Lewis wrote it harmonically on the blowing phase of it, the approach apparently grabbed him hard and obviously dug it as he told Oscar, "That's my Django but that's your Django for me." If ever there was a genuine musical gift to Europe, Oscar feels this composition serves as the premiere item of offering.

"Smudge"

This should have a familiar ring to devotees of the tune "Mumbles" featuring Clark Terry's vocalizing from the *Oscar Peterson Trio Plus One* album on Mercury, MG 20975.

Oscar relates how this unadulterated blues resulted from a second germinal background noodling in response to Terry's request "to cook for me … shout behind me on my out chorus." Chagrin reigned over the guys in the group and the listeners when Oscar omitted this blues segment, for everyone had been infected with the material; they would remark, "Hey, you didn't do that thing this time." Moreover, the young people at the Tivoli went through a whole bag of dances—the Frug, the Monkey, et al., to the tune. Thereby the name, "Smudge" was given in some prospect of the tune becoming a stimulus for a new dance.

Using "Smudge" as a platform for more thoughts, Oscar feels it's the blues with no excuse or qualification and the trio at its barren best. "Any jazz group should have the blues as a foundation—a primary concept of any group. It is the basis for being a group— happy or unhappy as I hear other groups—to exist or not to exist. Regardless of the so-called dimming jazz scene, my trio continues to exist because the trio persists with the catalytic seeding of the blues. It's much like surfing. When one is aware that the wave is going to break over—inevitably it will. I have demanded from all of my groups that they must swing and cook at any time without manufacturing it."

"Autumn Leaves"

This is essentially the "group" approach, a more conventional one, versus the loosely defined "serial" approach of that used on "Misty." Oscar finds a balance of the two directions desirable. "Autumn Leaves" by the trio has been a very big favorite in Europe for many years. "As a vehicle it is used two ways by the trio—at this moving, grooving tempo herein, the feeling to blow ourselves out to relax or at a slower tempo played late at night to express ourselves lyrically." Groups react differently at key locale or tempo changes, and listeners' reactions and temperaments likewise are altered."

The tune is one of the trio's "Steam tunes" (or from Lester Young's lovin' bag and sub-lexicon, "Pound Cake"), with only one predetermined set of figures on the opening and closing of the bridge. Yeah! This should burn up your rig … and wig.

"Moanin'"

Confessing that he didn't do Bobby Timmons' tune before in the midst of it being a hot winner several seasons ago because he was weary of it, "as I can be with other tunes that become too popular because everyone seems to go down the same drain," Oscar has lately rediscovered new things in the tune after the subsiding of popularity and following a more meticulous examination.

"Lovers' Promenade"

A thoroughly logical conclusion to this collection of tunes, this portrayal as a musical panorama of activities late in the day when young couples are walking hand in hand around the fountains, sitting in the restaurants, exiting various amusement concessions exhibiting a serene, warm satisfying feeling after a day's relaxation. Thus this original by Oscar was written from a first hand experience type of impetus and the title is certainly not a superimposition of a theme after a tune has been written.

If you will listen and re-listen to this varied program of music by the eloquent Oscar Peterson, you can't help but acquire a taste that is eloquent. Cop out on this invitation with some pseudo-hip attitude and you will be the one who will suffer impoverishment by abstinence. Dig it hard and you may find that O.P. is eloquently somethin' else!

Herbie Hancock

It's a rare occasion when a writer refuses to do liner notes for an album. But that was the case with a Blue Note recording I received for my review—the artist and album shall remain nameless—an assignment that soon turned from trash to treasure.

Francis Wolff, one of the founding partners who ran Blue Note, had sent me an acetate test pressing of a recording, along with his request that I do the album's liner notes. Well, the album sucked! I put it in the mail, returning it to Blue Note.

Before it had a chance to get there, I got a call from Francis, asking me what I had thought of the test pressing. I told him I had sent the disc back sans my contribution of liner notes. "This is trash, man … this is terrible … that's why I'm sending this disc back to you."

Taken aback, Francis paused for a moment, then responded. "Herb, thank you for your integrity and honesty about it. I promise you, I am going to find something that you're gonna get really excited about, and I don't think you're going to return it."

What Francis sent next was Herbie Hancock's *The Prisoner*, one of the best of Herbie's whole litany.

I did not return it.

Herbie Hancock—*The Prisoner*
Blue Note Records (BST 84321); 1969

"Generally speaking, I've been able to get closer to the real me on this album than on any other previous one." This is a value judgment of Herbie Hancock, the gifted young upper echelon jazz pianist-composer who left the charismatic and nutritious aura of the Miles Davis group to venture into leading his own band in order to cultivate his imagination and to shape his own musical concepts.

And what then does Hancock refer to when he mentions "the real me"? I recognize that no one can really define the real anybody, but on the other hand, clues and intuitive responses can be confirmed in various degrees to refine a view of someone. During the last couple of years Herbie and I have had several lengthy dialogues which I consider as helpful intake sources to discover what psychologist Benjamin Bloom calls the "cognitive-affective domains" of Herbie Hancock as they may relate to music. Therefore, I have included some excerpts and interpretations which may provide some insight to the Hancock mosaic.

Concerning his musical hopes and tendencies Hancock expressed, "I want my music to evolve toward a point where it can contain that part of me that is relatively most musical to people—but in a jazz climate that can communicate to the general public." He is referring to a flourishing residence in jazz while there is a cleanly easy-to-sing, easy-to-recall melodic line, but he also refers to correlates in rhythm and harmony. "I am trying to write hummable tunes with a kind of rhythmic element people can be infected with," he continued, "and one key to the rhythmic thing is duple meter." In this respect he discussed the duple meter of rock and the triple meter feeling of jazz. "People can identify more with duple meter, so the drummer does play duple meter but does not, however, play rock per se," he elaborated, "so you hear the drummer playing jazz." This metric flexibility is viewed as a resource for jazz percussion and Hancock has composed tunes using a type of bastardized bossa nova beat with a tinge of rock. He uses bossa nova which has duple meter because this metric trait is one that has made b. n. popular along with the inherently simple melodies. These appealing elements explain why Hancock uses them as communicative devices. As to harmony, he said, "Harmony is the element that offers even more flexibility. The differentiated positioning of chords in my *Maiden Voyage* is an example, and *Speak Like a Child* is somewhat like a pop ballad. It's an extension of the concept of simple melody and rhythm related to a more advanced harmony." In summarizing his rationale of exploring areas in this sphere, he offered, "It's like a huge door with a lot of little doors to the outside public and I'm trying different doors."

All of these key elements Hancock subscribes to in his response to the challenge of orchestrating for color are used to expand his color concept of the band. This partially accounts for his use of the bass trombone, bass clarinet, and the C flute in addition to the basic instrumentation of his sextet. Clusters, splashes, accents and sounds that create visual images and effects come out of his scoring. You can readily detect a close alliance of Hancock's orchestrations to those coloristic effects and sounds achieved so brilliantly by Gil Evans whose monumental collaborations with Miles Davis in particular created historical benchmarks. Hancock spoke admiringly, "I really dig Gil. Gil Evans is deceiving in the sound he gets because it sounds much more broad. The way he voices his chords is that he gets melodic movement on the bottom which goes beyond getting just functional movement ... his music is more buoyant, more colorful. There is a natural flow of melody leading into the sound."

Speaking of developmental influences on Herbie Hancock, aside from Gil and Miles, there is Bill Evans who was the first pianist Hancock could truly identify with. When Hancock started in jazz, George Shearing and Bud Powell were his forces of effect, and Hancock possessed a more emphatic harmonic approach before his melodic approach was secure. As for Bill Evans, Hancock exclaimed, "When I heard Bill, I knew that was it! Harmony has always gassed me. I was intrigued with different chord sounds and Bill led the way for me; he played a large part in my growth and development." Hancock's melodies are simple and he tries to get the harmony to sound simple too—in doing this he tries to get novel relationships between chords, each succession of chords presents an increment of surprise. In effect, there is no establishment of a strong tonal center. And in the way the chords follow each other, there is sufficient space and freedom between choral relationships so that soloists can feel free to comment comfortably and in the way they feel.

Concerning the musicians in his group, he selected those who play melodically ... this is not to infer that he wanted guys who thought less of the chord structure but it's a matter of having players who are decidedly more conscious of the sound. "All my soloists," he described, "play a different style but some part of each is related to each other, and I do some of all of their thing."

Joe Henderson is one of today's top saxophonists and he creates fire in the group. Flugelhornist Johnny Coles sounds like a young lion. Hancock mused, "Johnny moves by the moment. He plays things with such sheer beauty I wonder where it's coming from. He is just gifted enough to grab the notes he hears and get them out and it's pure soul that comes out. Coles' things are related to Miles' things, but Coles doesn't pick the same notes even though I believe they are conceptually similar." And trombonist Garnett Brown who has been very active in the New York studios and prominently featured with the Thad Jones/Mel Lewis Orchestra is considered a lucky circumstance for Hancock as Herbie feels that Garnett's experience is very valuable to the group.

Drummer Al "Tootie" Heath spent a good number of years in Europe as an American jazz expatriate before returning home last year, and upon the recommendation of Ron Carter, Hancock brought Heath into the fold. Hancock observes as others have, "Tootie is playing things I never heard him play before; he uses the drums as a total involvement and he can really swing … very tasty, very flexible and his big ears listen to everything!" Buster Williams seems to be playing everywhere—with Nancy Wilson, with The Jazz Crusaders, et al. He performs the basic function of the bass in supplying the foundation, but he also functions beautifully as a horn. Hancock feels that Buster's style is perfect for the group as he also understands formal chord structure and understands "the Hancock sound."

On this album wherein Hancock uses a nonet, he cited the merits of Hubert Laws in particular, pointing out that Laws is one of the finest flute players in classical or jazz; Laws is used by the New York Philharmonic Orchestra and other classical units for flute solos just as he is heavily featured on numerous jazz settings.

This album's title, *The Prisoner,* sets a thematic direction for Hancock to express how Black people have been imprisoned for a long time. The opening tune's connection with the late Dr. Martin Luther King is obvious. I first heard this piece as an untitled number when Hancock performed it at the 1968 University of California Jazz Festival. It has an airy singable line with the melody on top of the chordal structure; the first note of the melody is the 9th and as there are chord changes, an airiness grows out of the changes. Once again there isn't a pervasive tonal center in "I Have a Dream."

"The Prisoner" is in sections with an ABCB scheme. Joe Henderson's solo in the middle section shows the use of freedom and space provided by Hancock's writing. The interest here is on the sound. The composition was inspired by Stravinsky's "The Rite of Spring." Hancock's arrangement of Buster Williams' "Firewater" recalls Gil Evans' conceptual model. The title indicates the social duality of the oppressor and the oppressed. The fire and water idea symbolizes, for Hancock, the feeling of fire in violence and in power play and the feeling of water in Dr. King. Likewise, "He Who Lives in Fear" refers to the fact that King had to live in an atmosphere charged with intimidation. Via a skillful manipulation and reshaping of a very hip jingle Hancock did for a television cigarette commercial, he evolved a completely new piece with a melody and harmonic pattern. The juxtapositions he made came out beautifully with another Hancock gem. Finally, "Promise of the Sun," a fetching melody you won't forget easily, symbolizes how the sun promises life and freedom to all living things and yet Blacks are not yet free.

I think it's fortunate that affable, free thinking Herbie Hancock can so successfully amalgamate his powerfully creative influences and rich experience via people like Gil Evans, Miles Davis and Bill Evans. It is a bow of respect and warm admiration, too, for Hancock since it takes someone with creative powers to accomplish these processes. "The real Herbie Hancock" is neither a pipedream nor a prisoner. He is here for you to listen, to dig. And you'll be hearing from him many times on a motion picture score, a TV theme or another recording in the future as Hancock fills in more pieces to the Hancock mosaic.

McCoy Tyner

I got a call from McCoy Tyner one day in the early 1980s when I was with Palo Alto Records. He said, "Herb, I want to send you a cassette of a recording I've just done. I want to see if you're interested in it for your Palo Alto label." I told him to send it along and I would give it a listen.

Well, I listened to the cassette on arrival as promised and I immediately called McCoy back. "McCoy, I love your playing," I said, "but you're buried by the rest of your band. I want to hear *you*. You're the leader. You're the focus. I'm not in favor of you in this context. I think what you should do is this: I would like to hear *you* with a trio. I want to hear you—not the rest of the horns."

Two weeks later, I get a call from Israel and it's McCoy. Even through the phone, I could feel he was jubilant ... jumping for joy. I asked him, "What's the story, man?" And McCoy responded, "I followed your recommendations, Herb, and I have a trio and I love it and I want to thank you. You are astute about what I should do." I said, "Well, at some opportunity I'd like to record you." McCoy said, "You got it."

And that's how his album, *Just Feelin'*, came to be.

McCoy Tyner—*Just Feelin'*
Palo Alto Records (PA 8083); 1985

"I'm excited about the whole album—the material, the good mood and feelings— everything exceeded my expectations! It's one of my very best albums ever—I'm really very proud of it."

McCoy Tyner is effusive. "It's special to me because I haven't done a working trio album for such a long time and the level of communication between Avery, Louis and myself is just great. We play these tunes every night, so this record date is like catching us in a club. I've always wanted to do an album like this."

Including his six years as a member of the legendary John Coltrane Quartet, McCoy Tyner has been a major league jazz pianist for more than 25 years. With Coltrane he explored vigorously, using chords constructed in fourths, tonal clusters and chromatically altered chords. In doing so, he carved a road to the future of the piano.

After parting ways with Coltrane, he honed his individual style of seam-bursting intensity; his unique vernacular approach earned him a place in the circle of the world's top jazz pianists. As an unconventional architect of post bop piano and carrying the creative legacy embodied in Coltrane, McCoy became a guru to a generation of pianists, redefining the instrument.

When we first met in 1959 in San Francisco's Blackhawk, McCoy was a budding talent with The Jazztet, the fine newborn group co-led by Art Farmer and Benny Golson. His constant growth in stature since then is well illustrated in a wonderfully wide breadth of musical contexts—from unaccompanied solos to large aggregations.

But while McCoy has recorded prolifically in a mix of situations, there's little on record by an intact, working Tyner trio. Historically, pianists such as Oscar Peterson and Bill Evans have been easily identified with touring trios (despite their own share of other kinds of recordings); McCoy's career has no comparable trio identity. In May 1984, when bassist Avery Sharpe and Louis Hayes joined him, McCoy Tyner was poised to navigate a significant turning point in his career: he had his first regular working trio.

"I have more opportunity to play," he says enthusiastically. "I'm more in command of what's happening dynamically. And what's special is that we play very well together and enjoy playing together ... and enjoying it in turn motivates us to play, even better. I think it's just a wonderful situation." The phenomenon of "chemistry" between people is often dismissed as the stuff of fable, or at least mystery; that chemistry is an actual, physical release or absorption of energy is obvious after hearing these tracks. The telepathic musical communication between the three musicians demonstrates the concept eloquently.

McCoy points out the qualities he values in Avery Sharpe and Louis Hayes: "Louis is a seasoned drummer with lots of experience. He's adaptable and open for new things, and I insist on this quality." Louis amplifies, "We're free to express our uniqueness—there's no formalized 'follow the leader' syndrome."

"When I want to go back and play the blues," McCoy says, "Louis is super with the cymbal and really knows how to make if swing." Playing for years with the likes of celebrated groups led by Horace Silver, Cannonball Adderley, Oscar Peterson, and Freddie Hubbard, Louis is an accomplished drummer.

Young lion Avery Sharpe is multi-talented and an advanced master of his art. His credits include recordings or performances with Art Blakey, Woody Shaw, Archie Shepp and Pat Metheny. "Avery is mature beyond his years and he has fresh ideas," notes McCoy. "The combination of Avery's youthfulness and musical sophistication and Louis' rich foundation and openness—hey, we've got it!"

The band worked at Lush Life in New York and then in Israel, where McCoy experienced a spiritual and musically creative, uplifting period; we started shortly thereafter preparing to document the trio. During a week's gig at the Fairmont Hotel on Nob Hill in San Francisco, the trio cut this record.

The title tune, "Just Feelin'," recorded once before with horns, gets a markedly different treatment. "The earlier version was good, but this one is special," asserts McCoy. "There's a basic sort of gospel feeling and the trio captured the feeling I wanted." Louis' inventive cymbals, Avery's electric bass and guest Babatunde's percussion add flaring colors to the swells of McCoy's exuberance.

The familiar standard "I Didn't Know What Time It Was" a Tyner favorite, opens with McCoy's jubilant statement before his partners join him. "The way it moves is absorbing. Some tunes carry themselves by virtue of their structure—really a kind of natural phenomenon; the way it is structured motivates itself."

In memory of Count Basie, McCoy contributes a high spirited "Blues for Basie." McCoy describes: "I always admired the way his band sounded—a very tight sound. I liked his approach, so I tried to capture *that* sound, rather than mimicking Basie per se." In line with McCoy's intent, you can imagine hearing the orchestral sound of the Basie idiom—the glorious reed section playing with full ensemble fluency; the series of riffs, the incisive bite of the brasses and the uncluttered driving lines of the band—all swinging with the life-giving rhythm section. Check out Avery and Louis' handling of the brass swoops and McCoy's band fills and shouts.

Side two opens with Avery's Tynerish "Berliner" which features his large, warm bass notes and Louis' shimmering work. "Avery's a fine composer—this is one of his best. He was inspired to write in my style." The tune is reminiscent of one of McCoy's, "Elvin (Sir) Jones."

An album seems incomplete without a Tyner solo piece. His creative beauty is supported by authoritative musicianship. "You Don't Know What Love Is" was recorded previously with Coltrane but never as a solo.

McCoy's approach to a "standard" tune is to give it a fresh personality—to cultivate new blossoms on a dormant branch. I was turned on by the groove Avery's own group got into on "There Is No Greater Love," and eagerly proposed his arrangement for this album. Avery carries on the joyous tradition of Slam Stewart and Major Holley, two masters who have encouraged him: he bows solos in unison with his humming and singing.

McCoy has always been intrigued with rhythmic variety, and "Manha De Carnaval" winds up the program. "I recorded it once with a quartet but this is so different. I added a vamp with a mixture of Cuban, Mexican and Spanish flavors, to go into a Latin and bossa nova feeling. It creates a stronger interpretation."

Certainly the album is a colorful mosaic of many conversations. "Working with this trio night after night has given us the essence of experimentation and discovering what works," McCoy concludes.

It's clear it all works. McCoy Tyner plays feelin' music.

Marian McPartland

Marian McPartland called me one day, wanting to talk about jazz education. She said, "I know of your work. You are a pioneer. The next time you're in town, please come by." And so I did, several times.

We enjoyed many visits together. We talked about a lot of philosophical things, concrete things ... not necessarily related to jazz ... just a lot of things to discuss.

A Conversation with Marian McPartland
May 1998

Wong: Your National Public Radio show, *Piano Jazz*, has certainly made a significant contribution.

McPartland: I'm really lucky to be doing it and I'm happy to be doing it and getting some of the guests I've had. It's been a thrill, you know, and they just keep coming. Next year we are going to have a party in February ... like a twenty year party. It's hard to believe. It just started out and I'm thinking, well, maybe do thirteen shows or ten shows or something and then it'll be all over. And, you know, years later I'm still there.

Wong: It's like a gallery.

McPartland: It is, it is. So I'm enjoying it thoroughly.

Wong: I've been very interested to include you in this project of mine on the life of the creator. Adult creators actually do call upon their childhood experiences in the creative process. So I wanted to chat with you a little bit about your childhood foundation, first off. Could you describe your home environment in which you grew up as a child and how it was warm or nurturing?

McPartland: I would say it was fairly warm. But, you know, coming from a British family, my parents were really ... I don't know, as I think back, I guess they were fairly demonstrative. And actually I started listening to my mother play piano when I was about three, or even less. I mean, I remember, actually, I think I was about three years old. You know, in England they send you to school much sooner than they do here, and I think I might have been about three years old when they sent me to a ... it was like a convent school, but it was a day school; it was nearby, not a very long walk from my house. I don't remember anything too bad about it, but then I remember later my mother said that they took me away from there because they decided it was too soon.

Wong: This was in Windsor?

McPartland: No, this was after. Actually, the town I was born in is such a horrible sounding town and I always say it was near Windsor; the name of the town was Slough. And I was born there, but my parents moved when I was about three months old. I've been there since, and it's really a horrible town. But it's right next to Windsor, where a lot of my mother's relatives lived and worked. And that's where I always spent certain times in my childhood.

My childhood really ties in so much with playing, because my mother played piano and I just remember what she played at the time and getting up on the stool—which was a stool and not a bench—and trying to play this thing, which was a Chopin waltz. And I remember it very clearly. In fact, when I'm doing an interview, I can actually demonstrate and say, "This was the one I played."

Of course, I don't think I was anywhere near perfect. But then I remember making a trip to Windsor to see some relatives, and playing on their piano, which was a very ancient upright. Of course, at that time, I didn't have any ideas about what was a good piano or anything like that. But I just played from then on.

Then I did go to kindergarten. And then I just played. I learned everything by ear. The kids would sing and the teacher would play. It was actually a small school; like a one-room schoolhouse in the beginning, which sounds old fashioned, but that's what it was. I remember certain little things about it, but mainly I remember that everything I did really tied in with playing piano by ear.

Wong: How did you first get interested in jazz per se?

McPartland: From stuff I heard on the radio. I used to listen to copies of tunes all the time and hear the big bands and everything that they had on the BBC. A lot of tunes were ones that were popular here at first. They always wanted to be current with everything that was happening in America. But then when I was in my teens, I had a boyfriend who actually started out being my sister's boyfriend; but he was so interested in jazz—and she wasn't—that he kind of switched to me because I was so receptive to music and wanting to hear all the jazz greats. It just seemed like I assimilated everything that he brought over to the house, all the Fats Waller and James P. Johnson and Duke and Benny Goodman. I just listened to everything that I could lay my hands on.

I sort of had some intermittent piano lessons. And then, when I was actually much younger than my teens, my mother insisted I study the violin, which was really the only musical training I had as a kid. That was something that I really didn't want to do. I wasn't that interested in the violin.

Wong: That was a decision by your parents?

McPartland: Yes. And I just had to do as I was told. I mean, things in those days weren't like they are now. I think, even now, things are a little more civilized over there, although they're getting free. But we weren't. My sister and I, we had to really do what we were told and behave properly, and that's just the way things were.

Wong: How did you get into the profession itself?

McPartland: When I was finally getting to the age when I would be thinking about leaving school, I remember two things: being at the breakfast table when, I guess, I was maybe sixteen or something like that; I remember my mother saying, "Well, you better think what it is you want to do, because we can't keep you." She said it just like that. I don't remember saying anything in reply, just thinking—which I didn't seem to do much of in those days. Later on, I found out that a teacher at school said to my father, "What shall we do with her?" She went on to say to him, "This girl should be studying music." And he sort of said, "Oh, really. Oh well."

So then, I *did* get some real study at the Guildhall School of Music; I was there for about three years and I really got into it. I practiced all day; I would practice eight hours a day, and I really was very motivated.

Wong: Was that classical?

McPartland: Yes.

Wong: And what was the school?

McPartland: Guildhall School of Music. It's a very prestigious place in London. I was already into jazz at that time because I had already started listening to all these people that this guy brought over on records. And I was trying to play like them. Then, I had another boyfriend who had two pianos in his house, and I would go there and we would play tunes back and forth. It was, "Do you know this one and do you know this one?" So I learned millions of standards when I was a teenager.

While I was doing all this—playing classical music, playing scales, playing Beethoven and Bach—I was also taking composition. This went on for about three years. And then, I don't recall really thinking very clearly about this, but I went to see a guy who was very popular at that time, a guy who played … what you'd have to call "novelty" piano. He was very popular and he played a sort of jazz. I went over there to his studio just to sort of take a lesson and have him tell me how to improve my playing. And he heard me play—I remember a tune I played was "Where Are You?" Do you know that?—God, I mean, it's a tune that's still played today; very lovely tune.

I played that for him and he sort of showed me a couple of chords … and, at that time, he invited me to join a group. He was going out on the road with a four piano act, playing in vaudeville theaters. Immediately, I wanted to go! I mean, instantly I decided I must go. And my parents, of course, they were against it; it was such a family upset: "No, you cannot do that."

By this time I was about eighteen or nineteen, and I just went. I finished off at the Guildhall and promised I would go back and made all these promises, "Oh, I'll come back and I'll finish up," and all that stuff. Of course, I never did. I just went on the road with this group. And as I think back, I'm very glad I did.

Wong: What was the makeup of the group?

McPartland: It was this guy, whose name was Billy Mayerl. And he's still popular today, even though he's been long dead.

Wong: What did he play?

McPartland: Piano. He's got a lot of pieces which are sort of novelty, but they're nice. And then there was another man, George Lyttleton, a pianist. And two girls, myself and a girl who had sung a long time with one of the big bands in England.

Wong: So you went on the road around the country?

McPartland: Yeah, all over, good and bad. We played beautiful theaters and we played dumps. When I think about it, I mean, it's good my parents didn't see some of the places. I guess I was so naïve and green, you know, there's all this "stuff." I didn't get into any trouble, because I was just into the music.

We played all these vaudeville theaters. I met people who are quite legendary from over here, like Adelaide Hall was on the bill and Elisabeth Welch and The Peters Sisters.

Just a little while ago they did a special on the Nicholas Brothers, and I worked with them when they were all young guys. Kind of interesting to see them, you know, in their old age. That's what I did for maybe a couple of years.

After that, I did all kinds of odd things, like vaudeville or summer shows, and I did some two pianos. Then, when World War II came, all the women were called up to be in the army, and the only way I could get out of that was by being an entertainer; then you didn't have to go. I was in this group for entertaining the troops and then I joined USO camp shows and I went to France with the first group after they had the invasion.

That's where I met Jimmy, sort of barnstorming around, playing for the GIs all over the place. We would play in a field, or we would play on the back of a truck, or they would put up a stage for us somewhere. It was very exciting when you think about there being a war on and here was this group of us, really having a big time and being treated so wonderfully by all the officers and the GIs. Anyway, by now we're at 1944 ... was when I met Jimmy.

Wong: Then you came over a couple years after that?

McPartland: We got married there, in Germany, in 1945. When Jimmy got his discharge, they worked it out so that he could get discharged and join USO; so we stayed with USO for a few more months. We actually came back here in April of 1946, which was, of course, my first trip to the states. We stayed a little while, because Jimmy wanted to go to Eddie Condon's and go to all the jazz places. And then he introduced me to Louis Armstrong; I was like a kid in a candy store.

Wong: I'll bet.

McPartland: And I played. I wanted to play everywhere and let everybody know I knew all the tunes, and I could play all the Dixieland tunes they played at Eddie Condon's. But then we went to Chicago, where Jimmy's family were and still are. We put a little group together, a quintet, and we played around in Chicago. I think I've played in every bar and joint anywhere, especially in the Midwest. I can think of places that we've played that were really dumps; I mean, I've done everything. I'm sort of proud of it all when I think about it.

Wong: Do you have anything else to say about your childhood before we move on?

McPartland: As I think back, I probably had a pretty good childhood. Although my mother and father were not that demonstrative, I can only think of good things, really.

Wong: Do you ever consciously call upon your childhood experiences when you're creating jazz? Or did you leave that behind?

McPartland: Oh, I don't think you ever leave it behind. No, I probably do. When I think of music that I listened to then, one of my favorite composers was Delius. I suppose I often think of very bucolic things, like walking in the woods and flowers and meadows, because it seemed that that was something that I always liked. And the seashore. We went to different places for holidays at the seashore.

In fact, it's funny you would bring that up because, I don't know if you have it, but I just made a record with strings called *Silent Pool*. That title and the tune actually came from a place I used to go to as a kid with one of my aunts and uncles. I would go there to stay. They lived in a very rural area in the south of England. We would take walks and walked into this beautiful wooded area where this little pool was and that's what it's called, "The Silent Pool." So I would say, that's a direct remembrance of things that I did as a kid. It's funny, because the album came directly from that.

For the cover of the record, I had somebody try to duplicate what I told her I wanted.

I described the area and the trees … and the cover is really quite beautiful. I guess that was something else I was quite good at as a kid: I did paint and draw quite well. In fact, there's a whole bunch of my paintings that I did at school, somebody persuaded me to have framed. I never thought about this; they were laying in envelopes for forty years and somebody said, "Oh, you should frame those things," and so I did.

I suppose I was better at creative things; I was terrible at math, awful. But I have to thank my father for giving me good books to read and having a good vocabulary. I think I have a really good vocabulary and good grammar. I'm really very proud of that. I think kids nowadays are just short changed, they just don't know anything; it's just too bad.

Wong: I think the impact of environmental recollections and awareness certainly have been an enduring factor.

McPartland: Absolutely, absolutely.

Wong: You're illustration is perfect.

McPartland: In retrospect, there was a time when I thought my parents were so strict and so rotten and that they messed me up. And they really did.

As I think about it now, they were really very good and very responsible. I've got such deep sense of responsibility. It's only that it's the price of being neurotic, because they were so insistent on responsibility; at Christmas, I had to write thank you letters to everybody. My father would look at the letter and if there was any kind of mistake in it, I would have to do it over again. That has really stayed with me. You can imagine with all the mail I get and I have this compulsion to reply. I don't ever like to *not* answer people when they write or call. We were taught manners and everything. In fact, we were really hollered at for bad manners or not saying thank you or this or that. At the time, it all seemed silly, but now I'm glad I had all that stuff.

Wong: Since you were speaking about that one recording, what are those recordings that you consider the most important and memorable for you; those that you've done yourself? There are so many.

McPartland: I don't know. It's funny, I'm sort of fairly pleased with some things I do. I mean, I'm always knowing that I could do better. I guess there are some things that I've done that I haven't heard for years, like stuff at The Hickory House and I said, "Oh my God, is that awful!" You know, I'm listening to the chord changes … "What were you *thinking*?!"

I know that things about me have improved from my own awareness. But also, mingling with other musicians and hearing Bill Evans play—not deliberately trying to copy something, but able to hear something that I can use that is similar—but not trying to copy *everything*.

Wong: Besides Bill, what have been some of your most important historical associations with jazz musicians or jazz figures?

McPartland: Oh, well, Duke. I must have had good taste or something; or at least I knew what I liked. I remember as a teenager hearing some of these early Duke Ellington recordings. I can remember being absolutely aghast by the harmony, and then by him as a piano player. I've got a record he must have done in the '50s, maybe, a solo piano. In fact, I still have it downstairs, this LP of Duke playing solo piano. And some of his most beautiful tunes are on there, like "Reflections in D."

He was quite important to me as a fan, because he used to come to this club when I was there. The press agent for the club was also his press agent, so he used to spend a lot of time in there. I guess he liked the music and he would make comments to me about what I played. Of course, naturally, I learned millions of Ellington and Strayhorn tunes; actually, I probably already knew all the Duke Ellington tunes, but I would learn Billy Strayhorn tunes because he was sitting right there. I think tunes like "Lush Life" are some of the most gorgeous ever written. And you just don't ever give up playing those things.

Wong: Who are some other ones, other historical figures?

McPartland: Art Tatum, my God … I mean, I even was foolish enough to go a music store and buy a book of transcriptions from him. I never could read very well; I just wasn't that good a reader. And I would try to put these things out and I thought, oh gosh, this is ridiculous. Then, I just tried to pick stuff up off records. I spent hours with the record player, which in those days was a windup. I would sit at the piano and play a few bars and then try to duplicate them. Of course, I learned all the tunes of Fats Waller and I knew a lot of Benny Goodman tunes, and things that Teddy did. I always wanted to play like Teddy, play all those sparkling little runs and beautifully executed harmonies.

Wong: How would you describe your music from a stylistic point of view now?

McPartland: Well, remnants of bebop. Because, of course, I started out playing kind of straight ahead, I guess you could call it, sort of like cocktail piano. And then, of course, when Jimmy and I were together, I guess somehow…. I don't know how I knew all these tunes … but I did know them, so I could play. I've really got a Dixieland repertoire; I can play all those tunes that he liked to play, like "Louisiana" and "Basin Street Blues" and "Davenport Blues" and all those big things. I play all those.

Jimmy could see that I was getting into bebop and he really helped to get me started with my own trio. He really was such a great force in my life, in getting me started on my own. It was almost to his detriment, because he had got so used to having me play with the group, and I guess I was getting quite good at it, and then all of a sudden I started my own trio and he's going back to all the other piano players. There were plenty of them, but it was sort of a different thing. I guess he created a monster by helping me out with my own trio.

There's elements of bebop and elements of a little touch of fusion. I can go totally free and play with Cecil Taylor, and it all comes off. I can do that. But my own style is kind of with the most interesting harmony I can find, and I don't do much exploring. I usually kind of like to do things on the spot and see what comes out.

Wong: What do you think about when you're improvising?

McPartland: It depends. Sometimes I'm thinking about the next tune, like what would go here. Sometimes I'm thinking: Boy, all these people are in their 70s, what am I gonna play for *them*? I might be thinking that, but a lot of times, I'm just thinking about the actual tune, how not to play the same old shit—if you'll pardon the expression.

I try and be different every time I play a tune, whether it be changing the key or the tempo. A lot of things come out differently because of the rhythm section. I have a really adventuresome bass player who will do things that will spark me into doing something I wasn't expecting to do.

I may be thinking about the extra tune, or maybe the lyrics, a lot of times. A lot of us have talked about knowing the lyrics to a tune and how important that is. I think, probably, my favorite thing to do is to play ballads. I'm an absolutely ridiculous unabashed romantic Frank Sinatra fan. I've always got so much from all those tunes. I think probably one of my favorite tunes is that Harold Arlen song, "Last Night When We Were Young." That has such an interesting lyric, and it's not necessarily a tune I play all the time, but it's probably one of my favorite tunes. And a whole bunch of Ellington ballads, like "Prelude to a Kiss." I love that. I mean, there's millions of tunes that you can play.

Wong: Do you have problems or constraints that you meet in the process of improving? And if you do, how do you resolve those?

McPartland: The only problem I might have, and that's the beauty of jazz, is trying to execute some run or passage that I didn't do too cleanly. But you can really kind of play it, because with jazz you can play what you're capable of instead of having to play from a sheet of music and do what's there. So if there's something I can't do, I don't do it.

Wong: So beyond execution, you don't find any problems for your creating?

McPartland: Well, again, if I'm by myself it's different from if I'm with a rhythm section. Because, I do work with the same guys a lot. But, if for some reason you might have a strange bass player—I don't think I've had one in quite a long time—but if you had somebody that's new, that might be the only inhibiting thing. It might be what they would play that would force me to play the way they were playing, or miss a certain harmony that I would want to do. Because I have perfect pitch, it's helpful in that I can always hear every single note that's played. I always think it should be easy to play the bass, because they only have to play one note at a time. But some of them have problems getting from one note to the lick.

Wong: What are some typical conditions under which you're most creative? Are there some?

McPartland: This has a lot to with an audience or a room. I do definitely get vibes from the audience. And actually, I think the last few years, things have been really pretty good all the way around. Years ago I can remember playing in some clubs where people would be talking and not paying attention. And I haven't had a thing like that happen to me for so many years, I think I'd be in shock if it did. The only clubs I play now are one in Seattle called Jazz Alley … and at Yoshi's. And it's amazing: people are very silent, like they're at a concert. When I think of conditions at the Carlyle, when I was playing in the bar, and that was as late as the '60s and '70s, I guess … I mean, the people were so rude.

But I guess *I* was very rude. I would say awful things to people … and people remind me of things that I said, and I don't know how I got away with that. But it seems like all that's gone away, for me at least, when people would be noisy. In fact, I think that's when I really did make a career move, which was to get into the concert field, which I did by learning to play the Grieg "Piano Concerto." It amazes me that I was able to do that and play it, well, fairly creditably. I mean, it wasn't bad, it's wasn't quite Rubinstein, but it wasn't bad.

I played a bunch of symphony orchestras for several years doing that. That sort of got me out of nightclubs. I still do all those dates, but now I do them with an Ellington medley, a Gershwin medley, my own tunes; I've got some really beautiful symphony arrangements—some of them by Robert Farnon. In fact, I'm gonna do a date in San Luis Obispo in July … do you know Alan Broadbent?

Wong: I know him extremely well. I was going to mention him, because he wrote those beautiful string arrangements for you.

McPartland: That's the one I'm talking about, *Silent Pool*.

Wong: Alan and I have been friends since he was twenty-one, when he was still at Berklee College of Music, and then he was drafted by Nat Pierce for Woody's band.

McPartland: I think I met him when he was playing at Michael's Pub with Irene Kral, and she was so wonderful. She's another singer who would make me want to learn the songs—hearing singers do certain songs always has such an effect on me. Like Peggy Lee would do certain things. I've got albums of hers. I loved Peggy Lee; years ago, she did some gorgeous things.

Wong: Irene was so special.

McPartland: Yes, I've got about three albums of hers with Alan.

Wong: Alan is a rarity, isn't he?

McPartland: Oh, he is. And he did such a beautiful job with those pieces. I'm hoping we can do another one, because I didn't realize how many tunes I have that are just lying around. I was always so—oh, I don't know—*unbelieving* that I have written any good tunes. I didn't have any faith in what I'd written. As I look at some of them now, those I wrote years ago, I'm thinking, my God, that tune is really good. It's really funny, I very rarely play my own stuff. I've got a new record coming out and I'm playing only to satisfy myself that all the glitches were out. But the guy who did the mastering had taken out any bad notes. Then after the thing is out, maybe I'll play it once and I'd probably never play it again. Instead, I'm on to the next one.

Wong: How do other people stimulate your own creativity? Do you work it up yourself or it just happens?

McPartland: I don't know. I suppose sometimes it's like the carrot with the donkey. Somebody will say a couple of things … ideas … somebody asked me to write a piece for the New Jersey PBS station: "We need a piece that we're going to use as the ballet music for something or other." I was able to come out with this thing which worked out very well and it's one that I actually recorded on a thing that Alan arranged; it's called "A Delicate Balance."

I just sort of tell myself to do it. Like when I was doing the record, the music of Mary Lou Williams that we were doing. And I thought, I really should have something as a tribute to Mary Lou of my own on this record. So I just started thinking about her and how I've known her and what a sad thing it was that she had died, and all this stuff. And along came this tune, which is really a nice tune. And, in fact, it was just recorded by Nnenna Freelon.

Wong: I wonder: Is there a distinction between creating as a composer, for you, and creating as an improviser?

McPartland: I don't know, I've never thought about it. I just know when I'm playing a tune that I will try—especially if it's an *up* tune—to make it build and do different kinds of choruses, so that when the tune ends it will be on a high note or it will be…

Wong: Climactic?

McPartland: That's sort of what I'm thinking about. But a lot of times the creative thing will just come out of the air; I'll hear a phrase somewhere, maybe even something I can use as a title. A lot of things that I've written have sort of come from the title. And some of them have had quite romantic connotations. You know, the thing's actually drawn from life and you can sort of put the tune together. I've never tried to write lyrics. I've always felt my lyrics would be very kind of trite. But I can sort of put together some dummy lyrics to make the tune happen.

And then, I *do* get turned on by kids, I guess. I've done a lot of stage band clinics in the past. In fact, I'm thinking of one I did years ago. I know it's got to be years ago, because Pat Metheny was fifteen, and he was at the clinic and he wrote a big band piece for me and, God, and I don't know what I did with it; I've got it somewhere in my house. And I'd like to confront him with it one of these days. Anyway, I just felt that I had to do something to show that I could do something for the kids. It's being creative, but yet it's also, you're thinking, I just have to sit down and do *something*. And suddenly this tune of mine just fell into place that you might have heard, called "Ambiance"…

Wong: Oh, I love that thing!

McPartland: … and that just fell together that particular year, when Pat Metheny was fifteen and I was in Norman, Oklahoma, doing a stage band residency there with people like John Carter and Phil Wilson and … I forget who the rhythm section was. That's when I wrote that tune. It kind of fell together in less than an hour. I always think that, when people say they write something so quickly, I'm always thinking: Oh, shame on you, you didn't take any trouble. But then, sometimes it does happen that way, it just does fall together in a short time.

Wong: I remember some years ago you referred to this tune and you chatted about it. It was something that you held with a lot of special feeling.

McPartland: Not that one so much. That one was actually, I think at that time we were driving around and there was a Herbie Hancock record that was very popular at the time called, *Fat Albert Rotunda*.

Wong: Yes.

McPartland: I have that upstairs. And I don't know, there were some things on there that might have helped to sort of put together "Ambiance," although it's not like anything that was on that record. But I always sort of credit Herbie Hancock for putting me in the mood.

There's a couple of other ones: there's a nice ballad that I did, that Peggy Lee wrote a lyric for, called "In the Days of Our Love"; and, unfortunately, that's not one of the ones Alan did. But he did another one that I like called "Twilight World," that Johnny Mercer did the lyrics for. So I get a chance to do something else with Alan … and that's another thing: Sometimes you dream about doing something and you just have to make it happen.

Wong: The impetus sometimes comes from something obligatory?

McPartland: Yes, really, that's true. And then you think about something that you want to do. And you just think, oh, I really want to do that. But then, the hard part is thinking of ways to make it happen, and that has happened a lot in my life with things … like this thing with the Grieg. God, I don't know how I ever did that. I really did that particular piece was because I was mad at Alec Wilder. I had asked him to write something for me and he said, "Oh, my dear, I couldn't write anything for you. You don't read well enough." He was right, absolutely right. But then, on the other hand, I'm glad now that if he had written a piece for me it would have been something brand new that I would have no reference from anywhere else. It would be something that would have been so much harder for me to learn, so I'm glad. Then, I said immediately to myself: "Oh, the hell with you, I'm gonna learn the Grieg concerto." I started right out on it and I had a teacher work with me. I learned most of it from listening to a Rubinstein record, as a matter of fact, because my reading is so bad, but my ear is so good.

Wong: They're so good, they can become independently sufficient for you, it seems.

McPartland: I kind of wish I could be like Dick Hyman. He can read anything, even if it was a slice, then he'd make it sound good.

Wong: He's a pretty amazing guy.

McPartland: We've done a few things. We're doing a date in July with Dick and this classical pianist, Ruth Laredo. We've put together a sort of combination classic and jazz, because she's a wonderful reader and Dick writes out stuff for her. Like he wrote out "Dizzy Fingers" for her to play and, I mean, she reads it.

Wong: Speaking of classics, what recordings by other musicians do you consider indispensable classics of jazz? Essential? Just a couple or three …

McPartland: Oh, I think a lot of Bill Evans, like *You Must Believe in Spring* is one record I really like of his. I absolutely love that Chick Corea record, *Now He Sings, Now He Sobs*. I thought that was one of the best things I ever heard and it kills me that Roy Haynes is so totally up on everything. I mean, we had him as a guest and, who would know the guy is over seventy; he plays like a young kid.

Wong: Yes, he does.

McPartland: And, you know, any Art Tatum.

Wong: And Duke?

McPartland: Duke … probably the solo piano thing, and then some of his things that he's done, like "The Queen's Suite." Oh, and really, there are some tunes of his that don't get played all that much, like "Warm Valley." I love that tune, but the tune is hard. A lot of his tunes, you really have to have the right chords to go from the first part, because of the bridge. There are so many jokes in "Sophisticated Lady." If you don't get the right chords going into the bridge, you can fall off. And it's true, having played that with a whole bunch of different people. We're getting to that particular place, where I kind of wait and hear what the other person is going to do if it's somebody I don't know.

Wong: Let me ask you a very open question. What is this thing called jazz?

McPartland: I would almost think that jazz means different things to different people. That to some people jazz might mean something totally rhythmic. Whereas other people, like Bill Evans or George Shearing, might be more concerned with the harmonic end of it. But whatever your feelings are about it, there's a certain looseness that is not in other music. It's sort of like—I think I've said this before, but it's the only thing I can think of—like having a piece of string which will only stretch just so far and then having a rubber band which is more loose and you can kind of stretch it a little bit. And to me that's what jazz is like.

I think there are some things that people do in jazz that would be really terribly hard to notate, when you're crossing bar lines. Like playing with Ray Charles. I once said to him, "Now I can really find out what it feels like." Because he lays back so far that it's almost in the previous bar, you know. It's just ridiculous. So actually to play something with him, you get to know what he's feeling when he's doing that. You have to know where you are; you can't be like that unless you really know what you're doing. Like Anita O'Day used to do that. And to me, it's not something you can learn—maybe I'm wrong in saying that it's a sort of looseness …

Wong: Elastic.

McPartland: Yes, that's what it is, it is elastic. But if you were wrong, if you don't know what you're doing, it can be disastrous. I've sort of lost the question: What is this thing called jazz? That's all I can think of. I'm sure somebody like Chick Corea would give us a totally different answer. Everybody has their own answer.

Wong: In what ways do you feel you've helped jazz to grow or to progress? I think your shows, in their own way, have been highly significant contributions to furthering awareness, appreciation, and just revealing an enormous amount of insightful stuff.

McPartland: I never used to think about that, but I guess I'm forced to think about it. I do see this happening after being on the air so many years and hearing so many people play and their ways of playing and the things they say about their playing. And when you've got somebody like Dave McKenna, who's such a mainstream player, and then you're gonna have Bill Evans or you're gonna have Herbie Hancock or then you're gonna go all the way to Cecil Taylor, who I've never had really explain what he does. He always manages to wiggle out of it somehow. I always try to nail him on why he does certain things and he's got a wonderful way of speaking and explaining stuff, but he totally obfuscates everything he's saying. You never really know what it is he's doing. But I sort of love it in a way, because it's funny. I mean, I can go with it, I can play with him.

Wong: That's one of the amazing things. You're so adaptable. From one day to the next you can go from one extreme to the other. You're very remarkable.

McPartland: You're making my head swim.

Wong: Talking about elasticity, my gosh, you stretch, and you have to stretch so far.

McPartland: But it's never seemed hard for me and I don't know why that is. I think it's because I've heard, listened to and absorbed, not deliberately, but sort of by osmosis, hearing all kinds of music very early on, like on the BBC. And having all this stuff go in my head and trying to play it without any reason except for, it's a nice tune, I have to learn that. Or something on a record and I'd hear it and I'd play it. And I guess when I was very young I probably learned a lot quicker than I would now. I don't know, I seem to take forever when trying to take somebody's tune off a record and I'll be sitting there with a piece of paper and a pen. I think years ago I was probably just quicker.

I guess it's nice to know that you have done something. And, of course, it's because I've been able to have all these wonderful guests. I've just been able to kind of be the person that was able to bring them out.

Wong: Yes, that you do, indeed. Do you select all these people yourself?

McPartland: Yes, pretty much. Occasionally somebody will come up with it.

Wong: And you'll have musicians that are not necessarily pianists, and that's been very interesting.

McPartland: Well, I just thought that we should do that. There are so many people who are great musicians, but they're not necessarily piano players. But in the beginning we just stuck with people who did play, like Gerry Mulligan, like Gary Burton. And we got into Dizzy and then Milt Jackson.

Wong: Clark Terry.

McPartland: Clark Terry, but I don't think he could play any piano.

Wong: No.

McPartland: There's lots of people that really don't play, like Rosemary Clooney and Tony Bennett, who don't want to go near the piano. But then the rationalization was that, well, I still play, and even if they're not playing, they're singing, and I do extra playing maybe, or it'll just be different because of what they're going to bring to it. And we've had such terrific people. But, you know, having Tony was like having Beau Williams and they're so easy to work with. I can't think of anybody that's been hard to work with.

Wong: Lastly, do you have any view on jazz education today or for tomorrow? Because in your own way, that's what you're doing.

McPartland: Well, I don't know what to say, because unfortunately so many kids, because of what's happening on radio and TV, don't even know jazz exists, unfortunately. I mean, as Wynton said one time, they all play with what is enforced terms. That's what you listen to because it sells. I mean, marketing is a horrible word to me, because it means you're selling something which isn't necessarily good. I just hear some horrible music.

Wong: You don't have any perceived remedies? No one does?

McPartland: I wish I knew. I think all we can do is, if we see any kid that's gonna take even a moment to listen to what you or I are doing, just grab them and make sure they hear more. I mean, I started doing a date in the high schools here for no other reason except that I thought there weren't enough kids there that knew anything about jazz and that maybe if I got in there and did a concert with them it would improve them. And it has. I've been doing it for seven years now and there are a lot of kids who are really getting into it. I see a great improvement. There's a recording studio here that tapes the concert and gets it back to the kids. And they really are not as good as they should be for kids fifteen and sixteen, but every so often there's one or two that stand out from the bunch.

One would hope it will spread around. I keep in touch with so many of them that have either gone into music, or they haven't, or they become lawyers or whatever. I still keep up with them. And then there's a bunch of people that I've known for many years.

Sometimes somebody will come up to me and say, "Oh, you played at my high school and I remember thinking how good the group was," and stuff like that. It's nice to know that you did something that they remember. Maybe they will be better listeners when they're listening to records, because they will all listen to that.

Wong: What else would you like to do in the future that you haven't done yet? After all, you've done almost everything.

McPartland: I'd love to write more and I keep talking about it. See, I really just don't think at this late date I could ever learn to orchestrate, but I can sort of put down ideas. And I've had this woman, who I'm sure you'll hear about eventually, her name is Ellen Rowe, and she's a very fine pianist and arranger who used to go to the Eastman School. She's now on the faculty in Ann Arbor, Michigan. She's done a few very nice symphonic arrangements for me, and I want to do something, kind of a musical statement, about the environment.

I've talked about it so much that pretty soon somebody is gonna sit down and do it. They'll say, "Oh, that's a good idea," and they'll do it while I'm still thinking about it. I thought I'd get Ellen, who really is a terrific writer, and I would give her these ideas and how I think they should be. She's the best person I can think of. I've had a few people that I've worked with, but she's sort of the most constant, in that we've done things. In fact, when she was at the Eastman School, I called up Ray Wright and I said, "Well, who have you got who would do some symphony charts?" He recommended Ellen and she did one; she's done a lot of stuff for me. So, I thought maybe she'd have the time to work on this thing.

Wong: So it might be a symphonic piece?

McPartland: Yes, that's what I had in mind. But I really have to get off my ass and do it. You know, I've been talking about it for a long time and it's getting to the point that again, it's like the carrot and the donkey. If somebody said to me, "McPartland, if you write that piece we'll commit at such and such," that's probably what I have to do. I have to get somebody to say that.

Wong: Well, yes, it is about time.

McPartland: Yes, it is indeed.

— ·· — ·· — ·· — ·· — ·· — ·· — ·· — ·· — ·· — ·· — ·· — ·· — ·· — ·· —

Tee Carson

Tee Carson was probably one of best substitutes for Count Basie that ever existed. He knew the Count's library like the back of his hand. In fact, Tee was openly favored by Basie.

I recall a sample instance of that relationship: I was in the studio of Pablo Records—the personal label of Norman Granz—for a Basie band date. There was a passage in "Satin Doll" that was in contention between Granz and the Count. At one point in the session, Norman issued a comment on what he thought should be done with the passage and which musician should be playing it. It sounded more like an insistent directive than a helpful comment. A vividly angry Basie took issue with the point being made by Granz, objecting to the interference the suggested interpretation would cause to the fluidity of the arrangement. But, instead of playing the part the way *he* thought it should be played, Basie left the piano bench and invited Tee Carson to play it.

Norman played no further part in that discussion.

When Tee needed to supplement his income from gigs that were becoming more sporadic, he started working as a money market fund salesman in Palo Alto. That's how Tee Carson raised the funds needed to bring a host of Basie band members together for his own salute to the Count, *Basically Count*.

Tee Carson & The Basie Bandsmen—*Basically Count*

Palo Alto Records (PA 8005); 1981

> "Tee Carson is a marvelous jazz pianist—sensitive, fresh and tasty. Having him in a group means a guarantee to swing."
>
> —Billy Taylor

Amidst the pantheon of jazz giants, there is a special handful commanding universal respect. One of these favorites is Count Basie. The Basie tradition carries evergreen trademarks and getting a handle on the music is easy and direct; it's certainly not like trying to grasp smoke or fog.

Basie subscribes to an emphasis on swinging straight ahead—a generally uncomplicated brand of jazz. Its appeal is powerfully lively, communicating quickly with musicians in the band and with audiences. The remarkable sense of time, likened to the precision of a fine Swiss watch, comes out of Basie's style and fundamental piano qualities. His relaxed economical style packs a powerhouse swing that moves the sections of the orchestra into line—feeding soloists and ensemble logically and naturally. "The chief thing I do is pace-setting; you know, tempos … and I feed the soloists," Basie once said. "Other people use the piano for solos—guys who can really play it, but I use it as part of the rhythm section."

Vital to the mellow groove and dependable support to the band is the unfailingly tight alliance of the bass and guitar, charged in turn by the propulsive swing of the drums. The long tenure of guitarist Freddie Green with Basie is unique in jazz. Since March 1937, Green has welded the Basie rhythm section, providing supreme support to Basie's piano. His bright reputation as the best rhythm guitarist in the history of jazz is without challenge.

Considering Basie's assets, it is difficult finding a pianist-leader who can spell Basie in all that must happen from the piano bench. Failing health has plagued Basie in recent years and the need for a suitable surrogate has occurred at times.

Certainly pianist Nat Pierce has capably filled in for Basie now and then. However, a period in 1979 and again between May and September 1980 ushered Tee Carson into the band. Basie recently chose Carson to play "Satin Doll" on the orchestra's latest album *Warm Breeze* on Pablo Records (Carson did not receive due credit on the disc).

Carson has been familiar to Basie for many years as Carson was Ella Fitzgerald's conducting pianist between 1968 and 1971, intermittently playing opposite the Basie band. Carson had replaced the stalwart Jimmy Jones and then preceded Tommy Flanagan as Fitzgerald's accompanist. "On occasion I've tuned up Basie's band as well as doing some of his rehearsals, too," adds Carson.

Beckoned to duty when Basie was ill, Carson was welcomed with unanimous, warm respect from the band. This positive altitude is best represented through Freddie Green who holds the record for the longest membership in the band ... 45 years! Green generally offers praise conservatively, a perspective pertinent to appreciating Green's statement of confidence to Carson: "All the years that I've been with the band, a lot of guys have come around and wanted to sit in. But you've got my vote."

A native of Washington, D.C., Donald T. Carson's career has sparkled with jazz star associations beginning in 1946 with Ethel Waters. Leading a house band, he worked with numerous vocalists of historical stature, including Billie Holiday, Johnny Hartman, Herb Jeffries, Maxine Sullivan, Pearl Bailey and, of course, Ella Fitzgerald. Likewise, the string of luminary jazz instrumentalists Carson has played with is long, indeed.

Since his relatively recent move to the San Francisco Bay Area, Carson has enhanced many a jazz gig, besides his impressive stand-in work in Basie's band. For instance, the music of Philly Joe Jones, Benny Carter, Mark Murphy and Lorez Alexandria have all been graced by Carson's piano. His trio dates at the Monterey and Feather River Jazzfests featured Marc Johnson and Vince Lateano and then Frank Tusa and Shelly Manne—drawing compliments for his sun-glow musicality and ability to swing on turbo drive.

Tee Carson brings to this recording his well-crafted storehouse of strengths in union with nine other active Basie-ites right out of the current Basie orchestra. The top caliber of these musicians combined with the basic idiom of swing, blues and improvisation give the record a convincing feeling and a crisply fashioned Basie sound. The blues and the Basie tradition have been an inseparable blend for many decades.

The rhythm section rings authentic with Carson at the piano. He uses the keyboard end to end giving the session a wide palette of colors. Moreover, he lends judicious support to the ensemble via accentuations, expressions of urgency and encouragement—communicating directly with fans and musicians alike. Cleveland Eaton's big-toned bass suits the bluesy Basie type of music and Gregg Field supplies the requisites with aplomb, also.

Observe that the smaller band setting literally allows Green much more audible space (than in the full Basie orchestra) to reiterate his immutable excellence as per the Basie magic. In fact, everyone in the band is heard with keener definition ... yet the tentet sounds as dynamic as a big band of half again its size. Note, too, how the flexible ensemble sound and invigorating delicacy suggest a lineal descent from the late John Kirby's wonderful little band of about four decades ago.

Carson's style reflects an ability to choose the better chords intuitively and to adjust the rhythmic accents with ease. Make no mistake, Carson is a rich distillation of multiple lines of influence in jazz piano history and development, and is essentially his own man.

"Musicians are all inspired by others and you take the inspiration ... samplings of their flavor, and put them in a big vat, stir it, then add as much of your own self to it," says Carson. "The dexterity of Art Tatum and Oscar Peterson, the flow of Erroll Garner, the simplicity of Bill Evans, the stride of Fats Waller, the great styles of Nat Cole, Earl Hines and Lennie Tristano ... I try to carry but subordinate these influences and maintain my own identity on top."

The warm voicings, lyricism and finesse Carson gets are gained in part from his years of accompanying vocalists. "Restricted to a trio in a sense forced me to emulate a full band playing," notes Carson—accounting, too, for his comfortable adaptation to the Basie environment. Carson is indeed very much together when he plays the changes. He sculpts melodies into the chords and threads these phrases with poise.

Besides young Field and to some extent trumpeter Dale Carley, everyone in the band is a seasoned jazzman. In fact, half of the band has been in the Basie clan for at least 17 years (Bobby Plater, Eric Dixon, Bill Hughes, Grover Mitchell and Green). Veteran trumpeter Willie Cook spent many years with Duke Ellington's Orchestra, Carley with Clark Terry's Big Band and Cleve Eaton with Ramsey Lewis. Each brings a unique jazz voice to the music.

As for the tunes, the composer credits represent a good distribution among the writer-players. Except for Carson's sensitive ballad "E'naj," augmented by the voices of Acapella Gold, the groove tunes are all written with punchy section work and swash-buckling swing in mind.

Rather than singling out solos or peeling off a rundown of each tune, view them with a unified gestalt-ish perspective as there is so much satisfaction with them all. However, a few other highlights should be cited: the uplifting firepower trumpets of Carley and Cook, and the creamy fluidity and mature virility of Plater and Dixon's flutes and saxes.

And dig the classic riff lines with a dancing line of agile solos ... the spirited, supple vocal on Freddie Green's infectious "Until I Met You" by Mary Stallings who had sung with Basie's band for a couple of years. It's a tune I thought would be Stallings' groove, lending an added slant to the program of tunes. The band size drops to just Plater and Carley plus the four-man rhythm section. "Mary has always been a marvelous singer and she swings!" offers Count Basie.

The congenial, relaxed atmosphere pervaded the sessions and this unusual rapport among friends is reflected in the music here. Immediately after the session, trombonist Grover Mitchell observed, "It's better than I expected, man! It was a ball!" Carson quickly added: "Straight ahead! We just kept that dancing feeling going." You may agree that *Basically Count* is also Basically Tee! It swings from Tee Carson's first notes of his title tune to the clinging warm memories of the last notes of Plater's "Aw Shoosh" ... YEAH!

Dave Brubeck

In 1949, I had just returned from the armed services. I noticed that there was a course on jazz piano being offered by the music department at the University of California at Berkeley as a part of their extension curriculum. I thought, OK, I guess I'll go and check it out. Turned out it was Dave Brubeck and his wife, Iola, teaching the class. That's when I first met both of them.

Dave played the piano and the commentary was conducted by Iola; she made *all* the remarks. From my point of view, Dave was somewhat shy at the time, so he relegated the commentary to Iola and they gave the students a kind of an overview of the history of the jazz piano.

They were in dire straits and in desperate need of financial assistance in those days to the extent that, after one of the classes, Dave said to me, "Herb, can you lend me five dollars?" And I said, "Of course!"

I made sure I heard Dave whenever he played in the Bay Area and I tried to catch him when he had a gig wherever I happened to be visiting. Through the years our acquaintance grew until we got together in Monterey on the festival bill.

I used that opportunity to casually start up a conversation with Dave backstage, with ulterior motives in mind. During our chat, I changed the subject, mentioning in kind of a joking manner, "Dave, where's my five bucks? Do you remember when you borrowed it?" He said, "Yeah ... did I ever pay you back?" And I said, "No you didn't."

So Dave reached into his pocket, saying, "Well here, let me pay you back...." I held up my hands in mock horror. "No, no, Dave! I don't want you to pay me back. If you paid me back, I wouldn't have any story left to tell!"

And I never let him pay me back that infamous five bucks.

Conversations with Dave Brubeck

Monterey Jazz Festival; September 2002 (with excerpts from September 1998)

Wong: Welcome, Dave.

Brubeck: Thank you.

[To audience]

He was in my first class. I was the teacher. He was the student. Now look at him ... he's teaching me!

Wong: Well, Dave, those were memorable days.

[To audience]

This guy has so much vigor and creative vitality that it boggles the mind and stretches the imagination to its hilt!

Wong: For those who don't remember the conversation we had on these grounds, it might be useful to take a few moments to run through a quick recap of 1998, when we spent an hour-and-a-half here, with this place packed. Back in '98, we discussed your childhood culture ...

[Excerpt from 1998 Wong/Brubeck Conversation]

Wong: Dave, I know that a lot of people are familiar with your past or various parts of it, but perhaps if you could recount some parts of your childhood foundation in relation to how you were able to get into the career path of being a jazz pianist, since your family environment did not allow a radio or jazz records to be in the home. You want to bounce a little bit on that, Dave?

Brubeck: That's true, but what's even better than not having a radio or records is to have the real music. My mother said "any music in this house you have to make yourself," and that started before you were born. She believed in pre-natal influence, and my two older brothers were tremendous musicians. You were put in the crib next to the piano

Dave Brubeck and Herb Wong on stage during their 1998 conversation at the Monterey Jazz Festival (photograph by Andy Nozaka; courtesy Andy Nozaka).

and she taught music most of the day and then after dinner she practiced it seemed like … oh … 'til midnight. I was hearing the greatest piano literature every day.

On my way over here, somebody poked their head out the window and said, "Del Courtney says hello from Honolulu." Now, this is very important, because Del's band rehearsed every Thursday night in our house. So, I was hearing a jazz band from the time I was five or six in our front room. My brother and Del were roommates at the College of the Pacific and they worked at the ballroom, the Oakland Hotel Ballroom, and would drive up to Pacific. It was a rough life for them to keep that going. Later, my brother, Henry, worked with the Gil Evans Band, which is one of the most important bands in jazz. Most people don't realize that it came out of Stockton, California.

We were in Concord, California, where I was born, my brothers were born, my mother was born and their ancestors walked to from places like Indiana, across the plains. So I am a native Californian. My wife is fourth generation Californian, going back to 1835.

But the question is, where did I hear jazz? It was certainly at my house and next door. A fellow I've known since he was a half-hour old—because in those days you were born at home—is Bob Skinner. How many people know that name? You see, he was a great local pianist who has played all his life in the San Francisco–Oakland–San Rafael area. He's the one that would get the jazz records and I'd go next door. The first group I ever listened to, how many of you remember Billy Kyle? There you go, there's a few. He's played right here many times with Louis Armstrong. He was the pianist with Louis. He had a trio in, I would say around '36 or '37 called the Billy Kyle Trio. I played two pianos with my idol, Billy Kyle, right here on the fairgrounds when we did the show with Louis Armstrong. Louis's band was on the stage and my group, along with Lambert, Hendricks and Ross, Carmen McRae and Louis. Did any of you hear that performance? They say that it was one of the highlights of the Monterey Festival and it's been re-released on CD on Sony Records, which I'm very happy about.

Wong: In that 1998 conversation, Dave, we also talked about some of the formative areas of your career and your lifetime trail into the halls of the College of the Pacific; and some of the decisions that were made then that were very crucial to the rest of your life. We talked about your brothers, your family, the family values that were so important to you.

We talked about your work with Cal Tjader ... Paul Desmond ... all the rest of the people involved with your very important and very advanced-in-time ensemble called the Dave Brubeck Octet. We also talked about how you opened the gates to the campuses for jazz, the first person to pioneer the first jazz concerts on campuses.

[To audience]

It was Dave Brubeck who opened those doors.

[Excerpt from 1998 Wong/Brubeck conversation]

Wong: How about some comment on your study and work with Darius Milhaud at Mills College. I think this was a very pivotal experience for you.

Brubeck: There were so many great musicians that were interested in studying with Darius Milhaud. My brother and Pete Rugolo were Milhaud's first male students at Mills College and that's the way I got to meet Darius Milhaud. I had an interview and a lesson and I knew it was going to be years before the war was over, but I swore that I would come back and study with him. They had a wonderful program called the GI Bill and so, being that he was probably in the top three composers in the world ... there was Stravinsky, Bartók and Milhaud; you can place them where you'd like ... so we all wanted to study with him.

After the war, we went to Mills College and three of the guys were at San Francisco State: Cal Tjader, Ron Crotty and Paul Desmond. They came over to Mills and we formed the Octet, which I think was one of the most advanced groups that ever got together. We predated the birth of the cool and what was going on back in New York. I think we were a little wilder and maybe more inventive and maybe less jazz-oriented because we were interested in bringing the classical and the jazz together more than I think they were.

When we registered to go to Mills, Milhaud said, "How many of you are jazz musicians, would you raise your hands?" And I thought, here we go again, out the door, because there wasn't a college or university in the country that would admit to having any kind of jazz in their schools; whether it was Juilliard, or Oberlin, or Pacific, or Berkeley ... any place ... and here's this great musician saying "raise your hands."

We raised our hands and he said, "I would like you to write for the jazz instruments when you do your fugues and counterpoint compositions. Do it for the jazz musicians if you want."

My first known group was born at Mills College—a girls' school. It was very advanced and Milhaud said, "Why don't you play for the students at their assembly?" and our first concert was on the Mills campus. Then they asked me to go up to College of the Pacific, where I had graduated. We went up there with the Octet. It was a wonderful group.

Wong: Dave, I'm going to turn to some of the events and activities that have transpired since we were on stage here together four years ago. I thought I'd jump to the year 2000, which was a crucial year for many of the things that you've been involved with.

In April of that year—and I was privileged to be a part of the event—it was the sesquicentennial celebration of the University of the Pacific in Stockton, which was also the inaugural event for the great Brubeck Institute.

The music that you did with the University of the Pacific Choral Group and the Symphony Orchestra was transcendent; and you had another gig with the Stockton Symphony Orchestra. Can you give us some impressions about that particular event, because so many things were happening … a lot was going on there surrounding your life and music; can you share something about all of that?

Brubeck: The piece I wrote for the Stockton Symphony Orchestra was called "Millennium Interval" and, for me, in this millennium, the interval was the flat fifth. You musicians, you may know that interval: it's the one that became very prominent in all of bebop. It was prominent in classical composers, like Stravinsky in "The Rite of Spring."

I wanted to give a quick history of me leaving the cattle ranch and going to college, and the first thing I was aware of on campus was the campanile and the bells. So, I had those in there with a flat fifth. They didn't sound typical of the campanile, but they sounded good. Then I also sneaked in, with a lot of flat fifths, "California, Here I Come!" The whole symphony orchestra played that tune and I don't think they recognized it! And then I had the school song in, also with a lot of flat fifths.

The "Millennium Interval" had a lot to do with the interval that I still love. It was often referred to as "the Devil's interval." In classical music, you weren't supposed to use it; singers in choral music do not like to sing it—even great soloists don't like to sing it … [Brubeck hums example] … it's a hard interval to get in tune—so I had a lot of fun with it!

Wong: I'd like to turn to a celebration of your 80th birthday in London, where you were invited, along with your sons, on your 70th, 75th, and 80th birthdays. One of the by-products of your visit was this incredible recording with the London Symphony Orchestra with a Brubeckian repertoire…

[London Symphony Orchestra performing "Take Five" plays]

[Excerpt from 1998 Wong/Brubeck conversation]

Wong: I thought since hardly anybody who has heard your music has not recognized "Take Five" … we might ask you to talk a little about the birth of "Take Five" and somewhat into the anatomy of the tune itself—because it could have gone the other way and it might not have produced what we all know today—about that particular bridge and Paul and so forth. You want to talk a little about that? This was a 1959 recording, released in 1960 on the album *Time Out*.

Brubeck: When Joe Dodge left my group, it was truly a great loss … to this day, I love the way Joe Dodge played with the group. So, when Joe Morello joined the group, it was because Joe Dodge had left, and Morello was working in New York then, with Marian McPartland and Bill Crow, at The Hickory House.

Paul said to me, "You've got to go hear this guy Joe Morello; he is so fantastic." We were working around the corner at Basin Street East, so we went over to The Hickory House and heard Joe. Joe played all night with brushes. Really soft swingin' and Paul said, "That's what I want, a drummer who doesn't get in the way and play loud with sticks and drown me out."

I asked Joe if he would join the group and he said, "I'll tell you, I'll join the group. But your drummer and your bass player are out to lunch. You never let them do anything."

I said, "Well, that's the way we kind of approach it. The bassist and the drummer, they keep things together." He said, "I won't join unless you feature me."

So, the first night, I told Joe to take a solo and he took a solo and the whole audience stood up at the end. Paul came back to the dressing room at the end and he says, "Either he goes or I go." I said, "He's not going and I hope you're not."

The next night the band started as a duet and I was going to play that way all night. Pretty quick I saw Paul and Norman Bates come in and it was over, because they knew I wasn't going to let Joe go. He was the first guy that could play in odd time signatures perfectly. Joe had the ability to keep one rhythm in one foot, another rhythm in the other foot, another rhythm in one hand, and another rhythm in the other hand. I don't think there's been anybody who comes near Joe as far as being that complex.

He started playing in 5/4 backstage as a warm up. I said to Paul, "Why don't you put a melody over what Joe's doing in 5/4 time, because I'm doing an album now in all different time signatures and I'm going to call it *Time Out*." So Paul's assignment was to put a melody over Joe's rhythm.

Paul came to rehearsal in Oakland, where I was living, and the first thing he says is "I can't write anything in 5/4." I said, "Well, did you try?" He said, "Yeah, I've got a couple things." I said, "Let me see them." So, I looked at them … he played them … and I said, "We can put that together and make a tune." So that's the way "Take Five" was born. By Paul saying he *couldn't* do it … to me saying we *can* do it … it's there. You know, that's the most played jazz tune in the world.

Wong: You visit the UK quite often, Dave, and you seem to have a lot of activity there. They admire you tremendously and you've done a number of recordings there. Do you want to share what it is about the Britishers and your music?

Brubeck: We've just recorded four days in the Abbey Road Studios with the London Symphony. We did all this stuff I think nobody else will ever record. Hopefully, there will be an interest in some of my classical works that have been around a long time.

All of a sudden, this year, there's been more interest in my so-called "sacred" pieces. There's one called "The Gates of Justice." It has a cantorial tenor and a black baritone. At the time I wrote it, I was commissioned to try and bring these two cultures together, because there were some disturbing things going on in some major cities. They asked me to show the similarity between the African culture and the Jewish culture.

My wife and I took various things that showed the relationship, and I started discovering that African music and Jewish music are very much related. And then, you start thinking about it, they're still almost neighbors on the African continent.

Martin Luther King had given an address to the college students where my eldest son graduated. It was a long, wonderful address, but one thing that he said that I really thought was important—and I wanted to set it to music—was that "we must live together as brothers or die together as fools."

That is like part of the meat of this piece, because the black baritone sings this, and it's so obvious in the world that, if we don't start getting along with one another, we're going to destroy this planet.

There's always been people trying to lead us in the right direction, people like Martin

Luther King; and, usually, something terrible happens to the great leaders and they're silenced. But they don't have to be silenced if you remember what they said.

The heart of that is what I believe is the most important thing that Christ ever said, and he said it over 2000 years ago, and it could save us now. He said, "Love your enemies, do good to those that hate you."

Now you see, there's the only answer to the world's problems.

When I see something like that, I feel this is important for people to be aware of. Just think of a guy running for President, he thinks he's a good Christian, and he says, "My platform is to love your enemies, do good to those that hate you." Do you think he'd get elected?

Think about how important that is. We've tried everything else, but we haven't tried really—we've come close with the Marshall Plan, with MacArthur in Japan—and it worked. But then, it's forgotten that this is an approach that works. When somebody hates you, you dump so much good on them that they can't come up and do anything bad.

[Audience applause]

Wong: Wow! Brubeck for President!

[Audience laughter and applause]

Brubeck: That's why, this year, I'm recording the pieces that nobody else wants to record. Because when you've got the London Symphony, a great chorus, a wonderful children's choir, great soloists ... maybe 10, 20 years from now, somebody will put that out. I don't want to leave this place without getting those things recorded. So this year, I'm recording everything ... everything I've written that's not recorded ... so it's a great year.

[Audience applause]

Wong: Your serious and intense involvement with the synergies of secular and sectarian music, with classical and jazz and the polycultural aspects of life itself ... it seems very natural that the Brubeck Institute's curriculum includes a large component that is interdisciplinary in nature, that is articulated in ethnic studies, environmental studies, religious studies and other studies that fit into a trans-disciplinary perspective.

David, your social values, your clear cornerstone of family values, is much appreciated.

[Audience applause]

Brubeck: Herb mentioned "environmental," and another piece I want to get recorded is the Chief Seattle speech on the environment. I wrote that a long time ago and it's so important.

He said, "Will you teach your children what we have taught our children?" And he goes on to talk about how the Indian children were taught to respect the trees, the water, the fish, the air ... and he went on to name everything. And he made the President of the United States promise that all these things would be done—and we broke every promise.

So I think that Chief Seattle's speech on ecology and the environment is something that we should really respect; because it's part of our government to respect what we said we would do and what we would protect on this earth.

Wong: Wasn't that part of what you were doing when I heard you work with some folks in Berkeley at a congregational church three years ago?

Brubeck: We did this in Berkeley and Russell Means took the part of Chief Seattle.

If you want to see something noble and strong it was Russell Means doing the Chief Seattle speech. Then we did it in San Francisco and it seemed to be very successful with the audience that was there, but I want to try to get it into a recording so that it will always be around.

Another thing I've just set to music is what the Pope said in Central Park—at least what all the posters around New York said: "Do not be afraid. The power of the Holy Spirit is with you." I set that as a chorale and a fugue.

[Brubeck sings lyric and scats instrumentation]

Wong: While you delve into music of various idioms, Dave, it seems that, regardless of the pacing, the ambience, and whatever other quality we would like to ascribe to it … it always swings!

On July 6th of this year, you were at the International Festival of Montreal and on that last evening, in an encore, you played "Take Five." But on that encore, you knocked me out of my skull! Because you had Jim Hall on guitar, you had Toots Thielemans on there, and Angèle Dubeau was the violinist from the area. I never heard "Take Five" sound like that!

Brubeck: We do a lot of varied things that people don't know about. It's funny: Whenever we play the Montreal Jazz Festival, they ask me to do something and I'll say, "This will never work at a jazz festival!" And they always prove me wrong!

Can you imagine doing a Catholic mass at a jazz festival? And they demanded three of the sections be encored during the mass! That's a wild thing to have happen. You may not realize how wild. I thought, "My goodness, I don't think this is going to work, and they want to hear it twice?"

Wong: I missed the evening you and your group performed with the Russian National Orchestra at Montalvo, and that was reported to be exciting musicianship on their part … I hear it was fabulous … they played some of your tunes in the repertoire that they had played before; and there's also a recent release of a DVD, *Brubeck Returns to Moscow* … there's a lot of Russian things going on, Dave, a lot of "rushin' around" …

Brubeck: That was a great party! The Shostakovich String Quartet surprised me at the party and played "Take Five"—if you can imagine that! Then all these Russians came up and played, one after another; fantastic classical, but there are surprisingly fantastic jazz players in Russia. In fact, they're all over the world now, great jazz players.

[Brubeck pauses, then, to audience]

What's the date today?

[Audience responds with: "September 21st"]

My wife and I have been married 60 years today!

[Prolonged audience applause as Dave's wife, Iola, is recognized by audience and arrives on stage]

She has put up with me a long time … written so many of my so-called "serious" compositions. You're going to see on Sunday night, *The Real Ambassadors*, she conceived of that whole idea … in fact, I'm going to have Iola tell you about it.

Iola Brubeck: I think that's a dirty trick on our wedding anniversary!

Dave asked me to tell you about *The Real Ambassadors*. It was done 40 years ago, almost to the day, here at the Monterey Jazz Festival. Were you here, Herb?

Wong: Yes, I sure was.

Iola Brubeck: It was a night we will never forget, with the great Louis Armstrong.

I'll tell you a little story about that first night: Our rehearsal was, absolutely, a shambles! Nobody knew what they were supposed to do or what they were going to do.

Jimmy Lyons had a top hat and an attaché case for Louis Armstrong to carry on the stage, because he was "the ambassador." And Louis said, no, he didn't want to wear the hat and he didn't want to do this and he didn't want to do that. All he wanted to do was sing and do his part … he didn't want anything to do with these costumes and this acting bit. So, we said, OK. I mean, what else are you going to do at this point?

When it came time for *The Real Ambassadors* to start—when it came time for Satchmo to walk on stage—he strutted on stage, with the top hat on, carrying the attaché case. And, as he walked by Dave's piano, he said "Am I hammin' it up enough for you, Pops?"

The story of *The Real Ambassadors* is really a fantasy. It's a dream of the whole world being in harmony and we thought that Louis Armstrong represented that more than anybody else. This was a period when he had just begun to make the "world tours" … into Africa and other countries … and he was so acclaimed, more than any other American citizen, I guess.

The contrast with the acclaim that he received in the world outside of the United States and the prejudice he had to put up with and live with in the United States … that contrast was so great that we thought something should be done to address that. But we wanted to address it in a way that everyone could understand … and everyone loved Louis. So, if he said it, it was taken seriously by everyone.

That was the purpose behind *The Real Ambassadors*.

[Selections from *The Real Ambassadors* play]

Wong: I have but a few minutes left, and I want to do something very personal from your pen and feelings. I wonder if you could take a moment or two to share something that you did when you were at the IAJE conference in Long Beach. I heard you speak about you and Iola and how you two cats got together. And it was so beautiful, it was like a marriage made in heaven. Can you give a capsule of that … before I play the tune that you just know I am going to play?

Dave Brubeck: During World War II, a lot of us didn't know where we were going next, and a lot of my friends wanted to be married before they went. One day during that time, my mother said to me, "You've been in college four years and you've never gone to one formal occasion. So, I want you to go to this formal dance."

I said to my roommate, "As long as I gotta go to this dance, can you tell me who's the smartest girl on campus?" And he replied, "Iola Whitlock." I said, "Do you think she'd go out with me?" And he said, "Ask her."

So she went to this dance with me and—being that I'm a musician—I can't dance! All my dances, I'd been playing the piano, watching other people dance. So we danced around the floor once, and I said, "Let's get out of here." We went out on the levee behind the school, parked in my old Chevy. We talked for three hours and decided we should get married.

So that's what happened.

Wong: Beautiful! On this final example of your fantastic music, I'd like to have the audience listen to your personal dedication to Iola, entitled "All My Love."

I wanted to hasten to add a little backdrop to it: When you guys were on vacation in Maui, Iola asked you to "cool it" and don't work … don't mess around any more … really take it easy and relax. So when Iola was asleep, you grabbed a flashlight for illumination as you wrote this tune. What came out is this absolutely gorgeous piece of music...

["All My Love" plays]

— · — · — · — · — · — · — · — · — · — · — · — · — · — · — · — · —

Taylor Eigsti

I first met Taylor Eigsti when he was 10 years old. I remember sitting in on one of his sessions when Taylor played piano for tips at an Italian restaurant in Palo Alto. It didn't take long for Taylor Eigsti to make the leap from playing in that restaurant to playing on the outdoor stages at Stanford Shopping Center in a series of jazz concerts I had given birth to and produced in that upscale Palo Alto setting.

Taylor had been taking lessons from a piano teacher in a nearby neighborhood, but he was so capable, even at that age, he didn't stick to the lessons for long. And it wasn't long before people began discovering Taylor Eigsti, especially when he was showcased several times at the Mountain Winery in Saratoga, California.

It was backstage at that venue that I introduced Taylor to Dave Brubeck, before they played together on stage for the first time. Dave emphatically told Taylor how impressed he was with the young pianist's capability.

Live at Filoli was strikingly strategic for Taylor. Marian McPartland was scheduled to be the headliner at the Filoli Gardens engagement, a KCSM broadcast and recording session; but it turned out she couldn't make the gig. Taylor was asked to step in—and this, when he was only *16* years old! In fact, he turned 16 on the day of the concert, which was duly noted by the audience's rendition of "Happy Birthday" and the presentation of a birthday cake to Taylor onstage.

Herewith, Taylor's own mature-beyond-his-years comments on playing the gig and celebrating his special occasion:

Personal thanks to:
Bud Spangler, Madeline Eastman, and Mr. Charles Huggins, President of See's Candies, for offering me the opportunity to fill in for the great Marian McPartland at the Filoli Gardens Concert Series, and for trusting the recommendations of friends and fellow musicians John Shifflett, Anton Schwartz, Syd Hislam and my friend at "Jazz at Chardonnay," John Knipe. Many thanks to the incredible rhythm section of Jason Lewis and John Shifflett for all the fun they bring to every performance, and to Bud, for producing this recording, and overseeing the mastering along with Ken Lee.
To my longtime friend, Dr. Herb Wong, for making time in his extremely busy schedule to write the liner notes, and to David Benoit and Smith Dobson for their continuous support. To Grace Parker and Joy Sheldon for putting up with all of my delays, and for working on the CD design ... even with a broken wrist.
Thanks also, to my mother, for always keeping me on the right track, and to everyone who attended the Filoli concert and has waited so patiently for the release of this CD.
One final note of thanks to Paul Blystone and the volunteers at Filoli for the great birthday cake.

Even to this day, whenever I read Taylor's comments and listen to that CD, I still think, "This simply cannot be a *16*-year-old!"

Taylor Eigsti Trio—*Live at Filoli*
Syntropi Audio; 2001

Close your eyes and listen intently to this trio's tantalizing performance. It is clear the sophisticated pianist has an elegant touch and sound that you would assume has taken years to develop—qualities logically associated with a ripened artistic maturity. Likewise, the skin-tight interplay between the triangle of musicians featuring a leader/pianist whose intuitive leadership must be drawn from a long skein of seasoned experiences. Well, the amazing young jazz pianist is Taylor Eigsti (TE) whose 16th birthday was coincidentally reached on the day of this "live" performance recording at the Filoli Gardens in Woodside, California, south of San Francisco.

Followers of the precocious TE are keenly aware of his imperious wherewithal. Bear in mind, there is no acute shortage of young talented musicians, but out of the crowd emerge a few who will advance the art form. As pianist Smith Dobson notes: "Taylor may be one of those who make an important statement. He's been so far advanced since he was just a 10 or 11 year-old." That was about the time I first witnessed the prowess of this child prodigy. Subsequently I invited TE to perform in a Jazz Piano Gershwin Concert when he was barely 13. The program included piano notables Lou Levy, Michael Wolff, Larry Vuckovich and Denny Zeitlin; all five played in solo, duo and trio settings. Zeitlin exclaimed, "Wow! This kid can really play!"

When David Benoit met TE, at age 8, he was impressed! "We played together at Villa Montalvo when he was all of 12, and since then, Taylor's growth has expanded. He's going to go the full mile. His mind absorbs any and all music he wants to play. I'm proud to say I know him and that I have been an influence."

Since then, TE has played a long string of gigs—jazzfests from San Jose and San Francisco to Elkhart, Indiana and a host of jazz clubs and concerts (including those with Benoit and the San Jose Symphony Orchestra, with Dave Brubeck, Diane Schuur, James Moody, et al.) plus a special performance for President Clinton.

Besides his obvious intellect and giftedness, Taylor is very open minded, thoughtful, sensitive and candid. Playing and composing jazz clearly constitutes the propitious environment for his creativity, as it stimulates originality, experimentation, initiative and invention. His passion for music is such that his mind simply mops and soaks up everything.

While there are no boundaries to his interests, and the slate of tunes on this CD reveals rich variety and a strong eclectic perspective, TE strives for convergence. His penchant for bluesy colors reflects the strengths in the blues of major influence—pianist Gene Harris. And little wonder TE's music is threaded with soul.

Taylor's musical voice articulated in his playing is ever changing and growing due to his insatiable appetite. "I've listened to so many different people and styles—from Benny Green, Gene Harris and Chucho Valdés to Benoit, Charlie Parker and Cecil Taylor—when I improvise I don't consciously incorporate these flavors," explains Taylor. "I've been given the paints to put on my palette, so when I encounter a new canvas, I can use them naturally." Over the last few years of maturation, Taylor has accelerated the process … almost explosively—unifying subtle differences and he is "doing more mixing of my own palette." Incipient traces of purely Taylor Eigsti are showing up.

This CD is a happenstance result of Taylor taking the place of the great pianist Marian McPartland who was first scheduled to play at Filoli. The simpatico which bassist John Shifflett and drummer Jason Lewis maintain with TE is transparent and sheer aesthetic joy. His careful selection of tunes stretches across vintages, traditions, approaches and persuasion—well-paced to offer a profile of Eigsti music.

Opening with a great standard to blow on—the easily digestible "Have You Met Miss Jones?" is in a bebop groove. The inspiration of Gene Harris' indigo colors has the trio in a jubilant, accessible, funk and swing climate on "They Can't Take That Away from Me." A nice shuffle recalls its flavor in the late 1960s ... and Jason really cooks: John's bass, liberated from support role, enters the piece with the open, free intro.

Moving to the classic Thad Jones ballad "A Child Is Born"—it's a tasty choice. Taylor says: "I tried to get kind of bluesy but softly so every note is brought out." His appealing interpretation evinces beautiful balladic qualities. Juan Tizol's jazz evergreen "Caravan" carries the impact on Taylor by pianist Gonzalo Rubalcaba and Chucho Valdés: the net result is a deeper Cuban flavor as Taylor opens with the original montuno and revisits it. "Caravan" illustrates TE's resourcefulness. A very exciting and hip version!

Jerome Kern's 1933 "Smoke Gets in Your Eyes" is one of several ballad gems. I love how Taylor squeezes every single note of the smoky melody. Jason's brushwork lends an ambient effect. TE's solo piano is sampled on "Ain't Misbehavin'"—a popular Fats Waller 1929 classic. Another gorgeous ballad treatment is Duke Ellington's "In a Sentimental Mood." Just lean back and dig it! There's that marvelous Eigsti touch and sound again—magical!

Twisting around the melody of Eddie Harris' "Freedom Jazz Dance," it gets a vigorous rhythmic and funky feel. No surprise Taylor loves to play this fun tune as it allows so much experimentation. On Charlie Mingus' solid piece "Nostalgia in Times Square," Taylor is all over the tune vying for part ownership! Infusing much of Gene Harris' influence and other blues players, TE and his trio mates swing and sizzle together.

"Jason's got the best set of ears I've ever played with. He's always playing on the edge of his seat," asserts Taylor, "and John—whether on fast tunes or ballads, he picks the right notes!" Another perfect example of their synergy is on "My Foolish Heart" (a 1949 Victor Young favorite)—a standard played with grace and charm. Likewise, the trio's bond is felt on the spirited jam vehicle "Perdido," closing the set ... followed by a 16th birthday celebration!

This CD dramatically reveals how Taylor Eigsti already has more going on than many professional jazz pianists currently making recordings! Personally, I've been privileged by being an eye and ear witness to his star bright ascendancy.

Denny Zeitlin

Denny Zeitlin was one of a number of very talented musicians I signed and produced for Palo Alto Records and Black-Hawk Records. I always thought of Denny as a very creative musician—as were the other artists in that group. But Denny led a different life from the others; he's an M.D. specializing in psychiatry, evidenced in his playing by the reasoned, thoughtful and complex expressions on the music side of his life.

One of the artists in that Palo Alto/Black-Hawk group was bassist David Friesen, who used to talk to me about how he had dreamed of playing and recording with some of his favorite musicians ... Denny Zeitlin among them.

When Denny was playing at Pearl's in San Francisco's North Beach, I brought David to the club and introduced him to Denny. David was knocked out! That's the kind of impression Denny had on his fellow musicians. Yet Denny, himself, has always expressed a deeper concern with reaching the *everyday* listener with his music ... not just his fellow professionals.

Denny Zeitlin Trio—*Shining Hour / Live at the Trident*
Columbia (CL 2463); 1965; Reissued by Sony Music Entertainment

Shining Hour represents an important departure from Denny Zeitlin's previous Columbia albums, *Cathexis* (CL 2182/CS 8982*) and *Carnival* (CL 2340/CS 9140*). While those were performed in a studio environment, this is Zeitlin's first live session, recorded at the Trident in Sausalito, California. An occasional clinking of glasses, together with the reactions of an enthusiastic audience, produced an atmosphere of informal excitement and relaxed intimacy in contrast to the controlled, aseptic conditions of the usual studio recording.

Zeitlin, who received his M.D. degree from Johns Hopkins Medical School, is currently in residency at San Francisco's Langley Porter Neuropsychiatric Institute. He recorded this album in March 1965, during a week's vacation from internship. Despite his hectic schedule, Zeitlin is one of today's most astonishing jazz pianists. That his music is gaining him a wide, responsive public is proved by ever-increasing audiences whenever he appears at the Trident, by his many television appearances and concert performances, and by the highly enthusiastic reception he and the rest of the trio received from both audiences and critics at the recent Monterey and Newport Jazz Festivals.

An artist's philosophy inevitably enters into the equation of his total musical expression, and some comments that Zeitlin made to me in a letter recently (we were discussing some current problems in jazz) are worth sharing here: "In becoming 'respectable' and 'serious,'" wrote Zeitlin, "modern jazz is in danger of losing its audience. And the fault lies with both the musician and his public. The musical audience, threatened by the newness of the sounds, is largely unwilling to make the personal commitment of 'giving itself' to a new experience in the hopes of discovering new worlds of wonder and beauty. And the musicians (smarting at the lack of recognition that makes earning a living at their art a near impossibility) turn inward and to each other, presenting their backs to the audience …

"I am striving to develop an intensely personal music that at the same time aims at universality. It would please me as much, or more, if a janitor, flagpole-sitter, and secret agent were moved by my music than if three musicians were. The current 'thing' is for artists to say nothing in explanation of their art; I believe that the interested listener deserves all the help he needs. That is why I verbally explain aspects of many of the compositions we play at the Trident, and why we hope to hold seminars following many of the college concerts we will be doing in the coming year."

Zeitlin has nothing but the highest praise for the sensitivity and musicianship of his teammates Jerry Granelli and Charlie Haden. Jerry is a drummer who subordinates his flawless technique to a musical awareness that considers all possibilities and consistently reacts in a flexible and creative way. Charlie Haden blazed an entirely fresh approach to the bass violin during his tenure with Ornette Coleman in the late 1950s, and his work here reveals an increased maturity of style and a trait frequently missing in modern bassists—arresting power.

The selections:

"St. Thomas"

Following the Introduction by the Trident's manager, Lou Ganapoler, the session opens with an impromptu performance of this Sonny Rollins composition. Requested by a member of the audience, it was the first time the trio had played the tune. (Rollins named it after the best known of the Virgin Islands, in memory of his West Indian family background.). Although much of the tune's basic calypso flavor is retained, the trio freely extends the harmony and overall structure. Granelli's rich experience with Latin rhythms is a notable asset in this Caribbean setting, and Haden's warmth and firmness of time are impressive.

"Carole's Waltz"

Denny composed this piece the day of his first wedding anniversary in December 1964, and played it that evening at the Trident as a surprise for his wife, Carole. This performance is so alive with deep and tender meaning that it approximates an actual delivery of lyrics, conveying much of the soaring, gossamer yet regal quality of Carole Zeitlin.

"Spur of the Moment"

As its title would imply, this is an improvisation in response to a Trident patron's request for "some blues." The opening riff "just happened." Zeitlin builds a foot-tapping solo, followed by Haden's exploration of a "walking" bass line's possibilities.

"Where Does It Lead"

Denny's insatiable curiosity leads him into a variety of musical areas, so it is not surprising that a folk song should appear in this album. Carole, an accomplished folk singer and guitarist, first introduced him to it. Denny hopes that this reworking will evoke in its listeners some of the many images and meanings that the piece holds for him. An excellent use of space and a judicious use of the interval of the fifth results in a very "open" feeling.

"Lonely Woman"

Zeitlin comments: "For me, Ornette Coleman is the most significant jazzman to emerge in the past decade, and his music has had a powerful impact on my life. I first heard Charlie during Ornette's first gig in Chicago, and one of the first things I heard the quartet do was 'Lonely Woman.' It remains one of his most haunting melodies. Against the furious cymbal and Indian-like bass, I attempted to build layer upon layer of tension to generate an organic shape, improvising without preconceived harmonic, rhythmic or melodic structures."

"My Shining Hour"

This old and too-frequently neglected standard receives a "straight down the line" interpretation which sparkles with elation before fading away in the closing chord cycle.

"Quiet Now"

When I first heard the trio play this, I was profoundly moved. Haden remarks that it is one of the most beautiful ballads he has ever heard. Zeitlin, who is his own severest critic, rates it as one of his favorite compositions. A highly evocative work of great tenderness, it needs no further description.

"At Sixes and Sevens"

Zeitlin is deeply intrigued with the challenge of composing and improvising on different signatures and patterns, and the trio's current repertoire includes pieces in 5, 7, 10, 11 and various other time-signature combinations. This work consists of a bar of 7/4 alternating with a bar of 6/4, becoming 13/4 in the middle modal section. The angularity and unusual shifting character of the piece led to Carole's title suggestion. Haden's loose, comfortable time feeling complements perfectly Zeitlin's unusual phrasing which frequently seems to stretch, over hang and even obliterate the bar lines. Granelli's beautifully sensitive and highly-charged musical statement displays his remarkable adaptability to varied time signatures.

"What Is This Thing Called Love"

Zeitlin finds a constant source of stimulation in this jazz warhorse, and the trio uses it here as a vehicle for free improvisation. Denny points out that "sometimes what emerges is completely atonal, seemingly arrhythmic, and bears little resemblance to the shape or form of the tune. On this particular night we happened to adhere fairly closely to its form despite the shifts in tempos and alterations in harmonic structure." The track opens with a bristling, electrifying piano solo that is joined by bass and drums as the trio gathers its forces, then moves into a medium-tempo section in which Haden's bass catches fire. Zeitlin's piano takes over again in a furious, impassioned solo that leads into a closing statement of the theme.

In all, this balanced program provides a broad pathway into the musical soul of a young and dedicated pianist-composer-arranger who continues to generate music which ranks with the most significant sounds of our time.

Nat King Cole

There was a time when people had no idea of who the King Cole Trio was—or had even heard of its existence. But even back then, I knew they were special. When I first heard the Trio on those old Decca "race" records and on NBC Radio, I was immediately hooked. I knew this was *real* jazz … *real* jazz piano … *real* jazz trio music.

Once I heard Nat King Cole and his Trio, I never let go. I became known as "The King Cole Trio Hound," a title earned while chasing the group and following their gigs along with my brother, Woody, also a King Cole Trio devotee. When they would come to the Stockton area, I would be there for every minute of every show. And I loved every minute of it. Nat and his trio knew of my own special brand of emotion for them … and they never forgot it.

"Remembrances: Chasing the King Cole Trio"
The Jazz Review and Collector's Discography, March 1992

The recent outpouring of Nat Cole reissues, many of which are reviewed in this issue, has caused me to flash back to the early days of my passion for and pursuit of the King Cole Trio. My interest was strongly trapped as a young grade-school student when I first heard them on an NBC series in 1938. That powerful introduction served to ignite a life-long love for the Trio and for Nat Cole's piano and singing.

My brother Woody and I were devotees. As very young jazz-record collectors, we were captured by the groovy lyrics and the swinging, spirited sounds of the group. We promptly began a vigorous hunt for anything and everything we could find by the Trio.

We sold magazines and greeting cards, mowed and raked lawns, ran errands, and did whatever else we could to finance our special mission.

Their records were extremely hard to locate. Records then were generally sold through small record and sheet music departments of furniture and hardware stores. It was rare to find a shop selling only records. We probed stores from Stockton to the Sacramento Valley to the San Francisco Bay area. Salespeople would respond to our queries about the King Cole Trio with "King Who?" Some of these salespeople allowed me to browse their backroom stocks in search of titles by the Trio (as well as other lesser passions of mine, such as Louis Jordan and his Tympany Five, Billie Holiday, and The Harlem Hamfats).

Our first acquisitions included the likes of "Are You fer It?," "Call the Police," "I Like to Riff," "Stop! The Red Light's On," "Scotchin' with the Soda," and "Hit That Jive, Jack," featuring the Trio's vocals. But it was the smoky, warm voice of Nat Cole on such fresh, beautiful ballads as "This Will Make You Laugh," Nat's own "That Ain't Right," plus Cole's impressive piano and Oscar Moore's intuitive guitar that wiped me out on these first Deccas.

Another source for Nat's recordings was jukeboxes. We checked periodically with jukebox service companies to inspect the depositories of returns from jukeboxes. One side of a record would sometimes be perfectly clean though the other juked side was well-worn. We bought these 78 rpm discards for a dime. These were bargains considering that mint, blue label Deccas were retailed at 37 cents. Later on, before the Trio hit the big time with Capitol Records, we picked up new copies of the poorly distributed Excelsior and Premier/Atlas titles which had been released in limited editions.

It was our good fortune to have seen the King Cole Trio perform at a number of venues both in northern and southern California. Nat's facile fingering, joyfulness, winsome smile, and body language at the keyboard were remarkable.

My love for the King Cole Trio's music continued into adulthood. I first began sharing the musical wealth of the Trio while programming V-Discs and special broadcasts on Armed Forces Radio Service. Likewise, since I began broadcasting in 1959 on Radio KJAZ in San Francisco, a portion of my airtime has consistently been devoted to the Trio. I am currently focusing on the Trio as part of my teaching curriculum in a year-long course on the jazz piano trio at a nearby college campus.

I am extremely gratified to see the recent reemergence of the Trio's body of recorded works, much of it not available in the past. Let's hope that, bolstered by the ambitious efforts of Mosaic, LaserLight, Stash, and other companies, the King Cole Trio will receive much wider, overdue attention.

CHAPTER 11

Guitar

Often sounding like a combination of many different instruments rolled into one, the guitar offers a wide possibility of expression. With Charlie Christian's early influence and genius, you can hear the sounds of the saxophone in the guitar. At times, you can hear the piano in the guitar. In fact, in some recordings, the guitar becomes a "substitute" in place of the piano or other instruments.

The guitar is a self-sufficient instrument; but in collaboration, it lends a tremendously exciting voice to the band. In the right hands, the guitar is able to create a vast array of sounds, from luxuriant to raw. It can be very driven—or it can be cooled off into a very subtle, warm habitat.

It's tough to pick one guitarist as a leading example of the instrument, so my thoughts lean towards two: Jim Hall and Kenny Burrell.

Jim Hall

Jim Hall was a pure, model jazz guitarist, mystifyingly wonderful. He was part of the Chico Hamilton group in Los Angeles early on, before he moved to the East Coast, to New York, where one of his well-known duo partners was Bill Evans.

Jim Hall's harmonic conception is amazing; what he could do with those notes! His playing was so flexible, able to bend ... twist ... hammer ... whatever the tune needed. He would configure musical statements in his inimitable way, turning them into anything he wanted, from small to big assets.

Over the years, Jim Hall has been a subtle influence on many, many guitar players, mainly due to what I would call his "differentness"; the way he looked at what he played was just that—"different." As evidence of Jim's different nature, I would cite the recordings he did with Bill Evans. Anybody who could play a guitar with Bill Evans is someone special.

Special, too, was the way in which Jim served as the model for so many players in the past; even today, even the youngest talents, musicians like Julian Lage, claim Jim Hall as their hero. And it's easy to see why.

A Conversation with Jim Hall
September 1999

Wong: Reflecting a number of studies that have been made about creativity and childhood foundation, if you could recall your childhood to set the record straight ... you were born what day and year?

Hall: I was born December 4, 1930, in Buffalo, New York. In the same hospital that Mel Lewis was born in, and I think he was a year ahead of me. It was a Catholic hospital; he's Jewish and I'm a heathen.

Wong: Were you, or are you a member of a family that has brothers and sisters or are you alone?

Hall: No, I have a brother, younger.

Wong: And his name?

Hall: His name is Richard. He calls himself Dick. Richard Keith Hall.

Wong: Can you describe your home environment? Was it open and warm, was it encouraging, was it restrictive? Can you recall anything on that?

Hall: My home environment was pretty scattered. My mom was terrific; she just died a couple years ago. But my dad just sort of cut out; he just left when I was seven, and I saw him once ... I guess I saw him when I was 12. My mom raised my brother and me, and she was really terrific. She worked, sometimes two jobs, and we moved a lot, even before they got divorced or separated permanently. I don't know what my dad did for sure; he must have done something very unsuccessfully. But he worked with a bunch of things.

By the time I got out of school, I had been to ten different schools. Some of the moves were good; one was to the Cleveland Institute of Music that I actually chose, and then I got moved around ... this was in Cleveland, Ohio. I got put in a group of big bands for kids; something like that. After a couple of years I said, "I don't wanna be in this anymore," so I left. It was that kind of stuff.

Wong: Was this elementary school or ...?

Hall: Elementary and then junior high.

Wong: So you were in some kind of program for the gifted?

Hall: I was. It was embarrassing to me in a way, I didn't like it much and that's why I bailed out.

Wong: Your mother obviously was very nurturing to you.

Hall: So it seems, looking back, she must have been.

Wong: What was her name?

Hall: Her name was Louella and her maiden name had been Coles. And yes, she was nurturing; but this was in the 1930s and early '40s and it was pretty unusual, and probably not comfortable, for her to be unmarried. She was trying to, in effect, protect us. She was a woman and we were these two boys. It was probably pretty rough on her, but she did the best she could.

Wong: Do you recall, even under these circumstances, that your creative urges were cultivated at all? Teachers, friends, family?

Hall: That's a good question. I'm not sure; probably.

Wong: Well, certainly in school, to some extent, if they identified you as a member of that special group?

Hall: Yes, they did; we took these IQ tests.

Wong: Probably the Stanford Binet test.

Hall: Probably, that would be the one. I'm sure that I had some teachers that sort of looked out for me and everything.

Wong: Were you encouraged to listen to music? Or was there something at home at all?

Hall: Not particularly. As a matter of fact—again, I'm inferring this hundreds of years later—but I have a feeling that jazz music in particular was probably a little too sexy for my mom, especially raising two boys, she being a young woman. She kind of went for Guy Lombardo and Hawaiian music and that sort of thing, easy to listen to. She played a little bit of church piano.

Wong: How did you get interested in music, per se?

Hall: That's funny! I *just* played this tune, just this afternoon, called "Uncle Ed" and it's my mother's brother; my mother had two brothers. Uncle Ed played the guitar. I think he was very gifted, but he sort of went out on alcoholism and never came back. But he played the guitar and sang, kind of country music. And he always seemed to have cute ladies around him. So I was just thinking, hey, that might be all right. That was when I was, I think, nine, possibly ten. Then my mom bought me a guitar for Christmas, although her way of buying it was on the installment plan … you made a down payment on it and you paid it off.

Wong: Did you request a guitar?

Hall: I'm not sure that I did. I just don't know. I may have shown some interest, but she got me a guitar.

Wong: And you liked that?

Hall: I did, and I just started taking regular guitar lessons. It was at a store called Wurlitzer Musical Instruments in Cleveland, Ohio. And, again, I think it was part of the deal.

Wong: A part of the deal of the purchase?

Hall: Yes, you bought the guitar and you took a lesson. It was $1.75 per week, maybe, and, believe it or not, 75 cents went to the teacher and the dollar went for the guitar … or vice versa. I had a teacher who seemed to like me a lot, which was great. And he was very encouraging. I thought I was really fortunate there. I'm sure—again, I'm inferring this—but I assume that what I did was to look for and find father figures; first with a couple of teachers, and then with musicians who were maybe ten years older than me. When I reached my teens, they were in their 20s and 30s; they seemed like old geezers.

Wong: Were you with this private instructor for some time?

Hall: I think probably a couple of years.

Wong: Was there any instruction in school?

Hall: Later on there was, in junior high and high school. I played the string bass in the school, played in the orchestra. So there was a pretty good music program, both in junior high and high school in Cleveland. Elementary school I don't remember. I'm sure that there was some music, but I just don't remember.

Wong: What high school did you go to?

Hall: I went to John Adams High School in Cleveland, which, I think, has since been torn down.

Wong: Did they have a jazz ensemble at all … a dance band?

Hall: No, I don't think so. But on the other hand, I wasn't discouraged. Whereas, at the Institute of Music, there was no jazz and no guitar at all. It was just a regular conservatory.

Wong: And you chose to go there?

Hall: Yes, I did.

Wong: Did you know some of the people who had gone there? Is that why?

Hall: I knew one guy. I was working with a bass player whose wife worked in the office there, which is how I got the paid tuition a little ahead of time. And he had graduated.

He had a degree in music theory and possibly composition, and he raved about the school. And I'm sure he helped me get in. His name is Bill Adams.

Wong: Bill Adams? Boy, the "Adams" name keeps coming around!

Hall: Isn't that funny? I don't know if he's related to the composer or not. He could be his father, I'm not sure. But I was, maybe, 18 at the time, and I had been rehearsing with a group of guys in Cleveland. We had a quartet … good players. We all wore glasses so we called ourselves "Spectacles"—we were ahead of our time with that—nice, yes?

Wong: Oh, that's very good.

Hall: The idea was we were going to go around the globe with this group. We had vocals, four-part vocals, and …

Wong: You sang?

Hall: Yes, we sang a bit. I think I probably disappointed them, but I just sensed … I just assumed … that I was gonna be a musician and I said, "I want to be a better musician," and then I managed to get into the Institute of Music.

Wong: Prior to the formation or your interaction within this group, the "Spectacles," how did you get interested in jazz per se?

Hall: When I got into junior high school I'd been playing the guitar about three years, I guess. I got in a quartet with a guy named Angelo Vienna, a clarinet player; I hope he's still around. It was clarinet, drums, accordion and guitar. That was kind of a typical group. And I went to a record shop with Angelo one time and he was buying a Benny Goodman record. In those days, as you remember, you played the record …

Wong: … In the store?

Hall: Yes, that's right, in the store. So I heard Charlie Christian and it was like it was a spiritual awakening. It was great! I remember the tune; it was called "Grand Slam." And he had two choruses in blues and F. I wasn't sure what it was, but I said, "I wish I could do that." I say this a lot, but the great thing is, when I hear that record now, I have the same feeling: "Man, that's amazing! I wish I could do that." So that's what…

Wong: … First sparked you?

Hall: Yes, I think the quartet, the Angelo Vienna quartet, was probably kind of jazzy; I assume Angelo tried to be jazzy anyway. But we played everything: We played pop tunes and mazurkas and polkas … whatever.

Wong: Whatever you had to?

Hall: Whatever we had to. There were a couple groups that I ended up playing in.

Wong: Were there other records that were stimuli?

Hall: Later, after that, I bought an album of the Benny Goodman Sextet; I think there were maybe three records in it, and I didn't even have a record player! I remember carrying it around on the bus; it said "Benny Goodman Sextet" on the cover. One time I had it under my arm and you could just see the word, "Sex," and I said, "Oh, I better not." After that I heard Art Tatum and really got hooked on Art Tatum. And, of course, there was anything involving guitar. I listened to the King Cole Trio …

Wong: Oscar and Warren?

Hall: Oscar and Warren, right. Then, when I got to Los Angeles, I got to know him. In fact, I met him in Cleveland. I used to go to the Palace Theater, so I really kind of got addicted to jazz music.

Wong: Guitar specifically?

Hall: Yes, at first guitar. I would listen to the radio stations; some of the half-hour shows that they used to play. Then I hooked up with another teacher and I'm still in touch with him; his name's Fred Sharp. He lives in Florida now. And he was pretty advanced. He had been to New York and played with the Adrian Rollini Trio some time back. Then he moved back to Cleveland and he got me listening to Django Reinhardt and stuff, and playing through the transcriptions of Django's solos and Carl Kress and Dick McDonough also. So that was great. But again, I assume that I was kind of looking for father figures in a way through these teachers. But one of the guys in "Spectacles"—his name was Tony DiNardo—really introduced me to all these saxophone players who were a big part of what I still hear: Coleman Hawkins, Chu Berry, Lester Young, of course, Ben Webster, I got to work with him. Getting back to your original question, in the house I had Art Tatum records. I'd wait 'til my mom went to work and then I'd play them and the Benny Goodman Sextet and Coleman Hawkins.

Wong: And when you listened to the Art Tatum records, were those with Art Tatum and the Trio or were they just solo piano?

Hall: I think it was solo. As a matter of fact, I enjoy him best as a soloist. I got to know Tiny Grimes and he had some great stories. And then there were some terrific players around Cleveland. Benny Bailey was there. Actually, Tadd Dameron was from Cleveland. I didn't know him very well, but I'd see him sometimes. And Eugene Heard—"Fats" Heard—was a great drummer; got to play with him a lot. So there were some really good players there.

Wong: You really got into it for awhile back then.

Hall: Yes, that's when I was in my teens.

Wong: When you finished the Cleveland Institute of Music, did you leave town?

Hall: I'm still not sure why I did this, but I had finished a degree in music theory and I had written a string quartet. It sounds pretty good, actually, when I hear it. And Bartók was my hero. As I was starting on my Masters in composition, this buddy of mine, Ray Graziano, an alto player, and I had talked about going to California. He got a deal to deliver a car that he could drive across the country and just pay for the gas. And I think I got in one-and-a-half semesters or something toward my Masters and I bailed out; I'm still not sure why. My conscious reason was that I was already a professional at the time, and I wondered if I could do that successfully. I thought I might as well try it. And, also, I didn't really fit in in a school situation. Because the other choice was that I could get a job teaching in a college and writing music. The third element was this: Is this the direction you wanted to go in?

So I bailed out and Ray and I drove this Cadillac to Los Angeles. The reason I chose Los Angeles was because I had a friend out here, named Joe Dolny, who was a marvelous musician—I had studied arranging with him when I was about 16—and he had a rehearsal band, a really good band that played once a week at the Musicians' Union. A lot of really good players would come in just to get a chance play good music in a good band. So I knew I could do that. I had an aunt, my Aunt Eva, who's on my mother's side of the family; she was about 90 and she had been in Los Angeles for 50 years. She had an apartment, so I knew I had a place to sleep. So I went there. And then I hooked up with Chico. And the interesting thing for me, kind of regrouping, is that, in the last maybe ten years, I've been writing ... sort of continuing where I bailed out of school.

Wong: I could sense that.

Hall: I sort of got sidetracked playing the guitar.

Wong: When you mentioned the gentleman, Dolny, you said it was "teenage"; was it you that was a teenager or was it Joe Dolny?

Hall: He was maybe ten years older than I am. He had a group that was out on the road; he played trumpet and he played in some big bands. He was a marvelous arranger. I just studied big band arranging with him.

Wong: How did you connect with the Los Angeles area jazz community to garner a job with Chico Hamilton?

Hall: It's funny, Herb, this sounds facetious, but it occurs to me over and over how lucky I am and a lot of times I just happened to be at the …

Wong: … Right place, right time?

Hall: I was doing these once-a-week rehearsals at the Musicians' Union. Do you remember Johnny Gross?

Wong: Sure.

Hall: Johnny had a group or was forming a group, a quartet with Howard Roberts on guitar. I was at Johnny's house looking over his music when Chico called, just out of the blue. He said, "I'm looking for a guitar player," and Howard, who had the phone, said, "Here," and just sort of handed me the phone. So I went over to Chico's apartment and talked to him and played through some of his music. It was a perfect opportunity for me because I'd just gotten out of music school and …

Wong: … You were ready.

Hall: And with Buddy Collette playing on woodwinds, it was a perfect job for me. But it was just a shot in the dark, just happened.

Wong: Wow, that was lucky.

Hall: It really was. While I was playing with Chico, Jim Giuffre heard me; Jim was forming a group at that time. I almost went with Oscar Peterson then, too, because Herb Ellis was leaving; but I declined that job. I don't know if I was afraid or what, but I had a feeling I wanted to stay with Jimmy's group.

Wong: Well, now we're into the early '50s.

Hall: Middle, late '50s, actually. While I was with Jim, Jim was being managed by Norman Granz, who also managed Ella Fitzgerald. We did one tour where I played with Ella and with Jimmy both. Then I went to South America with Ella Fitzgerald; Roy Eldridge was with her, too. So, again, I was playing with my idol, I suppose, and I was still in my 20s. I don't really know how all that came about, but it was extremely fortunate.

Wong: How would you describe your music from a stylistic point of view? You were growing then. Were you listening to others? Or did you have some of your own ideas you were formulating?

Hall: I think what happened, Herb, was when I managed to get into the Institute of Music, the only kind of classical music that I was drawn to was stuff like Stravinsky, and I think Stravinsky probably reminded me of Woody Herman's band; I know he had written a piece for Herman's band.

Wong: Right, "Ebony Concerto."

Hall: I was really pretty ignorant about anything except maybe hillbilly music and jazz music; I didn't even know anything about hillbilly music. But in school, it was the best decision I ever made, because I was exposed to everything from Gregorian chants up to electronic music. That's really what I think opened me up and I came, I think unconsciously, to see music—not as Charlie Christian, Bartók, or Mozart—but as an art form and, in that sense, as a means of self-expression, which has helped nudge me. It has helped me to not get intimidated when I run into guys like Wes Montgomery. I said, "I'll never be able to do that," but I *can* do something different anyway; I don't *have to* do that. So it's helped in that way. I think it helped me to keep my balance in a lot of ways. And it also helped my improvising a lot.

Wong: How did you learn how to improvise? Did your teachers work with you on that or did it come later on from outside sources or models or influences?

Hall: It came from models. You're playing in a group and you're playing a tune, and you keep playing the melody over and over; and even *you* get bored after awhile, so you start screwing around with it. It probably started that innocently. And then, I heard Charlie Christian. For quite awhile I almost thought I should try to sound like Charlie Christian because I thought that was *it*; and then I thought about Django Reinhardt, maybe more for the accompaniment stuff. It's a personality thing, in that I'm not really good at playing something exactly the same way every time, or anything for that matter, doing anything exactly the same thing twice.

Wong: How do you go about creating an improvised solo? Do you think about certain things? What are those visions or inspirations?

Hall: I'm not sure if what I'm gonna describe came first—having done tons of counterpoint and composition, listening to pieces and being around good teachers, talking about the architecture of music, the shape—I think I became very aware of that, so that what I do, sometimes it's a little *too* conscious. For instance, maybe on the first tune we played this afternoon, it's just got an open section where the band plays a C tonality. So when I play an idea, three or four notes, that would register with me, and I could almost see it written out; and then I would try to react to that and take it a little further. Sort of like you're dealing with material. It's almost a visual thing. I see the motive and I try to extend that.

Another way of playing jazz is to have things worked out in the best licks that play it. Even as I describe that—I can tell, a little disdainfully—I try to make a composition each time in a solo. I hope to stay connected to what I've played before and I try to develop it. I think one of the reasons is that I'm fascinated by architecture. I've got a couple books of bridges and a book called *Spanning America*, about older bridge building, including a couple of chapters on the George Washington Bridge. The architecture interests me, especially when it's something about bridges; because what they *want to do* is fall down. As a matter of fact, I was on this one that fell down; I missed it by about an hour, ten years ago, when we were coming up to Yoshi's and had just driven over it.

Wong: So ... shaping and reshaping has a lot to do with your vision of your solos? And the analogies to formal architecture, per se, seems to have a nice intellectual input, given that connection?

Hall: It's probably a combination of architecture and painting.

Wong: Painting?

Hall: Maybe abstract painting. I have a lot of friends who are painters.

Wong: Do you paint?

Hall: I don't, but it's funny: In the last few years I've gotten really interested in Oriental calligraphy, the Chinese calligraphy, and I guess the Japanese use it the same way.

Wong: Yes, they do.

Hall: I've got all of the brushes and stuff, and I found a place where I can paint. And I've just never been able to get the time together to do it.

Wong: The Japanese adapted those ideograms from the Chinese, which is termed in Japanese as *kanji*.

Hall: I'm interested in that and I probably spend more time looking at paintings for inspiration. For instance, do you know Whitney Balliett?

Wong: Yes, of course.

Hall: His wife, Nancy, is a terrific painter. I have a couple of Nancy's cards on my piano and I keep her artwork. I have a little electric piano in the country and on there I have some pictures, photographs of bridges, and a card of Nancy's, and a great picture of a beetle from a book about Brazilian airlines. So that's what gets me!

But, when I listen to other guitar players I like to listen to, sometimes listening to people doing the same thing that you're trying to do can be discouraging or …

Wong: … Stumpifying?

Hall: Exactly, yes.

Wong: So … you use these visual things as creative idea sources? Or, they spark you and get your juices going?

Hall: Yes, they do, and probably more than if I were listening to music. There's just something about it; for me, a piece has to have a shape and I'm really interested in shapes. It should go someplace and turn. It's the same way I feel about paintings.

Wong: Are there some typical conditions that you seem to require for creating?

Hall: That's an interesting question. I still haven't sorted that out. Sometimes just a deadline will do it.

Wong: There are a number of people who say that: "The deadline moves me."

Hall: It's because you're thinking, "I've gotta get to it now, because I know I've gotta finish it." That's one catalyst. What I try to do is get up early, at six or so in the morning, and get in some time. And I make a point of not looking at the newspaper, because I get too distraught sometimes or distracted. So, I try to get an early start: Recently, Janie and I inherited a dog from our daughter from Denver, who had to move back to California. And he's great; he's an amazing little guy.

Wong: The dog … he has something to do with this … with your creativity?

Hall: Well, of course! He gets up fairly early, so then *I* have to start taking him out and everything; so I try to sneak in some work before he gets up.

Wong: I have a question to pose to you. Is there a distinction between your creative processes when you compose, as compared to when you are improvising, let's say a solo on stage? These are two different kinds of contexts in a sense, but you may still have the same principles in mind, such as shape and things. But how does that come about?

Hall: I think each one of them has advantages. When you're improvising, you can't really go back and change things or erase them. So I can say, a lot of times, "I'm making a living recovering from mistakes." I'll screw up and then I'll say: "Well, make it right." And then I can screw up again and nobody will know the difference! And then, when composing … Well, I'm hardly an expert at this because I'm just getting started.

My experience is that you *do* get to make things right, just the way you like them, so you *can* erase. But on the other hand, sometimes it will just come out and you'll not have to go back; that would be great, too! I think there are advantages, in a certain sense; improvising is instant composition, and then composition is just sort of slowed down improvisation. Sometimes I feel really good about an improvisation and say, that's good; I can commit that to paper.

Wong: Yes, sure, it's "re-capturable," in a way. You can reclaim things that you like, if it's notated or recorded or documented. If it's not, well, it evaporates and it's gone.

Whereas if you're sitting down and you're composing, you can revisit it anytime you want and change it.

Hall: Exactly.

Wong: Is there a difference in the kind of stimulation to get you going on either way, or is it pretty much the same?

Hall: I think it was a Hemingway quote where he said that if he was writing at night, he liked to stop writing when things were going well, so that when he woke up the next day he wouldn't be faced with a block. Sometimes I'll do that, I'll keep going until I hit a nice high; and then, when I start next time in the morning, that'll be there to wake up to.

Wong: That's good, because you can begin the day on a high note.

Hall: I also read a quote of Stravinsky, who was pretty good at it. He said that, for him, the most important thing was keeping the pencil moving. He said he would just sit down and wouldn't pull the pencil off until he was inspired. And he said, "Just keep the pencil moving." If he couldn't think of anything, he would just write his name or write his name upside down, just to sort of keep going.

Wong: Keep the momentum?

Hall: Keep the momentum, exactly.

Wong: You've tried that and it works?

Hall: I have and it does.

Wong: What recordings have been your most important? Historical recordings … your most prominent recordings?

Hall: Recordings that I've been involved in?

Wong: Yes, the ones in which you're most prominent; if you were to single a few out? Because you have such a long career, it's a lot to go through; there's this whole marathon of albums.

Hall: I like the Bill Evans duet, *Undercurrent*. And, of course, the stuff with Sonny Rollins, *The Bridge*.

Wong: There's that "bridge" idea again!

Hall: You're right, Herb. I hadn't thought of that. That was Sonny's record and I'm really proud to be on it. So, those two, and then I like some of the recent ones.

Wong: Any others stand out?

Hall: I like *Textures*.

Wong: I figured that was gonna come up.

Hall: And I like parts of *By Arrangement*.

Wong: What about the albums that you did on Artists House or Horizon?

Hall: I like those, too, and I especially like the trio album with Don Thompson and Terry Clarke. It was done at Bourbon Street. Actually, I think one of the reasons I like it so much is that Don Thompson recorded it accidentally. He had left his equipment on the stage for a couple of weeks, and we forgot we were recording, so it just came out so loose.

Wong: What recordings by other musicians do you consider essential, or maybe indispensable, classics of jazz?

Hall: Almost anything by Duke Ellington, the big band stuff, I love the total big band stuff. And the way that band sounded! It was kind of an improvising big band, too. I'd probably add in some Bill Evans things … and Miles Davis, of course.

Wong: In what ways do you feel you've helped jazz to progress or to grow or to develop as a musical art form? Do you have any ideas about that?

Hall: I don't really know. I don't mean this in a self-centered way, but I don't really see myself in any kind of large sense, except that I do notice that a lot of guitar players come and talk to me.

Wong: They sure do.

Hall: I think that I would have left music a long time ago if I was still trying to play the way I did in the 1960s. So I want to try to allow, not *make* myself, but *allow* myself to grow and stay open the same as if I were a painter or a writer. That's why I try to keep guys like Scott and Kenny around me, guys who provoke that. And, jazz being the family that it is, a lot of the younger players say that they listen to me, and now I listen to them. Maybe I'm setting an example for them, as an older guy who's still trying to grow.

Wong: What kind of equipment do you use? What's your guitar?

Hall: It's made by Jim D'Aquisto. He was relatively young when he died of epilepsy just a couple of years ago. He had been an apprentice to John D'Angelico when Jimmy was just a kid. He was experimenting all the time with instruments, right up to the very end. Each one of his guitars is a little different from the one before it. I'm using the Poly-Tone amp here, and they're good; they're really reliable. They're close to the old tube amp sound. So that's pretty simple stuff. It's never perfect, but …

Wong: Getting back to your relationship with art. I don't think I've heard that from anybody else yet … from the other musicians I've interviewed.

Hall: Painting, you mean, the visual element?

Wong: Yes, that was very fresh. I enjoyed it.

Hall: Parenthetically, at the Guggenheim Museum in Venice there's a whole room of Jackson Pollack's earlier stuff. This sounds like a real hick thing to say, but the guy could really paint, besides the drip thing. It was interesting to see his realistic paintings. And he just kept going and he evolved … that's one of the things I loved about Miles Davis, was that he kept growing and changing. A lot of people didn't like the directions that he was going in, big bands and stuff. But he was always searching and looking for new things. I really admire that. I also admire his use of silence, a lot.

Wong: How does it relate to this creative process?

Hall: I think probably the improvised part is important because jazz is a "pretty" term; and, in a way, I don't like the term. But, on the other hand, it's a way of improvising and you can improvise on really strict song, like maybe "Skylark" or something like that; or you could improvise just kind of freely together, just sort of looking at one another and just start out that way. It's kind of "instant composition," I would say. It may be an accent in music. It's become what I would call American music, I guess. And, again, an amalgam, it's a mixture of all different ethnic groups and age groups and genders and everything. That's the thing I love about it, I think, most. It doesn't know about boundaries.

Kenny Burrell

Kenny Burrell is the most steadfast guitarist in jazz. You can depend on quality music from him every time. His playing is so beautiful. His sound is perfect. He always contributes more than you would ever expect; with Kenny, you get more than you could ever hope for.

I always tried to catch Kenny whenever he played in San Francisco, every time I could. He was a regular artist in the city's jazz clubs, clubs like El Matador—at the time, one of maybe five or six jazz clubs located in just one block of Broadway in North Beach.

One day, back in 1967, I got a call from Kenny, asking me if I was planning on coming over to the club to hear him play. My response was a little unusual, maybe even unique: "Gee, Kenny," I said, "I don't think I can come over. Marilyn and I are getting married."

This seemed to catch Kenny by surprise, but he took it in his stride. "Oh, really?" he said. "When is that?"

"It's this Saturday," I replied.

"Jeez," he said, "I have a reservation to go home on Saturday. So, I guess you won't be making it to the club?"

To which I had to reply, "Kenny, it's just not possible."

Later in the evening, the phone rang and, again, it was Kenny. "Herb," he said, "I've changed my plans and we're going to come to your wedding."

I said, "What?"

And Kenny said, "Yeah, I was thinking of bringing my bass player with me."

I said, "Well, that's a surprise and it's wonderful!"

Then Kenny asked, "Can you name two or three tunes that I could play at your wedding?" And I suggested a few ballads.

Early Saturday morning, Kenny calls, yet again. "Herb, I have a favor to ask of you before the wedding. I forgot how the wedding march goes. Can you hum it for me?" I couldn't believe it! So I hummed "Da Da Dada … Da Da Dada."

And that's how Kenny Burrell happened to play for Marilyn and me at our wedding.

Kenny Burrell with the Gerald Wilson Orchestra—
75th Birthday Bash Live!
Blue Note Records (0946-374906-2-4); 2007

Crowning a 5-day gig at Yoshi's Jazz Club in Oakland, California, was the spectacular celebration of master guitarist Kenny Burrell's 75th birthday on July 31, 2006. Waves of anticipation wafted through the club creating a pervading buzz in the audience before musicians stepped on stage. The bewitching slate of Kenny Burrell and his combo, Gerald Wilson's legendary orchestra, guest stars Hubert Laws and Joey DeFrancesco, the birthday theme, and the live recording culminated in a dynamic attraction. A huge horde of fans outside Yoshi's queued around the block hoping to gain entry.

A brilliant exponent of the modern jazz guitar heritage, Burrell has been a protagonist carrying the torch of the jazz tradition cradled in bebop. He plays in settings from solo and small groups to orchestral ensembles, and his impressive artistry is illuminated by his extensive catalog of recordings and by his bright birthday performances. Little wonder that Duke Ellington cited Burrell as his favorite guitarist.

Birthday galas promise special gratifications and Burrell describes his joys: "I had so many happy moments from start to finish. It was heartwarming to see so many musicians, friends, family members, and students of mine who showed up to celebrate." (Burrell is Director of the UCLA Jazz Program.) "And the wonderful Gerald Wilson Orchestra! They played so great! It was a thrill to work with such a magnificent big band. Gerald made me bubble with inspiration and enthusiasm." Burrell and Wilson are NEA Jazz Masters honorees.

"I was so pleased to perform in varied settings," noted Burrell. His pluralistic leanings are expressed with felicitous chemistry and influence on listeners' imagination. With piquant surprises and introspective warmth, his improvisations are impulsively inspired yet formally elegant. This CD is a model of Burrell's uncompromising equation of swing.

The opening salvo by Burrell's kinetic, swinging guitar melded with the explosive Wilson arrangements quickly reached a seductive level. Wilson's popular 1962 signature composition/arrangement "Viva Tirado" is an apt opener, and Burrell captures the spirit of the great matador.

"I've wanted to record 'Stormy Monday Blues' vocally for years," says Burrell. "I told Gerald I'd like to do some blues, with 'Stormy Monday' in mind; I wanted something that fits as background for my singing while it also features the band." Consequently, "Stormy Monday Blues" was segued into Wilson's "Blues for the Count" featuring Burrell and the band. It's a fitting tribute to T-Bone Walker and Count Basie.

"Romance" is Wilson's beautiful song from *Theme for Monterey*, a 5-part suite in celebration of Monterey Jazz Festival's 40th Anniversary in 1998. "I like the piece a lot and we did it with a slightly different rhythmic approach," remarks Burrell. Pleased with a Brazilian flavor, Wilson said: "I love the way Kenny added a bossa nova beat."

Ardent admirers of Duke Ellington, Burrell and Wilson paid tribute to him via Ducal pieces—"Love You Madly," "Don't Get Around Much Anymore," and "Sophisticated Lady." Burrell revealed he had never recorded the latter tune as the only featured soloist. Wilson's attractive chart of "Lady" was textured with savory use of dynamics.

The small group segment begins with Wayne Shorter's trademark "Footprints." Its freedom of interpretations appeals to Burrell. The arrangement featured his bassist, Roberto Miranda, and drummer Clayton Cameron's articulate solo on brushes.

J.J. Johnson's lovely "Lament" served as a piece for Burrell and, for the most part, iconic flutist Hubert Laws, who blew a sensational solo with soft Burrell backing.

"'All Blues' is a tune I love to play as a trio," said Burrell. His guitar assumed dual roles as the lead and the accompanist on the storied classic.

"A Night in Tunisia" was perfect turf to ignite the fiery talents of organist Joey DeFrancesco, tenorist Herman Riley, altoist Jeff Clayton, and flutist Laws, joined by Burrell's trio. A flaming bebop ball!

Burrell had recorded "I'll Close My Eyes" with the late pioneer jazz organist Jimmy Smith. "We wanted to play something in tribute to James Oscar Smith and I love that song," said Burrell. "It was meaningful for Joey and I."

Consistent with the event's spirit, the closer, "Take the 'A' Train," was a Kenny Burrell stroke of joy. In response to shouting requests, he consented: "Surprising myself, I inserted those spontaneous lyrics. I was having so much fun with the guys." His scatting, influenced by Duke's singer Betty Roché's bop version, fueled the climactic groove of an unforgettable birthday bash.

A pertinent footnote on the event: An NEA grant for collaborative programming for Burrell and Wilson's Orchestra was awarded via Tim Jackson (GM, Kuumbwa Jazz Center). Peter Williams (Yoshi's Artistic Director) joined in staging the birthday bash.

Bola Sete

I was familiar with Bola Sete when he was playing at the historic Palace Hotel in San Francisco. He had practically no audience listening to him, whatsoever; he was pretty much playing there alone, a hidden treasure. I remember mentioning this to Dizzy Gillespie, noting that he would be intensely intrigued by Bola; and Dizzy did have a chance to witness what Bola was able to do with his instrument.

Dizzy then told the Monterey Jazz Festival's Jimmy Lyons about this great guitarist he'd heard and then *Jimmy* was intrigued. So much so that, in 1966, shortly after he was finished playing at the Palace, Bola got a groundbreaking gig at the Monterey Jazz Festival.

His performance was masterfully impressive! Bola seared the senses and burned a bulk of new ears for Monterey Jazzfest fans who had never heard a guitar played quite like Bola Sete played.

Bola Sete—*Bola Sete at the Monterey Jazz Festival*
Verve (V6-8689); 1966

This is a MAGNIFICENT album!

Guitarist Bola Sete has already recorded what can be considered a relatively bountiful legacy of gifted artistry; nevertheless, his starbright performance at the Ninth Annual Monterey Jazz Festival must be assessed as singular in its raging brilliance. Though I have thoroughly enjoyed Bola's playing in a wide variety of settings since I was first devastated by his solo work in the Tudor Room of the Sheraton Palace Hotel in San Francisco over half a dozen years ago, I don't question that the inhalation of this dramatic Festival appearance ranks as the most head-reeling, intoxicating encounter so far. What dozens of other musicians could not attain during the Festival or could at best waveringly approach, Bola's trio decidedly reached—the sublime station of inspired, universal communication.

Addressing themselves to an SRO audience, the Trio quickly engulfed the Saturday evening crowd of over 7,000 which had been warmed up by the MJF All-Star Orchestra led by Gil Evans, the Cannonball Adderley Quintet, and the Elvin Jones–Joe Henderson Quartet. Speaking of Gil Evans, I recall vividly the wordless admiration Gil displayed as he remained seated at the piano on stage, resting his chin in his cupped hand. As a renowned orchestrator whose musical strengths reflect an extraordinary sense of tonal textures, delicate harmonization, subtle blendings, and fresh imagination, Gil's apparent mesmerization was symbolic of the heightened demeanor of awe pervading the entire Festival arena—the onlooking musicians, the Festival staff, the vendors, the press and the patrons. Whitney Balliett writing in *The New Yorker* observed, "The Monterey audience almost lifted off its pad at the end of Sete's performance." Leonard Feather in the *Los Angeles Times* said, "It was standing ovation time for the Brazilian genius."

Bola Sete's given name is Djalma de Andrade. His Portuguese nickname "Bola Sete," means "seven ball"—the single black ball in the game of billiards as played in Brazil. He received this tag when he was the only Negro member of a small jazz group in South America. His conservatory training in Rio de Janeiro and his Segovia-inspired performances are evident in his diversified repertory which includes classical guitar and lute solos of Bach, Albéniz and Villa-Lobos.

Jazz writer Richard Hadlock, one of the first jazz people to communicate successfully with Bola in his native Portuguese, gave me some insight into Bola's approach. In essence, Hadlock feels that the charming thing about Bola's classical interpretations is that he brings to them his natural Brazilian warmth and the meaty traditions of *bossa velaj*. In addition to the classics, of course, Bola plays flamencos, bossa novas, and jazz per se. His jazz beginnings were inspired by jazz guitarists George Van Eps, Charlie Christian, and Django Reinhardt.

For a couple of years Bola performed and recorded with Vince Guaraldi's Trio. Last year he formed his own trio, the one heard on this album. His bass player, Sebastian Neto, polled as Brazil's top bassist prior to his residence in the U.S., has played with some of Brazil's finest musicians, among them Sérgio Mendes, João Gilberto, Antônio Carlos Jobim and João Donato: likewise, Neto has recorded extensively with American jazz-men—Stan Getz, Herbie Mann and Bud Shank—to name just three. Paulinho has, for the past decade, been recognized as Brazil's foremost drummer.

He has recorded with a wide spectrum of U.S. artists from Laurindo Almeida and Herbie Mann to Nelson Riddle—as well as doing a host of television and sound track assignments. Listen to Paulinho's sensitive, skillful use of percussion instruments. Dig the weird, organic, humanized sounds he produces. Unbelievable!

Bola's reputation for versatility was magnified recently by his appearances on concert programs featuring Nancy Wilson, Maynard Ferguson's big band and a variety of folk-rock artists such as The Animals, Sly and the Family Stone, The Harbinger Complex, The Association, and The Baytovans. The rare empathetic relationship of these three superb musicians must be judged as fundamental to the message they convey. The group is incomparable when rendering its exciting interpretations of authentic Brazilian material such as the wonderful medley from *Black Orpheus* on side one.

Bola is a total gas on "Soul Samba"! Incidentally, I never cease to relish watching Bola pour his soul into every single note of every single one of his performances. It's a warm, exhilarating, emotional experience to be able to peer into the raw, seemingly private and intimate interaction he has with his music; Bola's nimble fingers move like graceful dancers in miniature, his teeth grit with joy and pain, and the coolness and heat of his perspiration are all personalized parts of his inside portrait. Bola in person is a sincere, reflective, personable gentleman. Perhaps you have not had the opportunity to make his acquaintance. Fret not, for your one indelible aural souvenir of this perfectly marvelous and fantastic musician and his cohorts is contained within the sleeve of this album.

I repeat categorically—this is a MAGNIFICENT album!

Django Reinhardt

An internationally historic guitar player, Django Reinhardt had much to do with the influence of American music in France. He was just a genius; a brand new voice on the horizon.

He became one of the most storied guitarists of our time, partly because of his French gypsy background and partly because of his subsequent work with Stéphane Grappelli on their tour of the United States. Django's reputation preceded his visit to this country with Grappelli—he was an historic figure even before he stepped foot in America. But Django was unhappy with the tour. I don't know why, but he was just not grooving. He toured a little bit with the Ellington Band, too—Duke was one of his heroes—but with little visibility. He apparently just didn't want to do the tour and it showed.

Django Reinhardt—*The Versatile Giant*
Vogue P.I.P.; 1978; Reissued by Inner City Records (IC 7004)

Django Reinhardt was easily the greatest jazz guitarist of his time and his innovations were historically significant. Although he died in 1953, his influence continues to help shape the direction of his instrument.

His legacy is treasured by legions of jazz guitarists represented by long-standing players of high repute as well as youthful cadre in our schools. There is scarcely a jazz guitarist who would not acknowledge Django in a referent group of "the most inspiring jazz guitarists" or cite him among those having strong impact on their growth and development. Together with the likes of Eddie Lang and Charlie Christian, Django must be counted among the first generation giants of the jazz guitar. Early on, even Christian was an avid student of Django's solos. Homage to Django has been paid by a good many musicians, some via songs bearing reference to him; Joe Pass, for instance, composed and recorded "For Django." The best known composition might well be John Lewis' "Django."

A resume of some of Django's contributions must include his rich, distinctive, original melodies and his finely-shaped improvisations enlivened by fiery imagination. His unique tone is warm, romantic, clearly attractive, and his chords and runs are striking. Django's amazing technical fluency is even more impressive considering that he lost the use of the two smaller fingers on his left hand as a result of being badly burned in a fire in his gypsy wagon. Guitarist Charlie Byrd's comment is fitting: "Like all great players, it's musicianship that is crucial. If Django was as great as he truly was, he would be a genius even if he used a baseball bat!" He was a natural swinger.

Born in 1910 In Liberchies, Belgium, Jean-Baptiste Reinhardt was raised as a French gypsy musician. Self-taught, he played violin, guitar and banjo. By 1930, Django was intensely involved with jazz. Five years later, he organized his unorthodox yet highly successful Parisian quintet of a violin, three guitars and a bass—the Quintet of the Hot Club of France was created. Django became the popular object of visiting American jazz players; e.g., Rex Stewart, Benny Carter, Coleman Hawkins, Louis Armstrong and Dicky Wells. Django Reinhardt was easily the ranking jazz guitarist of the time.

It is eventful to discover heretofore unavailable or, at best, generally difficult to obtain recordings made by Django; some of these were released under discreet circumstances. "Tiger Rag," the opening tune, is one of these uncovered releases from 1934 which is, in fact, one of four versions produced by Pierre Nourry of the Hot Club of France. The last version makes its presence on this album; it was in the possession of Henry Bernard—one of France's earliest jazz connoisseurs. Nourry specifically made and sent the first three versions to other jazz critics including John Hammond and Hugues Panassié, to evoke wider interest in Django. All versions were cut with Django, his brother Joseph and the bassist from Martinique—Juan Fernandez.

Charles Delaunay (Django's biographer) and Panassié became staunch supporters of Django and the Quintet. Delaunay and Nourry joined in promoting the newly created Hot Club. Under the banner of Delaunay's Jazz, the spirited group featuring Stéphane Grappelli and the Reinhardt brothers recorded "I Saw Stars" and "I'm Confessin'" for the Odeon label. The Quintet takes the final tunes on Side One from the sound track of Marcel Carné's film *La Fleur de L'Age*.

In 1946, Django made his only American tour, playing with Duke Ellington's Orchestra. Of historical interest, some of the Chicago concert is documented here. Despite the "handicaps" of not having his own acoustic guitar and the below par audio quality, Django's inventive genius on electric guitar is fully worth including. Although the success of the brief concert tour fell short of its expectations, it was through this visit to the U.S. that Django became impressed with Charlie Parker and the bop movement. The imprint was later manifested by Django's recordings, signifying his ability to adapt to the times.

The final pair of tunes are 1951 broadcasts via French Radio RTF from the Club Saint-Germain in Paris featuring Django's Septet. This was when he was playing in excellent form in advance of his dwindling health.

Many records are available to Django devotees. This one highlights the rich diversity of *The Versatile Giant*, which is an apt title. Django's adaptability is expressed in this collective range of seventeen years—between 1934 and 1951. It presents a broad profile of a versatile giant of the jazz guitar who created a legacy—one which has become increasingly vital with age.

CHAPTER 12

Vibraphone

The vibraphone helps to complete the sound spectrum of the band. It was such an important part of Woody Herman's first Herd in the 1940s, when Red Norville—or Norvo, as he later became known—really set the tone for the instrument. Red was one of those rare musicians who had the speed ... the range ... the sound ... the whole ball of wax needed to master the vibraphone.

It is an instrument of very demanding facilities. That's why there are so very few musicians with a vibraphone in their holster and they are led, in my opinion, by Cal Tjader.

Cal Tjader

One of the best vibraphonists ever, Cal Tjader was actually Dave Brubeck's *drummer* in the earlier days of the late 1940s, and then he switched to include the vibraphone in his repertoire. I think Dave was surprised at Cal's immediate facility with the instrument!

For many years, Cal would send me the acetate for his new recordings and we would expose them for the first time on my radio show on KJAZ. That was, literally, the first time anyone had ever heard them played, beyond Cal in his own privacy.

Over the years, I had many, many conversations with Cal Tjader and we became close friends. That might be the reason he asked me to do the first liner notes I ever wrote, notes for his album, *Warm Wave*.

Once, when he was performing with his group at El Matador in San Francisco, Cal took a break—per a longstanding tradition of his—to let somebody else play the vibes, while Cal got a drink from the bar. I was standing there watching him during one of those breaks when he accidentally poked my elbow, and there went my drink—a non-alcoholic King Alphonse—spilling all over my camel-hair sport coat.

Cal was mortified and quickly said, "I'm so sorry, Herb, let me try to do something with this." While he was wiping away at my jacket, Cal continued, "You know, I have always wanted to do a tune in your honor, Herb ... and I'm going to do just that because I just screwed up." I said, "Cal, you don't have to do that!"

Cal's comment was based, in part, on a thing we had between us for a long, long time. Whenever Cal needed help with a title for a tune, we would sit down in a bar and I would grab a stack of cocktail napkins and start writing down all the tune titles that came to me. So, in this instance, Cal said, "I'm going to turn things around, Herb, and write a new piece of music you'll like ... especially the title!"

At the end of the night, Cal came back to me and said, "I've got it! How about 'Wong Way Street'?"

That was the first in a long list of pun-filled proposals Cal shot my way, a list that, with other musicians contributing over the years, eventually consisted of seven songs named and recorded in my honor: "Dr. Wong's Bag" (Woody Herman); "A-Wong Came Herb" (Roy Eldridge); "Dr. Herb's Herbs" (Larry Vuckovich); "Herbal Syndrome" (Mal Waldron); "Wong's Way" (Greg Abate); "Dr. Wong's Bird Song" (Dayna Stephens); and Cal Tjader's eventual title, "Daddy Wong Legs."

Cal Tjader—*The Prophet*
Verve Records (V6–8769); 1968

This is an ecstatically beautiful album. It is easily the most attractive Cal Tjader album since *Several Shades of Jade* (V6–8507) and *Warm Wave* (V6–8585). Cal has reported that these two older ones remain consistently high on the programming barometer of numerous radio stations. This status of classic Tjader music provides a more pivotal frame of reference for the comparable level of this new album, *The Prophet*.

The Tjader discography strikes a broad plate of ethnic music incorporated into his jazz concepts. His open attitude is reflected in the long chain of recorded jazz-environment interactions … sometimes victorious and other times short of the intended message; but, nevertheless, a sense of unity, of challenge and of learning seems to come through. Each album is a chronicle of Tjaderism, and this album represents one of the crests in the Tjader jazzlife.

Over and above the jazz idiom's core commonalities which are subject to environmental stimulation, Cal has displayed creativeness in terms of what Carl Rogers has summarized as "openness to experience, self-confidence, and the ability to toy with elements and concepts." Since Cal can be considered a veteran jazzman now, he is enjoying at least a pair of conditions that promote constructive creativity—one of them is psychological safety, a condition wherein Cal is accepted for unconditional worth while he functions in an environment of empathetic understanding. Psychological freedom, the other condition, refers to the extent to which Cal's composing and performing roles are fostered in a form of symbolic expression.

Cal had been ecstatic about the concept of the album long before it was hatched. Combined with the urge to extend the concept of the *Warm Wave* focus on beautiful tunes and the inspiration he had to involve João Donato's giftedness in composing lovely melodies, he made plans to collaborate with Donato. About Donato, Cal commented warmly, "João and I sat down and we were right into it. I'm very simpatico with his feelings and thinking. João has two bags that make him desirable—his gift for pretty Brazilian melodies and the fact that his tunes make for jazz adaptation. He is underrated as a composer." As for his successful relationship with Esmond Edwards the producer of the album, Cal noted, "Working with Es was great. He understood how I felt about playing and was very receptive to the concept. I did not want any pressure on current tunes, and I did not receive such pressure. Things that are necessarily important to the artists may not necessarily be important to the recording industry." This honest approach is evident in the music herein.

The quartet of Cal's vibes and the rhythm section recorded their tracks before the arrangements were conceived and dubbed in. This is a technique that avoids "over-arranging," Cal explained. "It is harder to concentrate on improvising while you are also trying to focus on the arrangement at the same time. Breathing space is needed. And Don Sebesky's skillful arranging was just right—sparing and tasteful!" This album is looser than *Warm Wave* and contains restrained power. It can be likened to how Ahmad Jamal makes powerful use of his rhythm section when he plays just a few notes or how Oscar Peterson played in pianissimo with Ray Brown and Ed Thigpen. Donato does not play like an organist with all the devices and stops; this accounts for the lack of intrusive elements characteristic of organ players who pour out all their wares. Cal remarked admiringly about Donato's judicious use of space, "João is like the Brazilian Count Basie, or like John Lewis in his feeling because of what he does not do; that is, absence is as important as presence." Bassist Red Mitchell and drummer Ed Thigpen mirror their seasoned experience in adapting to a broad palette of jazz persuasions. "They instinctively know what concepts you desire," Cal adds.

"Souled Out" is a little pseudo mambo, a jazz mambo wherein the middle section is based on a fairly familiar Latin montuna, A minor to D^7.

"Warm Song" is certainly one of the most attractive melodies Donato has written. It carries a strong ambience reminiscent of Neal Hefti's "Li'l Darlin'." In fact, Cal has begged Donato to send the chart to Basie for Hefti to arrange. The lovely melodic line also recalls for me "The Sleep Song," the old sign-off theme used by Glenn Miller.

The title selection, "The Prophet," was originally recorded almost four years ago, but this version makes it. A pretty Donato waltz is "Aquarius." It's the type of tune jazzmen like to play because of the harmony. Donato first recorded it in a Brazilian release.

"Cal's Bluedo" is simply "a desperate blues to round out the album." Ex-Kenton and Herman trumpet soloist Marvin Stamm sounds out here. It is appropriate to cite Hubert Laws who was also added via Sebesky's arrangements; Laws' flute work was the right touch and definitely is an ideal complement.

A superb ballad … Johnny Mandel, who is regarded by Cal as "the greatest romantic ballad writer today," wrote "A Time for Love." As a melody, it deserves no less attention than Mandel's "The Shadow of Your Smile." It is a tune that Cal's working group plays regularly which prompts me to state that Cal is, indeed, a magnificent ballad player. His vibes seem to take on added increments of luster and sensitivity when he waxes romantic.

You'll have fun listening to "Temo Teimoso." It is another of Donato's Brazilian beauties. Dig how Sebesky has added an appealing dimension of voices to the swinging sound. Finally, "The Loner" is the background music Cal provided for the flick *For Singles Only*.

This is an album possessed of evergreen atmosphere. And although Cal has mused, "I don't really care if it doesn't sell twenty copies—it's something I've wanted to do," it is an album that has inherent ecstatic power. It supports the psychological safety and freedom components for Cal's constructive creativity. Composer Roger Sessions has said, "Inspiration, then, is the impulse which sets creation in movement; it is also the energy which keeps it going." And Cal Tjader was truly inspired from the pre-conception to post-conception of this ecstatically beautiful album.

Bobby Hutcherson

I knew Bobby Hutcherson for some time, well before his first recording, which he did live for Palo Alto Records. I recruited Bobby to do the solo lines for a list of guest performers who played on that date, including Sonny Stitt on alto—not his usual tenor—along with John Handy and Richie Cole … that's three altos … and Bobby on vibes; plus the rhythm section of pianist Cedar Walton, Herbie Lewis on bass … and the whole thing was wrapped up by drummer Billy Higgins.

I had the group for two nights and, on both nights, fans formed long lines outside the venue but couldn't get in. Given a group of this caliber, it was a given that there would simply be no more space available in the club to accommodate more fans.

Speaking of Sonny Stitt, he had some serious dental problems and my brother Woody—who was to become known as "the jazz dentist"—had Sonny staying at his home for over a month to work on his entire mouth. I would go over to Woody's house and Sonny always seemed to be there, mouth open, with my brother working away. In subsequent gigs, Sonny would inevitably acknowledge that he sounded so much better than ever before and it was due to "Dr. Woody Wong."

Bobby Hutcherson—*Total Eclipse*
Blue Note Records (BST 84291);1969

"He is thoroughly distinctive." … "His progress is truly astounding." … "His playing is beautiful and exciting!" These reactions came from a group of vibists after a presentation labeled "A Generation of Vibers." The occasion was the 1968 Monterey Jazz Festival Sunday afternoon agenda. The program title, coined by Cal Tjader, was inspired by Philip Wylie's old *A Generation of Vipers*. Red Norvo, Milt Jackson, Tjader, Gary Burton and Bobby Hutcherson were the five vibe players involved. The above comments were made in reference to Hutcherson's imposing talents.

Tjader elaborated, "Bobby is a very dynamic player. Like Lester Young leading the way for extensions on his fresh approach with the tenor saxophone and like Coltrane setting things up for next steps, I think Bobby represents the next logical step in the generation of vibists through his tremendous emotional and physical involvement, his concept of freedom, his own sound, and his own brand of excitement. He is one of the young rabbits—playing straight through. And the way he gets to it—the feeling is beautiful." Young Gary Burton whose own musical development renders systemic terms inefficient, commented willingly, "Of all the new young vibists—Roy Ayers, Walt Dickerson, Lynn Blessing, and Mike Mainieri, for example—Bobby Hutcherson is the only one with a really different musical personality that indicates great evolutionary potential. Although his development stems from Milt Jackson roots, he has developed to the extent that this relationship is obscured most of the time because Bobby has moved on to become his own man. I respect him very much." Value judgments from his colleagues carry a high level of validity. Add to them Hutcherson's self-evaluation and we have a few more pieces of a picture of Hutcherson's music. He has continued to devote much time to self study for he feels that his search for more music is "within myself."

In the last couple of years, he has had under his own leadership several recordings principally made up of his compositions. In these albums, *Components* (Blue Note 84213), *Happenings* (Blue Note 84231), and *Stick-Up* (Blue Note 84244), Hutcherson's inventiveness and leadership have added to his growing stature. He has been an object of praise since the first of this decade when he broke into the jazz scene in California. In New York City, he was so impressive that he was in demand by numerous musicians—Eric Dolphy, Jackie McLean, Al Grey, Hank Mobley, Dexter Gordon, Archie Shepp, Grant Green,

Grachan Moncur, and Charles Tolliver to name some of them. Hutcherson has the ability to shape his playing to the ideas and concepts of other musicians. Another personalized asset is his ability to transcend the sound of the piano with his more open and freer sound on the vibes. His chime-like sound is different from the pianistic effects and tight pedaled approach that characterize most vibists. There is more harmonic permissiveness for other soloists in the group; this is due to Hutcherson's individualized comping style—his chords seem to suspend in space. Along with the clusters he plays, he does use space judiciously and beautifully. As he remarked, "The sound of space itself is truly beautiful." Certainly, it is understandable that so many musicians in the vanguard of jazz prefer to interact with the challenging and creative directions Hutcherson provides. In turn he finds that he must listen as openly as possible to others and to himself, thereby immersing himself in the total experience.

During the past year in particular he has continued to work in Gerald Wilson's orchestra whenever possible "to keep my ears open to orchestrations." This is a logical enterprise since Hutcherson uses his vibes orchestrally. Listen to him on two of Wilson's recent albums—*Everywhere* on Pacific Jazz and *California Soul* on World Pacific. Wilson, who has known Hutcherson since the vibes came into the latter's musical life, speaks enthusiastically, "Bobby is an exceptional soloist. He has accomplished an incredible amount in a comparatively short time. He is very thorough. Some people have it and some don't. Bobby's got it!"

Furthermore, Hutcherson has been co-leading a unit with Harold Land playing mainly in West Coast jazz hostelries and in concerts, and the future promises college concert tours beyond the Western borders. Early this year he and Land spent three weeks in New York City—a week at Slugs' and two in the Village Vanguard. This album was recorded following these club dates. Pianist Chick Corea reminisced about the brief association with Hutcherson and Land, "It was a marvelous experience. We played the way we felt—with complete relaxation. We played for ourselves the whole three weeks. Bobby is so lyrical, so easy to play with, so open. And each time we played a tune, it was a vastly different thing each time." Corea also holds great admiration for the tenor work of Harold Land. On this album Land's sound is fresh, confident and strong; his solos make up some of the many highlights on the date.

As to Hutcherson's esteem for Chick Corea, he responded warmly, "Chick can do whatever needs to be done and he puts his own thing into it. He's really fast and alert. He opens up things very well and blows my mind. He'll open up things so fast I have found myself wanting to shout out at Chick to wait up!" Corea has played with Blue Mitchell, Pete La Roca, Herbie Mann, Cal Tjader, Art Blakey, Willie Bobo, Stan Getz among others; he is currently a member of the Miles Davis Quintet. Like Hutcherson, Corea responds to a diversity of sounds. Bass player Reggie Johnson is empathetically keen and openly imaginative on the session. He switched from trombone to bass about five years ago. Johnson has played with Archie Shepp and Sonny Rollins. His big full sound is a vital part of this album's scintillations. As Shepp has indicated, Reggie Johnson is a formidable bassist.

Joe Chambers is a remarkable drummer. His sharply essential accents, colors and textures show why he has been teamed with Hutcherson on so many albums. His playing is tremendously rewarding for the attentive listener; his strength is discernible yet he exerts it without overpowering the listener. His contouring comes out in a natural manner and he is never gauche. In fact he is a very tasteful drummer. Chambers has played with

Freddie Hubbard, Eric Dolphy, Andrew Hill, Archie Shepp, Charles Lloyd, Joe Henderson, Jimmy Giuffre, and Donald Byrd.

It is obvious that this acutely probing group of contemporaries established a remarkable rapport. With the openness that they mutually required and gratifyingly enjoyed, this album presents a stimulating listening experience. New feelings, textures, shades, shapes and sounds come with every hearing. Hutcherson said, "I like to put people into a mood. The main thing is to set a mood by creating the sound that communicates the mood. Then the other musicians will jump into it. Some of the most simple things come out sounding intricate. It is delusive. I think simplicity is difficult to achieve. Each tune in the album has a definite mood which emerged." The album opens brightly with "Herzog" and it should place the listener in a receptive mood for the emotional vibrations. For Hutcherson, the tune conjures impressions of a duke … "a German duke."

The title selection "Total Eclipse" has an alternate unlisted title of "Mysterioso" because of the eeriness it apparently carries. It is aptly titled "Total Eclipse" as the last chord opens up with light and resolution somewhat like the phenomena of the sun's total eclipse by the moon. In the resolution there are sounds that prompt me to think of the vision of the corona—a beautiful cosmic halo surrounding the solar sphere. And at the edge of the sun's disk the solar prominences shoot out like brilliant tongues of flames up into the light of the coronal atmosphere. Man, it's an intriguing track in many ways.

"Matrix" is a twelve bar blues composed by Chick Corea who previously recorded it in a trio version. It has an infectious theme that swings. "Same Shame" has a long meter. The title was evoked by Hutcherson's reaction to the effect of "sameness." He explained, "it's the same as the sound of two chords. The first chord is really four different chords against the sound of the first chord creating the impression of an overall sound of just two chords."

A pretty waltz closes the album. Hutcherson used tiny bells on "Pompeian" because he feels that rhythm instruments not only provide more of a percussive sound with tonalities, but they lend themselves toward patterns. He enlarged on this thought, "We tried to develop extended patterns, and so on. This chain or expansion process is more easily done with rhythmic instruments." By the way, dig Harold Land's flute playing. Hutcherson believes Land will be attracting much attention on the flute eventually and admires Land's self discipline and self imposed demands in regard to the instrument. As he noted, "It is difficult to come through with clean sharp notes on the flute." Harold Land has expressed himself with much passion and warmth on the tenor for years and he is warming hearts with his performances on this album.

This album again demonstrates that Bobby Hutcherson is not merely a reflector but an explorer, a modifier whose relentless and patient efforts toward artistic perfection will make it impossible for his place in the generation of vibers to ever be eclipsed.

Milt Jackson

Milt Jackson has a real jazz strength in his playing; you can always tell who's playing when Milt's on vibes. He's a wonderful bebop vibraphonist—he's got that down—and he is such a swinger, a vibraphonist much more bluesy than any of his fellow vibists.

Milt Jackson was part of the group that was the precursor to the Modern Jazz Quartet. Prior to performing with that legendary group, Milt played on numerous albums of his own. His playing in those circumstances was very unlike what he did with MJQ; the projects Milt Jackson did on his own are so attractive because of their bluesy sounds— but when Milt played with the Modern Jazz Quartet, he was a beautiful balladeer. That group infused their song list with a kind of hard to describe feeling ... but you feel you know it's jazz.

Milt Jackson with J.J. Johnson—*A Date in New York*
Vogue P.I.P.; 1954; Reissued by Inner City (IC 7007)

Milt Jackson and J.J. Johnson are two of the most celebrated jazz musicians in the history of their chosen instruments. As artful, imaginative improvisers they are among the relatively small cluster of musicians who are literally distinctive in their style and personal in their sound. Both are bright illustrations of that rare breed of jazz musician who is predictably inventive and confidently at ease in practically all emotional settings. They are warmly expressive and articulate in any part of the sweeping array of contexts from soft, delicate, reflective ballads to highly charged, driving flag-wavers. The high quality of this inspired 1954 recording stands the test of time; it had won the French Jazz Academy's "Oscar" award for the best record of the year.

Augmenting the front line of the two principal soloists on half the program was Al Cohn whose style had reached a mature stage. Cohn had already counted experiences with Buddy Rich, Joe Marsala, Georgie Auld and the Elliot Lawrence Orchestras as well as the notable "Four Brothers" saxophone section of Woody Herman's "Second Herd." In 1954, Cohn, J.J. and Jackson were all busy, in-demand New York musicians of that jazz generation. They shared several prized qualities, giving this disc that special mark of allure and adventure—a strong melodic commitment, a sense of swing, a balance of composure and confidence and a deep-seated affinity for the blues.

In that year, the Modern Jazz Quartet had become a "permanent" organized unit, although it actually began as a performance group much earlier as a direct outgrowth of Dizzy Gillespie's big band. Milt Jackson on vibraphone was the strongest improvising voice in the MJQ; he and bassist Percy Heath—half of the MJQ—were on this French Vogue record date. It was organized by Parisian pianist Henri Renaud in New York City during his three-month stay in 1954. His modern approach, likened to Al Haig's bop conceptual direction, was boon to the total effort.

Fresh criteria and demands on other instruments were set as a result of the high standards of technical facility by the saxophone and trumpet boppers, thus challenging the slide trombone—a much less manageable horn. J.J. went beyond the legato style of the swing stylists. Indeed his well-developed, fluid staccato style and precision equipped him to make the tempos of blazing bop tunes—matching the high speed trumpets. "Indiana" is a good example of his remarkable control on a fast tune. "Jerry Old Man" is richly enhanced by his bop harmonies. J.J. speaks of his indebtedness to Lester Young for his linear approach. He also developed an unusual purity of tone which contributed to his overall position of historical importance.

Later in 1954, J.J. and Kai Winding joined to co-lead a two-trombone combo, reflecting in part the concepts of Diz and Bird. They reigned for two highly successful years, recording a good number of albums. Topping jazz polls in the U.S. and Europe, J.J. has been the foremost jazz trombonist for decades. This momentum of recognition lasted beyond his active, full-time playing days, straddling the later years when he was devoting most of his time to arranging and composing in Los Angeles.

Milt Jackson's illustrious career has likewise been feted with a long string of annual first place awards. As the strongest influence on his instrument since Lionel Hampton, who had a very different approach, Milt used a slow vibrato and a lean, linear and direct manner with no excess of fat in his solos. Along with others, "I'll Remember April" reveals his restless, swinging style with a keen sense of color, accent and timbre. Dig his bluesy work on "Jerry Old Man" and "Jay Jay's Blues." He takes charge of the blues authoritatively, like the classic blues player that he is. Even on such standards as "If I Had You," which has an exciting intro, Milt injects a blues sound. The tender "There's No You" shows his romanticism and his way of retaining the qualities of a ballad while improvising openly within a jazz context. Ditto for J.J. Both play ballads with moving sensitivity, whether the musical remarks are succinct or lengthy.

Milt was pianist/vibist for Dizzy's big band in the mid-forties and again with the 1950–52 band. I first caught 23-year-old Milt at Billy Berg's in L.A. in 1946 when he was part of Dizzy's front-running bop combo. That band also included Charlie Parker, Al Haig, Ray Brown and Stan Levey—one of the wildest racehorse bands I've ever heard. On this disc, Milt's piano is especially attractive on "Lullaby of the Leaves."

"Out of Nowhere" is an Al Cohn type of tune. He is one of the most natural melodic improvisers, with a knack for choosing the prettiest, most colorful notes. His tenor solos are meaningful statements, showing an arranger's sense of form.

Percy Heath's communicative bass is especially discernible as he announces his themes on "Out of Nowhere" and "I'll Remember April." Drummer Charlie Smith, who in 1954 was gigging with the Billy Taylor trio and Aaron Bell's trio, acquits himself very well on the album. His brushes on "April" call for notice.

As we step into the 1980s, this record, made over a quarter century ago, can be comfortably considered as a creditable jazz legacy. Its merit is clearly due to the presence of Milt Jackson and J.J. Johnson, who were already internationally acknowledged as premium artists on their respective instruments.

CHAPTER 13

Vocal

The vocalist carries a different concept than is conveyed by other players in the band. Vocalists carry not just a smattering of sounds, they carry messages seeped in meaningfulness—and they carry the insightfulness of what the lyrics are trying to tell us. The vocalist interprets and massages those lyrical messages, adding meaningful messaging to the sounds of the band.

There is an ongoing discussion in the industry as to whether one should be labeled a "jazz" singer or a "pop" singer. Most of the time it's a combination of both, which is not surprising and not illogical, especially when you consider the case of Carmen McRae.

Carmen McRae

I first discovered Carmen McRae when I heard her singing, early in her career, in San Francisco. She was playing a small club called Sugar Hill on the corner of Broadway and Montgomery, where Ben Webster and a number of other people played. The club had some interesting front line players, but it was Carmen who put Sugar Hill in its place as a significant jazz club; it was Carmen who put it on the map.

Originally, Carmen was a pianist. But, as she grew up musically, she started to get gigs for her voice and piano together. That ultimately led Carmen to devote full time effort purely to her singing. That was the basis of her popularity and, as the demand for her singing grew, it became a rare occasion for Carmen to even play the piano.

The key to Carmen's vocal style was that she would sing *behind* the beat. Her phrasing was different; she clearly was a jazz singer.

Carmen was a constant surprise. She had so many different ideas for so many different projects; she was able to freely go industry-wide with her ideas because people industry-wide wanted her. I don't think any other artist worked with the inventory of record labels that Carmen worked with; name a record label and chances are Carmen McRae is on it.

Carmen's *Dream of Life* CD was produced by Quincy Jones, who gave me the assignment to do the liner notes. It was an assignment I anticipated with joy because I knew Carmen had always wanted to record "Dream of Life"—ever since she composed it as a teenager and Billie Holiday recorded it.

To me, Carmen McRae—together with Lady Day, Sarah Vaughan and Ella—form the doyennes of women jazz singers.

Carmen McRae—*Dream of Life*
Qwest Records (46340-2); 1998; Reissued by Rhino Entertainment
Company / Warner Music Group

Carmen McRae was simply one of the most magnificent jazz singers in the world. Along with Billie Holiday, Ella Fitzgerald and Sarah Vaughan, Carmen McRae is a member of the pantheon of gifted jazz vocalists. Nominated for a Grammy on six occasions for her recordings, her artistic stature was likewise recognized by the National Endowment for the Arts when they awarded her the American Jazz Masters Award in 1994. Carmen was more than a special model of personalized singing. Her savior faire and excellence as a jazz pianist and a compassionate thespian in performance of every musical note, every syllable, every word, every phrase and every song—all contributed to Carmen's magical mosaic of artistry. With uncanny artfulness she bonded the meaning of the music, the meaning of the lyric plus a meaningfully fresh performance. She clearly represented the quintessence of jazz.

Born in New York City in Harlem on April 8, 1920, Carmen studied piano during childhood, and as a teenager she worked as a singer, self-accompanied on piano. Talented songwriter Irene Wilson Kitchings mentored Carmen and introduced her to Benny Carter and to Billie Holiday (Kitchings was married at the time to Teddy Wilson who was Billie's accompanist). At age 13 when Carmen heard Billie sing on the radio, she decided to become a singer. "She just knocked me out," said Carmen. Ultimately they became good friends and Billie remained as Carmen's major enduring inspiration.

Carmen won an amateur contest at the Apollo Theater at age 17. Later she was recruited to sing with Benny Carter's orchestra in 1944, followed by stints with Count Basie and Mercer Ellington until 1947. After playing piano and singing in Chicago in 1948, she returned to Brooklyn in 1951; subsequently she was intermission singer/pianist at Teddy Hill's Minton's Playhouse—one of the fertile bebop jam sites. She was in the thick of musicians' innovating explorations and venues where bebop ideas were being cultivated. In 1953, she sang as a standing solo vocalist—without her piano—on "guest nights" at Minton's. What she soaked up is reflected in her songs. The salient assets of her singing and her audacious improvisational skills took precedence over her piano. Also, under the effect of the new bebop movement, Sarah Vaughan became Carmen's second pivotal influence.

By 1954 her bright reputation and threshold recordings had finally attracted strong critical and popular acclaim, gaining her *DownBeat* magazine's "Best New Female Singer" award. Undeniably she was a hot emergent star. In due time her status became international, busy making impressive recordings and appearing worldwide with her band for the next three decades.

The venerable jazz icon Benny Carter said recently, "I first heard Carmen in 1940, about four years before she joined my orchestra, and even in those early days she had her own brand of vocal qualities. She knew what the songs were written about and knew the songwriter's intent—a rare insight. And she enhanced what he/she was trying to say." About lyric-sensitivity, Carmen had said that the lyrics were more important than the melody to her, "If I don't like the lyrics, the melody is meaningless" and "if a note doesn't lend itself to a lyric, I just go and change the note." She did not sing a song that she could not "feel" and enliven with earthy emotional heat. Guitarist John Collins who has played in bands led by legendaries Art Tatum, Roy Eldridge, Billie Holiday, Lester Young and some 15 years with Nat Cole was a very close friend of Carmen, beginning in 1938; he had also made recordings with her in the eighties. Collins said, "I used to tell her that she reminded me of Mabel Mercer in that she knows 9 million songs. She would pick songs carefully. Many were songs other singers wouldn't try—hard tunes, like those by Thelonious Monk. Her diction was incredible and she had immaculate taste—a tremendous artist!" Another long-term friend was trumpeter Harry "Sweets" Edison who spoke about a prevalent requisite in jazz. "Coming up in New York in the old days, your goal was to be an originator, not an imitator ... and Carmen was a heavyweight original."

The music on the recording at hand—*Dream of Life*—is the grand result of master bassist-composer-arranger John Clayton's suggestion to producer Wolfgang Hirschmann of the superb WDR (West German Radio) Big Band, when they were discussing who might be an exciting featured jazz artist to record with the band. JC recalled, "I mentioned I had traveled and worked with Carmen on the road and did some gigs when Carmen was in between bass players, and that we had become good friends and she would be a terrific prospect. Wolfgang flipped with the idea! Informing Carmen that I would write a whole new show for her with big band, she loved the whole thing." After the birth of the project, JC proceeded with field research going to her concerts to validate "what Carmen was comfortable with—just being herself, along with songs she wanted to do and hadn't done in a long time. I insisted she pick pieces from her show and I would have the big band be the backdrop. So the concept was basically Carmen and me putting our heads together."

John Clayton, Jr., is an extremely talented and admired bassist. He co-leads the Clayton-Hamilton Jazz Orchestra (with brother Jeff Clayton the alto saxophonist and Jeff Hamilton the drummer), among his amazingly large constellation of activities, he shines with his outstanding ability as a resourceful, creative arranger. About his influential forbearers, JC said: "When I was in the Count Basie band, I listened to the writing of Thad Jones, Billy Byers, Quincy Jones, Ernie Wilkins and Frank Foster. And I borrow things from all of them. Of course, Ellington is my hero." Whereas there are thumbprints and brush strokes remindful of their impact on JC, his artistic canvas is a pure John Clayton handprint. Note his acute affinity for the use of dynamics. "I love the extremes of dynamics—huge and minuscule," he affirms.

To play and interpret this body of work, JC conducts the WDR Big Band based in Cologne—easily the best ensemble in Europe. Bill Holman, Vince Mendoza, Quincy Jones or Bob Brookmeyer would bear witness to WDR's excellence. It boasts an eclectic international mixture of players with outstanding jazz soloists. "They swing like crazy!" said prominent pianist-composer Roger Kellaway. They surely underline swing on JC's charts as Carmen is brilliantly backed by the band.

The following is the program of eleven illuminating tunes on this album.

1. "In Walked Bud"

What an explosive, marvelous opener! "The opening figure was used in her trio arrangement, and I re-worked it for big band. It's power-packed but still light and airy," said JC. Catch the lead trumpet of Andy Haderer, the punching drums of John Von Ohlen and Henning Berg's trombone solo.

2. "Sunday"

JC shows wisdom in keeping the song "opened up," allowing bassist Scott Colley and pianist Eric Gunnison to solo just as the trio does on its "live" performances. Gunnison's fresh conception and lyricism are a great fit, and Colley's beautifully sounding bass integrates his notions into the texture. As members of Carmen's mainstay trio, they showed keen sensitivity. Thanks to JC for coaxing her to scat as this is the definitive "Sunday."

3. "For All We Know"

"When Carmen did this in a club, it was always spellbinding," reports JC. "Carmen had a little talk before she sang her song and I tried to capture the mood she set without losing that feel. Technically, I did it by muting the band—the warm bucket mutes for the brass, bass clarinet for a bari sax, and clarinets and flutes instead of saxes. I actually wrote a mood-setting tune as an intro." Listen to how JC contrasts the texture, cutting the band out as Carmen begins singing and lets the trio play. He paralleled his writing to her emotional curves nicely. "Knowing when she liked to build and climax, I just followed what she would do with it."

4. "I Have the Feeling I've Been Here Before"

Roger Kellaway wrote this pretty ballad over 20 years ago, originally labeled "Written for Carmen" until Alan and Marilyn Bergman added the wonderful lyrics. It was subsequently produced by Kellaway on a Blue Note album *I Am Music* in 1975. He said, "Anyone who works with Carmen learns about slow ballads. She was one of the thrills of my life. It's very rare to work with a singer that grew up through eras of care for musical depth, as you have grown up and you care about that—that's an absolute joy!" As an example of JC's strategy, he preserved an awareness of the lovely melodic line by "keeping in mind the romantic reflections."

5. "I Didn't Know What Time It Was"

This is another one in Carmen's book of preferred songs. "She had an arrangement for it and I honored it as a reference, so she didn't have to change what she was used to doing," JC described. "I kept her tempo and let her keep her phrasing ideas."

6. "A Song for You"

Leon Russell's tune was usually interpreted by Carmen in a rock-ballad feel, posing another kind of challenge for the writing. Developing contrasts is a vital JC process and product, and the piece illustrates this character. He spoke to it: "If it's going to be something soft and mellow, I want to contrast it either by having a thinner texture than she's used to, or a thicker, louder or softer one." Being a bass player, JC wrote out the bass part that Scott Colley played, reflecting a classical air. Carmen rises with hues and shades as the gigantic brass statement cools down to nothing except she and the bass.

7. "Miss Brown to You"

Carmen had sung this one for decades as it mirrors her adulation and love for Billie Holiday (who recorded it in 1933). "Sweets" Edison said, "Carmen was a Billie Holiday disciple and very close friend, and is the only one I know who could sing songs Billie used to do and yet Carmen was really just herself." Carmen had said it was not her wish to sound like Billie, but if she sang something that recalled Billie, she would do it in a way as if Billie were Carmen. The two spicy trumpet soloists lend extra value on this selection. The late Jon Eardley, who died in 1991, was an American expatriate, and young Roy Hargrove, only 20 at the time, was already showing his fiery wherewithal.

8. "Dream of Life"

The album's title tune is a Carmen McRae original written at age 17 and was recorded by Billie Holiday in 1939. The suave sounding trombone soloist is David Horler from Great Britain who evokes the sweet smooth sound of Tommy Dorsey. Eardley's warm muted horn is sensuous. Following Carmen's final note as the band takes control a few more seconds, JC sprinkles in a smart bit of dream dust from Henry Mancini's "Dreamsville."

9. "What Can I Say After I Say I'm Sorry?"

The rhythm section percolates and cooks under Hargrove's well-shaped solo. Carmen swings with well-enunciated lyrics while her tale is told so convincingly about remorse and shame.

10. "If the Moon Turns Green"

This song is a winsome choice. "This was my suggestion. She had done it on *The Great American Songbook* album (recorded on Atlantic Records at Donte's in North Hollywood in 1972) and I just love it! She said, 'I haven't done it in ages,' but she took on the challenge," explains JC. Gunnison and Colley reveal again their close communion with Carmen.

11. "You're a Weaver of Dreams"

This finale represents the encore format Carmen followed in her shows ... accompanying herself on piano as she had done exclusively in her dawning years. Roger Kellaway: "It's such a great experience in working with singers who can play piano. Carmen, like Sarah, was a very fine pianist and their whole relationship to chord changes is different; there's much more depth in the way they sing a melody." With just her piano and voice, Carmen emerges as a strong storyteller and consummate musician—a rare weaver of dreams.

Dream of Life, Carmen's last effort with a large ensemble, is unequivocally a landmark recording, one which will reward the listener with repeated dividends. It represents a triumph for John Clayton, Jr., as it does for Carmen McRae. Carmen McRae passed away on November 10, 1994, at age 74. Before her death she said: "All I want to be remembered for is my music." Essentially, *Dream of Life* is Carmen's valedictory statement with a large jazz ensemble. Moreover, it is a majestic, inspired memorial to the legacy of Carmen McRae.

A heartfelt tribute expression from lyricists Alan and Marilyn Bergman is valuable and pertinently symbolic: "At the outset, we have to admit to being prejudiced. We loved Carmen. She was funny—she was smart—and for lyric writers, she was a dream. She sang not only the lines, but she sang what was in between them. She peeled away every layer, not a nuance escaped her. And her musicianship goes without saying. We miss her."

Giacomo Gates

Giacomo Gates was like a secret waiting to be discovered. I say that because his talents were not able to be expressed far and wide from where he happened to be living—in Alaska, of all places—working in the construction business.

He started listening to guys like James Moody and Babs Gonzales, also known as "Professor Bop"—one of Giacomo's greatest influences—and then Giacomo started to sing. He was fussing around informally with recording himself, taping his voicings onto cassette tapes. Somehow, one of those cassettes made its way to me. I'd never heard of the guy before!

A true bebopper, Giacomo Gates developed into one of the major scat singers in jazz. He's able to weave fresh lyrics into traditional bebop tunes and when it came to his personal versions of standard tunes—songs from Tin Pan Alley—Giacomo would regenerate those tunes with his fresh approach.

I started to support him with performances and clinics in multiple appearances at the annual convention of the International Association for Jazz Education, because I thought he had something that was explosive—and I was right: Giacomo Gates is a dynamite singer.

Giacomo Gates—*Centerpiece*
Origin Records (Origin 82428); 2004

Dig this tantalizing tsunami of vocal bebop jazz flavors and tales served by the soulful vocalese singer-lyricist Giacomo Gates. With two recordings under his belt (*Blue Skies* and *Fly Rite* plus a key role on *Remembering Eddie Jefferson*), Gates continues to cement his place in the tight coterie of "main men" of jazz singing. Indeed, he is a standout member of an endangered species. His inventive manifestations on this CD reveal his mastery of this niche art form. Not only is he a natural talent, Gates is gifted with the temperament of a purist and a skilled craftsman of a high musical intelligence. Little wonder for the past eight years his performances have recruited rabid audiences of many stripes.

So what's his attraction? Promptly, he communicates earnest believability in his interpretations; he is downright fun and exciting to witness, as he infuses humor and surprises, maintaining allegiance to the pledge of swing and bebop. Real music breathes. Gates allows the music to ebb and flow—rush and drag a little bit so you don't forego the organic reality of the human condition, since we all occasionally rush and drag through our existence with passion.

Gates' phrasing is another attribute. Phrasing is a challenging element of singing. Spoken language and music have commonalities—beginning and stopping places, cadence, inflection, long and short sounds, and obvious places to breathe. Gates' phrasing is a commanding merger of spoken and musical languages—expressing bebop and lyrical ideas with his bilingual abilities. His sharp ear, jeweled voice box and feeling for words and phrases offer gemlike illustrations.

Moreover, his exuberance is caught on the disc. Gates' inspired performances include his vivid patter accompanying his delivery; he fulfills the wish of fans' enthusiasm for his raps. It's in this groove and spirit this CD is framed.

Essential to the quality is the acumen and interfacial powers of the musicians. Preceded by rich trails of experiences, the notable cast of Harold Danko, Ray Drummond, Greg Bandy, Vic Juris and Vincent Herring tether their trappings with Gates like hand in glove. His backdrop of influences is pertinent. "I listen to singers (Eddie Jefferson, Jon Hendricks, Dave Lambert, Annie Ross and Joe Williams) and horns (Dexter, Lester, Lee Morgan, Freddie Hubbard and Bird) and to sing like a musician, you must listen to musicians and think like one." Gates improvises as a horn soloist and functions as a band member, too.

With a neo-hipster status, it is a grand achievement to be hip without sounding dated. He provides a feast of traditions embodied in style, enunciation and choice of material; his carefully shaded dynamic palette permits great emotional subtlety. Gates reveals his reasons for the tune selections: "I like tunes that have a story. Many of these are favorites of mine and are also audience pleasers."

"Summertime"

A colorful agenda of some Eddie Jefferson lyrics ... shades of Miles via the whistling, "flute" and Gates' own spin.

"I Told You I Love You, Now Get Out"

Gates scats like a driving horn soloist—a perfect vehicle he heard ages ago—versions by Woody Herman (1947) and Jack Sheldon. Dig Danko's marvelous comping in his piano.

"Centerpiece"

Jon Hendricks' lyric set to Harry "Sweets" Edison's memorable blues with the lyric moved forward about 3½ beats." Engaging solos by Vic Juris' guitar and Ray Drummond's bass.

"How High the Moon/Ornithology"

In tandem the bebop anthem standard is blended with the noted bebop line, Gates makes a smooth segue that informs as well as swings—dig the rich variety of sounds he incorporates into his scat trajectories!

"You'd Be So Nice to Come Home To"

A markedly slowed down romantic interpretation, giving Cole Porter's tune more of a World War II nostalgic ambience—accented with sensitive rhythm section work and Gates' simulated horn lines.

"All of Me"

When Gates heard King Pleasure's lyric over Illinois Jacquet's tenor saxophone solo, he went wild! This old chestnut is a solid staple of Gate's repertoire.

"Lady Bird"

Done in rubato, Tadd Dameron's marvelous tune is enhanced with heartfelt lyrics by Stanley Cornfield—a rare treat to hear it sung and Gates does it with verve.

"Route 66"

A graphic coast-to-coast trip with Gates as tour guide offering the swinging commentary. "I'm imagining Bobby Troup (the tune's author) driving cross country with his wife, singer Julie London at 40–45 mph, in some old Buick ... everything for me is a picture."

"Scotch & Soda"

Written by Dave Guard of the Kingston Trio, it was their big hit and Gates says, "I 'hear' more of a Frank Sinatra approach for it—kinda dreamy and warm feelin."

"Lester Leaps In / I Got the Blues"

"Eddie Jefferson's take of Prez's masterpiece … it's James Moody's solo that Eddie Jefferson wordified. It's about being so wrapped up in someone that you'll do anything to prove it, but she won't let you, so … you got the blues." A true classic generated by tenor sax icon Lester Young.

"Milestones"

Gates' original lyrics are a gas. Asked how he produces his lyrics, he explained: "Most of mine come from the title and I have to be moved by the melody. That's how I got measurements on 'Milestones,' I tend to write philosophical lyrics. You've got to find joy in every moment, because there's always going to be a dawn." And the band is simply impressive.

"Hittin' the Jug / Swan Song"

"I've always dug Gene Ammons' great sound. He just blows one big long whole tone … blows everyone away. I stick closer to Jug's solo than King Pleasure did; I took his lyric, the vocal version—'Swan Song.' It's a sad, sad story with a farewell." A fitting closer for the CD.

Gates says in sum: "All the lyrics to all these tunes ring true for me, otherwise I wouldn't bother singin' them." It's a total ball for him to sing. He bubbles with effervescent joy and anecdotes reflecting the epiphanous character of his singing. Giacomo Gates is the ambassador of vocalese traditions.

Tierney Sutton

I was really excited about Tierney Sutton from the moment I heard about her working in the world of jazz education. She was teaching different aspects of voice and singing at USC at the time. On first hearing her sing, I was immediately taken by her presence and voice; I admired her adventure-filled performance and she backed it up with a fascinatingly equipped voice and control.

Tierney put together a trio that would just about kill any audience, and I've seen her do just that from Montreal to the West Coast. She always communicates with an incredible range and tone that any singer would dream to have as part of their repertoire. She is able to take a bebop tune and turn it into a classic, before your very ears.

Tierney Sutton—*Unsung Heroes*
Telarc Jazz (CD 83477); 2000; Reissued by Concord Records

The number of the great jazz divas is fading rapidly. There is a forceful message that motivation has cranked up dramatically for women jazz singers to pursue a coveted spotlight. The growing crowd of aspirants and voluminous flow of new vocal recordings are meaningful indices. Amidst this high density of vocal talent, a few have surfaced as top-of-the-cream standouts. That Tierney Sutton is among them, and is an extraordinary vocalist-musician, is manifest here.

Her incisive musicianly attributes are noticed promptly as they merge impressively with the fine musicians assembled for this CD. Tierney is a soprano but her voice descends into the alto range too. Then there's her very personal sound and style. Add her melodic imagination, amazing true intonation, lyricism and attractive choice of notes in shaping her solos—you wind up with an aptly successful balancing act of unfailing brilliant surprises and piquant expectations.

I first heard her perform at the 1998 IAJE (International Association of Jazz Educators) conference in New York City, and I simply flipped out! Likewise her debut recording *Introducing Tierney Sutton* has made an imprint, receiving generous enthusiastic response. Beyond all her captivating vocal assets, there is a warmly infectious and intangible something about her wherewithal. Listening to her sing on trumpeter Buddy Childers' Big Band CD opens even more windows of admiring perspectives: regarding Tierney singing lead over the band on "Boy from Ipanema," Childers waxes: "It's where most singers can't even get close to those notes, she's right on the money. She sings like a great lead trumpet player. Not only is she a terrific singer—but she's a great musician!"

Among other appearances with upper tier L.A. jazz players, she is often featured with Childers' Quintet as well as the Big Band: this is over and above her responsibilities as head of the USC jazz vocal department. Childers' high esteem for her is further expressed via an emphatic claim: "Tierney is the best singer I've ever worked with ... period! And I've worked with just about all the greats—Sinatra, Tony Bennett, Vic Damone, Ella Fitzgerald, Nat Cole, et al." He cites her marvelous voice quality and "she has perfect aim at a note—the best pitch and time of anyone since Mel Tormé."

Inspired by hearing many jazz notables who appeared on campus while she was at Wesleyan University, she became a quick jazz initiate and began performing inside of a year. After matriculating briefly at Berklee College of Music in Boston, she performed extensively in various high reputation jazzfests and venues here and abroad. In 1998, she was a semi-finalist in the Thelonious Monk Vocal Competition.

The conceptual rationale for this CD is enlightened by Tierney's working philosophy "As much as I love great singers—Bobby McFerrin and Al Jarreau—and no one's better than Sarah and Ella, my biggest influences were instrumentalists like Miles and Coltrane. And I've been doing lots of instrumental-ish tunes." At USC she followed her beliefs, making a curricular change—requiring tunes for singers to be the same required ones for instrumentalists—blurring the lines of separation. "Of course, singers must deliver the lyrics," she points out. "But in terms of getting jazz harmonies and jazz feel, you have to get into the meat of the instrumental music. So this CD is something l wanted to do because it was true for me."

The CD's program of tunes/heroes begins with tenor saxophonist Joe Henderson. After many years of lukewarm recognition for his prodigious talents, Henderson has in recent years finally received overdue plaudits. A Henderson favorite among musicians is "Recordame." Its reflective lyric is by singer Kelley Johnson, and Tierney was ultimately spurred by bassist Trey Henry's suggestion to do it "really slow." He arranged it with a meditative bass line cut off a bar, and stretched out the final measure over several bars, creating a suspended feeling at the end of each chord. Tierney's vocal is attractive as a somewhat dark, brooding mood is fittingly developed. The sensitive rhythm section of Christian Jacob, Trey Henry, and Ray Brinker is introduced with supportive interplay and warm solos. An engaging opener!

Johnny Mercer's lyrics were set to Ralph Burns' "Early Autumn," the programmatic epilogue to Burns' extended "Summer Sequence" written for the Woody Herman Orchestra in 1947 (featuring the famous seven-bar saxophone solo by Stan Getz). Pianist Bill Anschell had originally written a chart of the tune for singer Nnenna Freelon and sent it on to Tierney. In turn, she wrote a fresh arrangement for it—a medium swing. "It was fresh for me since I had worked at it as a ballad but decided on a straight-ahead groovy thing to balance uptempo and ballad numbers," Tierney notes. The swing feel is surely fulfilling and widens the diversity of the tune list. The beautiful harmonic colors and resourceful phrasing by pianist Jacob have strong appeal.

Pianist Jimmy Rowles' "The Peacocks" is a jeweled legacy. He recorded it as a duo with Stan Getz in 1977, and Getz had said: "There is no question that 'The Peacocks' is a classic—beyond time and place." Neither is it surprising. Tierney says: "It's my personal favorite—it's the strongest." She recalls how it happened for her. "My husband (Alan Kaplan), a studio musician, was in the studio with Gary Foster who had been given my first CD last year and liked it. When he heard about my new CD concept he sent an envelope with lead sheets of instrumental tunes with rarely sung lyrics. Generally I wasn't familiar with them, but I recognized 'The Peacocks' from Bill Evans' *You Must Believe in Spring*—one of my all-time favorite jazz albums. I thought, 'Someone's written lyrics!' A weird tune, the changes are so tense and the melody is so tricky Jimmy had someone trying to write lyrics with no satisfaction, so when he got the lyric from Norma Winstone, he said, 'This is the lyric!' And he wrote the lead sheet (on the last chorus—I'm singing the bridge and Gary plays a counterpoint melody—on alto flute—between each of my half step notes). Jimmy adapted the original melody to a piano arrangement so the piano would be playing those notes while the singer sings the other notes. Virtually everything we did was from Jimmy's hand ... close to what he would have wanted. It was extra special to have Gary Foster on the tune since he had recorded it with Jimmy shortly before his death." Obviously it's a tune one must work hard to master. Since Tierney had listened intently to the Evans' record so many times, it was natural and seductive when she sang it. Her performance is admirably effective in creating the haunting quality of the song.

"Bernie's Tune" has become a winning trademark selection for both Tierney and Buddy Childers. He had arranged it years ago for the late Diane Varga. "I just love singing it—it's so exciting to do it!" exclaims Tierney. It fits the concept of this album—an instrumental tune you don't think of as having words." Bernie Miller's tune is a fun tune to play, to sing and to listen to. It has been recorded by the Childers Big Band with Tierney on Candid Records. Incidentally, Childers' ignited horn dances in his high spirited flugelhorn solo work.

"I love 'Spring Is Here.' It's inspired by Kenny Barron's arrangement which I transcribed. I added the original verse, which sounds like an English folk tune. It's a striking contrast to the brooding quality of Kenny's arrangement," describes Tierney. "Kenny does the changes with pedal point over G and I do it over E." As an effect, Tierney has taken a song numerous singers sing, but she brings an unexpected novel perspective to it. Her treatment is wholly instrumental and organic, singing over it as an integral part of the band and not as a vocalist in front.

"Joy Spring" is a classic Clifford Brown barn-burner which enjoys healthy popularity in jazzdom ... a well-oiled arrangement Tierney has been doing for a decade. She scats the first two A sections of the melody and modulates a-plenty although each section seems deceivingly easy. Most singers avoid modulating because of the super difficulty it poses. Her consistent agility and crystalline tone make like the warm morning sun in spring—illuminating the body and spirit of the song Jamie Findlay's tasty guitar and her repartee with Buddy Childers' fluent horn lend enhanced energy and color the piece, making it a most rewarding vocal of the tune.

Wayne Shorter is one of the most gifted composers and most of his music is etched in the stone of jazz history. "All for One (Speak No Evil)" is one of Shorter's striking, epiphanous compositions from some thirty-five years ago; it is fraught with imaginative melodic and rhythmic ideas unbounded by convention. Tackling it vocally is a large challenge indeed. It exposes the intense focus Tierney exhibits both directly and by implication. She relates: "This was the hardest bridge in the CD. I spent a long, long time learning it. If I'm lucky, it doesn't sound as hard as it really is." It's a Vanessa Rubin lyric. The interpretive powers and telepathy of the trio of rhythm mates is evident in their swapping of furious punctuations and bristly rhythms: their artistry demands notice. Tierney continues: "This is great music, and my viewpoint is not that it has to be about me as much as it's about creating the kind of music that people will want to listen to again and again." With her commitment paying off majestically—her mission is accomplished.

The bebop entry is "Indiana / Donna Lee." "Donna Lee is one of the required tunes for my USC students. It is the only tune of their list I didn't know at first," Tierney shares. "So I learned it and did my best to embed it in my brain." Gary Foster's mercurial Bird-like alto solos lend extra ripping exuberance to the sum containing vivid memories of Tierney's explosive scat lines and exchanges with Foster—scything through Charlie Parker's domain. Dynamite!

Iconic jazz hero Benny Carter's popular "When Lights Are Low" is a treat of a medium swing treatment with pianist Shelly Berg's arrangement which invites a *par excellent* trombone solo by Alan Kaplan. Tierney's light improvising is delectable. I venture a wager that Benny would smile on this version of his staple.

Lastly, one of Dizzy Gillespie's outstanding evergreen pieces "Con Alma" is included via a happenstance. Trying in vain to ascertain the existence of authorized lyrics to "Con Alma," Tierney got an unexpected e-mail a week before the session from Judy Rafat, a jazz singer in Germany who had just recorded "Con Alma" on her own CD of Gillespie tunes. She had heard about Tierney and her first CD. (Dizzy was a Bahá'í and so are Judy and Tierney.). Ms. Rafat was kind enough to share the lyric. The piece is strongly classical as the first four bars, the bass line and the melody are the same as Bach's "Air on a G String," and Tierney sings "Con Alma" similarly in terms of bass and melody. Her immaculate unaccompanied voice creates a sublime aura.

Tierney enchants her listeners and pulls them into the core of her music. Both elegant and earthy, Tierney Sutton is contagious!

—————————————————————————————————

Dianne Reeves

I discovered Dianne Reeves' talents at an early stage in her career and I was blessed to nurture those talents when she recorded on my Palo Alto Records label. The longtime leader of Blue Note Records, the legendary Bruce Lundvall, once told me, "Dianne Reeves is the one artist you have on your label, Herb, that I would dearly love to have on mine." So when Bruce signed Dianne to Blue Note, I was happy to give her new association my blessing, and her sessions at Palo Alto Records became a Blue Note release during the label's re-issue renaissance.

Recently, I got a message on my answering machine from Dianne, phoning from a gig in Poland. She said to me, "Herb, I just want to tell you how I respect you as a man of integrity. When I was 15 years old," she continued, "you heard how I sang and you said, 'If I ever have the opportunity to help you, you'll be the first one I'd do something for.' And you did have the opportunity and you treated me as number one. And I'll never forget it. I would not be where I am today if it were not for you."

Dianne Reeves—*The Palo Alto Sessions / 1981–1985*
Capitol Records (CDP 7243 8 36545 29); 1996; Reissued by Blue Note

As the very small circle of jazz divas becomes even smaller as years go by, there is a swelling need for new generational successors to the likes of Sarah Vaughan, Carmen McRae and Ella Fitzgerald to keep the flames of singing jazz alive. A number of eligible hopefuls and prospects exist, but it is Dianne Reeves who is readily one of the top tiered choices to enter the pantheon of the jazz vocal universe. She sings superbly with a brilliant, consistently individual sound with the pure heart of her soul. Reeves is a paragon of perfect phrasing and flawless time management and control. Her unique musical identity is a rich product of background and open experientially filtered through her distinctive sensibilities.

While easily perceived as an eclectic singer due to a repertoire with no rigid walls, embracing many musical genotypes, Reeves is transparently rooted deeply and nurtured in a jazz soil and gestalt—brilliantly reinforced in her most recent Blue Note recording *Quiet After the Storm* (which has been nominated for a vocal jazz Grammy Award as of this writing). Whatever musical persuasion she chooses to sing in, expect the expected … also expect the unexpected. Her sounds of surprise articulates her commitment to a jazz behavioral ethic.

Since 1987, when Reeves began recording for Blue Note/EMI Records—a total of five to date—she has steadily expanded her fan base here and abroad. However, the bulk of her advocates may be unaware of her earlier recorded works. It is, thus, a rewarding circumstance that the disc at hand fills out the Reeves story illuminating her impressive beginnings as a sensational vocal artist, leading to her music and stature today. With the exception of the first track which Reeves recorded with the band Caldera, the remaining dozen selections are drawn from her two Palo Alto Jazz titles: *Welcome to My Love* and *For Every Heart*, circa 1982 and 1985 respectively.

I first heard Reeves in the late '70s in Wichita, Kansas, at a post-jazz festival session. She was still in her teens and sang a good many standards. She totally knocked me out! And I surmised with certitude that a bright future awaited her. I categorically promised her she would be beckoned if and when I found myself in a situation that could provide a recording opportunity. And indeed it happened as I assumed executive responsibilities with Palo Alto Records.

At the time, Reeves was based in Los Angeles singing in a variety of venues; e.g., Memory Lane, Vine St., The Driftwood Inn, The Lighthouse, Concerts by the Sea, and Donte's. "The band was named Night Flight—a cooperative group with Billy Childs, Billy Carroll, Joe Heredia, and Nick Kirgo," recalls Reeves. "A basically experimental group, we started working at the Comeback Inn, building a great following, but more significantly everyone's musical concept came out of that environment. Joey is the blueprint of any drummer I've ever had since then. He really knows how to accompany a singer and my improv inspiration came through his drums; my improv is more based on rhythm than on melody. I used to call him 'Mi Vida,' so I wrote it to recognize his importance."

Regarding her ten years of working with pianist-composer Childs, she says: "Billy gave me license to go anywhere musically. It wasn't just a backup group for me. It was a unified group which gave me a basis for my future. There was telepathy between Billy and me—we read each other's minds and my ears were broadened as a result."

The late Phil Moore, Jr., the pianist-composer-arranger and vocal coach was also Reeves' manager, and she was a member of his vocal workshop. Moore guided Reeves well and "he really helped me to be in touch with myself as an artist. I realized whatever you put on record is going to outlast you—hopefully, so I always need to put out my best."

As for standard tunes, "My Funny Valentine" on her first record was clearly the object of my affection and is the standard by which other vocal interpretations of the 1937 Rodgers and Hart evergreen should be measured—illustrating what Reeves describes as "taking standards and changing them to make some of them ours. And that arrangement came out of the group—something that happened one night and stuck." Conceptually the process has remained with Reeves as her footprints to the American songbook in subsequent recordings.

Moreover, she was also working with Sérgio Mendes—another piece of Reeves' mosaic of significant influences. The chief asset was singing in another language and culture. She adds: "Brazilian music was a great start. Sérgio turned me on to Brazilian artists and gave me a chance to perform in places like Israel, Latin America, Asia, and the Caribbean." Reeves' worldliness enlarged when Harry Belafonte presented her to European audiences. "Harry generously shared the stage with me and everyone contributed to the arrangements in a workshop setting he provided," remembers Reeves, "and it was my introduction to world music."

Regarding the impact of the Golden Age jazz divas on her, Reeves says: "Sarah was the beginning of everything for me. It was the way she approached a song (and she sang so many kinds of songs) and how she would color a song. When I listened to Carmen, I liked the way she interpreted lyrics. I came to love Billie Holiday later on—because no matter if it's a happy or sad song or just a life song anything good to strive for has some element of the blues. So I look at blues as wisdom, understanding and accepting life as it is. So I'm going to sing about it and it'll make me feel better getting it out. The music is itself positive and powerful, and if you approach it honestly, the blues element will be in it."

A number of factors comprise the Reeves equation. One of these values is improvisation. She possesses a personal form of improvisational singing. "Improv is the utterance of your soul—what you can't say with words you might say with utterances," she explains. Again, her improvisations come from a percussive perspective.

A very convincing and magnetic story-teller and songwriter, Reeves' lyric content relates to her predilections for imagery and retrospection. "I like imagery," she notes. "The majority of my songs have images, a kind of song that can make you feel something. Many of the songs are reflections of my childhood—times in my life I felt I had peace."

Peering back at the '80s, "my biggest struggle with critics was that 'I was too broad' or 'without a direction' but in reality on those first two records I was looking for my own voice. There's only one Sarah, Ella and Carmen, and certainly I needed to do my own thing. Listening to them I knew you must have your own voice." As a child of the '60s and '70s and when recording in the '80s, she was listening to jazz but also to the current music—the more fusion orientations of the '70s. Reeves tells about the first most exotic voices on the scene, Urszula Dudziak and Flora Purim who gained high critical and consumer respect. And Reeves was also paying attention to Chaka Khan and the earthy lyrics of Bill Withers among others. When she had the group with Billy Childs, they wrote their own music, too. "I was in my early twenties. I didn't know what I wanted to do but my heart was and is in everything I do!"

"I really hope that people will listen to the music from my Palo Alto Jazz period because all of my records are very connected; they come out of each other," asserts Reeves. The records then and now are woven by evolutionary threads, intertwining through all of her records as a single body of creative work. "Recently I listened to the two records—for the first time in about ten years—it just blew my mind!" she reveals. "I could hear the commitment. The records have a lot of dignity, like all of my records. I was very conscious of it then. It was like reading a diary. Both of these records, now on one CD mean a lot to me, especially the songs from *Welcome to My Love*."

The Reeves odyssey continues as she reaches out toward her stardreams. So welcome to her love of music and to her love of people, life and peace. Borrowing a little from her wonderful "Better Days" … Dianne Reeves is enjoying the spirit of better days.

— · — · — · — · — · — · — · — · — · — · — · — · — · — · — · — · — · —

Mel Tormé

I vividly recall an occasion involving Mel Tormé at the Monterey Jazz Festival.

One year, when he was one of the festival's featured artists, Mel went out on stage for his performance. He looked at the audience … he looked left … he looked right … and then, all of a sudden, Mel stormed off the stage, obviously pissed off at something he had seen.

What Mel had noticed were two video cameras off to the side of the festival's main stage—in his eye, a violation of his contract. I was backstage at the time and as I watched, my jaw dropping, Mel walked up to festival manager Jimmy Lyons and shouted, "What the hell are those things doing up there? I gave no permission, no release, nothing!"

And then Mel said, "I'm not going back on stage until I get $15,000 in cash!"

My jaw dropped even more.

And Jimmy? He just went out of his bird! He started running around, collecting as much cash as he could find, from every place and from every person he could conceivably find it, until he came up with the fifteen grand.

A little later, I walked down to one of the green rooms located beneath the festival's main stage. There was Mel Tormé, sitting on a cot, counting the cash! I mean $10 bills … $5 bills … $20 bills.

I said, "Mel, would you like some help? I mean, this is a hell of a chore … it's going to take forever!" Mel continued counting. "No thanks," he said, "I've got to do this myself."

And he did … counting every last dollar before he would return to the stage and get on with his performance.

Mel Tormé and the Mel-Tones—*It Happened in Monterey* [sic]

Musicraft Records (MVS 510); 1982; Reissued by Rhino Entertainment Company / Warner Music Group

The swing/dance bands of the pre- and post–World War II days in the 1940s were hospitable havens for vocal groups, as they were essentially functional parts of the big band entourage. Much in vogue and in comparative good supply, a backward glance reveals a wave of singing group stylists carrying on the tradition of the American song— popular songs, jazz songs and film/show tunes.

The Modernaires with the Glenn Miller Orchestra and the Pied Pipers, and later the Sentimentalists with Tommy Dorsey's band were among the most prominent. And remember the Snowflakes, the Stardusters, et al! Then there were dozens of "vocal-orchestral" groups who were self sufficient purely as vocal units.

I was duly attracted to the whole gamut during the vocal group dynasty, never missing a remote radio broadcast if possible, and in the service of Uncle Sam the Armed Forces Radio Service carried a rash of special shows spiked heavily with the music of the swing orchestras and vocalists. During a tenure as an AFRS jazz deejay I was alerted to every show and V-Disc extant.

There was no question then as well as now that Mel Tormé and the Mel-Tones etched the sharpest overall impression, despite the fact that the Modernaires, the Pipers and their stylistic descendants were of striking quality. When I first caught and loved the sounds of the Mel-Tones with Artie Shaw's Orchestra, they were doing Cole Porter tunes—"Get out of Town" and "What Is This Thing Called Love" on an AFRS show *Swing Time*. Then came the memorable original Musicraft 78 rpm records, providing the only commercial documentation of the Mel-Tones' bop era contributions. Long unavailable until Albert Marx resurrected the masters to compile first the repertoire with Shaw's orchestra with strings (Musicraft MVS-507) and second, the March–June 1946 sessions were assembled for reissue via the album in hand (MVS-510). And it was just a few months after these sessions in 1946 that the Mel-Tones disbanded.

The union of Tormé and the Mel-Tones was created from fortuitous circumstances. At age 17 in 1943, Tormé was doing triple duty as a vocalist, writing vocal group charts and holding down the drummer's chair in the Chico Marx road band. When Marx decided to quit the band business that summer, Tormé was left high and dry in "Tinseltown" trying to scrape up a gig.

Drummer-bandleader Ben Pollack, who was the Marx band organizer-manager at the time, must be credited as the matchmaker. He brought Tormé together with these five Los Angeles City College students, who had billed themselves as "The School Kids," singing informally in and around the campus environs. Their respective needs meshed as the group's bass singer and vocal arranger Tom Kenny was headed for a U.S. Army uniform. Tormé arrived on the scene as if on cue, and the first edition of the group was launched with Bernie Parke, Diz Disruhd, Betty Beveridge and Ginny O'Connor, plus Tormè, who doubled as arranger. Later Disruhd became another wartime draftee and was replaced by Les Baxter (whose reputation in future years as a composer-arranger elevated him to the heavy talent ranks in the industry).

They assumed a fresh name, "The Skylarks," which failed to achieve more than a modicum of success. They then tried the label "The Mel-Tones," which caught on as the key name for them and indeed, they flourished as the hippest modern sounding vocal group—appearing in several motion pictures and numerous sustaining radio shows. They ultimately expanded their name to Mel Tormé and the Mel-Tones in recognition of Tormé's dual role as the arranger and solo vocalist. As fate would often dictate, just when things were cooking and popping, Tormé also inevitably answered the call to the Armed Services in 1945, and the group broke up.

But his term of service was not long, and when he was discharged the following year he promptly picked up again with the Mel-Tones. Signed to Musicraft in 1946, the music on this album is evidence of the unerring excellence of Tormé's taste and knowledge and the glowing warmth and marvelous, firm swing feel of the group. Tormé attributes much of his arranging inspiration to the musical strengths of Vince Degen, the arranger for Six Hits and a Miss of the mid–1930s, and to Bill Conway, whose resourceful charts for the Modernaires were musical standouts.

Tormé has been a rare phenomenon throughout his long career. It is not surprising he was ahead of his time. So advanced were the harmonies and approach that the Mel-Tones could not sustain sufficient broad interest and ongoing economic support. Finally, in late 1946, Tormé struck out on his own solo career.

Note that the Hi-Los—the front-running vocal quartet in the '50s and '60s—recalls Tormé and the Mel-Tones in its inventive voicings and hipness. Clearly the Mel-Tones was the forerunner of the Hi-Los.

The music on this album adds to the body of vocal literature that should be particularly inspirational and valuable to the throngs of vocal jazz aspirants participating in campus vocal jazz programs. Models such as "It Happened in Monterey" [sic], the ingenious contrapuntal effect Tormé created via the tune "Ramona" scored as a counter melody, and the great scatting on "That's Where I Came In," reminiscent of the deftness of Buddy Stewart and Dave Lambert—and the evergreen quality of "Night and Day." And Sonny Burke's orchestrations are perfect for the vocal charts.

Pointedly all this was done back in 1946! My long standing joy and admiration for them aside, the ever remaining modernity of their wherewithal is impressive and satisfying. Mel Tormé is sui generis and The Mel-Tones are likewise a reflection of strong individuality.

Billie Holiday

My first memories of Billie Holiday coincide with my first memories of jazz.

When I was about 12 years old, I used to take the train from Stockton to San Francisco to catch jazz performances in the Bay Area. Jazz concerts were held in movie theaters in those days as a part of the program, and I remember having to sit through the entire billing at the Orpheum Theater in Oakland—a western, a cartoon, Tarzan, the newsreel, and then the main feature—just to hear Count Basie play live on stage.

Then I would move down to the front row and go through all that torture again—just so I could hear the band perform again!

Lester Young was my hero back then. I used to hang out outside of Jack's on Sutter Street in San Francisco to hear him perform. I couldn't get in, of course, because I was underage. After the shows he would come out, see me there once again, and exclaim, "What? Are you here again?"

And I responded, saying, "Using your words, Prez, 'I have eyes for your sounds.'"

On one of my visits to the City, a poster caught my eye: Lester Young was going to be playing with Billie Holiday at Hamburger Gus's in Oakland. And I thought, are you kidding? Prez and Lady Day at Hamburger Gus's? I could not and would not miss it.

On the day of the show, I brought a box from my grandmother's home, which was about seven blocks away from the club. When I got to Hamburger Gus's, I put the box on the curb outside the club and I stood on the box, peering over the top of the club's swinging doors so that I could see Lady Day and Prez performing. I could just about make out the tops of their heads.

At the end of the first set, Lester Young came outside with a chick on each of his arms. He sees me and says "What? You're here, too?" And I said, "Do you think that I would miss you and Lady Day?"

And then Prez dropped the two ladies from his grasp and put his arm around my shoulder. "You come with me," he commanded.

He proceeded to take me inside the club, where he grabbed a stool and put it in front of stage left. Then he lifted me up, put me on top of the stool, and said, "Here … sit here and dig it!"

That was the first time I ever saw Lady Day perform.

The last time I saw Billie Holiday in concert was at the first ever Monterey Jazz Festival in 1958. To our everlasting good fortune, two engineers from Ampex Corporation—the pioneering recording company—had some new equipment in hand that year, and they decided to test it in the outdoor arena at the inaugural Monterey fest.

At Monterey, Billie was backed by the same rhythm section she had at the Blackhawk in San Francisco: Dick Berk on drums; Eddie Khan on bass; Mal Waldron on piano. She had three special guests that night: Buddy DeFranco, Benny Carter and Gerry Mulligan.

When Billie came out from behind the curtain and advanced toward the festival stage, she experienced some serious problems with her stability. So Billie had to be assisted by Buddy and Gerry to make sure she was cool on stage.

It didn't seem to bother her—just as the roar of an overhead airplane landing at the nearby Monterey Airport didn't appear to faze her at all. In spite of the distractions, Lady Day went straight ahead with her set.

It was a short set as it turned out, and it was a privilege to see her in one of the last performances of her life.

Billie Holiday was mesmerizing. Everybody looked at her as a vocal symbol of what they would have liked to have achieved. To a person, they said, "I wish I could sing like Billie." But nobody could. Nobody could sing like Billie Holiday.

Billie Holiday—*At Monterey / 1958*
Black-Hawk Records (BKH 50701-1D); 1986

Any new, found addition to the body of recordings of Billie Holiday holds historical favor and unexaggerated large interest. This previously unreleased record is such an event. Billie Holiday defined jazz singing as an act with such originality that her legacy is of permanent importance. It has been axiomatic that Billie was the greatest woman jazz singer of all time. This recording stands as one of the very few documents of her performance less than a year before her death on July 17, 1959.

AT MONTEREY / 1958

Lent for Promotional Use Only. Any Sale or
Unauthorized Transfer is Prohibited and Void. Subject
to Return Upon Demand by Owner. Acceptance of This
Record Constitutes Agreement to the Above.

BILLIE
HOLIDAY

Album cover for Billie Holiday's _At Monterey / 1958_ (Black-Hawk Records [BKH 50701–1 D]) (photograph by Peter Breinig; illustration by Gail Aratani; art direction by Zand Gee).

Recorded "live" on October 5, 1958, at the first Monterey Jazz Festival, at an outdoor stage in a horse show arena, hers was the final act on the last evening before a wrap up jam session ending the 3-day MJF debut.

I had caught Billie and her trio several nights at her gig at San Francisco's Black Hawk the week before the festival. Mal Waldron, Eddie Khan and Dick Berk provided a strong, swinging trio; Drummer Berk who was just 19 years old recalls: "I was thrilled to be chosen to be in her rhythm section and we were really up for Monterey and Billie was too." Waldron's credentials were already impressive; Khan's work with Max Roach, Freddie Hubbard, Jackie McLean, etc., and Berk's impeccable time-keeping pleased Billie.

Introducing Billie and Friends to the 6000 people in the audience, M.C. Mort Sahl opened the set. Nearly half way into the set, Billie and her trio were joined by three giants of jazz—Gerry Mulligan, Benny Carter and Buddy DeFranco. Dig Gerry!

My own memories of the Holiday magic that evening remain lively. She held the musicians and audience magnetically as one as she sang eleven songs with hardfast determination even under the thunderous roar of an airplane flying low directly over the festival grounds, as it approached the Monterey Airport when she was singing "Good Morning Heartache." This is not an uncommon occurrence there; these few seconds of ad hoc noise are a part of preserving the integrity of the entire set.

As Jimmy Lyons, Founder of the MJF remembers: "I had admired Billie for so many years, playing her wonderful records on my radio shows and seeing her in person—I knew she would be important for our first festival … and she was!" We should rejoice that we are all beneficiaries of the circumstance. My gratitude is also extended to Pete Hammar of Ampex Corporation for his fortuitous discovery which has led to the finish of this album.

Index

Page numbers in bold italics indicate pages with illustrations.